HORSE-RACING IN FRANCE

A HISTORY

BY

ROBERT BLACK, M.A.

FORMERLY OF PEMBROKE COLLEGE, CAMBRIDGE

FRANCIA 'FARÀ DA SE'

1886

Copyright © 2013 Read Books Ltd.
This book is copyright and may not be
reproduced or copied in any way without
the express permission of the publisher in writing

British Library Cataloguing-in-Publication Data
A catalogue record for this book is available from the
British Library

Horses – Sports and Utility

The horse (*Equus ferus caballus*) is one of two extant subspecies of *Equus ferus*. It is an odd-toed ungulate mammal belonging to the taxonomic family 'Equidae'. The horse has evolved over the past 45 to 55 million years from a small multi-toed creature into the large, single-toed animal of today. Humans began to domesticate horses around 4000 BC, and their domestication is believed to have been widespread by 3000 BC. We, as humans have interacted with horses in a multitude of ways throughout history – from sport competitions and non-competitive recreational pursuits, to working activities such as police work, agriculture, entertainment and therapy. Horses have also been used in warfare, from which a wide variety of riding and driving techniques developed, using many different styles of equipment and methods of control. With this range of uses in mind, there is an equally extensive, specialized vocabulary used to describe equine-related concepts, covering everything from anatomy to life stages, size, colours, markings, breeds, locomotion, and behaviour.

Sporting events are some of the largest and best-known activities involving horses, and here – communication between human and horse is paramount. To aid this process, horses are usually ridden with a saddle on their backs to assist the rider with balance and positioning, and a bridle or related headgear to assist the rider in maintaining control. Historically, equestrians honed their craft through games and races;

providing skills needed for battle, as well as entertainment for home crowds. Today, these competitions have evolved into racing, dressage, eventing and show jumping – many of which have their origins in military training, focused on control and balance of both the horse and rider. Other sports, such as rodeo, developed from practical skills such as those needed on working ranches and stations. Horse racing of all types evolved from impromptu competitions between riders or drivers, and has since become a multi-million pound industry. It is watched in almost every nation of the world, in its three main forms: 'flat racing' (long, even stretches), 'steeplechasing' (racing over jumps) and 'harness racing' (where horses trot or pace whilst pulling a driver in a small, light cart). A major part of horse racing's economic importance lies in the gambling associated with it.

All forms of competition, requiring demanding and specialized skills from both horse and rider, resulted in the systematic development of specialized breeds and equipment for each sport. Horse shows, which have their origins in medieval European fairs, are held around the world. They host a huge range of classes, covering all of the mounted and harness disciplines, as well as 'In-hand' classes where the horses are led, rather than ridden, to be evaluated on their conformation. The method of judging varies with the discipline, but winning usually depends on style and ability of both horse and rider. Sports such as polo do not judge the horse itself, but rather use the horse as a partner for human competitors as a necessary part of the game. Although the horse requires specialized training to participate, the details of its performance are not judged, only the result of the rider's actions—be it getting a ball through a goal or some other task. A similar, historical example of sports partnerships between human and horse is 'jousting', in which the main goal is for one rider to unseat the other. This pastime is still practiced by some sportsmen today.

There are certain jobs that horses do very well, and no technology has yet developed to fully replace them. For example, mounted police horses are still effective for certain types of patrol duties and crowd control. Cattle ranches still require riders on horseback to round up cattle that are scattered across remote, rugged terrain. In more urban areas, horses used to be the main form of transport, in the form of pulling carriages, and are still extensively used (especially in the UK) for ceremonial functions, i.e. horse-drawn carriages transporting dignitaries, military personnel or even the royal family. Horses can also be used in areas where it is necessary to avoid vehicular disruption to delicate soil, such as nature reserves. They may also be the only form of transport allowed in wilderness areas, often because of the fact that horses are quieter than motorised vehicles, therefore impacting less on their surroundings. Although machinery has replaced horses in many parts of the world, an estimated 100 million horses, donkeys and mules are still used for agriculture and transportation in less developed areas. This number includes around 27 million working animals in Africa alone.

As well as these labour intensive uses, horses can also be incredibly valuable for therapy. People of all ages with physical and mental disabilities obtain beneficial results from association with horses. Therapeutic riding is used to mentally and physically stimulate disabled persons and help them improve their lives through improved balance and coordination, increased self-confidence, and a greater feeling of freedom and independence. Horses also provide psychological benefits to people whether they actually ride or not. 'Equine-assisted' or 'equine-facilitated' therapy is a form of experiential psychotherapy that uses horses as companion animals to assist people with mental illness, including anxiety disorders, psychotic disorders, mood disorders, behavioural difficulties, and those who are going through major life changes. There are also experimental programs using horses in prison settings. Exposure to horses appears to improve the behaviour of inmates and help reduce recidivism when they leave.

As a concluding note, one of the most important aspects of equine care is farriery; a specialist in equine hoof care. Horses aid humans in so many ways, it is important to ensure that they are properly equipped and cared for. Farriers have largely replaced blacksmiths (after this specialism mostly became redundant after the industrial revolution), and are highly skilled in both metalwork and horse anatomy. Historically, the jobs of farrier and blacksmith were practically synonymous, shown by the etymology of the word: farrier comes from Middle French *ferrier* (blacksmith), and from the Latin word *ferrum* (iron). Modern day farriers usually specialize in horseshoeing though, focusing their time and effort on the care of the horse's hoof, including trimming and balancing of the hoof, as well as the placing of the shoes. Additional tasks for the farrier include dealing with injured or diseased hooves and application of special shoes for racing, training or 'cosmetic' purposes. In countries such as the United Kingdom, it is illegal for people other than registered farriers to call themselves a farrier or to carry out any farriery work, the primary aim being 'to prevent and avoid suffering by and cruelty to horses arising from the shoeing of horses by unskilled persons.' This is not the case in all countries however, where horse protection is severely lacking.

We hope the reader enjoys this book.

PREFACE.

CIRCUMSTANCES rather than natural aptitude, taste, inclination, or deliberate design have made me for more than twenty years a close student of horse-racing, both English and French. Into those circumstances there is no occasion to enter, and I have not the slightest intention of being gratuitously tedious. Suffice it to say that my first experience of horse-racing carries me back more than forty years to a day of which I have still a vivid remembrance, when I saw an animal belonging to the famous Colonel (afterwards General) Peel run at a provincial race meeting; and that I believe I can still from mere memory give that animal's name (although it achieved no great celebrity)—'I-am-not-aware.' Since then I have witnessed a great many of the most memorable races ever run, and have had at least a bowing acquaintance with some of the most notable race horses, English, French, Austro-Hungarian, German, American, and others, that ever came to the post. I saw the hopes of the 'Rupert' Earl of Derby and his Toxophilite upset at Epsom by 'the lucky baronet' (Sir Joseph Hawley) and his Beadsman; I saw Buckstone and Tim Whiffler, General Peel and Ely, run their dead heats for the Ascot Cup; I saw Blair Athol win his Derby, the first time he ran in public; I saw Gladiateur win the Two Thousand, the Derby, the Ascot Cup, and indeed nearly all the races he won in England, and I saw him run for the Cambridgeshire, which no horse could have won under his weight; I saw the struggle between Lord Lyon and the then Bribery colt for the Derby, and the still closer struggle between Lord Lyon and the then Savernake for the Doncaster St. Leger. I have been a spectator of the doughty deeds done by French and other foreign horses on English ground from Hospodar to Boïard, Chamant, Rayon d'Or, Insulaire, and Iroquois; and, though I am a little hazy about La Toucques and Fille de l'Air (to both of whom I might, *mutatis mutandis*, apply the phrase 'Virgilium vidi tantùm'), I have a very distinct recollection of the fantastic Sornette. Other French and foreign performers on the English Turf, more or less numerous than the sand that is upon the seashore, I might mention as known to me by sight and by witnessed exploit (such as Dollar and his Goodwood Cup); but enough, no doubt, has been said to prove that I have personally 'assisted' at many eventful races and at some of the history I have attempted to put together.

As for books, such as it became a student of horseracing to read, mark, learn, and inwardly digest, I have

them by scores upon my bookshelves. I possess the
'Stud Books' (complete or up to some recent date) of
several countries—of England (from the first volume to
the latest, of course), of France, of Germany, of Austria-Hungary, of America (both Bruce's and Wallace's).
Of 'Calendars,' English, French, and other foreign ones,
I have a host—Heber's, Pond's, Tuting and Fawconer's;
many volumes of Weatherby's; some volumes of the
'Calendrier des Courses;' Mr. W. Pick's laborious
publications; Mr. Orton's 'Annals,' &c.; and I have
consulted them carefully when necessary. 'Histories of
the British Turf,' too, I possess; and thereby hangs my
tale.

For, although I have been constantly on the lookout, I have never been able to light upon a 'History of
the French Turf.' The nearest approach thereto that I
have been able to discover is the late Baron d'Etreillis's
('Ned Pearson's') book, called 'Dictionnaire du Sport
Français,' out of which a very good idea indeed may
be gleaned of the progress made by horse-racing in
France; but, from the nature of the case, the account
is not continuous or methodical, and would have to be
picked out piecemeal by anybody who should go to it
for information. Moreover it was published (and I am
not aware of any new and augmented edition) before
the extraordinary successes of the French and other
foreign horses had led to the controversy about 'reciprocity,' and consequently long before the double-barrelled achievement of Plaisanterie had brought

down upon French (and even Irish) horses the thunderbolt of exclusion from English handicaps, unless certain curious conditions should happen to be fulfilled.

It occurred to me, then, a few years ago, on a night when my sleep went from me, that I would undertake to supply, to the best of my poor ability, what experience and observation had led me to believe was a want.

It may be presumptuous for an Englishman to write a history of horse-racing in France; but, in extenuation of his presumption, let the Englishman plead that nobody else seemed to be inclined to do it; that the French Turf is really but an offshoot of the English; and that the success of French race horses in England or (in the Grand Prix de Paris) against horses taken over to France from England is the only satisfactory measure of the advance made by the French in their horse-racing and horse-breeding. From that point of view this history has been written.

The history, I think, will convince any unprejudiced reader that the French—notwithstanding many brilliant campaigns in England, and notwithstanding the fact that many countries (including England herself) have shown a disposition to purchase or hire French-bred stud horses from time to time—cannot yet 'go alone,' are not yet so much to be dreaded as the 'great citizen' of the Latin Grammar was 'dreaded by Otho.' There are signs, however, that our energetic neighbours intend to be perfectly independent some day, that a time will come when 'Francia farà da se.' Monsieur Edouard Cavailhon, of the French sporting journal 'L'Entraîneur,' in his lately published work called 'Les Haras de France,' very significantly remarks, 'Il faut encore pas mal de temps et de bonne volonté de la part des propriétaires de chevaux pour secouer le joug de la féodalité anglaise dans tout ce qui a rapport aux courses sur les hippodromes, mais dans les différents haras que je viens de parcourir *aucun Anglais n'est employé.*' We know too what efforts are being made by French owners, having at their head Monsieur A. Lupin (who holds that 'les sujets français sont aussi bons que les anglais'), to obtain a supply of native French jockeys, equal to Messrs. Archer, Wood, Barrett, Webb, Cannon, Osborne, Goater, and the rest of that glorious company of accomplished riders. All this gives a special interest to a history of horse-racing in France.

The narrative has been so arranged—year by year throughout a considerable, if not the greater, part of it—that readers who do not care to be troubled with details can 'skip,' without losing the continuity of what a great effort has been made to render a lively story; and that readers who do care for details may, with the further assistance of an index, either find all that they require or at any rate convince themselves that there are 'more where those came from' and be enabled to look up the more for themselves.

In the lists of sires imported from England into France it was frequently difficult to fix the exact date;

for sometimes the date is not forthcoming at all either in the English or in the French 'Stud Book,' sometimes the two authorities differ, and the preference given had to be determined by circumstances. Opportunity, however, may be here taken for saying how much inferior the French work, though undertaken by a Commission appointed with the usual flourishes by a Government, is (*me judice*) to the English, the outcome of private enterprise.

Lastly, let me hope that in speaking of persons, living or dead, I have said—as I certainly meant to say—nothing offensive or even disrespectful; and that as regards inevitable errors they may be found to be as few as could be expected in so laborious, so factful, so figureful, so nameful, so dateful, so diversified a work, designed and executed by a single unassisted and unprotected male.

LEAMINGTON : *Oct.* 7, 1886.

LIST OF THE PRINCIPAL PUBLICATIONS EMPLOYED MORE OR LESS FREELY FOR THE PURPOSES OF THIS WORK.

'American Stud Book, The' (Bruce's).
'Austro-Hungarian Stud Book, The.'
'English Stud Book, The.'
'French Stud Book, The.'
'German Stud Book, The.'
'English Racing Calendar, The' (Weatherby's).
'French Racing Calendar, The' (Bryon's).
'French (Official) Racing Calendar, The.'
'M'Call's Racing Chronicle.'
The 'Druid's' Works.
'La Chronique du Turf.'
'Austro-Hungarian Racing Calendar, The.'
'German Racing Calendar, The.'
'Le Journal des Haras.'
'Le Dictionnaire du Sport Français,' by 'Ned Pearson' (the late Baron d'Etreillis).
'Badminton Library' (Horse-Racing), The.
'History of Newmarket, The' (H. P. Hore's).
'Les Haras de France' (E. Cavaillon's).
Larousse's 'Dictionnaire Universel.'
'Le Figaro.'
'Turf Register, The' (by W. Pick, of York).
'Ruff's Guide.'
'Le Sport' and 'Le Sportsman' (*passim*).
'The Sportsman.'
'The Sporting Magazine.'
'The Standard.'
'The Times.'

CONTENTS.

CHAPTER		PAGE
I.	BEFORE THE DAYS OF THE SOCIÉTÉ D'ENCOURAGEMENT	1
II.	THE FRENCH JOCKEY CLUB	19
III.	THE FIRST STRUGGLES	50
IV.	THE INVASION OF PERFIDIOUS ALBION	60
V.	MONARQUE AND HIS SATELLITES	71
VI.	FRANC PICARD AND HIS TIMES	88
VII.	THE 'BIG STABLE'	107
VIII.	LA TOUCQUES—VERMOUT—FILLE DE L'AIR—GLADIATEUR	132
IX.	FROM THE 'TURN OF THE TIDE' TO THE 'DÉCHÉANCE'	156
X.	M. LEFÈVRE'S CAMPAIGN OF 1871—THE LAGRANGE-LEFÈVRE 'FUSION'—LORD FALMOUTH'S HOWL FOR 'RECIPROCITY'	182
XI.	FROM THE HOWL FOR 'RECIPROCITY' TO THE PRESENT DAY	217
XII.	A SUMMARY	333
XIII.	CONCLUSION	348
	INDEX	367

HORSE-RACING IN FRANCE

CHAPTER I.

BEFORE THE DAYS OF THE SOCIÉTÉ D'ENCOURAGEMENT.

DESULTORY horse-racing of course exists in all countries where there are horses to be ridden and men or boys (especially the latter) to ride them; and the commencement of such horse-racing dates, no doubt, from the earliest period at which the horses of those countries submit, either voluntarily or under compulsion, to bear riders upon their backs. Such horse-racing, therefore, is likely to have been practised in France quite as soon as in England, if not sooner. Such horse-racing, again, though still desultory, would, as time went on, inevitably lead to a custom of keeping certain horses more especially for that purpose, and, as a natural consequence, giving them a special preparation; and at this stage too there is reason to believe that France arrived as soon as England. At any rate there are, it is said, traces of French horse-racing in 1323 under Charles le Bel, and there is a story current about some 'running horses' (usually, but without unquestionable certainty, taken to mean 'race horses') sent, four centuries or so before Charles le Bel, by Hugh the Great, father of

B

Hugh Capet, to our king Athelstan, grandson of Alfred the Great. However that may be, it is quite certain that horse-racing as a regular institution, as a systematic pursuit, as both the sport of kings and at the same time a national pastime, as a means of contributing to the improvement of native horseflesh or to the replacement of it by a better breed, imported, acclimatised, naturalised, and propagated (when emulation—as it was sure to do—caused owners to seek for horses wherever the best were to be found), is of purely English initiation : it was known indeed in France, but known only to be lightly regarded and generally repudiated (with a few exceptions) until the formation of the Société d'Encouragement pour l'Amélioration des Races de Chevaux en France, commonly called the French Jockey Club, in 1833.

This is the more remarkable because to the French we were indebted for some of the very best sires that are named in the pedigrees of our thoroughbreds: for instance, St. Victor's Barb (the property of ' Monsieur St. Victor of France'), the famous Curwen bay Barb, the almost equally celebrated Thoulouse Barb, and the Godolphin Arabian (or Barb), whose history has been written by the great 'romancer' M. Eugène Sue, are known to have resided in France and to have belonged originally to Frenchmen. And since horse-racing on the English system has become an established institution in France great moan has been made by French sporting writers over the negligence of their predeceased compatriots, who permitted those ' sons of the desert,' presented to the Grande Nation by awe-stricken Eastern potentates, to slip into the clutches of perfidious Albion, thus laying the foundation of that supremacy on the turf which (as' well as every other supremacy), having been intended by Providence for France, has been diverted—for a while, if not for ever—to England and the English.

The first systematic efforts to improve the French breed of horses were made in the reign of Louis XIV. by the great minister Colbert, who founded the Administration des Haras, which has been continued to this day. The Administration, however, did not concern itself with horse-racing as a means of improvement; its chief, if not only, care was to provide at the expense of the State well-bred stud horses, whether Arabian or Eastern or other, whose services should be placed within reach of all and sundry on payment of an almost nominal fee. The 'demi-sang' or 'half-bred' horse, the 'cocktail,' as it has been commonly called, was all that was looked for at the very best: the 'thoroughbred' and the horse-racing by which alone the 'thoroughbred' can be tested were as yet disregarded by the Administration. It was not till after the Great Revolution, after the First Empire, after the second restoration and the death of Louis XVIII., when the Dauphin, son of Charles X., established his stud at Meudon, with the Duke de Guiche as Master of the Horse, with Mr. Corringham (a well-known English trainer) as director of the establishment, and with Rowlston (son of Camillus), purchased in England and imported into France in 1827, as 'chief of the stud,' that the Administration can be said to have obtained touch of such horse-racing as there was in France. It is true that, during the First Empire, from about 1806 to 1810, races were instituted, and there had been issued a 'règlement sur la réorganisation des haras et *des courses*;' that in 1820, after the Restoration, there had been published another decree concerning the age and height of horses 'admis sur l'hippodrome;' and that, moreover, in 1825, after the accession of horse-loving Charles X., there had been an ordinance classifying 'les chevaux de course;' but up to the eve of the Revolution of July the Administration des Haras seems to have dealt with French horse-racing and the French race horse in a fashion as desultory as the racing was itself. Moreover the Administration, even when it turned its attention more seriously to horse-racing, still clung to the 'half-bred' or 'demi-sang' heresy, and scouted the growing 'thoroughbred' ideas and the yearning after horse races on the English plan as sheer 'anglomanie;' and so it came to pass that the Revolution of July brought about a notable change not only in the dynasty but also in the affairs of the French Turf, so far as there can be said to have been any at that time. We are told that 'the first ministerial decree in which the words *pur sang* (thoroughbred) occur is dated 1832;' and certainly the French 'Stud Book' (or Register of Thoroughbreds, as it may be termed) owed its origin to an 'ordinance' of King Louis Philippe, dated 1833. In that same year was established the French Jockey Club, which had been for some time in process of incubation and was formed of members of whom the most prominent were diametrically opposed to the views and methods of the Administration des Haras, and were destined to triumph ultimately in the determined struggle that took place between the two parties as representatives respectively of 'pur sang' and 'demi-sang,' of so called 'anglomanie' and implied 'patriotism.'

Meanwhile, as has been stated already, there had been intermittent horse-racing from time to time in France; but the traces left of it, the records that remain of it, go to show that it had never become firmly and popularly established, as it now is; and that whenever, save in the very earliest times, there was a horse race of note, English grooms, or trainers, or jockeys, or horses, or practices, and sometimes all these together, were—or were considered—necessary for the accomplishment of the business. It will appear, perhaps, as the following paragraphs are perused, that but for the Great Revolution, which interfered with so many possibilities and probabilities, horse-racing on English principles might have become naturalised in France before the commencement of the nineteenth century, instead of having to wait for the Revolution of July 1830, the patronage of the popular Duke d'Orléans, son of Louis Philippe, and the foundation of the French Jockey Club in 1833.

As early as 1323, under Charles le Bel, or in 1370, in the reign of Charles le Sage, according to other accounts, there was horse-racing, apparently, at Sémur, Côte d'Or; but no 'Racing Calendar' of that date is forthcoming.

There were 'scratch' races in Louis XIV.'s time, as will appear from the following accounts.

Here is an extraordinary extract, taken, it is asserted, from 'the diary of Buisson d'Aubenay:'—

This day after dinner, March 15, 1651, a match for a wager of a thousand crowns was decided in the Bois de Boulogne between Prince d'Harcourt and the Duke de Joyeuse, both of whom mounted [? ran] horses that had been trained for the occasion in the village of Boulogne, on the Seine, in the same manner as English race horses. They had been fed for three weeks, or thereabouts, on bread made with beans and aniseed, in the place of oats, and two days previous to the contest taking place were each given between two and three hundred fresh eggs. They went the track from the barrier of La Muette, or

Meute, and passed along the highroad in the direction of St. Cloud. Turning, however, off to the right, within the enclosure of the main thoroughfare which leads back to the Château of Madrid, they came on at this spot neck and neck. Prince d'Harcourt was attired in a grey overcoat, made exceedingly tight for the occasion, with a round close cap, in which all his hair was rolled up, and carried three pounds of lead in his pockets to weigh as much as Plessis du Vernet, the riding-master, who took the place and rode the horse of the Duke de Joyeuse. But upon reaching the Madrid [a place so called in the Bois de Boulogne] they rode past the Sieur Dauphin, who was awaiting them at that place on horseback. According to their *puction* [agreement] the [*sic*] Plessis took the lead, and coming in about a hundred feet before his antagonist at the barrier of La Muette, was declared the winner. Many of the Court personages were present.

If no mistake have been made by the author and the translator of this extract, or by one or the other, the diet of the horses may be a matter of wonder, but the ' pact ' is more wonderful by far; the swindle is as incomprehensible as it was apparently barefaced.

Here is a little anecdote about another horse race, an 'international' race, open to horses of all countries. It was run in 1683 at Achères or St. Germain-en-Laye, 'before the eyes of ladies and of kings;' the Grand Monarque gave a plate of 1,000 pistoles for the winner; and it was won by England's representative, the celebrated Duke of Monmouth, who rode a gelding belonging to the Hon. Thomas Wharton. After the race the King wished to purchase the English gelding, and offered to give ' the weight of the horse in gold.' But the Hon. T. Wharton, in the spirit of Araunah, the Jebusite, when dealing with King David, would not sell, but would gladly have made King Louis a present of the horse. This King Louis, in the spirit of King David when dealing with Araunah, refused; but, as the Hon. T. Wharton was not so compliant in his courtesy as Araunah was, there was no 'deal,' and the Englishman kept his horse. Louis XIV., however, displayed such extraordinary favour towards the 'horsey' Englishmen at this time and such appreciation of their pre-eminence in the sport of horse-racing that he extended to the Hon. Bernard Howard (who was the 'Admiral Rous' of the English Turf in those days, a younger brother of the Duke of Norfolk, a 'pal' of Charles II.'s at Newmarket, and an ancestor of the present Earl of Suffolk and Berkshire) the privilege of driving right into the precincts of the Louvre, a privilege reserved for princes of the blood royal and a few favoured individuals.

Again we find that in Louis XIV.'s reign, in 1685, there was a race—not quite 'on the square' this time.

'One day,' says the narrative, 'when there was a horse race in the warren of Le Pecq (Le Vésinet), wherein a horse of MM. de Vendôme had run against a horse of M. Le Grand (le Grand Ecuyer), there was a warm dispute between those who had betted, the supporters of MM. de Vendôme asserting that the English groom who "ran" (*courait*) [or rode] their horse had allowed himself to be bribed by emissaries of the other party. And things were carried so far that the Duke de Grammont, who was among the supporters of MM. de Vendôme, having given a sort of lie to M. Le Grand, he replied to him with a sort of box o' the ear and pulled off his wig. It so happened that the Duke de Grammont had no sword handy, having got rid of his for fear it might be in his way as he accompanied the horses that ran the race; but his equerry and his supporters clapped hands to their swords against M. Le Grand, the Chevalier de Lorraine, and the other people of that party, and the disturbance would have gone very far had not Monseigneur [the Dauphin], who was close by, sent to stop it.'

This anecdote, which is said to be told in the

memoirs of the Marquis de Fourches, appears in 'Le Sport' (January 1877), and on it the writer who communicates it makes the following tolerably obvious observation: 'We remark that it was then, as it is nowadays, English jockeys who "ran" the horses, and that the rage for betting was already carried to such a pitch that the jockeys were accused, just as they now are, of allowing themselves to be bribed by the opposite party.'

In the next reign, that of Louis XV., during the close of which 'anglomanie,' everybody knows, was all the fashion, we find, as we might expect, a great deal of horse-racing in France, though the King, we are told, was led to forbid the sport in consequence of an incident reported by Horace Walpole, who writes to the Rev. W. Cole (February 28, 1766), 'To-day I have been to the Plaine de Sablons, by the Bois de Boulogne, to see a horse race rid in person by Count Lauraguais and Lord Forbes.' The Count's horse died, and was, of course, said by the French to have been poisoned (? by the English stable people); but the Count himself is stated to have 'quacked' the poor brute. This was the Count Lauraguais who was so well known (and disliked) at Newmarket; who purchased the famous English horse Gimcrack, and raced that celebrated 'crack' both in England and in France; who was brother to two of the King's many mistresses, and who was responsible for one of the King's many witticisms. Said the King to Lauraguais, 'What have you been doing all this while in England?' 'Sire,' answered Lauraguais, 'I have been learning how to think (penser).' 'Learning how to groom (panser), you mean,' rejoined the King. In the same reign the Duke de Lauzun (a nephew of the Duke de Biron, whose descendant, Duke de Gontaut-Biron, was president of the French Jockey Club from 1851 to 1883) ran horses in England (Taster, by Sweepstakes, and Patrician, by Matchem, for instance, in 1773). In this reign too we find from Jesse's 'Selwyn' that the Marquis de Fitzjames went with Guerchy (the French ambassador) and Lord March ('old Q.') to Newmarket, which he 'liked, and everybody liked him.' In fact, Newmarket about this time was positively infested by Frenchmen, insomuch that Lord Carlisle writes to Selwyn in 1768, 'I pity my Newmarket friends, who are to be bored by those Frenchmen;' and, according to Horace Walpole, the celebrated sportsman Mr. Hugo Meynell took it so much to heart that he said with grim humour 'he wished the peace were all over and we were comfortably at war again.'

It was in the reign of Louis XVI., however, just before 'the deluge,' that it seemed as if the French were about to settle down to their stride and commence their race with us both in breeding and running the thoroughbred; but circumstances beyond the control of any Jockey Club, French or English, postponed this pleasant prospect for about half a century. In 1783 horse-racing was in full blast at Vincennes and Fontainebleau; 'old Q.' and others of our leading racing men would send their horses (carrying extra weight) to run against the Count d'Artois (afterwards Charles X.), the Duke de Chartres (afterwards the Duke d'Orléans, known as Philippe Egalité), the Marquis de Conflans (godfather to the Conflans stakes at Brighton, then called Brighthelmstone, in 1785), the Duke de Lauzun, the Duke de Fitzjames, and other French notabilities, of whom several, including Philippe Egalité (who as Duke d'Orléans appears to have been an hon. member

of our Jockey Club), would run horses in England.
Other Frenchmen besides Philippe Egalité were also in
all probability hon. members of our Jockey Club; and
in course of time Philippe Egalité ran in England horses
'bred in France,' such as the two-year-olds Rouge,
Vert, and Glowworm, all by Glowworm, in 1785. Egalité as Duke de Chartres ran Cantator (bred in England,
however) for the Derby of 1784; and as near his
tragic end as 1790 was still horse-racing in England
(with Hocks, Lambinos, Fortitude, and Conqueror),
with a carelessness worthy of him who fiddled whilst
Rome was burning. At the French races the King
himself would attend, and would bet his modest 'petit
écu,' thinking, good soul, that the moderation of a
king might be a check upon the extravagant gambling
of courtiers, that example would be better than precept.

This was the time when several 'crack' English
sires were imported into France, not permanently for
the most part, but temporarily, both to run and to
serve as sires: such were the famous Comus (son of
Otho), sold to the Count d'Artois in 1776; Barbary
(son of Panglos), sold to the same purchaser about the
same time; Glowworm (son of Eclipse), sold to the
Marquis de Conflans about the same time; King Pepin
(son of Turf), sold to 'a French nobleman' (most likely
either the Count d'Artois or the Duke de Chartres) for
1,000 guineas about the same time; Pyroïs (son of
Matchem), sold (? to the Duke de Chartres) about the
same time; and Teucer (son of Northumberland),
purchased 'for Lord Rockingham, who sent him into
France to the Marquis de Conflans,' about the same
time. Mares too were imported by the French at that
period, whether for a permanency or only for a while:
among them were Sphynx (daughter of Marske), dam

of Count d'Artois's Biche (a great winner in France); Dulcinea (daughter of Whistlejacket), sold to Count d'Artois; the Duke de Chartres' Helen, by Conductor (temporarily), and many others. Here, then, were the means of propagating a French edition of the English thoroughbred, such as has since been acquired in France; but the Great Revolution supervened and swamped everything, so that scarcely a trace remains of the sires, the dams, and the progeny which the Count d'Artois and Philippe Egalité had been at so much pains to procure.

There was very little regard paid in France to horse-racing, to 'pur sang' or 'demi-sang' (that is, 'thoroughbred' or 'half-bred'), during the Terror, the Directory, and the Consulate, though the subject had attracted the attention of the celebrated Mirabeau when he was in England in 1783–5. In 1785 he, in fact, visited Epsom to see the races (as a gentleman of his kidney was likely to do), and under the pseudonym of 'M. Grossley' he published his views about the English and their 'horsiness.' It may not be everybody who is acquainted with his description, stale as it is to some of us; and it is, therefore, appended because of the evidence it affords of a French man of the world's mental condition as regards the race horse, the affairs of the Turf, and the sort of monopoly which Englishmen were evidently considered to hold in such matters. The paragraph concerning English ladies and their manner of riding is very amusing, as if French ladies either did not ride at all or were in the habit of riding *à califourchon*—that is, like a man. Here is the extract:—

> Horse-racing and cock-fighting are carried on here to a pitch of absolute madness, and many gentlemen of fortune ruin themselves by these pleasures. The course at Epsom is in the

middle of the Downs, intersected by three hills in parallel lines; in the vales between these hills the champions entered the list; the spectators came in coaches, which, without the least bustle or dispute about precedency, were arranged in three or four lines on the first of those hills; and on the top of all was a scaffolding for the judges who were to award the prize. This scaffolding was the goal which bounded the race, and the starting-post was at the head of the outer vale of the second hill. Four horses starting from thence ran in this valley, about the length of a mile; turned round by the next hill, to the height of the starting-post, and at length reached the hill on which stands the scaffolding, where he that came in first was declared the victor. The prize is not adjudged till after three heats; and to him only who has won two out of three. There are neither lists nor barriers at these races. The horses run in the midst of the crowd, who leave only a space sufficient for them to pass through, at the same time encouraging them by gestures and loud shouts. The victor, when he arrives at the goal, finds it a difficult effort to disengage himself from the crowd, who congratulate and caress him with an affection of heart which is no easy matter to form an idea of unless you have witnessed it. The deference to the victors is not confined to these transient honours. All the houses of the country gentlemen, all the inns, are lined with pictures of horses, painted or engraved, in various attitudes of strength or agility, with an account of the victories they have won, their names, those of the jockeys by whom they were trained; in fine, those of the noblemen to whom they belonged, and from whom they experienced all the care and tender treatment which favourite children can expect from a parent. So great was the crowd which covered the place where the horses ran that I could not see them except upon the ridge of the second hill. They kept upon the full stretch, without rising or darting forward, and seemed to resemble wooden horses fixed in full stretch upon the rim of the great horizontal circle, moving round upon its axis with the utmost imaginable rapidity. These race horses do not show their worth by their outward appearance; they are gaunt and meagre, and an awkward manner of stretching out their necks deprives them of all their beauty, the principal of which in a horse is to hold its head in a graceful attitude. The preservation and multiplication of this breed is owing to laws enacted by Henry VIII., and to prizes established in different parts of England for the victors at races. In short, these horses are, with respect to others, what gladiators were among the ancient Greeks and Romans. These races are not like those of Barbary horses at Rome and other cities of Italy. Each horse is ridden by a jockey, who is, generally speaking, only a common groom, unentitled to the least share in the honour of the victory, which is divided between the horse and the owner. The horses are sometimes mounted at races by noblemen who are willing to run the risk. They are less exposed to the danger of falling, bruising themselves, or dislocating a limb—a circumstance which occurred a few years ago to a young nobleman at his first race, at Newmarket—than to be deprived of respiration by the velocity of the motion. In order to cut the air, the groom, who almost lies upon the neck of the horse, holds the handle of the whip fixed before him, or shakes it above his mouth. Previously to the commencement of the race, the jockey, the saddle, and the whole trappings of the horse are weighed in the presence of the judges, and care is taken that all the horses admitted to run be of an equal weight. Victory is often due to the knowledge which the jockey has of his horse, and to the direction he gives him forward, or managing him properly. . . . The English in general have a degree of friendship and affection for horses which few men ever show for their own species. They seldom or never strike them. They seldom even speak to them except in a gentle and affectionate tone of voice. The horses of gentlemen of fortune, both in town and country, mostly die in the stable where they were foaled. They are treated like old friends, who, when advanced in years, are taken care of in consideration of past services. The English are as fond of riding as the Italians are of music. It rouses them; it prevents, suspends, and removes the effects of melancholy upon the constitution; it is an habitual want and a necessary remedy. The English ladies frequently ride on horseback, though they sit sideways upon their horses. This manner of riding they have derived from Anne of Luxembourg, consort of Richard II., whose example caused it to be introduced as the most becoming manner of riding for women. Thus mounted, they travel long journeys at a smart trot.

'They seldom or never strike them' is good, very good; Mirabeau had evidently never heard of Mr. William Clift (born in 1763) and other jockeys of the 'old school' who are said to have had 'heavy punishment' for their only creed.

But let us get on to the First Empire, when horse-racing in France was not much better than before. Napoleon the Great certainly said, in his omnipotent way, 'Let there be races,' and there were races, chiefly in the Department of the Orne, with a 'hippodrome' at Le Pin, where is the 'haras' founded by Colbert at the time of establishing the Administration des Haras; but the racing was of no account as sport, or as a national institution, or as an aid towards the improvement of French horseflesh by propagation of the Anglo-Arabian breed. It may have had some good influence upon the horses of the French cavalry, and that is all that Napoleon would have cared about; just as, probably, it was all that William the 'Dutchman' cared about when he bestowed no little patronage on Newmarket and the 'sport of kings.'

At the Restoration and the return of the Count d'Artois it may be supposed that there would have been a recurrence of old times, with another Comus, another King Pepin, and so on; but Humpty Dumpty is not easily set up again after a fall. However there were signs of what was soon to come both in breeding and in racing, as may be seen at a glance from looking at the early numbers of the 'Journal des Haras,' which was published for the first time in 1828. Not only was there the Dauphin's stud at Meudon (where Rowlston

stood in 1827), under the management of the Duke de
Guiche, but there were private breeders scattered about
the country during the years between the Restoration
and 1833, besides the Government studs at Le Pin, in
the north, and (a 'jumenterie,' for mares only) at Pompadour, in the south, to say nothing of Rosières-aux-
Salines. Prominent among these breeders were the
Duke des Cars (who is commemorated by the Prix des
Cars to this day), the Count de Tocqueville (who had
a private 'hippodrome' of his own near Dieppe), and
others; and there were the 'dealers' as well as breeders,
such as MM. de Royères, Crémieux, and others. One
of the most remarkable of these personages was an
ex-archbishop, M. l'Abbé de Pradt, who had been
created Archbishop of Malines (Mechlin) by Napoleon I., and who is probably better known to the
world in general as a 'trimmer,' a time-server, and a
voluminous writer of stuff and nonsense than as a
breeder of horses. To horse-breeding, nevertheless, he
took in his latter days; and he was warranted (by himself) to breed any sort of horse, of any size, any shape,
and any colour that anybody pleased; but it does not
appear that he could be warranted by himself or by
anybody else to breed a horse that would 'go.' But at
none of the breeding establishments (unless, perhaps, at
that of M. Ricussec, who had been breeding horses at
Buc, near Versailles, and afterwards at Viroflay, as
early as 1805) was there a single earnest desire to produce the true Anglo-Arabian thoroughbred, such as the
French now have in perfection. Some of the breeders
affected the natural 'Arab' (term applied to any pure
son or daughter of 'Eastern breed'), others the 'half-
bred,' or 'demi-sang,' or 'cock-tail.' With the Revolution of July and with the reign of the 'Citizen King'

another era was to commence for French horse-racing and horse-breeding. The French Jockey Club was to spring up in 1833 and France was to have a new institution.

It may be well to conclude this chapter with a list of the principal English thoroughbred sires introduced into France from the date of the Great Revolution to the foundation of the French Jockey Club. They were Abron (by Whisker), in 1828; Ad Libitum (by Whiskey), in 1817; Aldford (by Pavilion), in 1822; Alfred (by Filho da Puta), in 1828; Atom (by Phantom), foaled in 1818 (but the exact date of introduction is not always recorded); Barelegs (by Tramp), in 1828; Belmont (by Thunderbolt), in 1831; Ben Nevis (by Paynator), foaled in 1808; Bijou (by Orville), in 1818; Borysthenes (by Smolensko), in 1830; Brigand (by X Y Z), in 1826; Camerton (by Hambletonian), in 1818; Captain Candid (by Cerberus), in 1825; Carbon (by Waxy), in 1828; Charon (by Woful), in 1828; Cinder (by Woful), foaled in 1820; Claude (by Haphazard), foaled in 1819; Clayton (by Overton), in 1815; Coriolanus (by Gohanna), in 1818; Diamond (by Highflyer), in 1818 (died in 1819, aged twenty-seven); D.I.O (by Whitworth), in 1818; Doge of Venice (by Sir Oliver), in 1825; Dominechino (by Vandyke, junior), foaled in 1818; Eastham (by Sir Oliver), in 1825; Easton (by Stamford), foaled in 1805; Egremont (by Skiddaw), in 1819; Electrometer (by Thunderbolt), in 1828; Young Emilius (by Emilius, dam Sal), in 1832 (the other Young Emilius, dam Cobweb, was not imported till 1834); Enamel (by Phantom), in 1831; Farmer (by Pericles), foaled in 1819; Félix (by Comus), in 1826; Fulford (by Orville), in 1820; Young Gohanna (by Gohanna), in 1820; Hamlet (by Hambletonian), in

1818 ; Harlequin (by Cervantes), in 1831 ; Holbein (by Rubens), in 1826 ; Homer (by Catton), in 1826 ; Knight Errant (by Sancho), foaled in 1810; Linkboy (by Aladdin), foaled in 1823 ; Libertine (by Filho da Puta), in 1831 ; Lockell (by Selim), foaled in 1822 ; Locksley, *alias* Stamford (by Smolensko), in 1827 ; Lützen (by Gustavus), foaled in 1824 ; Young Merlin (by Merlin), in 1827 ; Middlethorpe (by Shuttle), in 1818 ; Milton (by Waxy), foaled in 1813 ; Minister (by The Prime Minister), in 1825 ; Mohican (by Woful), in 1832 ; Monkey (by Shuttle), in 1830 ; Mustachio (by Whisker), in 1828 ; Myrmidon (by Partisan), in 1824 (returned to England in 1826) ; Parchment, *alias* Tring (by Thunderbolt), in 1824 ; Paulus (by Sir Paul), in 1818 ; Peter Liberty (by Amadis), in 1825 ; Phosphor (by Meteor), in 1819 ; Piccadilly (by Buzzard), in 1814 ; Piccadilly (by Reveller), foaled in 1828 ; Premium (by Aladdin), in 1825 ; Rainbow (by Walton), in 1823 ; Rembrandt (by Vandyke, junior), in 1831 ; Rowlston (by Camillus), in 1827 ; Young Sir Joshua (by Rubens), in 1825 ; Smolensko (by Stamford), foaled in 1811 ; Snail (by Stamford), in 1819 ; Spy (by Walton), in 1818 ; Statesman (by Rockingham), in 1811 ; Young Staveley (by Sir David), in 1819 ; Streatlam Lad (by Remembrancer), in 1818 ; Swallow (by Skim), foaled in 1821 (died in 1835); Tigris (by Quiz), in 1818 ; Toil and Trouble (by Manfred), in 1828 ; Tooley (by Walton), foaled in 1809 ; Tozer, ex-Mistake (by Fyldener), in 1818 ; Trance (by Phantom), in 1831 ; Truffle (by Sorcerer), in 1817 ; Turcoman (by Selim), foaled in 1824 ; Vampire (by Waxy), in 1830 ; Young Vandyke (by Vandyke, junior), in 1827 ; Vanloo (by Rubens), foaled in 1817 ; Velvet (by Sorcerer), in 1818 ; Vivaldi (by Woodpecker), in 1801 (returned to England in 1817 and died the same year) ;

Warkworth (by Filho da Puta), in 1828; Zoroaster (by Sorcerer), foaled in 1805.

What feats were performed in France by the immediate progeny of all these sires there is no saying, as the records of French horse-racing were not regularly kept and published before the days of the French Jockey Club; but in two or three cases—those of Rowlston (imported by M. de Guiche for the Royal Stud of Meudon), Rainbow (imported by M. Rieussec, of the Viroflay stud) and Holbein—the deeds of the progeny remain on record in several instances; for Volante (by Rowlston) and Corysandre (by Holbein) won the Grand Prix at Paris in 1836 and 1838, and Félix, Franck, and Lydia (all by Rainbow) won between them the Grand Prix at Paris in 1834 and 1837, the Prix du Cadran in 1838, and the Prix du Jockey Club (French Derby) in 1836 and 1837. As for Rainbow (whose memory is kept green by the Prix Rainbow at Paris Spring Meeting), it is related that, when he stood at Viroflay, the French public would flock to see him, and pay a franc for the privilege, as eagerly as the British public used to flock to the Zoological Gardens to gape upon the miraculous Jumbo, the elephant.

CHAPTER II.

THE FRENCH JOCKEY CLUB.

THE true fathers of the French Turf (as it now is) were the original members of the French Jockey Club, or rather the original members of that body which formed the first Race Committee of the Société d'Encouragement, founded in 1833. There had for some time previously been that 'something in the air' which is always abroad when a new institution is about to come into existence; but it was in 1833 that the 'something' took definite shape and presented itself in the form of an aristocratic, influential, wealthy, and powerful association.

The origin of the Association or Club seems to have been on this wise: Before the year 1833 there had existed at Tivoli, Rue Blanche, Paris, 'an English Jockey Club and Pigeon-shooting Club,' the founder and secretary, and apparently proprietor, whereof was a Mr. Thomas Bryon, an Englishman. Among the eighteen members in 1830 there were four Englishmen, including the very eccentric Lord Henry Seymour, a native and resident of Paris, who, though he is said to have never set foot in England, was of English descent in the male line (being a son of the third Marquis of Hertford and of that Maria Fagniani whom it is well known that both George Selwyn and the 'old Q.' Duke of Queensberry, believed to have a daughter's claim upon them, and to whom they both consequently left a fortune), and had an Englishman's tastes and peculiarities, including a touch of 'horse upon the brain.' It appears to have struck him and some of his associates that the time had come for ameliorating the breed of French horses, and that it would be a good idea to relinquish the mongrel sort of establishment which combined a kind of 'Red House at Battersea' with a travesty of the 'English Jockey Club,' and to found a new Club, a 'Members' Club,' which should be both what the English Jockey Club is and what it is not— namely, both a tutelary guardian, as it were, of the Turf and a luxurious and fashionable lounge. At any rate that is what the French Jockey Club, after shifting quarters from Rue du Helder to Rue Grange Batelière, has become in its own house at the corner of the Boulevard des Capucines and Rue Scribe (where they built their magnificent rooms in 1863), 'horsiness' being now not required as a qualification on the part of a candidate, apparently, and the 'horsey' business being confided to a Race Committee, which has had no regular titular president since the lamented death of Viscount Paul Daru in 1876, though there is still a titular president of the Jockey Club, who by virtue of his office is always (since about 1865) an hon. member of the English Jockey Club. Lord Henry Seymour was the first president of the Club, which consisted of twelve substantive members (one of them being treasurer and two vice-presidents). Associated with him as original members were Count Maximilian Caccia, Count de Cambis (equerry to the Duke d'Orléans), M. Casimir Delamarre, Count Demidoff, M. Fasquel of Courteuil, M. Charles Laffitte (treasurer of the Club), M. Ernest

Leroy, the Chevalier de Machado, Prince N. de la Moscowa (vice-president), M. de Normandie, and M. Rienssec (vice-president). The King, Louis Philippe, was patron of the Association, and the Duke d'Orléans and the Duke de Nemours were honorary members, making the number fourteen altogether.

Let us see what manner of men these more or less illustrious personages were, and what they did to 'ameliorate' the French breed of horses and to promote French horse-racing.

Place aux rois! Let us commence with the Royal Family.

Louis Philippe, as a son of old Egalité, would naturally take to race horses and racing; but he had 'other fish to fry,' and to his son and heir, the Duke d'Orléans, to whom the King had ceded the *haras* of Meudon, which had been purchased from the ex-Dauphin, it is said, for 250,000 francs (10,000*l*.), was left the duty of developing the hereditary taste for horseflesh. That the King was lukewarm in his patronage of horse-racing may be gathered from one sporting paper at least of the day; but, on the other hand, he is credited with having sent M. Thiers to England on a mission which included an enquiry into the English system of managing a breeding stud, he decreed the formation of the French 'Stud Book,' and he took a certain interest in his son's horses, though his opinion of them does not seem to have been very high, to judge from the remark he is reported to have made after an inspection of the son's stables: 'You haven't a single horse, Orléans, with what I call a leg.' It has even been asserted that the patronage accorded by the King to the infant Jockey Club was prompted rather by policy than by a love of sport or a regard for horseflesh; but the blood of Egalité makes that assertion doubtful.

As for the Duke d'Orléans, the popular Prince, whose promise was such that, had he lived, he might have preserved the throne of France to his dynasty in 1848, and whose premature death brought to mind the touching lines of Virgil with the hackneyed 'Tu Marcellus eris,' he was undoubtedly a sportsman every inch. And, as if he had been a second Hippolytus, the horses he loved, it will be remembered, were his destruction; they ran away with his carriage, from which he leapt, receiving fatal injuries, in 1842. Then the newly established Jockey Club mourned its first and its greatest loss by death, and the French Turf, in its infancy, lost the best, if not the most enthusiastic, of its early 'fathers.' But he had already done wonders for the new-fledged institution. It is little to say that through his influence the French Jockey Club obtained leave to hold meetings regularly in the Champ de Mars; for the course there was about as bad as any could be, except, perhaps, that of Satory-Versailles, which is described as sheer cruelty to men and horses. The Duke d'Orléans did far more; he brought about the formation (in 1834) of the racecourse on the Duke d'Aumale's property at Chantilly (the Duke d'Aumale being but twelve years old), which was the best course in France (notwithstanding some drawbacks) until the creation of Longchamps (in 1856-57), and still remains the best of all in certain respects, especially picturesqueness and ability to withstand the effects of rain. At Chantilly was run the first Prix du Jockey Club (French Derby) in 1836, and the first Prix de Diane (or French Oaks) in 1843, and there those two races have been run ever since (except the memorable year 1848, when they were run at Versailles)

At Chantilly were the training-stables of the Duke d'Orléans; and there in 1839, with George Edwards, an Englishman, for trainer, with a staff of English grooms and stable lads, and with Edgar Pavis, English to the backbone and brother of the more celebrated Arthur Pavis, for principal jockey, the Duke had a score or more of horses in training, kept by pairs, two in each stable, with a picture of a horseshoe (or a real horseshoe) on every stable door, it is said, and the performances of each occupant painted upon the door within the shoe. The stud, as has been stated, was at Meudon, under the Duke's Master of the Horse, Count de Cambis, who had succeeded the King's Master of the Horse, Marquis de Strada, who had taken the place of the ex-Dauphin's Master of the Horse, Duke de Guiche. It may be roughly asserted that the racing of the French Turf from 1834 to 1842 was, but for the occasional intervention of M. Eugène Aumont and a few others, a duel between the Duke d'Orléans and Lord Henry Seymour. Of the score or more of horses which the Duke had in training in 1839, the most distinguished were Esmeralda, Romulus, Nautilus, Gigès, Quoniam, and the English-bred Beggarman, who won the Goodwood Cup of 1840, beating such 'illustrations' as Lanercost, Hetman Platoff, Charles XII., and Pocahontas (the dam of dams that bred Stockwell, Rataplan, and King Tom), and who, on returning to France under the care of Count de Cambis, was the hero of a ridiculous adventure, the zealous officials at Boulogne promptly seizing both horse and Count and committing them to durance vile, on suspicion of being the charger and equerry respectively of the Prince Louis Napoleon Bonaparte, who was just then giving trouble to the authorities. The Duke d'Orléans, in the name of Count de Cambis or in his own, won the Grand Prix, at Paris, with Volante (by Rowlston) in 1836, with Nautilus (by Cadland) in 1840, and with Gigès (by Priam) in 1841; the Prix du Cadran, at Paris, with Nautilus, in 1839, in 1840, and in 1842; the Poule d'Essai with Gigès in 1840, the Poule des Produits with Cauchemar (by Royal Oak) in 1841, and the Prix du Jockey Club with Romulus (by Cadland) in 1839. Of course he won many other successes, but they were of minor importance.

Of the Duke de Nemours it will suffice to say that he encouraged horse-racing regularly by his appearance at the races, and that it was he who came forward, his brother being employed on military service at the time, to receive the acclamations with which Beggarman's victory in the race for the Goodwood Cup of 1840 was greeted.

Such was the connection of the House of Orleans with the French Turf, such the countenance shown by that House to the institution during its first struggle into existence. To that House it must be acknowledged that the French Turf and the cause of the French thoroughbred (which is the English naturalised) owe not a little, if not quite so much as old Rome owed to the Neros. This, therefore, is a proper place for enumerating the chief English sires imported into France under the auspices of the House of Orleans from the birth of the French Jockey Club to the upheaval of thrones in 1848 :—

Abraham Cowley (by Jerry), foaled in 1836; Ægyptus (by Centaur), in 1834; Allington (by Gustavus), in 1833; Alteruter (by Lottery), in 1836; Anglesey (by Sultan), in 1837; Arthur (by Dick), in 1848; Ascot (by Gaberlunzie), in 1845; Young Bedlamite (by Bedlamite), in 1834; Beggarman (by Zin-

ganee), in 1839 ; Bizarre (by Orville), in 1840 ; Bon
Ton (by Phantom), in 1838 ; Brabant (by Lapdog), foaled
in 1836 ; Brocardo (by Touchstone), in 1848 ; Brookland
(by Filho da Puta), in 1839 ; *Cadland* (by Andrew), in
1834 ; Canton (by Cain), in 1845 ; Chance (by Lottery),
in 1837 ; Clarion (by Catton), in 1834 ; Copper Captain
(by Bobadil), in 1835 ; Count d'Orsay (by Dr. Faustus),
in 1836 ; Crispin, ex-Caspian (by Lottery), in 1835 ;
Dangerous (by Tramp), in 1836 ; Darlington (by Cleveland), in 1835 ; Delphi (by Elis), in 1842 ; Dick (by
Lamplighter), in 1836 ; Edmund (by Orville), in 1835 ;
Young Emilius (by Emilius, dam Cobweb), in 1834 ;
Fang (by Langar), in 1834 ; Farmington (by Cain), in
1844 (?) ; Faunus (by Whalebone), in 1836 ; Felix (by
Accident), in 1847 ; Freystrop (by Uncle Toby), in
1846 ; Frogmore (by Phantom), in 1838 ; General Mina
(by Camillus), in 1839 ; *Gladiator* (by Partisan), in
1846 ; Glory, ex-Bold Archer (by Glycon or Assassin),
in 1847 (by M. des Cars) ; His Highness (by Filho da
Puta), in 1839 ; Hœmus (by Sultan), in 1834 ; Hurricane (by Cain), before 1840 ; *Ibrahim* (by Sultan), in
1835 ; Ionian (by Ion), in 1847 ; Jason (by Centaur), in
1834 ; Jonas (by Whalebone), in 1835 ; The Juggler
(by Wamba), in 1837 ; Little Rover (by Cydnus), in
1837 ; *Lottery*, ex-Tinker (by Tramp), in 1834 ; Mahomet (by Muley), in 1835 ; *Mameluke* (by Partisan), in
1837 ; Marcellus (by Selim), in 1838 (?) ; Mariner (by
Merlin), in 1834 (?) ; *Mr. Wags* (by Langar), in 1838 (?) ;
Mendicant (by Tramp), in 1840 ; Minster (by Catton),
in 1835 ; Morotto (by Gustavus), in 1834 ; Muezzin
(by Sultan), in 1837 ; Napoleon (by Bob Booty), in
1834 ; Novelist (by Waverley), in 1835 ; *Nuncio* (by
Plenipotentiary), in 1847 ; Pagan (by Muley Moloch),
in 1846 ; Paradox (by Merlin), in 1834 ; Pegasus (by

Tiresias), in 1835 ; Petworth (by Little John), in 1835 ;
Physician (by Brutandorf), in 1842 ; Pickpocket (by
St. Patrick), in 1836 ; Polecat (by Bay Middleton),
in 1846 ; *The Prime Warden* (by Cadland), in 1847 ;
Prince Caradoc (by The Colonel), in 1847 ; Rabat-joie
(by Sir Hercules), in 1846 ; Roebuck (by Venison), in
1847 ; Romager (by Venison), in 1847 : Romeo (by
Emilius), in 1835 ; Royal George (by Royal Oak), in 1837 ;
Royal Oak (by Catton), in 1833 ; The Scavenger (by
Slane), in 1846 ; Secundus (by Scipio), foaled in 1836 ;
Sir Benjamin, *alias* Sir Benjamin Backbite (by Whisker),
in 1835 ; Skirmisher (by The Colonel), in 1837 ; Slang
(by Sober Robin), in 1835 ; Spatterdash (by Sir Benjamin), in 1842 ; Spectre (by Phantom), in 1834 ;
Sting (by Slane), in 1847 ; Tancred (by Selim), in 1834 ;
Tandem, ex-Multum in Parvo (by Rubens), in 1836 ;
Tetotum (by Lottery), in 1834 ; *Theodore* (by Woful),
in 1838 ; Tipple-Cider (by Defence), in 1846 ; Tourist
(by Dr. Syntax), in 1836 ; Tragedian (by Sir Isaac), in
1847 ; Tyrius (by Laurel), foaled in 1836 ; Vanloo (by
Waterloo), in 1836 ; Windcliffe (by Waverley), in 1836 ;
Worthless (by Camel), in 1846.

Of these names some are printed in italics, being the
names of very distinguished horses, such as Ibrahim,
winner of the Two Thousand ; Cadland, Dangerous, and
Mameluke, winners of the Derby ; Theodore, winner of
the St. Leger (a 'sensational' winner, though he never
did anything else) ; Lottery, Mr. Wags, Royal Oak, and
Sting, greater as sires than as performers, though Lottery
was a 'tickler' when his savage temper did not spoil
him and turn him simply into an 'eccentric genius ;' and
above all Gladiator, perhaps the very best sire the
French ever had from us, notwithstanding that Royal
Oak produced so many winners of French races and was

the sire of Poetess, who was the dam of the celebrated Hervine and of the great Monarque, who was the sire of so many 'illustrations,' including the fabulous Gladiateur. It is due to the Administration des Haras to mention that to them the French owed the purchase of Gladiator at a cost of 62,500 francs (2,500*l.*); but it was a private individual—Lord Henry Seymour—who purchased Royal Oak. Under the House of Orleans, then, it has been made plain that the Government had begun to launch out, to aim high, to bid for winners of our great races, and, what is more, to show judgment in buying at good prices well bred horses that had distinguished themselves, though they had not won our great races.

Let us now pass on to the other 'foundation members' of the French Jockey Club, or of the Race Committee thereof, giving the first place, as of right, to Lord Henry Seymour. This extraordinary personage was born in 1805, and died at Paris, which was also his birthplace, in 1859. It is said that he never so much as set foot in England (which was, *Hibernice*, his native land, though he was not 'raised' there); but Paris never knew a visitor or resident who displayed more of the 'madness' which foreigners consider natural to Englishmen. He was supposed, as has been already mentioned, to be related on his mother's side to 'old Q.' or George Selwyn, or both, and from either or both of them he might well have inherited some of his odd humours as well as his taste for horses and the Turf, inasmuch as both George Selwyn and 'old Q.' were members of our Jockey Club as well as men of strange humours, and 'old Q.' was one of the most famous gentlemen jockeys of his day, besides being one of the most prominent patrons of the Turf. How Lord Henry would drive about Paris and its neighbourhood with four horses, postilions, outriders, and bugle horns; how he would sit at the window of the noted 'Vendanges de Bourgogne,' in company with other *viveurs*, to see the 'descente de la Courtille,' the return from the 'barrier ball,' in the early morning after 'Mardi Gras;' and how (being a pleasant gentleman who liked his gold to be burning hot before he gave it away) he would scatter among the crowd of returning 'maskers' and others a copious 'friture d'or,' may be learned from such works as 'Les Salons de Paris sous Louis-Philippe,' by Viscount de Beaumont-Vassy. What curious testamentary documents, and how many of them (something over a score between 1855 and 1859), Lord Henry drew up or caused to be drawn up, and what trouble he created (not unintentionally, the cynics have suggested) by his handsome bequest of 72,000*l.* to be divided between the 'hospices' of Paris and London, may be gathered from the reported case of 'Wallace *v.* the Attorney-General.' He may have been considered by his friends a 'fellow of infinite jest;' but, as there were few, if any, mourners (beyond four or five members of the French Jockey Club) at his funeral, according to the accounts, or at any rate one account, his intimate friends were probably at last estranged; and certainly his fun was frequently of a questionable sort, akin to the worst kind of practical joking. He is said to have been the original of Balzac's 'droll,' who would administer drastic medicines furtively to his dearest friends and derive intense enjoyment from the very unpleasant results. He delighted, it is said, in the humane and ingenious pastime of giving away cigars with something explosive inserted in the extremity, and watching the effect when a light was applied by unsuspecting smokers. It is almost a pity that he did not live in the days of dynamite;

he might have had what the Americans call a 'good time,' and the newspapers might have had a charming variety of catastrophes to record. He was much comforted in his last moments, it is related, by a neat device he hit upon for making the loss of him felt and regretted by his servants: he left not a penny to any of them, expressly that they might miss him. It has been hinted, however, that he had another reason—that he knew how he had been plundered by those servants during his lifetime; that he had submitted uncomplainingly, for the sake of peace and quietness, as long as he lived; and that his apparent want of generosity was merely his 'playful way' of showing that he had not been so blind as they had supposed. However that may be, he was generously and tenderly mindful of his favourite horses, leaving annuities to four or five of them, together with an injunction that they should be exempt from saddle work (presumably from any kind of work). And it is Lord Henry's connection with horses that gives him prominence here.

He may be said to have 'encouraged' horse-racing almost from his cradle, both by example and by precept, by personal performance in the pigskin upon the 'amateurs' ride' in the Bois de Boulogne and by proxy in the form of a professional jockey to whom he gave instructions; and when, in 1833, he and some of his associates said to one another, 'Go to! let us found a Jockey Club after the English fashion (only more gregarious) and a Society for the Amelioration of the French Breed of Horses,' he threw himself enthusiastically into the work and set about improving his stock and his stables (whether at Sablonville, or Glatigny, or elsewhere), which had already attained considerable celebrity.

He at once imported Royal Oak (son of Catton and sire of Slane), who, though he had been but a very moderate performer on the racecourse, became a very king of the stud in France and was the sire of quite a galaxy of French celebrities.

But it was not by the importation of Royal Oak, or of Ibrahim (winner of the Two Thousand in 1835), or of any other horse, that Lord Henry did so much for horse-breeding and horse-racing in France as to deserve the title of 'the father of fathers of the French Turf;' it was by the importation of men, of Mr. Thomas Carter, the famous trainer, and in his wake or under his wing, as stable assistants, Messrs. Henry and Thomas Jennings, *par nobile fratrum*, and afterwards an equally notable pair of trainers; for though Mr. Carter may have introduced the two great brethren, yet Lord Henry introduced Mr. Carter, and so led to the importation of the twain.

Lord Henry won the Grand Prix at Paris with Miss Annette (by Reveller) in 1835 and with Franck (by Rainbow) in 1837; the Prix du Cadran, at Paris, with Franck in 1838; and the Prix du Jockey Club (French Derby) with Franck, Lydia (by Rainbow), Vendredi (by Cain), and Poetess (by Royal Oak) in 1836, 1837, 1838, and 1841, besides numerous or innumerable smaller affairs, including all sorts of matches; his winners, however (such as Miss Annette, purchased from M. Crémieux), do not all—or even most of them— seem to have been bred by him or begotten by sires imported by him, but they were mostly trained by Mr. Carter, to whom they probably owed their success (though Poetess is said to have been trained by R. Boyce). The colours of Lord Henry Seymour, which were orange and black cap, disappeared from the French Turf about a year after the French Derby had been won by his famous Poetess in 1841, and she also disappeared for a while, the double disappearance being connected, no doubt, in some way with a 'scandal' which arose out of the French Derby of 1840, and which will receive due notice hereafter in the proper place. Oddly enough, notwithstanding Lord Henry's great success, his two chief stud horses, Royal Oak and Ibrahim, seem to have gone a-begging for some time after his retirement, both in England and in France. Perhaps he put too high a price upon them; but they eventually found a home in the French Government's studs, where they both died in 1849. The great things achieved by Lord Henry Seymour for the French Turf are kept in memory by the Prix Seymour at the Paris Summer Meeting, and the Prix de Glatigny, the Prix Royal Oak, and the Prix de Sablonville at the Paris Autumn Meeting.

Besides the president, Lord Henry Seymour, there were at first two vice-presidents of the French Jockey Club—Joseph Napoleon Ney, Prince de la Moscowa, and M. Rieussec.

The Prince de la Moscowa was the eldest son of Marshal Ney, 'the bravest of the brave,' and the eldest brother of the Duke d'Elchingen (whose son, the second Duke d'Elchingen, died so mysteriously some few years ago at a miserable sort of house in the suburbs of Paris) and of Edgar Ney (the friend and equerry of Napoleon III.), who himself in 1857 received the title of Prince de la Moscowa. The former Prince de la Moscowa, at first vice-president and afterwards president of the French Jockey Club, though his memory is kept green upon the French Turf by the Prix de la Moscowa at the Paris Summer Meeting, and though he was a famous 'gentleman rider' and both owned and bred race horses, is probably better remembered as an accomplished musician and composer and as a writer of various works (whether about horses or upon other subjects), as well as a magnificent *viveur*, than as a patron of horse-racing and horse-breeding. His name is not conspicuous among either the winners of the great French races or the importers of horses that became famous as sires. His colours—yellow, blue sleeves and cap—never showed (according to the records) in the first place among the runners for the French Oaks or the French Derby. On the other hand he was the composer of the opera ' Régine ' (to mention none other), and he wrote the ' Histoire du Siège de Valenciennes,' to say nothing of ' horsey ' treatises. He was born in May 1805 and died in July 1857; he married the daughter and only child of the French ' king-maker,' Jacques Laffitte, the banker, who in mockery of his son-in-law's title called himself ' Prince du Rabot ' (' Prince of the Plane,' for his father had been a carpenter), and who made the celebrated reply ' C'est trop tard ' to the reluctant overtures of Charles X. It seems but the other day that we were reading the distressing story of the Prince de la Moscowa's widow and her behaviour towards her daughter, who had married the Duke de Persigny and shared his ruined fortunes at Nice, and were wondering whether, what with the fate of the ' bravest of the brave,' what with the sad end of the second Duke d'Elchingen, and what with the public scandal concerning the Princess de la Moscowa and her daughter, there was ever a family whose fortunes were such a mixture of brilliancy and misery as those of the Neys.

As for M. Rieussec, the other vice-president, he was a notable man in many ways, and his death is historical. In point of years he was about the 'father' of the French Jockey Club, and he had been improving the breed of French horses, to the best of his ability, for some thirty years before 1833. He was apparently a prosperous timber merchant, or something of that kind, and at the latter part of his life a lieutenant-colonel in the National Guard. As early as 1805, or even before, he had formed a stud at Buc, not far from Versailles, whence he removed to Viroflay, where there had always been a stud within the memory of man, and where his efforts were seconded by the Government until the events of 1815 interfered with his progress. He recommenced his labours, however, as soon as possible, though with scantier means; made three trips at least to England, and brought home with him several English thoroughbred mares and horses, including Rainbow, already mentioned, with whose son Félix he won, in 1834, the Grand Prix at Paris, which of course must not be confounded with the Grand Prix de Paris. Unfortunately M. Rieussec had but comparatively little chance of seeing his colours—sky blue and red cap—borne to the front, for he was one of those eighteen who fell victims to the murderous attempt made by Fieschi upon Louis Philippe's life on July 28, 1835. His daughter, Madame Cazalot, however, won several races with his horses; and he had already set his mark very distinctly on the French Turf, whereon his memory is perpetuated by the Prix Rainbow, the Prix Rieussec, and the Prix de Viroflay at the Paris Spring Meeting. 'M. Rieussec,' said an obituary notice of him, 'un des premiers employa ses connaissances et sa fortune à former un haras modèle en France dans sa belle propriété de Viroflay. Sa mort est une véritable perte pour notre naissante industrie chevaline et pour

D

les nombreux ouvriers dont il était le père et le soutien.' He was materially assisted by an Englishman named Palmer (well known in English 'horsey' circles of his day), who was at one time his head man, who is reported to have made a good thing in francs by exhibiting at so much a head the celebrated stud horse Rainbow on Sundays to the Parisians and others (who 'gaped upon him as on a thing miraculous'), and who seems to have been identical with the founder of 'Palmer's New Betting Rooms,' one of the earliest precursors of the 'Salon des Courses,' at Paris. And so within two years of its certified existence the French Turf lost one of its earliest and most enthusiastic 'fathers.'

Very different was the case with M. Charles Laffitte, the first treasurer of the French Jockey Club and one of the original 'foundation members.' He lived to 1875 or 1876, and had been known, when he died, as a sportsman of some fifty years' standing, having established that character before the date of the Société d'Encouragement. As early as 1829 he is found racing, sometimes on the principle of 'every man his own jockey,' and in 1831 he appeared as plaintiff in an action against Madame veuve Crémieux (widow of the celebrated breeder and dealer and sister of M. Chéri-Salvador, the first French 'Tattersall') about a filly misrepresented as being 'by Merlin' instead of 'by Morisco,' and recovered damages. He is described in the 'case' as 'M. Charles Laffitte, of 36 Rue Laffitte, Paris;' he is understood to have been a nephew of the celebrated Jacques Laffitte, father of the Princess de la Moscowa, and was himself a banker, in which capacity he was well adapted for his post of treasurer to the Jockey Club and for the useful part he is said to have performed afterwards when the grant for the Grand Prix de Paris was discussed by the municipal authorities. M. Charles Laffitte, yielding to the epidemic which was so prevalent in his country at the time, married an Englishwoman, Miss Fairlie Cunningham, who seems to have had a near relative of her own name (perhaps her father or brother) among the early members of the French Jockey Club, and who held an acknowledged position among 'the beauties of Chantilly.' Not as Charles Laffitte, however, the man of business, the worthy banker, but as dashing 'Major Fridolin,' or 'Colonel Fridolin' (as he was sometimes called), the fashionable military gentleman, was 'the treasurer' known, at first on the French Turf and then on our own. It was not, nevertheless, in the springtide of his sporting career, when his colours appear to have been sky blue and black cap, but long afterwards, when his white jacket and sky blue cap were almost as well known and formidable in England as in France, that he can be said to have exercised a perceptible—though always a truly paternal—influence upon the breed of French horses and the progress of the French Turf. It was not, indeed, until the year 1864 or thereabouts, when, the Lagrange-Nivière partnership, known as 'la Grande Ecurie,' having been dissolved, 'Major Fridolin' became joint owner with Baron Nivière of the La Morlaye stable and the Villebon stud, that he began to be conspicuous. After that Gontran, Bigarreau, Sornette, Franc-Tireur, and others, some of them as well known and almost as much thought of in England as in France, were horses that did him extraordinary credit. The best hits made by the first treasurer of the French Jockey Club, whether we call him M. Charles Laffitte or Major Fridolin, or promote him to Colonel Fridolin, were the purchase of Light ('bred in France'), sire of both Bigarreau and Sornette (who won the French Derby, the French Oaks, and the Grand Prix between them, all in one year, 1870), and still more, perhaps, the importation from England of Tournament, sire of many good sons and daughters, including Franc-Tireur, Sabre, and Tyrolienne. 'Major Fridolin' and his breeding stud are intentionally or accidentally commemorated by the Prix de Villebon at Paris Autumn Meeting and the Prix de Château-Laffitte at Chantilly Autumn Meeting, not to mention the Prix Charles Laffitte at Dieppe. M. Charles Laffitte appears to have been a 'deputy' and likewise a 'count;' but he seems to have despised or at any rate to have neglected the title, as became a nephew (as he is said to have been) of old 'Prince du Rabot.'

We now come to the eight 'foundation members' of the Jockey Club (or of the Comité des Courses), who originally held no special office.

Count Max. Caccia, the first in alphabetical order, betrays his Italian origin and his natural proclivities by his very name, which means 'hunt' or 'chase,' or even 'sport.' He appears to have been that Count Maximilian Caccia who, though of Piedmontese birth and family, received his early education in Paris, was a captain of French hussars in 1846, in which year he wrote a book entitled 'Les Vertus Militaires,' dedicated to the Duke de Nemours (himself an honorary foundation member of the French Jockey Club), and who subsequently, when the affairs of Italy demanded his services, served as colonel in the Piedmontese army and was lost, so far as any trace of him remains in the records, to the French Turf. He was both a breeder and an owner of race horses, as well as a noted rider. He had a 'haras,' as appears from the newspapers of the day, and from it he supplied even Lord Henry Seymour with certain horses, including the half-bred Clérino. He is the hero too of a curious 'sporting event' for a bet of 50 louis between himself and Lord Henry. The Count was a pupil of the Ecole Royale d'Equitation de Paris, and, to maintain the excellence of the riding taught in that school, he made the aforesaid bet that he would ride at the trot ('au trot anglais'—that is, no doubt, without 'pacing' or 'ambling,' but at the true diagonal trot) and 'bare back' (in French 'à poil') from the Porte Maillot to the Porte de Boulogne, in the Bois de Boulogne, a distance of something over two miles. This he did, and 'realised the stakes,' on November 27, 1829, triumphantly vindicating the cause of the Ecole d'Equitation de Paris, though his friends were afraid that 'the long and rapid descent towards the Porte de Boulogne' would be rather too much for him and his riding-master. However none of the great French races and none of the illustrious sires or dams of the French studs appear to have been assigned to Count Max. Caccia.

We now come to Count de Cambis, who died in Paris in 1874 at the great age of eighty, and was described at that time as 'ancien officier supérieur.' The Count derived his chief importance, of course, from the fact that he had the management of the Meudon stud for the Duke d'Orléans (himself honorary foundation member of the French Jockey Club). He was equerry to the Duke, and afterwards honorary equerry to the infant Count de Paris. Count de Cambis, after the death of the Duke d'Orléans (who frequently, if not generally, ran in the Count's name), won the Prix de Diane (French Oaks) in 1847 with Wirthschaft (by Gigès), but in his capacity, no doubt, of manager of the Meudon stud, where she was foaled. The Count's prominence in matters of the Turf, however, is shown by his appointment as one of the very first 'Commission of the Stud Book.' He is not to be confounded with the Marquis de Cambis d'Orsan, created a peer of France in October 1837. As manager of the Meudon stud Count de Cambis ranks among the very chiefest 'fathers' of the French Turf. His curious adventure, or misadventure, on returning to France with the Duke d'Orléans' Beggarman after this horse had won the Goodwood Cup in 1840 has already been mentioned.

The next on the list is M. Casimir Delamarre (quite a distinct personage from Count Achille Delamarre, some time president of the French Jockey Club), who was a cavalry officer at first, then a banker (having married the daughter of M. Martin Didier, of whose banking house he became the head in course of time), and at the same time proprietor of 'La Patrie,' which newspaper he purchased and may be said to have raised from next to nothing to a real power in the State. M. Delamarre did not become conspicuous either among the great winners or the great breeders of his day, but he worked for 'the cause;' and it is recorded that at the sale of M. Crémieux's 'Madrid' stud, Bois de Boulogne, in 1831, he gave 8,195 francs (about 328*l.*)—a sum never before paid in France, it is said, for so young an animal—for the yearling Fra Diavolo, which found its way into the omnivorous stables of Lord Henry Seymour, but has left no name to conjure with, and, in fact, was at last 'added to the list' in 1849 (*v.* French Stud Book). It was, nevertheless, from a Delamarre (whether related to M. Casimir or not) that, strange to say, the English were to receive their first 'knockdown blow' in their fight with the French for the glories of horse-racing; for when, in 1864, there was no blinking the fact that the winner of the English Derby (and a winner so idolised—without sufficient cause, perhaps—as Blair Athol) had been beaten fairly and squarely, full weight for age, over a distance that was an undeniable test, by a French horse, not only bred in France, but never sent out of France for a whiff of the Newmarket breeze, or a gallop on Newmarket Heath, or a change of air and a bit of exercise on English downs, the owner of that horse, Vermout by name (and a very bitter sort of 'pick-me up' he seemed), was M. Henri Delamarre.

As for Count Demidoff, who comes next in order, he is made out to have been that Count Anatole Demidoff (created Count or Duke of San Donato by the Grand Duke of Tuscany) who married Princess Mathilde (cousin of Napoleon III.) in 1841 and separated from her by mutual consent in 1845. The Count, whose family derived fabulous wealth from the Ural mines, was born at Florence in 1812 and died at Paris in 1870. His father had imported Arabian horses into the Crimea, and he himself imported English thoroughbreds into Russia, France, and Italy. His name is found in connection with that of the celebrated Sir Joseph Hawley in the chronicles of horse-racing at Florence. Count Anatole, or Prince Anatole, as he afterwards became, is far better remembered as a great traveller (which made his horse-racing desultory), as a munificent patron of art and literature, and as no mean man of letters himself, than as one of the 'fathers of the French Turf.' No wonder, then, that his colours—green and orange fringe, blue cap—were not seen very often in the front at French races. Among his published works may be mentioned a 'Voyage dans la Russie Méridionale et la Crimée, par la Hongrie, la Valachie et la Moldavie' and (posthumously) 'Prisonniers de Guerre des Puissances Belligérantes pendant la Campagne de Crimée.' Among English thoroughbreds that belonged to him may be mentioned Paradox (for the sake of the name, which has since become famous), by Merlin, imported into Florence in 1831 and transferred to France in 1834, and Tim, by Middleton, imported into France (by Count Demidoff, it is presumed) in 1836. Howbeit none of the French horses that have made a reputation can be readily traced to the importations of Count Demidoff.

Pass we on now to M. Fasquel ' of Courteuil,' so distinguished, not only to keep him from being confounded with another M. Fasquel (Alcibiade), an owner of horses, but also and no doubt chiefly for the sake of the excellent stud he possessed in the very earliest days of the French Turf, a stud which the princely and aristocratic visitors at Chantilly at race time would go over to see and admire and take a lesson from. In 1834, indeed, a high, if not the very highest, rank was assigned to the stud of M. Fasquel, who is described as 'propriétaire et agriculteur bien connu' at the village of 'Courteuil, near Senlis (Oise),' where he not only had factories but also a large estate 'pouvant produire en abondance tout ce qui est nécessaire au cheval.' Mr. F. Kent appears to have trained for M. Fasquel, who was a great purchaser of horses both in Normandy and in England, or of animals imported from England, or of the produce of animals imported thence; but, in proportion to his exertions, he was perhaps the most unfortunate of all the early 'fathers' of the French Turf. His colours, red and black cap, were certainly borne to victory by Minuit in the Grand Prix at Paris in 1842, by Tomate in the Prix du Cadran in 1846, by Fort-à-bras in the Prix de la Ville de Paris in 1859, and on sundry other more or less unimportant occasions by the aforesaid or by sundry other horses; but not once did French Oaks or French Derby fall to the lot of this indefatigable gentleman, and his success, in comparison with his means and pains, must be considered infinitesimal. He seems to have died about 1873, but his memory, or that of his stud, may be said to be preserved by the Prix de Courteuil at Chantilly Spring Meeting.

We have now arrived at M. Ernest Leroy, who died at Maisons-Laffitte on November 16, 1880, at the great age of eighty-two, having been (with the exception of the Duke de Nemours, who was originally an honorary foundation member) the only 'original member' left alive after the death of M. Charles Laffitte. M. Leroy was a noted 'gentleman rider' in his day, and was for some time on the Commission of the Stud Book. Though his colours, blue and black cap, were not conspicuous in the principal contests, he occupied a foremost position among the early promoters of French horse-racing and horse-breeding, and by his agency were introduced into France many valuable sires from England. He was apparently the titular purchaser—chiefly, no doubt, on behalf of the French Government—of Ægyptus, by Centaur; Darlington, by Cleveland; Sir Benjamin Backbite, by Whisker; Elthiron, by Pantaloon; Womersley, by Irish Birdcatcher; Hernandez, by Pantaloon; Lanercost, by Liverpool, &c.; and certainly, if his purchases were left to his own judgment, he did not do badly for his clients, though it was not he, but M. Thannberg, it is said, who got Ion so cheap at 450 guineas, and M. le Chevalier de la Place who obtained Gladiator, about the best bargain the French Government ever made, for 2,000 guineas, or (according to a French authority) 2,500*l*. (62,500 francs).

The next 'item' is Chevalier de Machado, who, as his name would indicate, was a Spaniard, though he was settled at Paris. Perhaps he belonged to the embassy; anyhow he was a gentleman of position and influence, as is to be inferred from the fact that he was employed by his Government, at the time of the Carlist disturbances in 1834 or thereabouts, on a political mission in London. He may have promoted the interests of the French Turf to a greater extent than the writer of these words wots of, but little or no trace of his personal participation is to be found in the generally accepted records of French horse-racing and horse-breeding.

There remains to be noticed M. de Normandie, a very prominent personage among the 'fathers of the French Turf.' He would occupy an official position now and then at the flat racing, and in steeple-chasing he was regarded (not so much by his rivals, perhaps, save in their secret hearts, as by his friends and himself) as *facile princeps*. *Princeps* is said advisedly, for in one French publication certainly, if not in more, he is styled 'Duc de Normandie,' a slight mistake with which his colours, being 'all white,' suggesting some connection with the Royal Bourbons, may have had something to do. Even the 'fifth-form schoolboy,' whom Lord Macaulay was fond of crediting with a miraculous amount of knowledge, is no doubt aware—much more should a French publication have been—that since the ducal seal was solemnly broken in 1469, and Normandy declared inseparable from the crown of France for ever, the title of Duke de Normandie has been borne by nobody but Louis XVI.'s second son, more commonly known as the ephemeral Louis XVII. It is in quite a different direction that we must look for the family of

M. de Normandie or Denormandie, for the latter is the form adopted by the gentleman who was some time Governor of the Bank of France and a member of the Senate, and who is understood to have been a nephew or other relative of the redoubtable 'father of the French Turf.' M. de Normandie, the great 'gentleman jock,' is said to have been long resident in England, where he imbibed those tastes, contracted those habits, learned to advocate those doctrines which were ridiculed as 'anglomanie' by Frenchmen who were opposed to the ideas of the new Société d'Encouragement and attached to the views of the Administration des Haras. Anyhow M. de Normandie, as has already been stated, acquired the reputation of being the 'crack' gentleman rider, the French 'Arthur Coventry,' of his generation, able to hold his own against English gentlemen and English jockeys, equal to 'showing the way' to such horsemen as MM. Edgar Ney, the Prince de la Moscowa, Ernest Leroy, the Count de Vaublanc, the Count de Morny, the Viscount de Hédouville, Charles Laffitte ('Major Fridolin'), and even Mackenzie-Grieves, the demi-French Scoto-Englishman, who has justly been regarded as 'the father of French racecourses.' M. de Normandie won what is said to have been the first regular steeple-chase ever run in France on English principles. It took place in 1829 or 1830 near St. Germain, in the commune of Jouy; and M. de Normandie came in first, having behind him the Prince de la Moscowa and six others, including two Englishmen (Captain Locke and Mr. Tomlin). M. de Normandie was also the winner of an improvised race which took place at Chantilly in 1833 between himself, Prince Lobanoff, Viscount de Hédouville, and others, and which is said to have suggested the idea of forming the racecourse there. M. de Normandie frequently acted in the earliest days of the French Jockey Club as steward, judge, and starter; and thus, though he does not appear to have introduced any famous strain of blood into the studs of his country, left his impress ineffaceably upon the French Turf.

Such, then, were the men who founded the Society which has become, whether this were the original intention or not, a large and fashionable Club as well as an Association for the Encouragement and Improvement of French Horse-breeding; such were the men who were the 'foundation members' of the French Jockey Club and formed its first Comité des Courses or Race Committee.

It will be seen at a glance that the French Jockey Club, at its institution, consisted, for the most part, of such members as belonged to our own Jockey Club at its origin: there were Royal Princes (like our 'Culloden' Duke of Cumberland), noblemen, men of rank and wealth, men of property without high rank, all having considerable influence, all or nearly all deeply interested in horse-breeding and in the improvement of the breed of horses by means of horse-racing (the only safe guide towards a 'selection of the fittest'), and all or nearly all practical horsemen, riding their own horses on occasion. In other points, besides promising auspices, influential connections, and personal enthusiasm, there was a resemblance (arising, no doubt, from express imitation) between the new French Jockey Club and the long-established English. There were the three stewards of the French Jockey Club, the rules and orders of the French Jockey Club, the rules of racing (applicable only to races under the Club's own management), and so on. As regards election, place of meeting, and subscription, however, the French Jockey Club seems to have been formed only speciously—if at all—on the model of the English, and with very different results. In both the number of members is understood to be nominally unlimited, but whilst there is virtually a limit to the number in the English Club the French has grown like a grain of mustard seed. It is doubtful whether the English Club ever numbered (all honorary members included) a hundred, and they have always had some—however far away—connection with horse-racing; the French has reached its thousand or two, and it is said that the only horse that most of them have anything to do with is a clothes-horse. The English Club, too, for a long while had no regular meeting-place in London until Messrs. Weatherby went to 6 Old Burlington Street; the Club would meet at the Star and Garter, Pall Mall, or at the Thatched House, St. James's, or at Tattersall's, or at one another's houses (as is the case now sometimes, on business). The French Club, on the contrary, seem to have always had a regular Club House in Paris, though it had one or two other local habitations (in Rue du Helder, Rue Grange-Batelière, and Rue de Grammont) before settling down at the corner of Rue Scribe. The twelve 'originals' were not long in adding to their number, as they might do (according to their programme) to an unlimited extent; and it is probable that the modest payments which were fixed in the first instance facilitated their progress. Two hundred francs entrance and one hundred yearly subscription appear to have been the amounts to be paid at the outset. Then, when 'Société' was distinguished from 'Cercle' (or 'Jockey Club'), so that it became possible to belong to the former without being a member of the latter (but a member of the latter must belong to the former), the payments for the first year amounted apparently to 500 francs. One black ball to five white was fixed as the measure of exclusion. Various changes have been made, always (of course) in the direction of higher payments, especially as regards the entrance fee, which is said to be, or lately to have been, 1,050 fr. (40 gs.), with an annual subscription of 500 fr. (20*l*.) In certain respects the French Club has for many years been more liberal than the English: ambassadors and foreign ministers may be admitted—on application—without ballot, and any member of the English Jockey Club—on application—can obtain admission to the French Jockey Club's stand at races, and can—or could in 1870—be admitted to the Club for a month. This apparently greater liberality can, of course, be easily explained: the English Jockey Club has so few members comparatively (and consequently is not likely to overcrowd the French stand), and has no large or even fixed Club House such as the French Club has, to which temporary members could be admitted; and if it had the French visitors might be numerous enough to swamp the place.

However that may be, the liberality displayed towards strangers, whether English or other, by the French Jockey Club was not extended to the conditions of the races (under the Club's management), which were confined to horses 'bred in France,' with a few insignificant exceptions; and this restrictive spirit led in time to that English yell for 'reciprocity' which will receive due notice in the proper place. It should be remembered, however, that the infant French Jockey Club could not hope to compete at first with English antagonists, would have disgusted the French people with horse-racing in which victory must almost certainly have remained in every case with the foreigner and with foreign horses, and would have ruined at the outset the very cause the Club was instituted to promote. Besides, the Club required funds to found prizes; and the only way to get those funds was to have 'gate meetings,' at which few Frenchmen would be likely to pay their francs simply to see their native horses beaten, and at which few French owners were likely to subscribe heavy sums of money to be carried across 'the silver streak,' so that it would have been hopeless to look for any considerable 'race fund' from an accumulation of 'entries' and 'forfeits.' Moreover the Club was in direct conflict with the State as represented by the Administration des Haras (ready enough to offer small 'prix' at races on the 'demi-sang' or 'pure Arab' and anti-English plan), so that no subvention of any importance was to be hoped for from that quarter; not to mention that the Administration would have been more determined than the Club itself to limit the competition to horses 'bred in France.' Yet it was quite clear that 'prix' or 'added money' would be required to coax French owners to pay even a moderate 'entry' before they would incur the expenses of training and racing, and that 'gate meetings,' at which French self-respect or even vanity must not receive any violent shock, were the best means of providing resources for 'prix.' Whether a 'gate' were charged at the very commencement or not matters little; it soon became the universal —or all but universal—practice, and in course of time the funds of the French Jockey Club were so large that the 'prix' or 'added money' for the Prix du Jockey Club, or French Derby, fixed originally at 5,000 francs (200*l.*), had risen in a few years to 20,000 francs (800*l.*), and in 1878 had reached the handsome amount of

50,000 francs (2,000*l.*)—at which it still remains—so that in 1886 the French Derby was worth nearly 4,500*l.*, only about 200*l.* less than the old, rich English. It must be acknowledged, then, on the whole, that the French Jockey Club exercised a sound discretion in restricting its ' prix ' to the competition of horses ' bred in France ' only ; for though perhaps at the beginning the ' prix ' would not have been attractive enough in value to tempt the best English horses, yet inferior English horses would have been quite good enough for the purpose then, and either the French would have lost their interest, through sheer disgust, in the sport forthwith, or, as the 'prix' became more valuable and attracted still better horses from England, the French would have been similarly affected at a somewhat later period. Anyhow this fundamental difference remains between the English Jockey Club and the French : that the latter contributes, and from the first did contribute, as ' added money ' a very considerable portion— if not the greater part—of every one of the most valuable prizes in France, whereas the former contributes, and always did contribute, nothing at all to the most valuable prizes in England ; and that the latter literally reared the infant institution of the French Turf from a weakling to a giant, whilst the former found the English Turf a full-grown and flourishing but somewhat wild and erratic monster and promptly assumed the guidance of it.

The fourteen ' foundation members ' of the French Jockey Club (or of its first Race Committee), who have been named and described, took to themselves, either immediately or from time to time—or as they themselves dropped off had their places supplied by—men who were more famous than they upon the French Turf. The Race Committee came to consist of fifteen 'foundation members,' as they continue to be called, and fifteen 'subsidiary members' (or 'membres adjoints'); and among the earliest and most notable of these were Prince Marc de Beauvau (of the La Morlaye stable and Viroflay stud), Messrs. Fould (of Chantilly, Ibos, and Le Nivernais), Viscount de Hédouville, Viscount Paul Daru (president of the Race Committee), M. Auguste Lupin (importer of a multitude, with comparatively little success), Baron N. de Rothschild (owner of Baroncino), Baron de la Rochette, Count F. de Lagrange (owner of Gladiateur), Henri Delamarre (owner of Vermout), Baron Schickler (the lucky purchaser of The Nabob, sire of Vermout and Bois-Roussel), M. Charles Calenge (founder of Caen races to all intents and purposes, though there was racing there as early as 1837, before he took matters in hand), Mr. Mackenzie-Grieves, and others, *quos nunc describere longum est.*

CHAPTER III.

THE FIRST STRUGGLES.

When the French Jockey Club commenced their patriotic and Herculean task in 1833 it may be said that, save here and there in the provinces perhaps (as in the North at Le Pin, where there had been racing 'off and on' since 1805, and at Dieppe, where Count de Tocqueville, as has already been mentioned, had a private 'hippodrome' of his own, and, it may be, at Pompadour, where the Administration des Haras had for many years a breeding stud, at Tarbes, and at other places in the South), there were in France no racecourses on which a conscientious owner could invite a respectable horse to risk his limbs in a serious race, or any human jockey to expose his flesh and blood and bones (especially his collar bone) to what that flesh and blood would have to bear. There had been steeple-chasing at Croix de Berny as early as 1832, and at La Marche there were regular steeple-chases not long afterwards; and, as we have seen, there had been all kinds of horse-racing at odd times (before and after 1783), whether at Vincennes or at Fontainebleau or elsewhere; but, according to excellent authority, the 'hippodrome' of Chantilly, when it was first laid out (1833–34), was 'unique in France.' In the Champ de Mars and at Satory-Versailles, the chief places of racing near Paris (before the 'venue' was moved to the Bois de Boulogne), the ground was simply detestable. The Champ de Mars was bad enough, but things were still worse at Satory-Versailles, where, in wet weather, the course was 'so deep in mud that the horses could hardly move,' and in dry weather 'so hard as to endanger the strongest legs,' not to mention that 'when the horses galloped the jockeys were blinded by a cloud of dust and small pebbles.' Of course the same difficulties, in a modified degree, have to be encountered sometimes in England on the very best courses, but the Champ de Mars and Satory-Versailles seem to have been intolerable.

In those early times, when the 'duel' between the Duke d'Orléans and Lord Henry Seymour (with an Aumont intervening now and then) was the main feature of French horse-racing, the noteworthy meetings were very few in number, comprising scarcely any beyond the Paris Spring Meeting of four days, the Chantilly Spring Meeting of three days, the Versailles Summer Meeting on two consecutive Sundays, the Chantilly Autumn Meeting of two days running, and the Paris Autumn Meeting of three days. And if the number of meetings was small, so was the number of competing horses, and so was the value of the 'prix.' Hence, to make a good many races with very few horses, the practice of running races in 'heats' was grossly abused. What was the state of things in 1840 may be gathered from a letter in which Madame de Girardin remarks, 'The races on Sunday were favoured with superb weather, and the extraordinary sight was seen of nine horses running together—nine live horses, nine rivals—a rare spectacle in the Champ de Mars. Generally one horse runs all alone, contending against no opponent, and always coming in first. But this does not signify; it excites the admiration of those who love sport, and especially of the philosophers among them: it is so noble to strive against and overcome —oneself!'

As for the value of the 'prix,' a plate of 100*l.* would have been handsome, but it was sometimes enhanced by the addition of some crockery-ware from Sèvres, by way, says a French cynic, of 'encouraging at one and the same time the ceramic as well as the hippic industry; but the owners of horses did not much care for it, as they could not cover their expenses with these cumbersome works of art.'

We learn, on trustworthy authority, that 'the average number of horses running every year, which had been but 59 from 1833 to 1840, rose to 125 between 1841 and 1848, and soon afterwards to 140 and even 160.' Some of these animals appear to have been kept a long while in training, and to have been sent long and troublesome journeys to pick up sums of from 60*l.* to 80*l.* Old Hervine, for instance, who had won the Prix de Diane (French Oaks) for M. Alexandre Aumont in 1851, was seen running, it is recorded, at Chantilly in 1855—ten weeks after foaling too—for what we should call a plate of 120*l.*, which is only twice 60*l.*

As regards owners of horses, we are told on good authority that in the very early days of the French Jockey Club there were but twenty-four owners of race horses in France known to fame: but by 1845 the number had doubled, or more than doubled, and the chief among them were M. Alexandre Aumont (soon to be succeeded by the never to be forgotten Count F. de Lagrange), M. (and afterwards Madame) Latache de

Fay), M. Auguste Lupin, Prince Marc de Beauvau (whose establishment at La Morlaye and elsewhere was kept rather as a great lord keeps anything fashionable than because the owner's heart was in the matter, though he was successful enough through the agency of Mr. Henry Jennings, the trainer), Baron N. de Rothschild, Count des Cars (a very old 'horsey' name among the French), Count de Morny, MM. Reiset (whose services in the cause of the French Turf are commemorated by the Prix Reiset at Paris Spring Meeting), Fasquel (of Courteuil), Mosselman (of Verberie, near Compiègne), de Terves, de Baracé, Baron A. Schickler, and Henri Delamarre; and in the South Count de Coux, M. de Vanteaux, the Marquis de Roffignac, M. Achille Fould (the celebrated Minister of Finance), M. de Béhague (a notable breeder), and in the 'Circonscription de l'Ouest' M. Robin (breeder and owner of Souvenir, the first 'Western' horse to 'illustrate' the provinces, as he did by winning the French Derby in 1862), together with one or two others.

As for the trainers, on whom so much depends, they were English to a man, or almost to a man; and of them there were at Chantilly alone about this time a score or more, among whom the most prominent were (besides Messrs. Corringham, Palmer, and the 'old originals') Mr. Thomas Carter, employed by Lord Henry Seymour originally, and afterwards by M. Reiset and Baron de Rothschild; Mr. T. Jennings and Mr. H. Jennings (both introduced under the wing of Mr. Thomas Carter originally, as has already been noticed), the former employed by M. Aumont, the latter by that easy master Prince Marc de Beauvau; Mr. Boldrick, by Madame Latache de Fay Mr. R. Cunningham, by

M. Auguste Lupin; Messrs. Lamplugh, Hurst, and—soon to be very celebrated indeed—Charles Pratt, first a jockey under the wing of Mr. H. Jennings and then that trainer's successor.

Of jockeys the most noted were (as early as 1826) Hall, Webb, North, Boast, &c.; and afterwards (from 1835 to 1859) Edgar Pavis (brother of Arthur Pavis), Edwards, Flatman, Spreoty (whose name is indelibly associated with Monarque), Boldrick, and Lamplugh (both of them trainers as well as jockeys, and the latter celebrated as both trainer and rider of the almost fabulous French steeple-chaser Franc Picard), C. Pratt, Chifney, J. Bartholomew, and especially Kitchener (who was in later days to become distinguished beyond the rest by his two victories in the Grand Prix de Paris, on Vermout over T. Chaloner, on Blair Athol and on the moderate Glaneur over G. Fordham on The Drummer, and by his triumphs in the Goodwood and Brighton Cups on the back of Dollar). These jockeys were English to a man; and they and their 'mates,' together with the aforesaid trainers and their 'mates,' by marrying and giving in marriage, by settling in 'la belle France' and bringing over their brethren and sisters and cousins and connections, established what is called 'the English colony' at Chantilly, a colony so prosperous, powerful, numerous, and increasing that the 'natives' are said to be 'nowhere,' to play second fiddle, and to have had to learn the English language for greater ease of communication if not in sheer self-defence.

Howbeit there were even in the earlier days, both before and after the first twenty years of the French Turf, which the French Jockey Club laid down (so to speak), some native jockeys, 'bred in France,' of no mean reputation; to wit, Pierre Chabrol, Cornelier, Antoine, Z. Caillotin (he who rode Honesty, winner of the French Oaks in 1854), Pierre Prunet, Joseph, and more to the back of them. And it is a little remarkable that French jockeys should apparently have been in greater esteem then than they are now, though races have been instituted in France to be ridden by jockeys of French parentage only, both by father and mother, for the express purpose of encouraging a breed of indigenous jockeys. The attempt has not been so successful as it might have been; and the secret of the comparative failure is stated by a 'compatriot' to be that the French nature abhors an abdominal vacuum, the French jockeys 'trouvant trop rude l'obligation de se faire maigrir.'

Meanwhile the French Jockey Club had been making way surely, if slowly. Under the auspices of that body a few really notable races had been established and regularly run, with a few breaks from various causes. The Grand Prix at Paris (not, of course, the Grand Prix de Paris), which seems to have been an institution of the Administration des Haras (by whom or by which the race was won with Corysandre in 1838, and in 1839 with Eylau, both bred at the Administration's own 'haras' at Le Pin), was patronised by the members of the French Jockey Club, and lasted from 1834 to 1860 (both years included), and much the same remark applies to the Prix de la Ville de Paris, which dates from 1844 but was turned into a handicap in 1864: but the French Jockey Club had established on their own account the Prix du Jockey Club, or French Derby (first run in 1836), and the Prix de Diane, or French Oaks (first run in 1843), at Chantilly; the Prix du Cadran (first run in 1838); the Poule d'Essai, sometimes called the French Two Thousand (first run in 1840); the Poule des Produits (first run in 1841) at Paris Spring Meeting, and sundry others. It would not be long before they began to feel strong enough to 'have a shy,' in sporting language, at perfidious Albion herself.

In the meantime they had already enjoyed their 'Derby scandal,' after our 'Running Rein' fashion, in 1840, thus preceding us by four years. This may be taken to show either how nicely they were coming on with their horse-racing or how naturally the iniquities of horse-racing come to mankind, so much more naturally and easily than any other part or characteristic of that 'sport of kings.' The story is on this wise:—

Whereas in 1840 the French Derby had been considered a 'moral' (which means, in the language of the Turf, a 'moral certainty' and has nothing to do with virtue) for Lord Henry Seymour's Jenny (by imported Royal Oak and imported Kermesse), it was won by M. Eugène Aumont with a filly described as Tontine (by Tetotum and Odette), Jenny being second only. As in the case of 'Running Rein' in England before the Derby of 1844, so in the case of Tontine in France before the French Derby of 1840, there had been sinister rumours abroad concerning a meditated *coup*, and as General Peel afterwards did in England so did Lord Henry Seymour in France: he promptly objected to Tontine, declaring that she was not bred in France at all, but was (with a change of name only) an English filly called Herodia (by Aaron and a Y. Election mare). The case was investigated both by the French Jockey Club and by the 'tribunals,' and the result was a curious paradox. The race[1] was not awarded to the

---

[1] The charge, of course, being 'not proved' to the satisfaction of the French Jockey Club's stewards.

second, so that the so-called Tontine's name remains for all time among the winners of the French Derby; but, on the other hand, the proofs of substitution were considered (too late, perhaps, for different action, or because the 'tribunals' differed from the French Jockey Club and other Turf or stud authorities) so strong that the name of Tontine (by Tetotum and Odette) appears among the brood mares in the French Stud Book without any remark or any progeny, though it is said to be well known that the mare which won the French Derby under the style and title of 'Tontine, by Teetotum and Odette,' had a pretty long string of foals. What became of those thoroughbreds? It is clear that they may have been found very useful as 'extras' in the accomplishment of other *coups*.

This chapter may be properly concluded with a few observations touching the means within reach of French breeders about the time of the 'Tontine scandal' and the subsequent years until the first French victory in the Goodwood Cup with an animal 'bred in France' was won by M. A. Lupin in 1853 with Jouvence.

It is worthy of notice, first of all, that the stud horses of any value belonged almost exclusively to the State. 'In the [French] Stud Book of 1843,' says the authority, 'figured sixty-nine thoroughbred English sires. Three only of these belonged to private individuals. . . . . In 1854 the State put at the disposal of breeders 345 sires of Eastern or English thoroughbred origin.' The chief of these latter were Ion, imported in 1851; Strongbow, in 1852; The Prime Warden, in 1847; Elthiron, in 1853; Nautilus, 'bred in France,' foaled in 1835; Eremos, 'bred in France,' foaled in 1845; Nunnykirk, imported in 1850; The Baron, imported in 1849; Caravan, imported for the use of the cavalry school at Saumur about 1843; Iago, imported in 1853; Lanercost, in 1853; Nuncio, in 1847; Womersley, in 1853; and, above all, the short-lived Emperor (imported 1850, died 1851), the esteemed Sting (imported in 1848), and the famous Gladiator (imported in 1846), of whom it might almost be said by the French, as was said long ago of the 'Godolphin Arabian' among ourselves, 'There is not a *superior* horse now on the Turf' without a cross of him, 'neither has there been for many years past.'

The prices paid for these sires to the English sellers were (with the exception of Gladiator, for whom the French Government wisely paid about 2,500*l*.) so low, for the most part, that the State could well afford to all but give their services away, and are enough to astonish a generation which is familiar with such princely outlay as 14,000*l*.—a small fortune—for a Doncaster, or upwards of 12,000 guineas for a Blair Athol. The price of Strongbow was but 7,600 francs, or about 304*l*.; of Nuncio but 4,000 francs, or about 160*l*.; of the great (but poisoned) Lanercost but 12,000 francs, or about 480*l*.; of the 'fashionably' bred Womersley but 350 guineas or thereabouts; of that excellent sire Sting but 15,450 francs, or about 618*l*. True a little over a thousand guineas was given for The Baron, and about a thousand for Nunnykirk, who is said to have never covered anywhere but in France, and who, though he was sire of Potocki (winner of the French Derby in 1857), was not a very great bargain. We, however, are accustomed to see a thousand guineas paid for yearlings that never face the starting-post.

The fees paid for the services of these sires were sometimes quite ludicrous, calling to mind the 'jeremiad' that was sung by a sporting writer over the fallen fortunes of the once famous horse The Wizard (winner of our Two Thousand in 1860) when the son of West Australian, being an exile in Germany, 'was reduced to smiling on half-bred beauty for fifteen shillings (five thalers).' The fee for Ion, for Lanercost, for other 'cracks' apparently, was but 200 francs, or 8*l*. ; for Nuncio but 150 francs, or 6*l*. ; for Nunnykirk but 75 francs, or 3*l*., for some seasons ; and for the rest on a similar scale. The time was not yet foreseen when a native French sire, as Flageolet in 1880, would be advertised at 5,000 francs, or 200*l*., a mare, as if he were a Stockwell or the peer of The Hermit, son of Newminster.

CHAPTER IV.

THE INVASION OF PERFIDIOUS ALBION.

THE history of French horse-racing and its progress is the history of a French invasion of England. We brought our horse-racing to its height of excellence, our thoroughbred horses to as near perfection as possible, by our own strength alone, by judicious importation of Eastern blood and by competition among ourselves. There was no established 'Turf' in any part of the world to which we could go to test our horses against antagonists of acknowledged superiority. We occasionally, from the commencement, had tried our Anglo-Arabian or Anglo-Eastern horses, bred and trained on English principles, against the pure 'son of the Desert' both at home and abroad, and against indigenous foreign horses (as when, in 1825, Sharper made an example of two Cossack horses in a race of fifty miles on the public road hard by St. Petersburg), and always, or nearly always, to our enormous advantage, to the establishment of our indisputable supremacy. But it was different with the French. They, with commendable perspicacity, so far as they were represented by the Société d'Encouragement, or French Jockey Club, had seen at the outset that they would save some fifty years or more of gradual development by adopting our ready-made thoroughbred, brought to its high state of perfection by the only method that any people, nation, or language (save perhaps the 'children of the Desert,' and they with but small probability of success) could be expected to employ to any purpose; and having determined to proceed by the said adoption, they had but one way of discovering how they were getting on, and that was an invasion of England, a descent upon English racecourses open to all the world, and a contest between the true English thoroughbred and the French edition of it on that English thoroughbred's native heath. We could not very well go over to them; for, even if the metal had been more attractive, the rules of the French Jockey Club precluded us. No doubt, as we have seen in the case of the French Derby in 1840, there might occasionally be reason to believe that an English thoroughbred had run, under false pretences, against the best native 'Frenchmen,' and beaten them handsomely; but such instances, even had they been less rare and more openly confessed, could hardly be considered quite satisfactory. Now, when the mountain will not or cannot go to Mahomet, Mahomet has to go to the mountain; when the English 'cracks' would not or could not go over to France to 'try conclusions' with the French 'cracks,' the latter had to come over to us in England. This invasion may be said to have commenced in earnest, as a regular series of campaigns, about the year 1852.

Up to that date desultory descents had been made upon our racecourses by the French, who, moreover, had not only imported but run English thoroughbreds against their own native produce in small, chiefly provincial, affairs (in steeple-chases, no doubt, and in races instituted by the Administration des Haras, though the runners were mostly 'demi-sang' and 'Arabs'); but they had seldom met any English 'cracks,' either on English or on French soil.

We have seen that old 'Egalité' ran horses 'bred in France' in England before the first Revolution, and that English and French horses ran against one another at Vincennes and elsewhere in France on the eve of 'the deluge.' After 'the deluge,' during the Restoration, we do not find any mention of horses 'bred in France' running in England, and there is scarcely a trace of any Frenchman running any race horse at all in England. After the Revolution of July 1830, however, we find Baron Teissier (who was naturalised in England, a member of the English Jockey Club, a resident at Epsom, and a steward of Epsom races) nominating, in 1833, a filly (English) for the Durdans Stakes; and after the establishment of the French Jockey Club, in 1833, we find Lord Henry Seymour (who for all racing purposes was a Frenchman) running Elizondo (English) in 1836 at Newmarket, in 1838 Scroggins (English) at Bedford and Newmarket, and Oakstick ('bred in France') in 1841 at Goodwood. Meanwhile the Duke d'Orléans, as we have seen, had won the Goodwood Cup in 1840 with Beggarman (English); and he had run Nautilus ('bred in France') unsuccessfully for the Goodwood Cup in 1841. M. Eugène Aumont also had run Mr. Wags (English) at Canterbury in 1839; and Mr. T. Carter (domiciled in France with Lord Henry Seymour) had run Brabant and Creusa (English, but imported into France) in England in 1838, on behalf, no doubt, of Lord Henry Seymour. Such were the chief efforts made by French owners in the years immediately succeeding the foundation of the French Jockey Club.

Indeed, the Germans, oddly enough, may be said to

have 'made the running' among the foreigners (including Russians and Austro-Hungarians) with Messrs. Lichtwald (who got 'warned off' in consequence of the 'Leander business' in 1844) and with Count Hahn, who won the Stewards' Cup and the Chesterfield Cup at Goodwood in 1850 with Turnus (bred in Germany), before the French won anything with any horse bred in France.

However, to return to the French: From 1841 to 1851, both years included, the ' crack ' French horses were the Duke d'Orléans's Gigès (by Priam), M. Fasquel's Minuit (by Terror), Prince Marc de Beauvau's (Lord Henry Seymour's) Jenny (by Royal Oak), Baron N. de Rothschild's Drummer (by Langar), M. Alexandre Aumont's Cavatine (by Tarrare, imported by M. Eugène Aumont) and FitzEmilius (by Young Emilius), Prince Marc de Beauvau's Prédestinée (by Mr. Wags, imported by M. Eugène Aumont), M. Jules Rivière's Morok (by Beggarman, imported by the Duke d'Orléans), Mr. Thomas Carter's Dulcamara (by Physician), Prince Marc de Beauvau's Sérénade (by Royal Oak, imported by Lord Henry Seymour), M. Auguste Lupin's Messine (by Attila, by Colwick), M. Eugène Aumont's Déception (by Royal Oak), the Duke d'Orléans's Nautilus (by Cadland, imported by the French Government and dead within four years), Mr. T. Carter's Annetta (by Ibrahim, imported by Lord Henry Seymour), Prince Marc de Beauvau's Nativa and Baron N. de Rothschild's Edwin (both by Royal Oak), M. Fasquel's Tomate (by Lottery, imported by the French Government apparently), M. Alexandre Aumont's Liverpool (by Liverpool, sold to the French Government for 2,000 guineas, but he died before delivery in 1844), Mr. T. Carter's Nanetta (by Alteruter, imported by the French Government apparently), M. Alexandre Aumont's La

Clôture and Hervine (both by Mr. Wags), M. Auguste Lupin's Fiammetta (by Actæon or Camel, her dam, Wings, a winner of the Oaks, having been purchased by M. Lupin ' in foal ' in 1837), Prince Marc de Beauvau's Commodore Napier (by Royal Oak), M. Célestin de Pontalba's Philip Shah (by The Shah, the dam—a Catton mare—having been imported ' in foal ') and Tronquette (by Royal Oak), M. A. Lupin's Gambetti (by Emilius, the dam—Tarantella, a winner of the One Thousand—having been purchased by M. Lupin ' in foal '), Mr. T. Carter's Expérience (by Physician, imported by the French Government apparently), M. A. Lupin's St. Germain (by Attila, by Colwick), M. Latache de Fay's Firstborn (by Nuncio, imported by the French Government from Belgium, whither he first went from England), Count de Cambis' (the Duke d'Orléans') Cauchemar (by Royal Oak), M. A. Lupin's Angora (by Lottery), Mr. T. Carter's Governor (by Royal Oak), M. A. Lupin's Myszka (by Bizarre, winner of the Ascot Cup two years running, 1824 and 1825, imported by the French Government apparently), Baron N. de Rothschild's Fleet (by Bizarre) and Gland (by Royal Oak), Prince Marc de Beauvau's Lioubliou (by Alteruter), M. A. Lupin's Capri (by Physician), Count de Hédouville's Babiéga (by Attila), Mr. T. Carter's Illustration (by Gladiator, imported by the French Government), M. A. Lupin's Ratopolis (by Lottery) and Suavita (by Napoleon, bred in Ireland, imported by the French Government apparently), Baron N. de Rothschild's Meudon (by Alteruter), Baron de Pierres' Mythème and Djali (both by Caravan, imported by the French Government), Prince Marc de Beauvau's Lanterne (by Hercule—a son of Rainbow—bred by M. Rieussec in France) and Dorade (by Physician or Royal Oak),

Count de Cambis's (Meudon stud's) Wirthschaft (by Gigès, 'bred in France'), M. de Perceval's Vergogne (by Ibrahim), Prince Marc de Beauvau's Fleur de Marie (by Attila), Lord Henry Seymour's Poetess and Viscount E. Perregaux's Plover (both by Royal Oak), M. Célestin de Pontalba's Renonce (by Young Emilius), and M. A. Lupin's Amalfi (by Gladiator or Young Emilius).

Of these French 'cracks' very few indeed up to 1851 (included) had put in an appearance on any English racecourse, and very few of their owners had tried their strength against English opponents on English ground, whether with French or English horses.

The Duke d'Orléans won the Prix du Cadran thrice—in 1839, 1840, and 1842—with Nautilus; but Nautilus, as we have seen, with all his allowance of weight, could not get a place for the Goodwood Cup; and of the other French 'cracks' (which do not include, of course, Cameleon, run by the Belgian Société Verviétoise [or de Verviers] unsuccessfully for the Goodwood Cup of 1844), Baron N. de Rothschild's Drummer (unplaced for the Goodwood Cup of 1845), M. Aumont's (Mr. T. Gibson's) FitzEmilius (unplaced for the Goodwood Cup of 1848), and Mr. T. Carter's Dulcamara (ran for the Doncaster Stakes in 1850) were about all that were enterprising enough to face an English starter on English ground; for such animals as Jessy or Jessie (daughter of Ion and Cyprienne, and bred in France), who ran several times in England in 1850, were sold out of France and were by no means 'cracks,' belonging to another category altogether.

The year 1852 was to see the commencement of a new era.

The French had hitherto made very gingerly approaches—had proceeded *à tâtons*, as they themselves would say—but at last they were beginning to feel their feet and to see their way. By means of Nautilus and other horses that had dared to compete with English thoroughbreds at Goodwood now and then, and by means of Beggarman and other English horses that had been used for running as well as for stud purposes in France (where, at Boulogne, La Clôture—by Mr. Wags —' bred in France,' had in 1850-51 actually beaten an English horse of no account) the French had been able to measure their improvement up to a certain point.

Now in 1852 the indefatigable M. Alexandre Aumont (who founded the famous *haras* of Victot, near Caen, in horse-loving Normandy, and who had taken over the stables of his brother, M. Eugène Aumont, when the latter fell under a cloud in consequence of the 'Tontine scandal') had a four-year-old filly, Hervine by name, a daughter of Mr. Wags and the celebrated Poetess (herself a winner of the French Derby and the dam of the famous Monarque); and the said Hervine was considered a perfect marvel of horseflesh.

There were few, just a few, two-year-old races in France at this time, and perhaps the best two-year-old performer of 1850 was First Born ; but in 1851, at three years of age, Hervine had won the French Oaks, in 1852 she had won the Prix du Cadran, and when it was determined to send her over to compete for the Goodwood Cup in 1852 she was regarded by her compatriots as 'the ever victorious filly,' having carried all before her both in France and in Belgium. Moreover her owner, M. Alexandre Aumont, was a sportsman *bien éveillé*—very wide awake indeed—and generally knew what he was about.

Why the French should nearly always have chosen the Goodwood Cup for their first object of attack is easy to understand; for the conditions of that race gave immense advantages to horses 'bred on the Continent,' as well as to 'pure Arabs' and to horses 'bred in America,' &c. And so Hervine had a considerable 'pull' in the weights, carrying but 6 st. 11 lbs. to the 7 st. 4 lbs. (car. 7 st. 6 lbs.) of the winner, Kingston, a year her junior.

Weight excepted, however, it must be owned that Hervine had everything against her. She suffered, it is said, from the sea voyage (for though horses cannot vomit they can suffer terribly from *mal de mer*, to the extent of dying of it, like the celebrated French mare Gabrielle d'Estrées in 1867), and arrived in anything but good trim at Goodwood. Then it was found that her 'frequent pardner,' Mr Spreoty the jockey, who was to have ridden her and who knew her · little ways,' was nearly 10 lbs. over weight, and the mount had to be given to somebody else. This somebody was certainly 'Tiny Wells,' than whom since Castor, Bellerophon, and 'that lot' a better could not very well (without prejudice of pun) have been obtained. But even a Wells cannot divine by the light of nature or learn at a moment's information the peculiarities of a sensitive animal he has never before bestridden. Suffice it to say that Hervine, the 'ever victorious filly,' could not obtain so much as a place among such redoubtable competitors as Kingston, Little Harry, Teddington, Hernandez, the great Newminster, and Stilton. So M. Aumont and his friends were obliged to content themselves with the reflection that in so illustrious a 'field'

       'Tis better to have run and lost
       Than never to have run at all.

Howbeit the French were now beginning to 'burn,'

as the children say in the game of 'hide and seek;' the year 1853 was to be memorable in the annals of the French Turf.

In that year Hervine again went down to the sea in ships, braved *mal de mer*, and made another bid for the Goodwood Cup. This time she had the services of her old friend Mr. Spreoty, who rode her; but again she was unfortunate. She was five years old (though she is called 'aged' in the English Calendar), and she carried 7 st. 1 lb.; yet she, who is described by one of her compatriots as 'la perle de notre parure chevaline,' could only obtain second place, having behind her, however, such horses as Kingston, Muscovite, and Weathergage. And—what was balm indeed for 'la belle France'—only the French could beat the French, for the winner was M. A. Lupin's Jouvence, 'bred in France,' but trained partly in England.

Jouvence (daughter of Sting and Currency), was three years old in 1853, carried about the lightest weight (5 st. 9 lbs.) ever borne by a winner of the Goodwood Cup, had already run in England (third for the City and Suburban at Epsom Spring Meeting, where M. Lupin had also run Cassique, 'bred in France'), and had won both the French Oaks and the French Derby. Great were the rejoicings in Paris over this first victory of a French-bred horse in England; the French Jockey Club was illuminated and Waterloo was almost forgiven. Nor was this all. Both Jouvence and Hervine ran after this in the same year (1853) in England; the former (with success twice at Egham, where she won a Queen's Plate) several times, and the latter once (unsuccessfully in the Cambridgeshire). Nor, again, was *this* all; M. Lupin anticipated his compatriots by running a French-bred two-year-old (Benvenuto, at Epsom

Autumn Meeting) in England. Nor was even *this* all; for, measured through Hervine and Jouvence, there were in France three other French-bred animals foaled in the same year as Jouvence—namely, M. Alexandre Aumont's FitzGladiator and Royal-quand-même (winners of many races in France and Belgium), and Count de Hédouville's Moustique (winner of the Poule d'Essai, or French Two Thousand, in 1853)—worthy of competing (at any rate with an allowance of weight) with English horses on English ground.

In 1854 the chief French 'cracks' were Hervine (six years old), Trust (five years old), Aguila (five years old), Royal-quand-même (four years old), Jouvence (four years old), FitzGladiator (four years old), Moustique (four years old), Papillon (four years old), Echelle (dam of Orphelin, four years old), Honesty and Celebrity (both three years old, both by Gladiator), Nancy (three years old, by Mr. Wags), Lycisca (three years old, by Sting), Valéria (three years old, by Sting), and perhaps there may be added a two-year-old, Rémus (by Garry Owen), belonging to M. Adolphe Fould. Of these representatives Hervine was to have run for the Cambridgeshire, but fell lame, with her usual ill luck (for she was then in great form); Fitz-Gladiator was to have run for the Goodwood Cup, but could not stand the preparation; Valéria ran hopelessly behind Virago for the Goodwood Cup (for which there were only three runners) and behind Winkfield for the Brighton Stakes; Aguila ran hopelessly for the Great Ebor Handicap and the Great Yorkshire Handicap; Jouvence had no fewer than six vain trials on various English courses; Lycisca, the shifty, ran to no purpose in the City and Suburban (won by the invincible Virago); and the bright hopes of the French had surely been extinguished but for the 'place' obtained by Trust both in the Stewards' Cup and in a Handicap Plate at Goodwood, and for the fifty sovereigns won by Rémus at Epsom Autumn Meeting.

But it is darkest before dawn: the very same year was to see the first appearance (on any Turf) of Monarque.

CHAPTER V

MONARQUE AND HIS SATELLITES.

The coming of Monarque, the sire of sires of the French native produce, marks a new era in the history of French horse-racing. The dam of Monarque was the celebrated Poetess (by Royal Oak), Hervine's dam; for sire he required three single horses rolled into one—to wit, The Baron, Sting, and The Emperor. There are reasons, however, for allotting the chief honours of so distinguished a sireship to the short-lived Emperor (short-lived in France, indeed, and only ten years old altogether; foaled in 1841, imported into France in 1850, dead in 1851); and in the very name of Monarque one can trace an intention of expressing conviction as to the true paternity.

Monarque was a 'bay 'oss,' foaled in 1852 at M. Alexandre Aumont's famous Victot stud, near Caen; and M. Aumont's property he remained until 1857, when the great Anglo-French or Franco-English devotee of the Turf, Count Frédéric de Lagrange, of the Dangu stud, purchased the whole of M. Aumont's racing stable.

Monarque did not 'come out' till he was three years of age; but he ran at two, three, four, five, and six years. At two years of age he was beaten, it is stated by the authority (with his pocket-handkerchief to his compatriotic eyes), for the Grand Critérium for two-year-olds, in 1854, by Allez-y-gaîment (another son of The Emperor, by the way), belonging to M. H. Mosselman; and that was the only occasion, it is said, on which Monarque was ever beaten in France by a French horse at even weights or at weight for age. So too the great West Australian was beaten once at two years of age by his natural and feudal inferior Speed-the-Plough. At three years of age, however, Monarque took ample revenge on Allez-y-gaîment, in 1855, in which year the 'monarch of all he surveyed' won the Poule d'Essai of 6,000 francs, or 240*l.*, the Poule des Produits of 3,500 francs, or 140*l.*, the French Derby of 52,000 francs, or 2,080*l.*, the Grand Saint Léger at Moulins of 9,900 francs, or 396*l.*, and other events, including the Continental Derby at Ghent.

In England, however, in 1855 Monarque, having been sent to give his perfidious neighbours a taste of his quality, was a dead failure. His reputation had gone before him, but his works did not follow him. He was honoured with the top weight among the three-year-olds in a field of twenty-nine for the Stewards' Cup at Goodwood, but, as he started at odds of 20 to 1 against him, it looks as if the somewhat 'onerous' compliment were due rather to French brag about him than to genuine English respect for him. At any rate he did not get so much as a place, and the excuse made for him was that he 'got off' badly, and that in so short a race a bad start is often fatal. However the Cesarewitch course, which he tried towards the end of the same season, is not open to the same objection; yet for the Cesarewitch, again, for which also he carried the highest weight among the three-year-olds, he did not get a place, though he is said to have finished close up with Sultan, who carried about four pounds less than he, and who won the Cambridgeshire with 7 st. 6 lbs. (7 st. in the Cesarewitch) about a fortnight later.

On this visit Monarque had with him a satellite or stable companion, one Peu d'Espoir, whose paternity, oddly enough (for he too is described as by Sting, The Baron, or The Emperor), rested under the very same shadow of doubt as Monarque's. This Peu d'Espoir, though he was thought something of in his own country, could get no nearer than third among a very moderate lot (three-year-olds) for 50*l.* at Newmarket Second October Meeting. That there was something in him nevertheless he showed some ten days after his return home by running and winning a very trying race at Paris, beating Ronzi (winner of the French Oaks, by Sir Tatton Sykes) and Monarchist (yet another son of The Emperor). It was a race in 'heats' at Paris for a Prix Spécial. Peu d'Espoir won the first heat, ran a dead heat with Ronzi in the second (so that it went for nothing), was beaten in the third, and with great difficulty won the fourth ; so that the 3,500 francs, or 140*l.*, he gained by his prowess might be fairly termed ' very hard cash.'

Of the other French horses that were 'in attendance' on Monarque at his visits in 1855, or that came over to England at all during that year, M. Adolphe Fould's Rémus, the two-year-old hero of the preceding year, ran once (for the City and Suburban)—to no purpose. Hervine, now 'aged,' ran second for the Goodwood Stakes; M. Adolphe Fould's two-year-old Ramadan (by Garry Owen) was a 'bad third' for a sweepstakes at Bedford, and afterwards seventh and last for the Criterion Stakes; but, as if to mock

Monarque, the Goodwood Cup was won by Baron N. de Rothschild's Baroncino (yet another son of The Emperor), who had been second to Monarque for the French Derby. This Baroncino, like M. Lupin's Benvenuto (a candidate for the Epsom Autumn Handicap the year before), ultimately remained by purchase or transfer in England, but neither of them did any good in the land of their adoption. Oddly enough, Monarque on returning to France won three races in one week, as if to show that 'it was the climate.'

In 1856 we notice that it is no longer Monarque who rules the roast in France, but Madame Latache de Fay's Ronzi (winner of the French Oaks in 1855); and that Hervine, Jouvence, Trust, and Royal-quand-même have disappeared from the scene. In 1856, in fact, Ronzi stood at the head of affairs, winning (in stakes) twice as much as Monarque, whom she defeated in the Prix de l'Empereur at Chantilly, for which, however, she was in the receipt of 10 lbs. Behind her and Monarque was Lion, three years old, receiving a stone from Monarque and, sex considered, 6 lbs. from Ronzi.

This Lion, son of Ion and Miss Caroline, English sire and English dam, both imported, was one of the very best and most remarkable of all the French horses, and, but for his early death in 1857 (when at four years of age he broke his leg), might have attained a reputation, both as a racer and as a sire, not inferior to Monarque's. Lion belonged to Prince Marc de Beauvau (or to the confederacy of which Prince Marc was the titular head), and he had won a very sensational French Derby in 1856 after a dead heat with a very inferior animal, Count de Morny's Diamant (son of Young Emilius and Naiade), whom he completely 'lost' in the 'run off.' But Lion, like Bay Middleton and many other 'brilliant cripples,' was always very 'queer' about the legs and consequently difficult to train and to keep 'in form.'

Close up with Lion in the aforesaid Prix de l'Empereur was Vermeille (ex-Merveille), a daughter of The Baron and Fair Helen. She had been trained in England up to the date of the French Derby (for which she made a fair show behind Lion); but, though her racing career was not dishonourable, her honours were won at the stud, where she became the dam of M. Henri Delamarre's Vermout (who was 'one too many' for Blair Athol), Vertugadin, Vérité, and Verdure.

In England the French breed of horses was represented in 1856 by none or next to none but Baroncino, a 'resident,' and Peu d'Espoir and Monarque, 'invaders;' the first ran once (for the Craven Stakes at Epsom Summer Meeting), but did not get a place, and the same fate overtook Peu d'Espoir in the Goodwood Stakes (when there were twenty-five runners, eight horses fell, and four jockeys were seriously injured), but Monarque ran third both for the Stewards' Cup and the Goodwood Cup. Of course it was discovered that he must have won if the orders given to his jockey had been more 'judgmatical,' but his compatriot very impartially observes, 'There certainly are untoward chances on the Turf, but somehow Monarque never encountered them in France; yet he had made three trips to England with the same want of success.'

His day nevertheless was coming, and with a change of owners he was to have a change of luck.

About the middle of October 1856 a rumour went abroad that M. Alexandre Aumont, who had performed such wonders of breeding and racing in France, who with Hervine, Peu d'Espoir, and Monarque had made such gallant attempts on English racecourses, who, as one of his compatriots eloquently puts it, 'had caught a glimpse of the promised land, but was not to enter it,' and who had announced an intention of disposing of his stud by auction, had come to a private arrangement with a wholesale purchaser. This purchaser was a gentleman who soon became as well known and as formidable on the English as on the French Turf—Count Frédéric de Lagrange. The horses sold comprised Monarque (four years old in 1856), Peu d'Espoir (four years old), Brutus (son of Sting and Loterie, two years), Mademoiselle de Chantilly (by Gladiator and Maid of Mona, two years), and others; and, what was more or what was most, they were accompanied by the renowned trainer Mr. T. Jennings, who had done so much for M. Aumont and was to do so much more for Count F. de Lagrange. Monarque at once foreshadowed the victorious destiny of the new colours by winning a Prix Impérial at Paris Autumn Meeting, having, however, only one (somewhat sorry) opponent to beat in Madame Latache de Fay's Valbruant (son of Nuncio and Wirthschaft).

In 1857 Monarque, who had won the first success for his new colours, maintained his supremacy in France (winning the Prix du Pavillon, the Prix des Haras at Chantilly, the Prix de l'Administration des Haras and the Prix Impérial at Boulogne, the Prix Impérial at Moulins, and the Prix Impérial and the Grand Prix Impérial at Paris, &c.), but on two memorable occasions he nearly lost it actually and virtually lost it quite. On May 17, the day on which Mademoiselle de Chantilly won the French Oaks for the new colours borne by Monarque, the great horse won a terrific race at

Chantilly from Lion with great difficulty, Lion being in receipt of only two pounds. A week afterwards, at Chantilly again, the two horses ran a race in heats. Monarque (giving as much as ten pounds this time) won the first heat by a head only; and in the second he was already beaten when Lion (a year his junior) broke his pastern within sight, though not quite within reach, of the winning post.

This was the day of the French Derby, and a very memorable French Derby. Among the competitors were M. A. Lupin's Florin (winner of both the Poule d'Essai and the Poule des Produits); Count F. de Lagrange's Mademoiselle de Chantilly (winner of the French Oaks and of the Prix de l'Empereur, now the Grande Poule des Produits, at Paris); and Prince Marc de Beauvau's Duchess (winner of the Grand Critérium at Paris the year before). Florin was thought likely to win, and M. Lupin (who had two other candidates, named Paladin and Potocki) declared to win with Florin. This horse was the son of the celebrated Surplice and of Payment (imported by M. Lupin when she was in foal with Florin, and destined to be afterwards the dam of the very distinguished Dollar); but he was an unlucky beast, a *bête à chagrin*. He had lost an eye from inflammation brought on by a cold, and just after the start for the French Derby he crossed his legs, came down heavily, and fell upon his rider, Kitchener, who was picked up insensible. Now was seen the advantage of having two, or rather three, strings to your bow; for Paladin immediately took up the running on behalf of Potocki, made the pace a 'cracker,' and resigning his place to Potocki at the distance, enabled the latter to win easily by two lengths. Second was Count F. de Lagrange's late purchase,

Brutus; Prince Marc de Beauvau's Serious was third; Mademoiselle de Chantilly, Duchess, and Lastborn, half-sister to Ronzi, could not obtain a place. There are authorities who say that Potocki (who was a son of the Baron or Nunnykirk and Myszka, by Bizarre, and had already won the Prix de la Ville, now the Prix de Lutèce, beating Monarque, at a difference, however, of more than 3 st.) was intrinsically a better horse than Florin, but he died in 1859 and could not prove it (though he won the Prix du Cadran in 1858) by his produce.

As for the French invasion of England in 1857, France was better represented than ever before on English ground; and the chief, if not the whole, of the representatives were Monarque, Potocki, Florin, Paladin, Ronzi, Mademoiselle de Chantilly, and a two-year-old filly, Chevrette, belonging to Count F. de Lagrange. Potocki, carrying 7 st. 1 lb., which was more than was carried by any English horse of his age, and Paladin, carrying the almost feather weight of 5 st. 12 lbs. (though there was an English horse in the race with 4 st. 5 lbs., carrying 4 st. 7 lbs.), were 'nowhere' for the Goodwood Stakes, and Paladin ran to no purpose in another race at Goodwood. Florin ran in vain for the Goodwood Cup and the Chesterfield Cup at Goodwood; Ronzi ran in vain for the Cesarewitch (which, oddly enough, was won this year by a 'foreigner,' the American Pryoress, after a dead heat of *three*), for two Handicap Plates at Newmarket Houghton Meeting, as well as for one at the Second October, and won a Handicap Plate of fifty sovereigns at the Houghton; Mademoiselle de Chantilly had the honour of starting equal second favourite for the Cambridgeshire, but was not placed; and Chevrette ran three times, and won once, a Handicap Sweepstakes for two-year-olds and three-year-olds of about 130*l*. at Newmarket Houghton Meeting.

Monarque was the hero of the campaign; at last he won the Goodwood Cup, the only event for which he was a competitor, and he had behind him the prodigious Fisherman (winner of twenty six Queen's Plates during his career) and the 'Americans' Pryor and Pryoress, as well as his compatriot Florin. As it was, Monarque (five years, 8 st. 9 lbs.) won by a head only from Riseber (three years, 7 st. 2 lbs.) second and Fisherman (four years, 9 st. 1 lb.) a 'bad third.' This victory, as a candid French authority admits, was nothing for the Gallic cock to crow over, especially as Monarque was or may have been served by a 'scrimmage' in which Gemma di Vergy, the favourite, Gunboat, and Florin were 'upset' both literally and figuratively. The French authority's candour may be accounted for partly, perhaps, by the fact that the Frenchmen did not profit much by Monarque's victory; the 'francs' were on the unlucky Florin.

The result of the French invasion of England in 1857, then, may be summed up thus: a victory, nothing to boast of, in the race for the Goodwood Cup, two other (very small) successes, and several failures.

Meanwhile, on the other hand, there had been an English invasion of French soil, to the great discomfiture of the French. On September 30 Fisherman, Saunterer, and Commotion had gone over 'for a lark' to Chantilly, to run for the Prix de l'Empereur against Monarque, Ronzi, Mademoiselle de Chantilly, and Duchess. The English horses gave away 'lumps' of weight to the French; yet Fisherman won easily and was followed home by Saunterer and Commotion second and third, not a single 'Frenchman' obtaining a place. Howbeit Mademoiselle de Chantilly ran Commotion to a head. It must have been a rare sight, with the best of the French horses of various ages contending against some very good English, also of different ages; and it is a pity that the French have no longer so attractive an international race, at Paris or Chantilly —the Grand Prix, as everybody knows, being for three-year-olds only.

Nevertheless our neighbours were pretty well pleased with their progress, as appears from an official report, dated February 27, 1858, wherein it is written—

We are a long way ahead since the days when English horses of very moderate quality, selling-platers (to be sold for 10,000 francs, or 400*l*., and no doubt not worth so much, as they could not find purchasers at that price), would win the Prix d'Orléans, though they conceded weight to our horses. The French horses sent to England acquit themselves nowadays after a highly significant fashion. Twelve or fifteen years ago Nautilus, Drummer, and Fitz Emilius, with a great advantage in the weights, could not get a place at the end of the 4 kilomètres ($2\frac{1}{2}$ miles) at Goodwood; but within the last five years Jouvence, Baroncino, and Monarque have won the Cup, even with some diminution of the former advantages; Hervine has come in second; Ronzi, Chevrette, and Rémus have won prizes of less importance; Trust and Mademoiselle de Chantilly have distinguished themselves.

As if to emphasise these remarks, Monarque began the French invasion of England in 1858 so auspiciously that he won (six years, 8 st. 9 lbs.) the Newmarket Handicap of 845*l*. on April 6; and just ten days afterwards his stable companion Mademoiselle de Chantilly followed suit by winning the City and Suburban of 1,030*l*. in a field of 26. This was a pretty brilliant beginning of the season, full of promise for Count F. de Lagrange

and his compatriots; but its exceptional brightness,
as so often happens, was but the precursor of a deeper
gloom than ever prevailed before, to continue till the
autumn of 1860.

Balagny, Goëlette, Etoile du Nord (winner of the
French Oaks and a stable companion of Mademoiselle
de Chantilly), La Maladetta, Nuncia, Phœnix (the fore-
runner of a more famous and more notorious Phénix),
Ventre Saint-Gris (who started first favourite for the
Goodwood Cup), Wedding, and Zouave, as well as
Martel-en-Tête (who was to win the Prix du Cadran the
next year), all 'bred in France,' of all ages from two years
to six, had run in England once or oftener (Zouave no
fewer than five times, twice ' placed') without doing any
good; Mademoiselle de Chantilly herself had dimmed
the splendour of her opening success by two subsequent
failures; and, sad to relate, the same Epsom Spring
Meeting which had seen her triumphant had seen
Monarque 'break down' in the race for the Great
Metropolitan. There is an end, they say, to everything
but Cromwell Road; and so there was an end of
Monarque's racing. He had been ' hard at it' since
1854; he had certainly ' beaten more than beat him,'
and at the stud he was about to commence a career
which would throw his performances on the racecourse altogether into the shade. The estimate given
of him as a race horse by a fair-minded compatriot
is as follows: 'It is certain that, though he always
displayed an indisputable superiority in France, and
though he achieved two brilliant [?] successes in England, he was not fit to compete, without a considerable advantage in weight, against English horses
of the first rank.' There was good reason to say so;
for this year 1858, again, Saunterer went over to

G

Chantilly, where he was opposed by the best French horses for the Prix de l'Empereur (for which, of course, Monarque, having broken down, could not run), and he won easily, giving, four years old as he was, 10 lbs. to Miss Cath (five years old) and nearly 20 lbs. to the three-year-olds Ventre Saint-Gris (winner of the French Derby), Gouvieux (winner of the Poule des Produits and of what is now called the Grande Poule des Produits), and Zouave (a good horse but a true son of The Baron, shifty son of a shifty sire). Of Ventre Saint-Gris, by the way, it is to be noted that he, like our Blair Athol, won his Derby the first time he ran in public; like Romulus and Amalfi (winners of the French Derby in 1839 and 1851), never won another race; and, like our Bend Or, had his identity disputed and established by enquiry.

But to return to Monarque: As regards his personal appearance Monarque is described as a bright bay, with a beautiful head, a long neck, a deep, well-sloped shoulder, rather weak loins, and defective thighs: a magnificent stem, in fact, but rather a weak stern. At his full height he stood, it is said, 1 m. 62 c. (about 16 hands). He had a considerable turn of speed, but his great point was his gameness.

'Never,' says one of his admiring compatriots, 'did he ask for mercy, never did he cry, "Hold! enough!" His courage, on the contrary, seemed to increase with the demands made upon it: he always and everywhere showed a readiness to meet all comers. The tasks imposed upon him were sometimes beyond his powers, but never attained the limits of his courage. Before the struggle Monarque would pace the paddock, walking easily and calmly with that light and measured tread which is peculiar to horses of noble blood; head low, tail dancing, indifferent he seemed to all that went on around him. When his clothing was removed to saddle him nobody could ever detect in him the slightest sign of that nervous trembling or of that feverish moisture which with weak and timid animals betray their apprehension of the coming contest. His neat, intelligent head was raised with an expression of confidence and defiance, and he walked on to the course as calm and resolute as an ancient gladiator.'

That something was expected of Monarque at the stud may be inferred from the fact that he was soon advertised, at a fee of 500 francs (about 20*l*.), in the English Calendar, being probably the first horse 'bred in France' that had yet arrived at such distinction; and his produce soon justified his pretensions. In 1860 were born to him Hospodar (who won the Clearwell Stakes and Criterion Stakes in 1862, and was first favourite for the Two Thousand and equal second favourite for the English Derby in 1863), Fornarina, Infante, Le Maréchal, and Villafranca (all winners in England as well as in France); in 1861 Béatrix and Gédéon (winners in England as well as in France) among others; in 1862 there was born to him Gladiateur, beyond whom it is not necessary to go, for he was a phenomenon, an Eclipse, a Bay Middleton, a horse that marks an era, though he may have been foaled in a comparatively 'bad year.' But it may just be added that Monarque was also the sire of Young Monarque, Auguste, Longchamps, Le Sarrazin, and Boulogne (winners of the Prix du Cadran and other notable events), Trocadéro and Henry (winners of great things in England as well as in France), Patricien and Consul (winners of the French Derby), Le Mandarin (a good horse, but suffering—as Nunnykirk suffered from being in 'the same year' with The Flying Dutchman—from being of the same age as Gladiateur), Don Carlos (a fine stayer, winner of the Prix Gladiateur in 1871), and others too numerous to specify. It may be worth while to note that Monarque was far more fortunate in his colts than in his fillies, of which latter none but Reine (winner of the One Thousand and Oaks in 1872) ever won the Oaks (whether French or English). Dangu was the scene on which Monarque played the part of 'King of the Stud,' and where he died, at 22 years of age, in 1874. The following effusion will serve to conclude this chapter appropriately. It should be borne in mind that Count F. de Lagrange had no children, but had several nephews, some connected with him in matters of horse-racing.

Souvenirs de Dangu.

' A qui sont ces cours d'eau, ces fermes, ces herbages,
Ces champs et ces taillis, ces fiefs, ces apanages ?
A qui, dans leurs paddocks au profane mûrés,
Ces troupeaux de poulains galopant dans les prés ?
Et là-haut, émergeant d'une épaisse verdure,
Ce château dont au loin j'aperçois la toiture ? '
  Ainsi s'exprimait en chemin
   Un voyageur l'autre matin.
Dans le wagon, en face de notre homme
(Vous trouverez au bas le nom dont il se nomme),
Un gentleman, bien mis, bien portant, bien nourri,
Répondit : ' C'est Dangu, domaine favori
  De notre oncle Lagrange.'

   * *
    *

Le train ralentissait ; on était arrivé.
  Le gentleman, déjà levé,
   S'apprêtait à descendre,
Quand l'étranger lui dit : ' Oserais-je prétendre
A la faveur d'entrer avec vous au château ?
Je suis touriste et grand admirateur du beau.
Des splendeurs de Dangu, cicerone fidèle,
Ouvrez-moi les trésors de ce haras modèle.'
  ' Soit ; mais surtout soyez discret
   Et gardez un profond secret

De tout ceci. Venez, parcourons cette terre,
Où je vais vous sacrer Chevalier du Mystère.
Vous verrez les juments, les poulains, les yearlings,
Que doit dresser bientôt le grand Thomas Jennings,
Tout, jusqu'aux étalons, immortelle phalange
      De notre oncle Lagrange ! '

* *
*

Pour monter au château, l'on traverse d'abord
Un parc de l'ancien temps, un merveilleux décor.
En face du perron est l'endroit où repose,
Sous la verte pelouse, au pied d'un massif rose,
Celui qui fut *Monarque !* Ah ! que les *Tournament*,
Les *Dollar*, les *Vermout*, près de ce monument,
      Sont des seigneurs sans importance !
— Sous les rameaux, que la brise balance,
Tu peux dormir en paix dans ta tombe de fleurs :
Aucun n'a depuis toi fait de *Gladiateurs !*
Tout ici de ton fils conserve la mémoire,
Tout chante ses hauts faits et consacre sa gloire.
Sa généalogie, inscrite sur le mur,
Atteste que son sang coulait antique et pur.
Partout, dans les salons, des coupes burinées
Rappellent le héros des batailles gagnées !
Phénomène déjà, c'est dans ce pré, là-bas,
      Qu'on admirait ses premiers pas.
Son compagnon d'alors, traînant une voiture,
Aux poulains aujourd'hui porte la nourriture.
Renforcés comme lui par un grain généreux,
Nous les verrons un jour, dignes de leurs aïeux,
Illustrer de *Consul* la race refleurie
Et donner des *Nougats* à la Grande Ecurie !

* *
*

Plus loin, sous le coteau, quel est ce vétéran,
Qui nous regarde à peine, et semble un vieux sultan
Fatigué du sérail, rêvant l'apoplexie
      Alors que les sultans
      Pouvaient vivre longtemps,

A l'abri des ciseaux, dans leurs palais d'Asie ?
Spectre d'un grand vainqueur, vénérables débris,
  Saluons : c'est *Ventre Saint-Gris !*
Par son maître choyé jusqu'en sa solitude,
Il mourra sans avoir souffert l'ingratitude.

* *
*

Quand ils eurent ainsi tout visité, tout vu,
D'un bout à l'autre de Dangu ;
Après avoir longtemps par la porte entr'ouverte
Contemplé dans leur box *Tolla*, la *Reine Berthe*,
Vivid, *Fille de l'Air*, et cent autres commères,
  Et puis, après les fils, les pères,
Consul, *Le Sarrazin*, *Peut-être*, et cætera ;
A la grille, pensif, l'étranger demeura :
' Je vous quitte,' dit-il ; ' merci de ma journée,
Grâce à vous si complète et si bien terminée.
Vous direz de ma part au maître de ces lieux
Que j'eusse été sur terre un homme bienheureux
Si le ciel m'avait mis, ô bonheur sans mélange,
Au nombre des neveux de votre oncle Lagrange.'

Le Baron de Calibre XII.

Besides Monarque the French 'cracks' of 1858 were Miss Cath (five years), Gouvieux (three years), Serious (four years), Duchess (four years), Goëlette (three years), Forest du Lys (four years), &c., purchased from Prince Marc de Beauvau by the new comer Baron L. Nivière, who at once with their assistance took a leading position on the French Turf; Mademoiselle de Chantilly (four years), Etoile du Nord (three years), Ventre Saint-Gris (three years), Zouave (three years), &c., belonging to the other new comer, Count F. de Lagrange ; Count P. Rœderer's Brocoli (three years, by Gladiator), and Potocki (four years), La Maladetta (three years), &c., belonging to the 'old hand' M. A. Lupin, who ran La Maladetta thrice that year in England, but could only get second with her to

Sunbeam (who won easily) for the Coronation Stakes at Ascot.

There is something sad about the latter years of Monarque's life. He was left (according to information kindly given by the editor of 'Le Sport') at Dangu during the 'évènements,' and, though Count de Lagrange was there (with something else to think of, no doubt), was allowed to be at grass all the while, and was found in a deplorable state at the peace, with his hoofs grown to inordinate length and with feet terribly diseased. However he was brought round to some extent and performed stud duties for two years longer, till he died (as has been stated) in 1874 : in fact, Agile (foaled 1873), Avenante (foaled 1874), Avocat (foaled 1874), Chimène (foaled 1873), Confiance (foaled 1872), Falaise (foaled 1874), &c., had their parentage (on the male side) ascribed either to Monarque alone or to him ' or ' some other sire. The neglect of Monarque recalls the case of King Herod, whose owner—Sir J. Moore—had not the same excuse as Monarque's.

CHAPTER VI.

FRANC PICARD AND HIS TIMES.

IF any justification were needed for harking back a few years, and leaving 'the flat' for a 'spin across country,' the history of the legendary French steeple-chaser Franc Picard ('Frank Pickard,' of course, among his English friends and enemies) would be ample; for, steeple-chaser though he was for the greater part of his life, he was thoroughbred, and perhaps did more than any other creature on four legs to eradicate the heresy of 'demi-sang' (the 'half-bred' theory) and to fix eternally in its place—among the French—the true creed of 'pur sang' (the 'thoroughbred' theory). Moreover his history will take us to racecourses other than those on which the great French races were run, and will give us an opportunity of observing how 'hippodromes' had been increasing and multiplying, as well as improving, in the various parts of France from the earliest days of the French Jockey Club to the era of Monarque.

We will retrace our steps, first of all, no further back than the year 1846, in which there was foaled at the stud of the Marquis de Saint-Clou (it is said) a thoroughbred colt (by Royal Oak or Nautilus and Niobé, the dam 'bred in France') to which was given the name of Babouino. At three years of age he ran without success in all manner of races on the flat. In

1850 he was 'added to the list,' and was offered for sale at the price of a cavalry 'remount,' but could not obtain a purchaser, although, oddly enough, he was within an ace of being purchased by the famous 'gentleman jockey' Viscount A. Talon (well known in England), owner and rider of the celebrated steeplechaser (half-bred) Emilius, who in course of time had to play second fiddle to the 'cast-off' thoroughbred. In 1851 Babouino at last found a buyer. This was M. de la Mothe, a celebrated 'gentleman jockey,' a patron of steeple-chasing, and at one time inspector to the Administration des Haras. He gave 5,000 francs (about 200*l.*) for the despised gelding, changed the horse's name to Franc Picard, and handed him over to the trainership and jockeyship of a well-known Englishman, Lamplugh by name, who speedily justified the saying of the Arabs, 'Sire and dam make the foal; trainer and rider make the horse.' Franc Picard was a small, insignificant-looking bay, and, it is said, a 'roarer' withal; but, under the care of Mr. Lamplugh, he is stated to have got cured of his very 'roaring,' a cure which has been known to be effected by exportation to the Cape or elsewhere, but seldom, if ever, by any treatment in Europe. At any rate his 'roaring' did not prevent him from doing ample justice to the pains bestowed upon him by Mr. Lamplugh, who learned to thoroughly understand the horse, his cleverness, his honesty, his docility, and to husband and make the most of his resources to the last puff of wind.

In 1852 Franc Picard revealed his precious qualities as a steeple-chaser of great address, making fewer 'blunders' than any of his contemporaries. He was successful at La Marche, Le Pin, Craon, and Saumur, twice beating Emilius and Viscount Artus Talon, the 'knowing' gentleman who would not purchase him. This Emilius, by the way, was the very opposite, they say, of Franc Picard; for the former was half-bred, a 'cocktail,' a great, strapping, leathering animal, and the defeats he suffered in his contests with the little thoroughbred Franc Picard went a long way towards changing public opinion in France, which had inclined to give the preference to 'demi-sang' over 'pur sang,' especially in steeple-chasing, with its long distances and often heavy 'going.'

In 1853 Franc Picard began badly, but he won during the year some 29,000 francs, or 1,160*l.*, including the value of an *objet d'art*, given by the Emperor, at Caen, the amount of the two Grand Steeple-chases at Spa and of the races he won at Dieppe, where he commenced a career which has made his name to be indelibly associated with that place in quite a legendary manner.

In 1854 he won 48,850 francs, or 1,954*l.*, having been twice victorious at Dieppe, twice at La Marche, once at Bordeaux, once (if not twice) at Longchamps (during the first unsuccessful occupation of that 'hippodrome' before the French Jockey Club took it in hand), and elsewhere. His winnings were not surpassed even on the flat by any horse but Royal-quand-même, who won 50,700 francs (2,028*l.*)

In 1855, on March 25, he put in an appearance at La Croix de Berny on the revival of steeple-chases there after a lapse of eleven years. The revival, however, was a dead failure, in consequence of the execrable weather, the ground being converted into a swamp and the spectators being drenched to the skin. Moreover Franc Picard at the very start put his foot in a hole and was pulled up lame; M. Delamarre's

Flying Buck (not by Venison, but by Economist, the
'Irishman'), a life-long rival of Franc Picard's, went to
the front and was winning easily when he blundered
and fell at the last jump, and the 12,700 francs, or 508*l.*
(the value of the 'chase'), fell to a very ancient
customer, one British Yeoman. After this, when
Franc Picard was recovered of his lameness, came a
long duel between him and the competitors from
M. Henri Delamarre's stable. On April 1 Franc
Picard ran a dead heat with Lady Arthur (English
thoroughbred) at La Marche, and 'divided' with her,
taking, however, the lion's share (7,175 francs out of
12,350). On May 17 he was beaten by Flying Buck
at La Marche, and after that again at Spa. He then
went to Dieppe, and there, on 'his own' ground,
he triumphed over Jean Duquesne (recently imported
from England), Peter (a noted English steeple-chaser,
sent over expressly), Lady Arthur, and others; and on
the same day he turned the tables on his 'frequent
pardner,' or rather 'frequent opponent,' Flying Buck.
This year he brought his owner some 23,000 francs, or
920*l.*, in specie, and 3,000 francs' worth, or 120*l.* worth,
of 'crockery.' The aforesaid Peter may or may not
have been a different animal from the celebrated half-
bred Peter Simple and a so called Simple Peter, against
both of whom (according to the French Calendar) Franc
Picard also ran.

In 1856, during the Spring, Franc Picard crossed the
Channel to try conclusions on the enemy's own ground
in the Liverpool Grand National; and such respect had
he acquired by his defeat of Peter (? Simple) that he had
to carry the top weight, which he did unsuccessfully indeed but not dishonourably, as he carried 12 lbs. more
than the three placed horses. At Coventry he was not

more, though not less, successful ; but at Birmingham he won the Grand Steeple-chase with the top weight. Then began French chanticleer to crow very naturally to the following tune : 'So a French horse, trained at Chantilly too, can win over the Channel. Such a triumph is satisfactory in all respects ; for it is a French horse, trained in France, and belonging to a French owner. Regarded from this triple point of view it is the race—of all others in the annals of the Turf—most gratifying to the pride of hippic France.' On returning home the 'Despised One,' the former Babouino that went a-begging for a purchaser, gained more victories, including of course the Grand Steeple chase at Dieppe.

In 1857 he was almost equally victorious at Spa, at Valenciennes, and, needless to add, at Dieppe.

In 1858 he underwent a temporary eclipse. Clever as he was, he actually fell at La Marche and again at Spa ; he did not go—for a wonder—to Dieppe ; and his winnings took the reduced form of two prizes, worth only about 5,800 francs, or 232*l*., between them.

Nor was 1859 a much better year, for he was beaten at La Marche, at Warwick (whither he went on a goose's rather than a horse's errand across the Channel), and at Valenciennes (where he was crushed by the weight); but he made his usual trip to Dieppe, and, as usual, won the Grand Steeple-chase, beating six competitors (one English).

In 1860, to his compatriots' astonishment, grief, and even indignation, he really lost 'his own' Grand Steeple-chase at Dieppe ; but then he carried 77 kilos. (about 12 st. 3 lbs.) and gave away 38 lbs. to the winner, Surprise. However he won three races or chases, notably the Grand Steeple-chase at Spa.

In the Spring of 1861 he again crossed the Channel,

and was not placed for the Liverpool Grand National; but he was second, with 5 lbs. the worse in weight, to Red Rover for the Windsor Grand Handicap. On returning to France he was beaten a second time by Surprise, the mare having on this occasion only 9 lbs. advantage in weight. He was second to his stable companion The Colonel (by Pantaloon) at La Marche, and second to Trembleur (a thoroughbred 'Frenchman,' by Young Emilius and Miss Tandem) at Saumur. All this looked as if the end were at hand; and it was—but a glorious end. August came, and at Le Pin he won the steeple-chase, showing his heels to Pacha, Governor, &c., and making 11,500 francs, or 460*l*., by the performance; and at Dieppe, where he was so much 'at home' and so greatly beloved and respected, he gave away weight to eleven opponents, ran one of his finest races, and came in an easy first, though he broke down some 500 metres (about two furlongs and a half) from the post, having Waterloo, The Premier, and other English horses behind him. 'The old conqueror,' says the report in 'Le Sport,' 'ended his career with a glorious victory on the ground on which he had always shone. He broke down so badly that the long list of his triumphs is closed at last. The incident affected the spectators deeply, and damped the enthusiasm which caused Lamplugh to be received year by year, on returning to weigh in, with an ovation. A noble career could not have been more worthily terminated; Franc Picard maintained to the last his title of Steeple-chase Champion of France.' He broke down, like Monarque; but, more happy than Monarque, he disappeared in a blaze of triumph, and yet, less happy than Monarque, he could not perpetuate his name by a line of illustrious descendants.

Franc Picard, during his ten years' work, won something like a hundred prizes, worth more than 230,000 francs (about 9,200*l*.), to say nothing of 'crockery' under the style and title of 'objets d'art.' This is a large sum for France in those days, though they have 'altered all that.' Within the space of nine years Franc Picard was seven times a winner of the Grand Steeple-chase at Dieppe, and at Spa he was hardly less successful. He did not make much of his ventures in England, but he ran honourably; it might be said of him that 'all was lost but honour' (though indeed he did win something noteworthy in England), and in his own country or in Belgium he constantly triumphed over the English horses that were sent or were imported to measure strength with him on his own soil.

And now that steeple-chasing has been touched upon it will not be impertinent to mention, on the authority of 'Le Sport,' that Count de Morny's Diamant (who ran a dead heat with Lion for the French Derby of 1856) was expatriated to England, where he developed a taste, or at any rate a capacity, for steeple-chasing, won some 'chases' in his new home, and 'exhibited to the last that endurance which had been his distinctive characteristic on the flat.'

Small excuse is necessary for 'wandering out of the record,' for deserting the main track of this narrative (which is concerned chiefly, from the nature of the case, with flat racing, the 'legitimate' part of horse-racing), to follow Franc Picard over 'obstacles;' for it will have been noticed that he was in his way a good 'standard of measurement' for the French, whether they tried French or English horses against him : that he advanced the cause of the 'thoroughbred' by that example which is so much better than precept; that his history has caused mention to be made of M. Henri Delamarre, who began his 'sporting life' as a steeple-chaser, and was probably induced to turn his attention to the breeding of thoroughbreds and to the 'legitimate' flat racing (which is the only means of testing them) by observation of Franc Picard and his and other thorough-bred steeple-chasers' performances; and that the same history has led to casual notice of certain provincial 'hippodromes' (on which none of the great French races were run), thereby presenting a favourable opportunity of dealing with French 'hippodromes' in general, their increase and improvement, since the institution of the French Jockey Club. But before we leave Franc Picard altogether, let one observation be made: his mean appearance and his comparatively splendid and fabulous career combined are a paradox which, as in the case of some celebrated English steeple-chasers, such as Salamander and Emblem and Emblematic (no use on the flat, and apparently unfit to carry even a feather weight over a long distance and in ugly ground), is always puzzling to both initiated and uninitiated observers of horseflesh. It seems to be more common among thoroughbred horses than among any other living creatures, and is not unreasonably supposed (though it is one of those things that 'no feller can understand') to arise from the fact that 'bon sang ne ment pas,' that a well-bred horse is always good for something—if not to win the Derby, yet to make a first-rate steeple-chaser, or a marvellous hunter, or a prodigious trotter, or an invaluable hack, or, it may be, though himself of no account, a very Abraham of winners (like the Godolphin Arabian, or Bartlett's Childers, or Snake, or, in more modern times, Young Melbourne, who for some reason or other did not run themselves, but were very much the cause of running in others), or, at the very worst, an excellent 'pièce de résistance' at one of the establishments called 'Bouillons Duval.'

And now a word or two about French racecourses, commonly called 'hippodromes.'

It has already been noted that as early as the time of Louis XIV. (in 1651, 1683, and 1685) there were evidently racecourses, whether temporary or permanent, at the Bois de Boulogne, at St. Germain-en-Laye (Achères), and at Le Pecq (Le Vésinet); that in Louis XV.'s time there was a racecourse at the Plaine de Sablons; and that in Louis XVI.'s there were constantly used racecourses at the Plaine de Sablons, the Royal Park of Vincennes, and Fontainebleau. Then came a sort of blank till the time of the Empire, when races were 'decreed' at Le Pin and elsewhere; but there is scarcely a vestige left of them, and there is hardly a scrap of information before 1819, from which year there were Prix du Roi, or Prix Royaux, or Prix des Princes, or all three sorts, run for regularly at the Champ de Mars or elsewhere.

From 1776 to 1833 (the close of it) there were horse races, and therefore racecourses or 'hippodromes' of some kind, at the following places (and perhaps at others not set down in the 'books'):—

Town.	Department.
1. Arles	Bouches du Rhône.
2. Aurillac	Cantal.
3. Bordeaux	Gironde.
4. Bourbon-Vendée	Vendée.
5. Chantilly	Oise.
6. Fontainebleau	Seine-et-Marne.
7. Jouy (steeple-chase)	Seine-et-Oise.
8. Limoges	Haute Vienne.
9. Maisons-sur-Seine	Seine-et-Oise.

Town.		Department.
10. Mont de Marsan	. .	Landes.
11. Nancy . . .	.	Meurthe.
12. Paris { Bois de Boulogne / Champ de Mars }		Seine.
13. Pin (Le) . .	. .	Orne.
14. Poitiers . .	. .	Vienne.
15. Sablons (Plaine de)	.	Seine.
16. Semur . .	. .	Côte d'Or.
17. St. Brieuc . .	. .	Côtes du Nord.
18. Strasbourg .	. .	Bas Rhin.
19. Tarbes . .	. .	Hautes Pyrénées.
20. Trèves . .	. .	Sarre.
21. Tuble . .	. .	Corrèze.
22. Vincennes .	. .	Seine.

And what has been the growth since the Société d'Encouragement began their propaganda in 1833? Some of the 'old originals' have—naturally—'gone under;' Arles, Bourbon-Vendée, Sablons, Semur, Trèves, and one or two others have disappeared from the list, but, *en revanche*, so many more have been added that the number of 'hippodromes' for 'courses plates,' or 'flat racing,' was 133 in 1885, which is actually 63 more than was then the number in the still United Kingdom, according to 'Weatherby.'

To the twenty-two 'originals' may be added, if anybody please, Count Victor de Tocqueville's private 'hippodrome' near Dieppe; but it is not probable that there were many other private 'hippodromes' up to the day when M. E. Blanc set up his at Chapelle-en-Serval in 1879.

The principal proprietors of horses during this period (from 1776 to the end of 1833), and those most known to fame, were the Count d'Artois (Charles X.), the Duke de Chartres (Duke d'Orléans, 'Philippe Egalité'), the Prince de Nassau, the Prince de Guéménée, the Marquis de

H

Conflans, the Duke de Lauzun, MM. *de Royères, Rieussec,* the Count de Narbonne, Raymond de Cantal, *Crémieux, Chédeville, Benoît,* de Maulmont, de la Place, *de Vanteaux,* La Vigne, Rabion, Neveu, Leconte, the *Duke de Guiche,* Souchey, Cazalot, the Baron de la Bastide (mayor of Limoges), the Count (Duke) *Descars,* Delarroque, Desmaisons de Bonnefond, the Count de Castellane, Desgrands, Périer, *C. Laffitte,* the Prince de la Moscowa, the Count de Sarrazin, Husson, Chéri-Salvador, *J. G. Schickler,* and above all *Lord Henry Seymour* (whose first appearance was made about 1826). Italics distinguish the names now best remembered.

As for the twelve founders of the Jockey Club, they had by the end of 1833 (or soon afterwards, in 1834-35) taken unto themselves a host, of whom the most notable names were the following:—

Louis André, Ernest André, the Count d'Aure, the Baron de la Bastide, the Count de Beaumont, the Prince de Belgiajoso, the Count Léon de Bernis, the Count Gaston de Blangy, the Marquis de Boisgelin, Achille Bouchet, *J. Bowes,* Lord *Bruce,* Caillard, E. Cailiard, the Viscount Adolphe de Carbonnières, the Count de Champlatreux, the Count de Châteauvillars, Collinot (de Long-Périer), the Count de Cornelissen, the Marquis de Croix, the Count de Croix, the Viscount Paul Daru, the Count Dalton, the Count Dubourg, the Count René du Pylle, the Baron Durand, the Viscount Melin Dutaillis, Dutheil, the Prince d'Eckmühl, Major *Fancourt,* Alcibiade Fasquel, De Fleuriau, Achille Fould, Major *Frazer,* the Marquis de Grammont, the Baron Millin de Grandemaison, General Count de la Grange (father of Count Frédéric), the Marquis Conrade de la Grange, the Viscount Frédéric de la Grange, De Gricourt, Henri and Charles Greffulhe, the Count de Halley Coëtquen, the Count Eugène d'Harcourt, the Viscount de Hédouville, the Viscount d'Hinnisdal, the Viscount Hocquart, the Duke d'Istrie, the Marquis Fernand de Laferté, De Lajeunevraye, the Marquis de Lavalette, Auguste Lupin, Lecouteulx, Lévy, the Marquis des Ligneries, the Count de MacCarthy, Edouard Manuel, Léopold Manuel, the Marquis de Marmier, the Marquis de Miramon, Edmond de Montguyon, Fernand de Montguyon, General the Baron Morell, the Count de Morin du Sendat, Alfred Mosselmann, the Chevalier de Nogent, the Count Edgar Ney, the Viscount Léonce Odoart, Louis Paira, Théodore Patureau, Casimir Périer, Paul Périer, the Count de Plaisance, Couret Pleville, Charles de Poupilliers, the Count de Pracontal, the Viscount Rampon, *Ricardo*, the Baron G. de la Rifaudière, Jules Robin, Antoine de Rothschild, the Count de Roydeville, Sir Cavendish *Rumbold*, De Saint-Cyran, the Marquis de Sainte-Croix, Saint-Valliers, the Baron Auguste Sanegon, the Baron Paul Sanegon, Achille Scillières, the Count de Septeuil, Eugène Sue, the Count Charles de Béthune-Sully, Auguste Thuret, Henri Thuret, the Count Guy de la Tour du Pin, the Count Ludovic de la Tour du Pin, the Marquis de la Valette, the Count de Vassy, the Count de Vauban, the Count Adolphe de Vaublanc, the Prince de Wagram, the Count Walewski, and the Earl of *Yarmouth*; according to the authority, the orthography, and the titularity of the 'Calendriers' published at the time.

The names printed in italics are, of course, Englishmen's (Mr. John Bowes, of Streatlam, who won the Derby at Epsom with Mündig, Cotherstone, Daniel O'Rourke, and West Australian, who lived most of his time in Paris, and who died but a few months ago, being most remarkable among them). The name of

M. Eugène Sue, the novelist, is worthy of a passing remark: he was a very 'horsey' gentleman indeed, and in his capacity of romancer wrote a highly effective account of the Godolphin Arabian, a 'romance' quite up to the author's level as an imaginative writer whose motto was 'Tant pis pour les faits.'

It will be observed that a Rothschild (to whom might perhaps be added Barons James and Nathaniel, who were among the very first to join) is associated with these earliest members of the Jockey Club; and there too appear the names of M. A. Lupin and Count (then Viscount) F. de Lagrange (written La Grange), who were the first to make a mark in England. It was not likely that the list would be swelled by any of the Aumonts, who, as it were, set up Count de Lagrange with a stock of race horses; for—even if there were no other reason—none of them was yet distinguished or even known among breeders and owners.

The chief 'haras,' or 'breeding studs,' in France up to 1883 were—

1. The old-established place at Le Pin, called Haras Royal du Pin, in existence since the days of Louis XIV., Colbert, and the infancy of the Administration des Haras; there at some time or other, from 1818 to 1834, were stationed the English imported stud horses Tigris (winner of the Two Thousand, by Quiz), Streatlam Lad (by Remembrancer), Mustachio (by Whisker), Napoleon (by Bob Booty), who became the sire of Eylau, &c., besides the Arab Massoud, &c.

2. The Dauphin's Haras de Meudon (with fourteen thoroughbred mares, in 1828, and the stud horse Rowlston, imported from England).

3. M. Rieussec's, first at Buc and then at Viroflay, with the famous Rainbow for stud horse in chief.

4. The Duke Descars', first at Château de Sourche (Sarthe) and then at Château de la Roche (Vienne), to which it was transferred in 1827 (with Tooley, son of Walton and Phantasmagoria, Trance, son of Phantom and Pope Joan, and Sidi-Mahmoud, a pure Barb, for chief stud horses).

5. M. de Kertangui's (at St. George, Morlaix, Brittany, for the production of 'demi-sang' chiefly).

6. Count Victor de Tocqueville's (at Château de Gueures, near Dieppe, for 'Arab blood' chiefly, but with the imported English sires Domenichino, son of Vandyke, Junior and July, and Zoroaster [who ran in the name of Knave of Clubs and stood in England under the name of Prince Regent], son of Sorcerer and Louisa, for stud horses too).

7. The versatile Abbé de Pradt's (ex-Archbishop of Malines), at his breeding establishment in Le Cantal, where he offered to supply any sort of horse 'to order,' as a tailor would supply a coat or a hat-maker a hat, of any size, any colour, any number of legs—up to three —that anybody pleased.

8. Haras Royal de Rozières (under the management of the Marquis de Vaugiraud, where the animals bred were remarkable for being under-sized). It is said to have been broken up in 1844, but must have been re-organised.

9. M. J. G. Schickler's (in the neighbourhood of Paris, probably with Tandem, formerly Multum in Parvo, son of Rubens and Jannette, as stud horse in chief).

10. M. Crémieux's (who was a great breeder both at his Haras de l'Allier and at his Haras de Madrid, Bois de Boulogne, and to whom, as well as to M. J. E. Schickler, the stud horse Tandem, ex-Multum in Parvo, seems to have belonged for a time).

11. MM. Hémart's (at La Charmoye, near Epernay, with Atom, son of Phantom and Mite, for stud horse in chief).

12. Lord Henry Seymour's (at Sablonville, with Royal Oak, son of Catton and sire of Poetess, who was the dam of both Hervine and Monarque, for stud horse in chief).

We have already seen that, at the foundation of the French Jockey Club, there was no decent public race-course (so far as the man in the street or the members of the Club themselves knew) in France until the idea of making one at Chantilly—an idea which arose, it is said, out of a 'scratch' race between Prince de Labanoff (or Lobanoff) and some of his friends (including Viscount de Hédouville and the celebrated rider M. de Normandie, the winner of the race)—was adopted by the Duke d'Orléans, representative of the Duke d'Aumale (to whom the property was bequeathed by the Prince de Condé) and promptly carried out—so promptly that by the end of the year 1833 a programme was drawn up for the spring of 1834, though the French Derby (Prix du Jockey Club) did not (and could not very well, if the condition of entry as yearlings were to be observed from the start) take place till 1836. The modest 5,000 francs given by the Club as added money, indeed, were not voted before June 24, 1835; but probably the name and conditions had previously been settled. The Prix de Diane, or French Oaks (with similar conditions and a smaller 'dotation'—only 3,000 francs for some years, though it was 6,000 'by subscription' the first year), did not begin till 1843, when Prince Marc de Beauvau's Nativa won).

All this time the Paris meetings remained without any 'hippodrome' at which the merest plater would not have been justified in turning up his nose; and so

they were destined to remain for some years to come,
with nothing but the Champ de Mars to knock the
horses about upon.

At last, in 1856–57, the Société d'Encouragement
(which was a sort of Esau to its twin brother the
French Jockey Club in point of birth) commenced a
new era, were enabled to turn over a new leaf or a
new lease. They obtained (chiefly through the Duke
de Morny, that great patron of the Turf, the creator
of Deauville, the originator of the Grand Prix de
Paris) from the Government and the municipality of
Paris a promise that a 'hippodrome' should be included
in the projected plan for transforming the Bois de Boulogne into an earthly paradise. In the Longchamps
meadows, then, on the borders of the Seine, they obtained an allotment of ground, levelled indeed, but perfectly bare, and, by an arrangement with the municipality of Paris, the Société became lessees of the racecourse for fifty years (the lease expiring in 1906), and
undertook to pay an annual rent, as well as to build
stands, which at the expiration of the lease should
become the property of the city. The stands were
erected by the city's own architects, MM. Bailly and
Davioud, at an expense of 420,000 francs (16,800*l*.), and
subsequent expenses (turfing and what not) brought the
amount up to 1,284,981 francs (about 51,395*l*.). The
enclosure was opened on the last Sunday in April 1857,
and the opening was a vast success, though the weather
was not quite 'conformable.' Seven hundred 'voitures'
(which may, of course, have included the humble
'growler' of Paris as well as the 'eleven four-in-hands')
and two hundred and fifty 'cavaliers' were counted on
the ground, and Alphonse on foot was there in his
thousands. The first race was then, as it still is, La

Bourse; and it was won, in accordance with the fitness of things, by M. A. Lupin (winner of the first Goodwood Cup—the first notable race ever won in England by a Frenchman—and the 'doyen' of the French Jockey Club and of French 'hommes de cheval') with Eclaireur, son of imported Mr. Wags and home-bred Lanterne.

At the same time that the Société leased Longchamps a contract was made with the State for the direction and management of the autumn races, which had hitherto been under the authority of the municipality and the Administration des Haras jointly; and thus the organisation of the races, in all their details, rested in the hands of the French Jockey Club.

'The ground,' we are informed, 'measures about 66 hectares in superficies. Its vast extent admits of marking out upon it several courses different in shape and dimensions, avoiding too sharp or too frequent turns, and giving the horses every facility for allowing full play to their powers without any hindrance. The course is covered with turf, the ground as good as artificial soil can be. Thanks to the care of Mr. Mackenzie-Grieves and to those expenses from which the Société never recoils, it has become as good as can possibly be desired.'

There is always an Englishman, if only a Scoto-Franco-Englishman, with a finger in the French horse pie; the trainers, the lads, the jockeys, the grooms have always been English almost to a man, and now the very racecourses need the supervision of a perfidious Briton.

However, here we have Paris at last with a 'hippodrome' worthy of her (at least so the 'compatriot' quoted above considers), and it is certainly as prettily situated as heart or eye could desire.

We may now, then, return to our muttons and follow the progress of French horse-racing, having first appended a list of the places at which race meetings were held last year (1885), and which have grown out of the original twenty-two (in existence between 1776 and 1833) with a rapid multiplication worthy of the famous 'men in buckram.'

Agen, Abbeville, Aire, Aix-les-Bains, Aimargues, Amiens, Angers, Angoulême, Antrain, Auch, Aurillac, Auxonne, Avignon, Avranches, Bagnères de Bigorre, Bagnères de Luchon, Barbezieux, Bayonne-Biarritz, Bazas, Beaumont de Lomagne, Beaupréau, Beauvais, Bernay, Besançon, Bergerac, Bordeaux, Boulogne-sur-Mer, Bourgoin, Cabourg, Caen, Carhaix, Carpentras, Castillonnès, Castelsarrazin, Cavaillon, Cazaubon, Chalais, Chalamont, Châlon-sur-Saône, Chantilly, Chateauroux, Châtillon-sur-Chalaronne, Cherbourg, Cholet, Condom, Corlay, Courseulles, Craon, Dax, Deauville, Dieppe, Dinan, Dorat, Douai, Dunkerque, Eauze, Evreux, Feurs, Fleurance, Fontainebleau, Gémozac, Grenade-sur-l'Adour, Guérande, Havre, Hyères, Jullouville, La Brède, La Foux, La Guerche, Langon, Lannion, Laon, La Roche-sur-Yon, La Tour du Pin, Le Mans, Lesparre, L'Isle, Libourne, Limoges, Lille, Lyon, Mansle, Marmande, Marseille, Maubourguet, Meslay du Maine, Mirambeau, Montaigu, Montauban, Mont de Marsan, Montélimar, Morlaix, Moulins, Nancy, Nantes, Narbonne, Nevers, Nîmes, Niort, Pau, Périgueux, Paris (Bois de Boulogne), Pertuis, Pin, Poitiers, Quimper, Redon, Reims, Rennes, Rochefort-sur-Mer, Roubaix, Rouen, Royan, Sables d'Olonne, St. André de Cubzac, St. Brieuc, Saintes, St. Jean d'Angély, St. Lô, St. Nazaire, St. Ouen des Toits, Saumur, Tannay, Tarbes, Toulouse, Tourcoing, Tours, Valence d'Agen, Valenciennes, Vannes, Vernon, Vic-Bigorre, Vincennes.

No doubt some of these meetings—a dozen or more

—would not be recognised by the Société d'Encouragement in the official 'Calendrier;' but they serve, nevertheless, to show how the French have come on with their horse-racing since the establishment of that energetic association in 1833.

By the way, opportunity may here be taken for mentioning the succession of secretaries to whom the Société have been so much indebted since its foundation. Mr. T. Bryon himself probably acted in that capacity at first; but in 1837, when the Club was at No. 2 Rue Grange-Batelière, the office was filled by M. Joseph Grandhomme. In 1848 the Club had so expanded that, it would seem, there were two secretaries required; M. Grandhomme remained secretary to the Société d'Encouragement, and M. Groszos (who died, aged 68, in December 1883) appears to have become secretary or assistant secretary to the Jockey Club (Cercle). M. Grandhomme (who died at 79 years of age on April 10, 1885) retired in 1877, and was succeeded by his son, M. Georges Grandhomme (the most urbane and considerate of correspondents, as the author of this work wishes to testify), who died about eighteen months before his father and was succeeded by the present secretary, M. G. Madelaine.

CHAPTER VII.

THE 'BIG STABLE.'

Towards the close of the year 1857 there had occurred an event of very great importance in the history of French horse-racing: the confederacy of which Prince Marc de Beauvau had been the head (with Prince Etienne de Beauvau, Count Wladimir de Komar, Count Manuel de Noailles, and Viscount Onésime Aguado as his chief associates) had broken up, and Baron Nivière had become the purchaser of the whole stable (La Morlaye). In 1860 Baron Nivière and Count F. de Lagrange joined their forces and formed the redoubtable association known as the 'Big Stable' (la Grande Ecurie). The Baron had retained the services of Mr. Henry Jennings (at La Morlaye), just as the Count had retained the services of Mr. Tom Jennings (M. Alexandre Aumont's trainer), and the two brothers had the direction of the 'Big Stable,' Henry being in charge of the French branch and Tom of the English, with an establishment (which became famous as 'Phantom Cottage') at Newmarket.

But this is making the running a little too fast. We will return to the year 1859, the year after the retirement of Monarque.

In 1859 the most notable French horses were, among the older, Tippler (who developed from a nonentity at three years of age into a 'crack'—a French 'crack,' that is—at four), Martel-en-Tête, Zouave, Gouvieux (winner of the Poule des Produits in 1858), Fort-à-bras, Goëlette, and (in the South) Sylvain ; among the three-year-olds Black Prince (winner of the French Derby), Géologie (winner of the French Oaks), Union Jack (winner of the Prix de l'Empereur, now Grande Poule des Produits, at Paris), Nuncia (who had been a very promising two-year-old), Bakaloum (winner of the Poule d'Essai), Précurseur, the celebrated Light (son of The Prime Warden and Balaclava, though he had not as yet shown what was in him—that he would win nineteen races 'right off the reel' and would become the sire of Bigarreau and Sornette), and (in the South) Bissextil and Marianne.

Nevertheless the annual French invasion of England was in 1859 a dead failure. The campaign began badly at Warwick when Count F. de Lagrange ran Tramp (two years old) and Etoile du Nord (winner of the French Oaks in 1858) to no purpose ; and the last French performance of the year in England was that of Baron Schickler's Martel-en-Tête, who was second for the City and Suburban (won by Glenbuck, three years old, with the preposterous weight of 4 st. 10 lbs., car. 4 st. 12 lbs.) just five days before he won the Prix du Cadran in the Bois de Boulogne. At Ascot Baron Nivière ran Miss Cath (six years) and Wedding (three years) in vain ; the former was said to be not 'wound up,' the latter to have been badly ridden (by Pantal, a French jockey apparently). At Goodwood, whither Count F. de Lagrange sent Mademoiselle de Chantilly (five years), Union Jack (three years), and Aboukir (two years), the Frenchmen were grievously discomfited ; neither the Count, nor Baron Nivière (with Miss Cath), nor the Baron's associate Count de Prado (with Gouvieux), could nearly win a race, whether it were the Stewards' Cup, or the Goodwood Stakes, or the Findon Stakes, or the Goodwood Cup, or the Bentinck Memorial Plate. It should be mentioned, however, that Mademoiselle de Chantilly had made a *faux pas* or met with some sort of accident *en route*, and so merely walked in with the crowd to see what had won the Goodwood Cup, having previously been unplaced for the Stewards' Cup. This year, again, English horses, Gaspard and Lifeboat to wit, went, as in previous years, to run for the Prix de l'Empereur at Chantilly. The French were represented by Goëlette, Black Prince, and Fortune among others; Lifeboat was naturally made favourite; but Gaspard won, Goëlette (much indulged in point of weight) was second, and Lifeboat only third. The victory of the English horse was received by the French, it is said, in ' dead silence' (' morne silence'). This year too Géologie (winner of the French Oaks and of the Grand Prix at Baden, but defeated for the French Derby) was sent by Baron Nivière to run for our Cambridgeshire, but was not in the betting or stood at 66 to 1, and indeed was ' not in it' at all. Thus, then, a ' compatriot' tersely but accurately sums up the history of the season: ' Produce very indifferent: success in England—none.' The year, however, was memorable for the importation into France of the Flying Dutchman by the Administration des Haras, at a cost of 104,000 francs, or upwards of 4,000*l*. (the highest price the Government had ever paid for a stud horse), and of Pyrrhus the First (winner of the Derby of 1846) by M. de Nexon.

The year 1860 was notable for the disappearance from the Turf of M. Alexandre Aumont, who, when he sold his horses to Count F. de Lagrange in 1856, had undertaken not to race for three years. The time was now over, and already, in 1859, M. Aumont had shown that he was in his old 'form' by winning the Grand Criterium at Paris with the two-year-old Mon Etoile, who seemed to have *de l'avenir*. The bright prospects, however, vanished at his death, which occurred early in the year, before the season opened ; and though his son, M. Paul Aumont, immediately stepped into his place, Mon Etoile was disqualified through her nominator's death for the French Derby and other engagements in the great 'Poules' at Paris.

On French soil Géologie began the campaign of 1860 by proving that, notwithstanding her sorry exhibition in the Cambridgeshire of 1859, she was the best animal of her year : she won the Prix du Cadran in a common canter against Black Prince and Nuncia, and she scored a victory once every succeeding Sunday during the Paris Spring Meeting, beating on May 3 the indefatigable Mademoiselle de Chantilly, who had lately returned home from an unsuccessful competition for the City and Suburban. At this Paris meeting Count F. de Lagrange's Pierrefonds won the Prix de la Ville from Madame Latache de Fay's Beauvais (who turned the tables upon him in the French Derby) ; and Baron N. de Rothschild won the Poule d'Essai as well as another race with Gustave (beating Pierrefonds, Prétendant, &c.), insomuch that sanguine Frenchmen began to have visions of another Baroncino and another Goodwood Cup. At Chantilly the French Oaks was won by Baron Nivière's Surprise (who was to be the dam of Sornette, by Light), and the French Derby, as already mentioned, by Beauvais. The fact, however, deserves a second mention, because it was the first and only time the French Derby was won by Madame de Fay, who struggled so 'widowfully' to do the deed which had been so long attempted without success by her late husband. In the summer and autumn the French horses showed excellent form, especially M. Benoît's Capucine and M. P. Aumont's Mon Etoile, at home, in Belgium, and at Baden, where Capucine won the Grand Prix and the celebrated Cosmopolite, more famous as a steeple-chaser than as a flat racer, a worthy compatriot of Franc Picard, distinguished himself.

But it was in their annual invasion of England that the French gave the most significant signs of improvement, though the campaign in itself was not much to boast of. The year 1860 is the date of a new departure, for in that year the French for the first time ran a horse 'bred in France' (though old Philippe Egalité had run or nominated an English horse, Cantator, in 1784) for the English Derby. Count F. de Lagrange, in the spirit of the French 'sapper' to whom 'nothing is sacred,' boldly ran Dangu (bred in France) for the 'blue riband of the Turf,' and though the horse started at the hopeless odds of 200 to 1 against him he was placed fourth by the judge, a long way, it is true, behind Thormanby and The Wizard, but in front of such horses as the 'American' Umpire, Buccaneer (so famous as a sire), Nutbourne, and High Treason. Dangu was a son of that excellent sire FitzGladiator, but did not do much to 'illustrate' either himself or the race of Gladiator. Still it was evident at last that the French 'meant business.'

This year Count F. de Lagrange ran Mademoiselle de Chantilly for the Newmarket Handicap, the City and Suburban, the Cambridgeshire (for which she ran Weatherbound to a head), and a Handicap Sweepstakes at Newmarket Houghton, but she won nothing; Baron Nivière ran Goëlette to no purpose at Newmarket July, but won two races at the Houghton with Prétendant (son of Faugh-a-Ballagh) against some reputed English 'flyers' and made the astonished Britons rub their eyes; and Baron N. de Rothschild not very nearly repeated 'the Baroncino trick' with Gustave, for the 'Frenchman,' though second to Sweetsauce for the Goodwood Cup, was ten lengths 'to the bad.' Of the other horses 'bred in France' that ran in England this year (1860) Zouave was third for both the Stewards' Cup and Goodwood Cup; Fort-à-bras and Viroflay were 'not placed' for the former, as also Fort-à-bras and Nuncia were for the Chesterfield Cup, and Héliopolis for the Findon Stakes and subsequently for three races at Newmarket; much the same remark applies to Angélo, but Négro (afterwards Massa) won a small sweepstakes at Newmarket Houghton, as also did Isabella (winner of the Grand Criterium at Paris), a two-year-old; the celebrated Gabrielle d'Estrées, another two-year-old, was fourth but 'not placed' for a Nursery Handicap at Newmarket (which was little enough for a future winner of the French Derby); the wonderful Light (sire of Sonnette), who had won nineteen events 'off the reel' in France, until his uninterrupted victories had been stopped by Mademoiselle de Chantilly at Caen, was 'not placed' for a plate at Newmarket Houghton, but started first favourite at 2 to 1 for the Liverpool Autumn Cup and was second, only a neck behind The Brewer, an 'aged' horse carrying 12 lbs. less than the four-year-old Light; and finally Cosmopolite, who was always 'partem in utramque paratus,' as ready to run steeple-chases as flat races, flat races as steeple-chases, wound up the season honourably for the French by winning 'Le Grand Steeple-chase d'Hereford,' as the French authority hath it.

Meanwhile, in the early autumn, the dreaded coalition had taken place; Count F. de Lagrange and Baron Nivière had made common cause, creating a great sensation, exciting wide apprehension, insomuch that men talked in France of a 'Turf deluge,' in which the smaller establishments should be overwhelmed by the 'Big Stable.' It was even whispered that the Emperor himself, who was known to be partial to horse-racing on the English plan, had an interest in the 'Big Stable' and was its real head; but for the latter insinuation there appears to have been no sufficient ground. Minds, however, were somewhat tranquillised on reflection, when it was remembered that the smaller stables had done pretty well; that Madame Latache de Fay (who died in July 1861, and was succeeded by M. Teissière) had won the two biggest French prizes (the Grande Poule des Produits, as it is now called, and the French Derby); that Mon Etoile and Capucine had brought considerable grist to their owners' mill; that Count de Morny had made a good show with Violette (winner of the Poule des Produits); that M. Henri Delamarre had been to the fore with Papillotte (who was to be the dam of Patricien); and that of the small owners Baron Schickler alone could be considered quite out in the cold, though MM. Fould, Lupin, de Vanteaux, Rothschild, and Nexon were not much better off. There was still more relief felt when it became manifest that the 'Big Stable' was about to put forth its chief strength not in France but in England, where the more powerful branch of it would henceforth have a local habitation and a name.

The 'Big Stable' lasted about two years only, and its achievements justified partly the fears which had been expressed, partly the reassurance which had afterwards been acquired.

In 1861 the Count and the Baron together won in France, it is stated, 118 races and 497,000 francs (about 19,880*l*.), and in England stood fifth (with 7,440*l*.) in the list of winning owners, but in 1862 had dropped in France to 78 races and 352,808 francs (something over 14,000*l*.) and in England to the seventh place (with 6,440*l*.), whilst M. Robin (owner of Souvenir, the winner of the French Derby) had come up to 129,000 francs (5,160*l*.), M. P. Aumont to 90,000 francs (3,600*l*.), and M. Delamarre and Baron Schickler to about 80,000 francs (3,200*l*.) apiece; so that the alarm which might well have been created by the successes of the 'Big Stable' in 1861 was reasonably modified by its falling-off in 1862 and the corresponding improvement made by smaller private owners acting single-handed.

In 1861 the most notable of the horses 'bred in France' were Prétendant (four years, winner of the Prix du Cadran), Mon Etoile (four years, winner of the Grand Prix de l'Impératrice, afterwards called Prix Rainbow), Surprise (four years, winner of the Grand Prix de l'Empereur, afterwards called Prix Gladiateur, and dam of Sornette), Good-bye (three years, winner of the Prix de Longchamps and the Poule des Produits), Finlande (three years, winner of what is now the Grande Poule des Produits and of the French Oaks), Isabella (three years, winner of the Poule d'Essai), La Diva (three years, winner of the Prix de la Ville de Paris), Gabrielle d'Estrées (three years, winner of the French Derby), Palestro (three years, winner of the Grand Prix du Prince Impérial, afterwards called Prix Royal Oak), Compiègne (three years, second for the Grand Prix at Baden), and the two-year-olds Partisan (by Launcelot),

Gemma (by Womersley), and Stradella (by the Cossack or Father Thames), winners of the three principal 'Critériums' in France.

Of this number Palestro and Gabrielle d'Estrées were the most remarkable, for reasons which will be given hereafter.

Meanwhile let us see how the French, led by the 'Big Stable,' acquitted themselves in England, the arena in which they were constantly testing their growing strength.

The 'Big Stable' ran Héliopolis (at Coventry); Palaiseau and Grenadier (at Warwick and all over the country); Cosmopolite and Mademoiselle de Chantilly (at Northampton and very many other places); Light, Angélo, Gabrielle d'Estrées, Prétendant, and Marignan (two years old, the first foal, it is said, ever bred at Dangu under the new 'departure' of Count F. de Lagrange) at Epsom Spring Meeting (and at many other meetings); Gouvieux, Isabella, Dangu, Alba (two years), and Lyciscote (at Newmarket Craven, &c. &c.); Boran (by Ion, at Newmarket First Spring); Baliverne (at Chester, &c. &c.); Wedding, Royallieu (for the Derby), and Surprise at Epsom Summer Meeting, &c. &c.; Absinthe (two years) and Alerte (two years, winner of the Biennial for two-year-olds) at Ascot, &c. &c.; La Vapeur, Fabius, Mistral (two years), Flaub (two years), at Newmarket July, &c.; Shingle (English gelding) at Goodwood and Lewes; Généalogie (two years) for the Gimcrack Stakes (for which she ran second) at York, &c.; Hadji Stavros (two years) at Warwick Autumn Meeting, &c.; Allez-y-rondement (two years) at Newmarket and Liverpool; Mayfield (English gelding) at Newmarket and Worcester; Palestro at Newmarket; Exactitude (two years), Benjamin (two years), and

Mademoiselle de Champigny (two years) at Newmarket, &c.; Finlande and Herculaneum (two years) at Newmarket; and M. Aumont, who seems to have been the only Frenchman besides the 'Big Stable' to run in England this year, had 'a shy' at the Goodwood Cup with Mon Etoile, but she did not obtain a place, taking a back seat with her compatriot Royallieu.

Of the horses mentioned as having run in England the following only were winners on English racecourses: Palaiseau (three events and 222*l*. at Doncaster and Newmarket); Cosmopolite, the 'horse of all work,' a gelding (eight events and 1,905*l*. at Warwick, Newmarket [Great Eastern Handicap], and Doncaster); Light (one event, 50*l*., at Epsom); Angélo (two events and 170*l*. at Chester and York); Gabrielle d'Estrées (one event and 140*l*. at Shrewsbury); Marignan (four events and 845*l*. at Epsom, Manchester, and [the Fernhill Stakes] at Ascot); Baliverne (five events and 515*l*. at York, Malton, Newton, and Wolverhampton); Wedding (one event and 50*l*. at Epsom); Surprise (one event and 250*l*. at Epsom, the Cup); Alerte (one event and 705*l*. [Ascot Biennial]); Palestro (one event—the Cambridgeshire—and 2,225*l*.); Exactitude (one event and 60*l*. at Newmarket); Mademoiselle de Champigny (one event and 190*l*. at Bedford): upwards of 7,000*l*. in all.

The campaign had not been very brilliant perhaps, but it was enough to set a 'compatriot,' who dwelt rather upon victories than defeats, singing a song of satisfaction on this wise: 'There can now be no doubt of the progress made in French horse-breeding. It is not ten years since old Hervine's first attempt at Goodwood was described as madness; and now the French horses have to be taken into account wherever they put in an appearance.' Especially did the victory of Palestro in the Cambridgeshire (for which Count de Lagrange had made so close a bid the year before with Mademoiselle de Chantilly, a head only behind the winner, Weatherbound), having his 'compatriot' Gabrielle d'Estrées second, in front of the great Asteroid, tickle the Gallic fancy: so that the Administration des Haras by the pen of General Fleury delivered itself of a sermon on horse-breeding, proclaiming that, with the view of producing other thoroughbreds in the likeness of Palestro, the Government had 'founded a model training school at Le Pin' (where, as we have seen, there had always been a 'haras' from the time of Colbert). But 'model institutions' generally come to grief, and General Fleury's 'foundation' seems to have been no exception to the rule.

And now a few words about the most remarkable French horses that appeared on the Turf, whether on the Continent or in England, in 1861.

Let us begin with Palestro, who was a sort of Franc Picard of the 'legitimate business.' He was foaled at the stud of a M. Chédeville; he was a son of that wonderful sire FitzGladiator and of Lady Saddler (who died the very year she foaled him, 1858), herself 'bred in France,' so that he was French every whit. Palestro, like Franc Picard (who was originally called Babouino), had his original name 'Coquet' altered to that which he was to make celebrated; and, like Franc Picard again, there was not much of a rush to buy him at first (for he was purchased as a foal by M. Alexandre Aumont, a consummate judge, for 420 francs, or about 16 guineas, reminding us of the more modern Plaisanterie, a winner of the Cambridgeshire, as well as Cesarewitch, purchased for 32 guineas as a yearling).

Like Franc Picard, furthermore, Palestro, after he had been tried (at Mont de Marsan, in the South), did not please, and would have been sold with alacrity for 4,000 francs, or 160*l*., but no man would have him. He had come into the hands of Count F. de Lagrange (when M. Aumont was under an engagement 'not to run' for three years from 1856), but he was not included in the partnership between Count F. de Lagrange and Baron Nivière, it is said; he nevertheless entered the La Morlaye stable, presided over by Mr. Henry Jennings, who determined to give the horse a chance, tried him with Finlande and other 'good ones,' and came to the conclusion that there was 'something in him.'

On May 8, 1861, he was a 'bad third' for the race for which he was entered; on the 17th he won 'easily' the Prix de l'Empereur at Poitiers; on September 10 he was a 'bad third' for the Grand Prix at Baden; after that he won 'easily' the Grand Prix de l'Empereur at Chantilly; and then he 'broke out' and won the Cambridgeshire, having won other races in France, such as the Prix du Trocadéro and the Prix du Prince Impérial at Paris: in fact, the 16-guinea foal won some 4,000*l*. or 5,000*l*. at three and four years of age within the space of a few months, having won in 1862, in the spring (after his victories in the previous autumn), the Grand Prix de l'Impératrice (now called the Prix Rainbow) of 16,200 francs (about 648*l*.) at Paris and a sweepstakes of 400*l*. at Newmarket. Palestro ended as curiously as he began. It was his destiny to serve the hated German, the enemy of his country, having been purchased by Count H. Henckel, of Donnersmark. Nor were his vicissitudes then over, for in 1871 he was sold to the Imperial-Royal Stud Depôt, Stuhlweissenberg, Austria-Hungary. But neither in France nor in

Germany, nor in Austria-Hungary, does he appear to have begotten any little 'Palestro' to 'illustrate' his name.

Let us next recount the sad story of Gabrielle d'Estrées, daughter of FitzGladiator (sire of Palestro) and of Antonia (by Epirus), the dam of the right honourable but extremely savage Trocadéro. Gabrielle was running up to seven years of age—that is, to the end of 1864—and nevertheless went out of training without a stain upon her character for soundness. At two years of age she ran and was seen (not to advantage) in England; at three years she won (as we have seen) the French Derby, but she shared with the illustrious, though 'goose-rumped,' Caller Ou the misfortune of being unplaced behind Brown Duchess for the Oaks at Epsom; and she went on running with more or less success (rather less than more, perhaps) assiduously, having run at least ten races, some of them in 'heats' (as the Prix Impérial, for instance, which she won at Chantilly), at six years of age. Endurance and 'bottom' (which the French call 'fond') were, therefore, her strong points, and that made her melancholy end the more regrettable. She had been sent over to England on a visit to Gladiateur, and at her return, in 1867, she had so bad a passage that she fell sick and died, having produced (alive) but one filly (exported to England, according to the French Stud Book) and one colt, Mademoiselle de Vendôme and Commandeur. Her evident liability to suffer from *mal de mer* may have accounted for the poor show she always made in England. What made her loss so much deplored in France was that she (save Antoinette, supposed to be 'lost, stolen, or strayed') was the last daughter left of Antonia, who, singularly enough, died the same year as her ill-starred daughter, Gabrielle, and who had produced the great

Trocadéro. Howbeit Antonia, being twenty-six years old, cannot be considered to have died prematurely.

We may now turn to Compiègne, one of the 'stars' of the French horses of 1861, though he did not pay us a visit in England. He was another of the 'Fitz-Gladiators.' He won in 1861 the Prix de la Ville de Spa, the Saint-Léger de Moulins, the Saint-Léger de Bade, and the Prix de Lichtenthal at Baden 'right off the reel;' and he was to win the Prix du Cadran the next year. Moreover he was to be the sire of the celebrated Mortemer, for whom the Americans would one day pay a 'parlous' amount of dollars. But 'whom the gods love die young,' and Compiègne (like Attila, son of Colwick in 1846) died at seven years of age—in 1865.

And now for the legendary Light, five years old in 1861. He was in many respects the most wonderful of all the group. Light, a bay son of The Prime Warden and Balaclava, was foaled in 1856 at the Marquis de Talhouët's stud, and was purchased as a yearling by Baron Nivière. He did not run at two years of age, and at three years he met with several defeats before he won his first race—at Amiens; he then easily defeated Fort-à-bras at Boulogne, at equal weights; and he terminated his first year's racing with an uninterrupted series of successes at Le Pin, Caen, Abbeville, Le Mans, and Blois. Next year (1860) he won *nineteen* events in succession, including the Prix Biennal and the Prix de Suresnes at Paris, the Prix de l'Empereur at Angoulême, three 'prix' at Poitiers, a 'prix' of 5,000 francs (200*l.*) at Chantilly ('heats' of 4,000 metres, or about two and a half miles each), the Prix de Satory at Versailles, and the Prix Impérial at Boulogne, Rennes, and Tarbes, but at last, having crossed the Channel, he was beaten (as has been mentioned) for the Liverpool Autumn Cup. In 1861 he won a race at Epsom and the Prix de Boulogne. After that he went into the retirement of the 'haras.' No doubt Light did not beat the best horses of his date or win the 'classic' events of his country, but he did wonders; and he was the sire of Bigarreau and Sornette (winners of the French Derby and the Grand Prix in 1870), who did what their sire had omitted to do. That is quite enough for glory, to have begotten two such 'clippers' in one year. Light had his 'haras' at Villebon, 'Major Fridolin's.' The following is the description of Light's personal appearance: 'middle height, regular formation, a total absence of any blemishes to signify;' and it is added that 'his aptitude for developing his superiority over all sorts of courses, his perfect temper, and his uncommon energy gave him a claim to high rank among thoroughbreds,' and that from him might be expected a valuable stock of 'steeple-chasers, chargers, and hunters.' It may have been so; but there have been few great race horses to 'illustrate' his name, and his excellent but fantastic daughter Sornette 'suicided herself' before she had a chance of producing a foal to reflect honour on 'the children of Light.'

It has been mentioned that in 1861 the 'Big Stable' ran Royallieu for the Derby in England, the 'second time of asking' on the part of the Frenchmen. It was a bad year for so bold an attempt; for it was the year when men betted the three 'D's' against the three 'K's' (Dundee, Diophantus, and Dictator against Kettledrum, Klarikoff, and Kildonan), any one of the six being considered good enough to win the Derby. However Royallieu (another son—like Dangu in the year before—of the wonderful FitzGladiator) was not disgraced; indeed, according to his 'compatriots' he ought to have won, so that, as he was not by any means the best horse of his year in France, our Derby of 1861 should have been at the mercy of the French (especially when Dundee was left with only three legs to run upon) had they but entered the 'right un.' Here is what a 'compatriot' has written on the subject—

Royallieu was going very well half a mile from home when he came in contact with Atherstone, nearly fell, and cannoned against Dundee. . . . Royallieu came in scarcely more than two lengths behind the winner. He had recovered his lost ground in a wonderful manner, and there is reason to believe that, but for the accident, he would have been placed among the first three. This was a result all the more honourable for French breeding in that the son of Eusebia (Royallieu) was certainly not the best horse of the year.

Even in the English accounts Royallieu is made out to have finished level with Klarikoff (that good but unfortunate horse, always being 'messed about,' and at last burnt to death in his travelling van), 'close up' with Aurelian, who was but a neck behind Diophantus, who was a mere head behind Dundee, who was just a length behind Kettledrum. Clearly, then, the French were 'burning,' getting near the coveted prize. But they were not to 'find' yet awhile, and the 'trick,' when done, was not to be done by the 'Big Stable.'

Before quitting the year 1861 let a tribute be paid to the memory of that wonderful French gelding Cosmopolite, who ran (six years old) no fewer than nineteen times (counting 'the flat' only) in England alone this year, and who is said never to have started until he was five years old, in consequence of an accident he met with in the stables of the well-known and highly respected Viscount Paul Daru (vice-president and afterwards president of the French Jockey Club's 'Comité des Courses'), who was his original owner before he passed into the hands of Baron Nivière.

The year 1862 was an 'annus mirabilis' in the history of French horse-racing for many reasons, as will soon appear.

At the outset the 'Frenchmen,' whether belonging to the 'Big Stable' or not, were not very successful in England, though the 'Big un,' having now a branch establishment, a 'succursale,' among the perfidious Britons, might with comparative ease spread its horses like grasshoppers (as some of them were to look upon) all over 'Albion,' without risk of *mal de mer*, from Land's End to John o' Groat's. However Cosmopolite led off and won (w.o.) the Trial Stakes and (after a dead heat) the Sefton Handicap at Liverpool Spring Meeting (after that Viscount de Namur's Tippler and the 'Big Stable's' Attrape-qui-peut had been defeated twice and once respectively at Lincoln, Nottingham, and Derby); and then 'little Benjamin' won the Trial Stakes at Doncaster, but soon ceased to be a 'ruler.' Then Finlande ran third for the Great Northamptonshire, Allez-y-rondement won the Racing Stakes at Northampton, Gouvieux came in first for the Northamptonshire Cup Stakes, and Mademoiselle de Champigny for the Delapré Handicap at Northampton; but at this meeting Baliverne fell from her high estate and dropped into the ranks of the selling-platers, and Villafranca (own sister of the newborn Gladiateur—if indeed he had yet been 'dropped'—and one of the first of Monarque's progeny to appear in public) was third for the Althorp Park Stakes for two-year-olds. As for Gouvieux, though he had come in first the 'Big Stable' did not profit thereby, inasmuch as H. Grimshaw, the rider of Gouvieux, had 'repeatedly struck' Doyle, who was convicted of 'foul riding' (whereby he got his 'mount' Retento into the second place), and the first and second horses were consequently disqualified. At Epsom Spring Meeting the French horses—to wit, Palestro, Gentilhomme (two years), Le Maréchal (two years), Finlande, Gaulois (two years), and Mademoiselle de Champigny (then Mr. Angell's)—ran without much success or credit; but at Newmarket Craven (where the 'Big Stable' did badly with Baliverne, Attrape-qui-peut, Alerte, Finlande, Gabrielle d'Estrées, Royal-lieu, Gaulois, and Gisors [gelding], as also Mr. Lowther did with his French acquisition Exactitude) Absinthe won a sweepstakes in Count F. de Lagrange's name, and so did Le Maréchal (elder brother of the subsequently distinguished Consul).

Nor previously to the Epsom Summer Meeting did the 'Big Stable' or any other representatives of the French Turf show to advantage in England, though Baliverne in the name of Baron Nivière walked over and divided stakes with the noted Little Lady, and Palestro, Maubourguet, and Royallieu, in Count F. de Lagrange's name, won a race apiece, the two former at Newmarket First Spring (where also Le Maréchal ran a dead heat), the other at Chester (the Palatine Cup Stakes). By the way Royallieu was sold this year to go to the assistance of our horse-breeding colonists, friends, and kinsmen in Australia.

In France, however, it was a little different, for the 'Big Stable' (though beaten for the French Derby) won at the Paris Spring Meeting the Prix du Cadran with Compiègne, the Prix de Longchamps with Allez-y-rondement, the Grand Prix de l'Impératrice (now Prix Rainbow) with Palestro, and the Poule d'Essai (sometimes called French Two Thousand) with Stradella;

and at Chantilly Spring Meeting the French Oaks with Stradella (after a dead heat with Noélie), which Stradella, as men said, ought to have won the French Derby, for which she was beaten by Souvenir. Of the other principal Spring events at Paris Baron A. Schickler (who won the Poule des Produits—now Prix Daru—with Provocateur and what is now the Grande Poule des Produits with Choisy-le-Roi) and M. Henri Delamarre (who won the Prix de la Ville de Paris with Télégraphe) were the heroes. Moreover the victory of Choisy-le-Roi had been a great blow for the 'Big Stable,' which had run first and second with Benjamin and Généalogie; but they were both disqualified on the ground of a 'cross,' and the race was awarded to the third.

The French Derby, it has been said, was won by Souvenir; and thereby hangs a tale, a tale of North v. South and West, much as with us in the old times it used to be a struggle for supremacy on the Turf between the Northern and the Southern horses, both before and after the day when Phenomenon (then unnamed) was beaten for the Derby of 1783 by Saltram and others. For be it recalled to mind that France had been divided for all 'horsey' purposes once upon a time into three 'circumscriptions' or 'districts'— North (in which probably was merged East, as the latter is not specified), South, and West. The head-quarters of the North were at Chantilly, under the immediate patronage of the French Jockey Club; the South and West were more particularly under the wing of the Administration des Haras (with 'Arab' views and tendencies), and their horses, when sent to compete at Paris or Chantilly, were considered to be of such intrinsic inferiority that they received an allowance

of weight, which allowance, after the victory of
Souvenir in the French Derby (for which presumably,
as in the English Derby, there was never any difference
of weight between the candidates), was withdrawn, just
as the allowance once made to French horses running
in England was gradually withdrawn. The 'coming
event,' however, so far as Souvenir's victory was concerned, had duly ' thrown its shadow before.' At the
Paris Autumn Meeting in the previous year Saint
Aignan, a 'Western' horse, belonging to M. D. Caillé
and bred by M. Robin (breeder and owner of Souvenir),
had won the Omnium (sometimes called ' the French
Cesarewitch ') and had been second to Palestro for
the Grand Prix de l'Impératrice. Moreover M. Verry's
Vertu Facile, a filly from the 'Southern circumscription'
and winner of the Derby du Midi at Bordeaux, had
come to Paris and given Stradella some trouble to beat
her for the Poule d'Essai. So that the victory of
Souvenir and the 'South' or ' West' over the ' Big Stable '
and the ' North ' had been in a measure foreshadowed.

Now came the Epsom Summer Meeting, at which
the 'Frenchmen' were very much in the shade. They
did not even run for the Derby, and in the Oaks the
' Big Stable,' having been third on the Derby Day with
Baliverne for the Manor Plate, and second (and last)
with her for the Shirley Stakes the day after, could not
get a place with Alerte. Count F. de Lagrange certainly won the Two-year-old Stakes, against seven
opponents, with Vivid (who was to be third for the
Oaks next year); but then Vivid was not French, but
English. At Ascot the 'Frenchmen' ran pretty freely,
but got more kicks than halfpence or Cups: Gentilhomme
(two years), Brick (two years), Allez-y-rondement
(three years), Alerte (three years), and Palestro (four

years, for the Gold Cup) were all sent empty away.
At Odiham, however, our old friend and antagonist
M. A. Lupin won the Hurstbourne Stakes with Boute-
feu ('bred in France,' but trained for him in England),
who had previously been third for the Claremont Stakes
at Hampton. Now did the French star begin to rise
and shine a little: at Bibury Club Meeting Infante
(two years, by Monarque) won the Champagne Stakes;
at Stockbridge Meeting proper Le Maréchal (two years,
by Monarque), though carrying a 5-lb. penalty, lost
the Mottisfont Stakes by a head only (doing honour
to the new sire, Monarque); and at Newmarket July
Armagnac (two years) made his first appearance, and
was third (but a 'bad' third) to the 'cracks' Saccharometer and Blue Mantle for the July Stakes, next day
won the Exeter Stakes (for which M. A. Lupin's celebrated Dollar was but third), and avenged his 'compatriot' Le Maréchal by beating Weatherbow (winner
of the Mottisfont Stakes), and was unplaced (in company
with Dollar) for the Chesterfield Stakes; after which
Baliverne (three years) won a 'selling' stakes. At
Abingdon Fontenoy (two years) ran third for the Trial
Stakes, Armagnac won the Abingdon Stakes, and Alba
(now Mr. J. B. Hawke's) won the Ladies' Plate; at
Liverpool Odine (two years, by FitzGladiator, half-
sister by her dam, Pauline, to Fille de l'Air) won a
sweepstakes; at Stamford Alerte walked over for the
St. Leger and won the Kitton Stakes from a single
opponent; and at Goodwood Brick (two years, son of
The Flying Dutchman) won the Lavant Stakes (660*l.*)
and (carrying 6 lbs. extra) ran a dead heat, walked
over, and divided the 605*l.* for the Nursery Stakes
(handicap), afterwards winning 100*l.* (w.o.) at Brighton;
and Armagnac (carrying 5 lbs. extra) was second for

the Molecomb Stakes. It was at Newmarket Autumn
Meetings, however, that the French star culminated
in England. Fontenoy and Le Maréchal had done
fairly at York (where they both ran second—in the
Prince of Wales's Stakes and in the North of England
Biennial—and the latter won the Gimcrack Stakes of
365*l*.), and then came a regular display of fireworks
(chiefly in honour of Monarque) at the three Newmarket Meetings (after Gentilhomme, Valentine, and
Villafranca had not 'illustrated' themselves at Doncaster). First of all 'little Benjamin' and Columbine
did badly at the First October, but Baliverne won a
sweepstakes, Villafranca (by Monarque) 'split' Bohemia
and Turcos for the Granby Stakes, Gentilhomme won
a sweepstakes, and Villafranca and Columbine were
third and fourth for a sweepstakes; at the Second
October Hospodar (by Monarque) won the Clearwell
Stakes of 920*l*., Alerte was second to Lacydes for the
Select Stakes, Villafranca won a sweepstakes of 150*l*.,
Fornarina (by Monarque) received 100*l*. forfeit, Gentil
homme received 100*l*. forfeit, Fontenoy won a sweepstakes (selling) of 40*l*. only, Infante (by Monarque)
ran second to Welland for a handicap sweepstakes,
Armagnac (now Lord Stamford's) had been but three-
quarters of a length behind his only opponent, Taje, for
the Bedford Stakes, and Royallieu was third to Optimist
and Man-at-Arms for a plate; and at the Houghton
Meeting Gemma ran third for the Cambridgeshire (for
which, however, Stradella was not placed), Baliverne
(then Mr. Fuller's) was second to Xurullo for a sweepstakes, Valentine won a Nursery stakes, Souveraine
(by Monarque) ran a dead heat (but was beaten in the
'decider') for a sweepstakes, and above all Hospodar
(by Monarque) won the Criterion Stakes of 1,170*l*.,

thus running twice and winning twice in the season, and, for the first time since the days of Noë, established a French horse in the position of favourite for next year's Two Thousand and Derby, as Hospodar became for a time. And yet the French were not happy; indeed the 'Big Stable' had already 'split up' from unhappiness, an event which will be dealt with presently.

Meanwhile in France and on the Continent Alerte, who had returned for a while to her native land after her success at Stamford, had been picking up gold and silver (in francs—that is) in moderation, at Moulins and Valenciennes especially. But when the Baden Meeting came she was not considered strong enough for the work, and Stradella was despatched to win—as she did—the Grand Prix at Baden and the Baden St. Leger, beating all her 'compatriots' and a German horse, the most dangerous of her opponents—to wit, Count H. Henckel's Arthur (by Hartneitstein). Nevertheless the 'Big Stable' began to fall into the background at Baden, and the stables of MM. Delamarre, Aumont, Robin, and Viscount P. Daru began to assume the ascendency, commencing by carrying off several 'prix' at Baden, and afterwards taking the Omnium (won by Viscount P. Daru's Mazeppa), the Grand Prix du Prince Impérial, now Prix Royal Oak (won by M. Robin's Souvenir, son of Caravan), and the Grand Prix de l'Empereur, now Prix Gladiateur (won by M. Aumont's brilliant but uncertain Mon Etoile) at Paris Autumn Meeting. The most significant proof, however, of the high opinion gained at this time by French produce, especially that of the 'Big Stable,' was that it was attracting the attention of English purchasers, insomuch that the day after the Baden Meeting of 1862 Lord

Stamford purchased Armagnac (who ran in the English lord's name for the French Derby), Brick, and Le Maréchal, all together, for 150,000 francs (6,000*l*.)

About this time it was rumoured abroad that the 'Big Stable' was about to break up, and that all their horses might be had 'in a lump' for 800,000 francs (32,000*l*.) The break-up took place and the horses were sold, but not 'in a lump.' The chief 'lots' went as follows:—

The French Government took Gouvieux (aged) for about 200*l*., and Marignan (three years) for about 1,000*l*., and hired Palestro (four years) for a term, thus obtaining the first of his services before he was sold to the Prussians. Mr. Henry Jennings took Falendre (three years, ex-Magenta, and afterwards L'Africain, very well known in England by that name as a steeple-chaser; died in 1866), Mademoiselle Duchesnois (yearling), and Donjon (two years, exported to Belgium in 1866), for an average of 100*l*. apiece. Count Lehndorf, Baron d'Auriol, and M. Lunel purchased one or two each. The Duke de Morny bought Gédéon (by Monarque, a yearling, winner in 1864 of the Prix de Longchamps, &c. &c., and known as a two-year-old in England). M. H. Delamarre got Fidélité (by Monarque, a yearling) pretty cheap for 120*l*. Lord Stamford gave 1,000*l*. for Gemma (by Womersley, three years), who ran Bathilde and Limosina very close for the Cambridgeshire that same year. Finlande (ex-Faustine, four years) was withdrawn in favour of Baron Nivière (her breeder), and did not for some years afterwards become the property of M. A. Lupin, to whom she was one day to be so valuable a brood mare, the dam of St. Cyr and Fontainebleau. Count F. de Lagrange took Hospodar at the hardly remunerative price (as it turned out) of 5,000*l*., Compiègne (four years), Stradella (three years), Jarnicoton (two years), Villafranca (two years), La Reine Berthe (two years), Sonchamp (yearling), and others, including above all the celebrated Fille de l'Air (ex-Capucine II., a yearling), remarkably cheap (as it happened) at about 340*l*. And so, after some two years' existence, there was an end of the 'Big Stable,' which had accomplished, in that short period, for French horses and their reputation more than anybody would have thought likely to be done in much less than a generation. It was not a lucky 'split' for Baron Nivière; for there was Count F. de Lagrange left 'single-handed' indeed, but in possession of Fille de l'Air, the heroine of 1864, and Gladiateur (foaled that very year, 1862), the hero of 1865.

CHAPTER VIII.

LA TOUCQUES—VERMOUT—FILLE DE L'AIR—GLADIATEUR.

THE year 1863, in the history of French horse-racing, should have been 'Hospodar's year;' it was, on the contrary, 'La Toucques's year.'

The most notable fact of the year was undoubtedly the 'international race,' the Grand Prix de Paris, which, after much correspondence between Viscount P. Daru on the part of the wicked Frenchmen (who seem to think 'the better the day the better the deed,' and accordingly do the most important part of their horse-racing on Sundays) and Admiral Rous on the part of the religious English (who seem to prefer such profanation of their so-called Sabbath as is least like the profanation acclimatised in other countries), was at last definitively settled as an institution to be first brought into practice (notwithstanding vigorous Christian protests from the most unexpected quarters in England, in sporting newspapers and elsewhere) on Sunday, May 31, 1863. And brought off, accordingly, the race was, with results to be recorded hereafter. The moving spirit in the promotion of this institution is said to have been the Emperor of the French, represented by his 'familiar' the Duke de Morny (who is regarded as the 'creator' of Deauville). At any rate the 'Grand Prix' was to be ' an "objet d'art," the gift of his Majesty the Emperor, and 4,000l., given half by the city of Paris and half by the five great railway companies of France.' The 'objet d'art' has (perhaps happily) ceased to be given either by an emperor or by anybody else; but the 4,000*l.* are still given in the original proportions by the same donors, though there is yearly some difficulty in extracting the money out of the municipality of Paris by the most cunning and energetic alchemy. The conditions of the race, with a few slight alterations, remain the same as they were in the first instance; but the number of subscribers (of 40*l.* each, with forfeits in various smaller amounts down to 4*l.*) has increased so enormously that the 'prize' has become the most valuable in Europe as a rule, with the exception of what seems likely to be the intermittent and uncertain Eclipse Stakes ' of 10,000*l.*' at Sandown Park, and the similar 'big things' which are threatened at Kempton Park (in 1889) and at Manchester (the Lancaster Plate of 11,000 sovs. in 1888).

Even the first year, 1863, it was valuable enough to occupy the serious attention of many pious Britons who had conscientious objections to 'racing on Sunday,' and were quite prepared to 'blow the "objet d'art,"' but thought it a 'wicked sin' to let upwards of 4,000*l.* come their way without making at least a grab at it. If you might pull your ox or your ass out of a pit on the Sabbath day, surely you might pull your race horse out of his stable. And so did they, some of them.

With what notion the Grand Prix de Paris was instituted some doubt has been expressed. French authorities, speaking after the event and taking advantage of the light derived from what has since happened and from the controversy about 'reciprocity,' have tried to make out that it was intended as a delicate compliment and honourable amends, as a sort of anticipatory reply made to those Englishmen who, with Lord

Falmouth at their head, were some day to complain that, whilst all English races were open to the French, only a few paltry French races (not under the direct management of the French Jockey Club) were open to English owners; that there was no reciprocal spirit shown by the French. And the employers of the French argument have supported their statement by appealing to the notorious fact that the institution of the Grand Prix was objected to by many persons in France on the ground that it would be a sheer gift of 4,000*l.* or more to 'perfidious Albion,' an objection which seemed to be justified when Mr. Savile, an Englishman, won the first Grand Prix with The Ranger.

Saturnine Englishmen, on the contrary, will not have this explanation for a moment. If there were anything in it, they say, why was it not pointed out and acknowledged more generally by a grateful 'sporting press' in England at the time; and why was the race not set for a day less objectionable to the English people than Sunday? It is well known, says the saturnine Englishman, that some of the most formidable English owners (such as Sir R. Sutton, the 'lessee,' or General Pearson, the owner of Lord Lyon; Mr. Chaplin, the owner of The Hermit; Mr. Johnstone, the owner of Pretender, and Sir J. Hawley, the owner of Blue Gown and Pero Gomez; Lord Falmouth, owner of Kingcraft and Silvio; and the Duke of Westminster, owner of Bend Or and Shotover) either did not, do not, and never will, enter their horses or certainly did not, do not, and never will, send them to run for the Grand Prix, out of respect—in some, if not in all cases—for English opinion (whatever their own sentiments may have been) about horse-racing on Sunday; and the French were told that it would be so. 'Gammon,' therefore, is the familiar term applied by the saturnine

Englishman to the French pretext of compliment and chivalrous compensation. The origin of the Grand Prix de Paris is traced by the saturnine Englishman to French vanity, which the Emperor of the French and his 'familiar' the Duke de Morny knew very well indeed and were especially anxious to gratify. The Gallic cock, as we have seen, had been crowing loudly over the improvement of their horseflesh and their successes upon the Turf, both English and Continental, insomuch that at the end of the season of 1862 there was among the first favourites—if he were not the very first favourite—for the English Derby of 1863 a French colt, Hospodar. 'Go to,' then, said Napoleon and De Morny, according to the saturnine Englishman, 'let us have at Paris a great horse race, open to all peoples, nations, and languages; let a French horse run for it and win it, beating perfidious Albion (whose best horses may peradventure be absent because of her ridiculous Sabbath) and all the "cracks" of the Continent before the eyes of a polyglot multitude and in the sight of the Parisians, and Paris will be mad with delight, the glory of France and the Empire will be enhanced, the memory of Waterloo will be partly obliterated.' Of course the favouritism of Hospodar had not been revealed when the Grand Prix was projected, for the engagements for that race had to be made before July 1, 1862; but French chanticleer had been heard long before that and was 'spoiling' to 'show off' on his 'own dunghill' (if such a term may be applied to delightful Longchamps) before 'tout le monde' and particularly his own dear Parisians, with 'tout le monde' running horses against him.

In 1863 the most noted French horses were, in France, Alerte (four years, winner of the Prix du Cadran), Villafranca (three years, winner of the Prix de Longchamps), Souvenir (four years, winner of what is now called the Prix Rainbow and of what is now called the Prix Gladiateur), Stentor (three years, winner of the Poule d'Essai), Pergola (three years, winner of the Poule des Produits), Dollar (three years, winner of what is now called the Grande Poule des Produits), Guillaume le Taciturne (three years, winner of the Prix de la Ville de Paris), Orphelin (four years, a good but unlucky horse), and far and away above all La Toucques (three years, winner of both French Oaks and French Derby, of what is now called the Prix Royal Oak and of the Grand Prix at Baden); and in England Alerte, Alcibiade, Baliverne, Béatrix, Damier, Démon, Gabrielle d'Estrées, Fontenoy, Jarnicoton, Le Maréchal, Odine, Souchamp, Soumise, Stradella, Villafranca, and, most conspicuous of all, Fille de l'Air (two years), Hospodar (three years), and La Toucques (three years).

The dispersal of the 'Big Stable' and, besides that, the inclination to buy French produce had scattered French horses all over the country among English owners—but the 'Frenchmen' owned by Englishmen did not come to the front very much, and Lord Stamford had little joy of his 6,000$l.$ worth of French horseflesh in Brick, Armagnac, and Le Maréchal, though the last won three events out of six in 1863 (120$l.$ at Warwick, 125$l.$ at Newmarket, and 150$l.$ at Liverpool)—so that in 1863, more than ever before, we find French horses running at nearly all the English meetings from Lincoln (in February) to Warwick (in November).

Three, however, of these 'Frenchmen' overshadow all the rest—Hospodar by the prestige with which he began the year, La Toucques by her undoubted merit, and Fille de l'Air by her great performances.

Hospodar may be dismissed in a few words: he

was found to have lost his two-year-old form altogether. He ran (first favourite) for the Two Thousand, but did not obtain a place behind Macaroni, Saccharometer, and King of the Vale; he nevertheless started a better favourite (equal second with The Gillie, in fact) than any one of those three for the Derby, and again (in company with his stable companion Jarnicoton) did not obtain a place. He was fourth (behind Saccharometer, Judex, and Tom Fool) for the Ascot Biennial, not placed (in company with Jarnicoton again) for the Cambridgeshire, and received forfeit of 200*l.* from the great Saccharometer (in a match A.F., 8 st. 10 lbs. each). In his own country he had run unplaced for the Grand Prix, for which Saccharometer was third. He afterwards became a stud horse of some repute, sire of Capsule, Roquefort, Florian, &c.

La Toucques (daughter of The Baron and Tapestry) is a most interesting study—a real phenomenon, a meteor that comes, shines, and passes away, leaving scarcely a trace of its brilliant existence. She is described as a 'chestnut;' but, if memory may be trusted, she was so curiously marked with 'blazes' as to be reviled by Englishmen who 'sat in scorner's chair' as 'the piebald' and 'the circus horse;' she was accused, moreover, of the mysterious offence of being 'a three-cornered customer.' Her owner, Count A. de Montgomery (who did not have her trained at his own fine 'prairies' at Fervacques, Normandy, but sent her to be trained in England—at Middleham, by Mr. Fobert, if there be no mistake), is said to have tried to get rid of her for 200*l.*, but in vain (as had happened at first to the owners of Franc Picard and Palestro): his lucky star was dead against it. La Toucques, if known at all at two years of age beyond the limits of her stable and its adherents, was certainly unknown to fame when she came out to run her dazzling career (in her own country) as a three-year-old. She seems to have made her first attempt at York Spring Meeting, where she was beaten into fifth place (with six runners) for the Knavesmire Plate by Livingstone, Inverness, Lyra, and Fauconberg. She then went over the sea and 'took it out' on her 'compatriots,' winning the French Derby (for which Lord Stamford's Armagnac was favourite) with the great Dollar behind her, and the French Oaks (with Grande Dame, a 'good sort,' behind her), started first favourite (in preference to Lord Clifden, Saccharometer, The Ranger, Hospodar, &c.) for the Grand Prix de Paris, which, in the estimation of some of her 'compatriots,' she certainly 'ought to have won,' and returned to England. There she ran second by a neck to Isoline (three years, 7 st. 3 lbs. each) for the Goodwood Cup and won the Stockton Stewards' Cup. Afterwards she went back to the Continent, where she won the Grand Prix at Baden (again beating the great Dollar), the Prix de l'Empereur at Chantilly (beating the meritorious Orphelin as well as the highly respectable and respected Flibustier), and what is now the Prix Royal Oak at Paris Autumn Meeting. In 1864 she appears to have been in retirement; but in 1865 she ran neither wisely nor too well for the Chester Cup and the Northumberland Plate, being unplaced for both. At the stud, whither she speedily went, she was not a great success. She was the dam of La Calonne, Toucques, Henry IV., &c.; but she cannot be said to have done much to 'illustrate' her name, although her daughter La Seine did run third for the One Thousand in 1876. La Toucques won altogether six races, 5,360*l.* (about) and an 'objet d'art.'

We now come to Fille de l'Air, a marvel. at two
years of age (in 1863), and, as will be seen hereafter,
a greater marvel at three. In her case too, as in the
case of Franc Picard (ex-Babouino) and of Palestro
(ex-Coquet), a change of name seems to have had the
very happiest effect, for she was originally called Capucine II., after a noted mare (winner of the Critérium at
two years of age, &c.) bred by M. Benoist, who also is
said to have bred Fille de l'Air (ex-Capucine II.), and she
was the last foal of her dam Pauline, who was trained a
little but never ran. She became the sole property of
Count F. de Lagrange, as has been observed, at the
break-up of the 'Big Stable' and the consequent sale, for
about 340*l*. The rule prohibiting two-year-olds from
running in France before August 1 would have been a
bad thing for her and her owner had it applied to England; for she began her performances on May 19 at
Epsom, where she at once began to 'illustrate' her sire,
Faugh-a-Ballagh, by winning the Woodcote Stakes of
665*l*. After this she won the Molecomb Stakes of 650*l*.
(beating Scottish Chief), the Brighton Biennial (w.o.)
of 230*l*., a sweepstakes of 270*l*. at Newmarket First
October, and as a 'bonne bouche' the Criterion Stakes
(*à la* Hospodar the preceding year) of 1,120*l*. at the
Houghton (beating Prince Arthur, 'the beautiful' Ely,
Coastguard, and others). Here were five events out of
nine won, to the tune of 2,935*l*.—' wealth beyond the
dreams of avarice' to a French two-year-old as yet,
and a ' record' almost more creditable than Hospodar's
'unbeaten certificate' of the year before. ; for in the
races. in which she was beaten Fille de l'Air had
invariably been ' placed ' (whether giving away weight
or not) third for the Two-year-old Stakes at Epsom,
second to Ely for the Champagne Stakes at Doncaster,

third to Coastguard and Prince Arthur for a sweepstakes at the same place, and third for the Hopeful Stakes at Newmarket First October. Moreover she had beaten Scottish Chief and had turned the tables on Ely, Coastguard, and Prince Arthur once or more than once. Count F. de Lagrange and all the Frenchmen who were 'in the know' might well hug themselves in the belief that they would soon make perfidious Albion 'see sights.' Already this year, 1863, Count F. de Lagrange had run third for the Oaks with Vivid; but then Vivid was an English filly. Fille de l'Air, or 'Fiddler,' as she was liable to be called (in imitation of 'Parisian' speech), was French.

Among the most notable occurrences in the world of French horse-racing in 1863 was the new partnership formed, on the dissolution of the Lagrange-Nivière Association (called the 'Big Stable'), between Baron Nivière and M. Charles Laffitte ('Major Fridolin'), with Mr. Charles Pratt (instead of Mr. Henry Jennings, who became a 'public' trainer at La Croix St. Ouen, near Compiègne) for trainer, chief jockey, and general manager of the stable at La Morlaye, with a 'haras' at Villebon, near Palaiseau, which was first the property of Baron Nivière, then of the Baron and the 'Major' jointly, lastly of the latter alone, and with the yearling Gontran to oppose (hopelessly) to the yearling Gladiateur of the 'opposition stable' (Count F. de Lagrange's), but with nothing at all to match against Fille de l'Air.

The year 1864 was a glorious one for the French, both at home and in England, but, for all the prowess of Fille de l'Air, the honours of the campaign did not remain with Count F. de Lagrange among the French owners, and certainly not with Messrs. Nivière-Fridolin.

At the Paris Spring Meeting the principal events

were won as follows: the Prix du Cadran (for four-year-olds) by Baron A. Schickler with Guillaume le Taciturne; the Prix de Longchamps (for three-year-olds) by the Duke de Morny with Gédéon (by Monarque); the Grand Prix de l'Impératrice (now Prix Rainbow) by M. A. Lupin with Dollar (four years), just a head, and a short head, in front of Count F. de Lagrange's Stradella; the Poule des Produits (for three-year olds) by M. H. Delamarre with Bois-Roussel (by The Nabob); the Poule d'Essai (for three-year-olds) by Baron N. de Rothschild with Baronello; and the Prix de l'Empereur (now Grande Poule des Produits, for three-year-olds) by M. H. Delamarre with Bois-Roussel. At Chantilly Spring Meeting the principal events were won as follows: the French Oaks easily by Count F. de Lagrange with Fille de l'Air, and the French Derby by M. H. Delamarre with Bois-Roussel. At Paris Summer Meeting the Prix de l'Empereur was won by M. A. Lupin with Dollar (four years), beating Count F. de Lagrange's Stradella (five years) by a neck, as well as the Count's Jarnicoton (four years) and M. Lupin's Pergola (four years); and the Grand Prix de Paris by M. H. Delamarre with Vermout (by The Nabob), beating Blair Athol (winner of the English Derby), Fille de l'Air (winner of both French Oaks and English Oaks), Bois-Roussel (winner of the French Derby), and Baronello (winner of the Poule d'Essai), so that the Seine was fairly set on fire. At Paris Autumn Meeting the Grand Prix du Prince Impérial (for three-year-olds, now Prix Royal Oak) was won by Count F. de Lagrange with Fille de l'Air (beating easily her only opponent and late defeater, Vermout), the Grand Critérium (for two-year-olds) was won by Count F. de Lagrange with Le Béarnais, and the Grand Prix de l'Empereur (now Prix Gladiateur, for four-year-olds and upwards) was won by the Duke de Morny with Noélie (five years), beating Dollar and Orphelin among others. At Baden the Continental St. Leger had been won by Count F. de Lagrange with Fille de l'Air, beating her only opponent, Vermout, again; but, *en revanche*, the Grand Prix at Baden had been won easily by Vermout, beating Dollar and Fille de l'Air (second and third) among others; so that, on the whole, the honours of the season (in France) may be said to have remained with M. H. Delamarre, run hard by Count F. de Lagrange, with M. A. Lupin, the Duke de Morny, and Baron N. de Rothschild 'close up.'

In England neither Vermout nor Bois-Roussel put in an appearance, and of the other French 'cracks' Fille de l'Air was the only one that did anything 'particular;' and she did something very 'particular' indeed, so that she was called 'the French Crucifix.' She started first favourite for the Two Thousand at Newmarket and was not placed, whereupon she took a trip to France and got beaten for the French Two Thousand (Poule d'Essai) also, but won the French Oaks easily, and, as if her health had been improved by a taste of her native air, she returned and won the Oaks at Epsom, causing a disgraceful riot. There was 'scandal against Queen Elizabeth:' it was murmured that Fille de l'Air was 'very elder than her looks,' and at length her mouth, to the indignation of her owner—who, however, was willing enough to have it done—was examined, but there was 'nothing in it.'

This opportunity may be taken of regretting that among Englishmen, who are so boastful of their 'fair play,' this sort of suspicion, when a foreigner wins an English race of importance and exhibits decided superiority, should be so common; it was so afterwards

with Gladiateur, and it had been so already with the
'American' Umpire. No doubt it is usually the 'tag,
rag, and bobtail' that raise the outcry or whisper the
suspicion, but not always.

To resume: Fille de l'Air could not give the weight
to Ely in the Prince of Wales's Stakes at Ascot, won
the Brighton Biennial, won both Newmarket Oaks and
Newmarket Derby, won a free handicap at Newmarket
Houghton, and succumbed not ingloriously (under her
greater weight) to Master Richard and Baragah in
another free handicap at the same meeting. Her
defeat in the Grand Prix de Paris was expected by the
friends of Blair Athol of course, but the race was supposed to lie between these two, winners of the English
Oaks and English Derby, and the defeat of the latter
has been regarded as a 'fluke,' due partly to the effects
of the sea voyage and partly to the fact that his jockey
confined his efforts to beating Fille de l'Air, forgetting
or neglecting Vermout altogether. But, as we have
seen, Vermout, measured through Fille de l'Air in subsequent contests, was no mean antagonist; and it is not
impossible that Bois-Roussel, if he had not 'broken
down,' might have beaten the three. Vermout too,
strangely enough, became the sire of Boïard, who himself, in 1873, defeated another winner of the English
Derby (Doncaster, beaten also by Flageolet) for the
Grand Prix de Paris.

At four years of age Fille de l'Air did wonderfully
well in France and in England, winning the Grand Prix
de l'Impératrice (now Prix Rainbow) and La Coupe at
Paris, and several events, including the Alexandra
Plate, in England, though she was beaten for the Ascot
Cup, for which Ely and General Peel ran their famous
dead heat. She then went to the stud at Dangu, where

she died in 1878, her first foal having been Eole (foaled 1868, a 'cripple,' by Gladiateur) and her best, perhaps, Reine (by Monarque), winner of both One Thousand and Oaks in England, but an unsuccessful runner in France, in 1872.

That Fille de l'Air was a 'puzzler,' subject to strange variations of 'form,' is true; but that should not have astonished the countrymen of Caller Ou. It is common with both colts and fillies, especially with the latter, as the 'compatriots' of Sérénade (winner of the French Oaks in 1848), Prédestinée (winner of the Grand Prix at Paris in 1847), Jouvence, and Mon Etoile (both well known in England) are aware. But fashionable jockeys, on whom insolence is apparently considered to sit so well, are sometimes responsible for confirming suspicions by the manner in which they receive good-natured comments. 'She looks very different now to what she looked at Newmarket,' said a gentleman to Mr. A. Edwards, the fashionable jockey who rode Fille de l'Air for both Two Thousand and Epsom Oaks, and 'What the hell's that to you?' was the insolent response in a tone and with a manner suggestive of 'something not quite straight,' though there was probably nothing more than sheer rudeness meant.

Of the French 'cracks' in the 'same year' with Fille de l'Air it may be mentioned that Vermout became a great French sire, that Bois-Roussel was purchased for Austria-Hungary (Kisbér) in 1865, that Baronello was 'added to the list' in consequence of the double portion of temper he inherited from his sire (The Baron), that Gédéon became known as a stud horse in England, and that Guillaume le Taciturne did not greatly 'illustrate' the Martinvast stud (Baron A. Schickler's) in France.

Dollar, very highly distinguished among the French

'cracks' in 1864, was a year older than Fille de l'Air; Gladiateur, Le Béarnais, Le Mandarin, Gontran, all more or less distinguished, were a year younger, and the greatest of them was Gladiateur, whose history belongs to the next year, and of whom it might have been said, in the words of Horace, 'Unde nil majus generatur ipso; Nec viget quidquam simile aut secundum.' But his time has not yet arrived.

Dollar (son of The Flying Dutchman and Payment, both 'importations') had not run in England in 1863, though he had run twice—very moderately—as a two-year old in 1862. In 1864 he began the year well for M. A. Lupin and the French by winning the Great Northamptonshire Stakes and, after running second for the Worcester Stakes, he and his 'frequent pardner,' Kitchener (the hero of the 2 st. 12 lbs. 'bodily weight' for the Chester Cup of 1844), won the Goodwood Cup and the Brighton Cup and ran second for the Wolverhampton Handicap. This was the first year in which a French horse, carrying full weight for age, had won the Goodwood Cup; and there was a sort of poetical justice in the fact that the feat should have been performed in the colours of M. A. Lupin, who had been the first Frenchman to win the Goodwood Cup at all, in 1853, with an animal 'bred in France,' having a liberal allowance of weight, such as was accorded to Jouvence. What a sire this same Dollar became witness a vast galaxy of winners, including the wonderfully good racer and sire Salvator.

All this, added to the doings of the two-year-olds 'bred in France,' several of which have been mentioned, made 1864 a glorious year for the French Turf. But this glory was about to be completely eclipsed by the glories of 1865, in which year the history of horse-racing both in England and France is almost summed up in the single word Gladiateur.

Vermout, who had defeated the winner of the English Derby, was very well; and Fille de l'Air, who had run the winner of the Derby almost to a standstill and had won the Oaks at Epsom as well as at Chantilly, had been all very well; but there had been a bitter drop in the cup of French bliss, for in both these cases, though the dams had been bred in France, the sires (The Nabob and Faugh-a-Ballagh) were English, more or less recently imported from England. Gladiateur was free from any such reproach; his sire, Monarque, was 'bred in France' at the celebrated M. A. Aumont's stud at Victot, and his dam, Miss Gladiator, was 'bred in France' at the celebrated Mr. Thomas Carter's stud (at Vineuil, apparently), and afterwards purchased by Count F. de Lagrange. This it was, this complete 'Frenchiness' of Gladiateur, which made his victories over all the flower of English horsedom so doubly delightful to the race of Charlemagne, so 'crowful' to the Gallic cock, so grateful to feelings still suffering from the memory of Trafalgar and Waterloo.

Gladiateur was foaled at Dangu, and of course (as men afterwards remembered when he grew great) there were wonders connected with the birth of such a prodigy. He is said to have been produced by a manœuvre worthy of the astute Jacob, the patriarch, who played such clever tricks with the hazel rods and the cattle and sheep of his father-in-law, Laban. If it had been his mother-in-law (who notoriously has no friends, poor soul) it would have been considered quite fair, no doubt. Well, an enthusiastic 'compatriot' gives the following account of Gladiateur's birth, an account which breathes the spirit of a Grecian dithyrambic poet recounting the birth of winged Pegasus, of divine origin.

'The birth of Gladiateur,' we are told, 'has this peculiarity about it, that Monarque (his sire) had always displayed a sort of abhorrence for Miss Gladiator and, on the other hand, had exhibited a sort of passion (strange as it may seem to employ such a term in speaking of a horse, but there is really none other applicable) for Liouba, dam of Le Mandarin (by Monarque). To bring Monarque, therefore, to consent to the union from which Gladiateur was to spring he had to be left to feast his eyes—in an ecstasy—for a while upon his favourite; he was then blindfolded and Miss Gladiator was substituted for the Liouba of his choice.'

In fact, Monarque was treated as shamefully as Jacob when Leah was substituted for Rachel, and without any explanation or apology. 'This circumstance,' the 'compatriot' continues, 'though of little consequence in itself' (as if it were nothing to trifle with the affections and predilections of the 'Grand Monarque'!) 'must not be lost sight of by those who enquire into the secrets of Nature. Who knows whether this protracted longing, this defrauded expectation, had not something to do with the qualities transmitted a hundredfold by the sire to the son?' 'Gladiateur,' the 'compatriot' goes on to say, was 'like' his sire, only 'different;' he reminded you of Monarque, but 'only as a hundred reminds you of twenty:' he was, in fact, a considerable multiple of his sire.

That something out of the common was expected of Gladiateur from the first by his friends may be inferred from the significant fact that he was entered for *all* the great English races for three-year-olds, and some of those for two-year-olds.

He first came out, at two years of age, for the Clearwell Stakes, which he won (like his 'compatriot'

Hospodar in 1862) against a field of poor quality; he then ran a dead heat (with the very moderate Longdown) for the third place in the Prendergast Stakes (behind nothing better than Bedminster and Siberia); and, finally, he was unplaced (9 st. 2 lbs.) for the Criterion Stakes (which Hospodar had won in 1862) behind Chattanooga (8 st. 10 lbs.), &c. Consequently he retired into winter quarters without much of a reputation and certainly with less prestige than had been acquired by Hospodar. Indeed, Le Mandarin (also by Monarque), a stable companion of Gladiateur's and Gontran (a son of FitzGladiator, belonging to the Nivière-Fridolin confederacy), to say nothing of Argences (by Moustique), would probably at this time have been put very nearly upon a level with him by good judges.

In 1865 Gladiateur first appeared as a candidate for the Two Thousand. He was not saddled in the 'birdcage,' but apart, 'behind the ditch;' there were few to watch his 'toilet,' and of those present the majority voted him an 'ugly great coach-horse.' The next time he appeared in public there would be a goodly crowd to attend upon him, in a few weeks he would be the observed of all observers, and in due time it would be discovered that, instead of being an 'ugly great coach-horse,' he was (for all his Roman nose) one of the finest specimens of the thoroughbred ever seen.

Well, he came out for the Two Thousand, and he was not at all 'fancied.' Bedminster, for some inexplicable reason, was favourite; Breadalbane (own brother to Blair Athol) and Liddington (the best horse of the year, perhaps, but for his 'roaring') were equal second favourites; and then Gladiateur and a wretched 'impostor' called Kangaroo (for whom the unfortunate young Marquis of Hastings had been deluded into paying 6,000 guineas, it is said, not long before the day of the race) were favourites at 6 to 1 each. It was a rare finish; Bedminster, as a spectator remarked, 'galloped hisself to a common cob' and was soon 'done with,' to the evident dismay of his jockey (Wells), but Gladiateur (H. Grimshaw), Archimedes (T. Aldcroft), Liddington (J. Daley), Zambesi (H. Covey), and Breadalbane were all together in that order at the end, two 'necks' and two 'heads' being all that divided Gladiateur, the winner, from Breadalbane, the fifth. As to whether the race was won easily or not there was a divergence of opinion.

Then came the Derby.

There was still a disinclination to believe that a French horse, of French-bred sire and French-bred dam, could win the Epsom Derby on Banstead Downs, with the ghosts of so many previous winners, from Diomed to Bay Middleton, from Cotherstone to West Australian, gibbering at him and mocking at his pretences.

Nevertheless there was no getting over the fact that he had won the Two Thousand in good style, and that his stable companion Le Mandarin (who notoriously could not hold the stable lantern to him this year) had just been second to Gontran for the French Derby; and so he started, as by right, first favourite at 5 to 2.

How he won was never forgotten by eye witnesses: how he was 'shut in,' and how his jockey (H. Grimshaw) deliberately 'went round' and won 'by two lengths easy' was a sight to be remembered. He was followed home by Christmas Carol and Eltham, the latter a 'rank outsider,' which made some people think it was 'all wrong,' whilst others declared that it was a 'bad year,' and that the winner was 'very lucky' to have such horses as The Duke, and Liddington, and Wild Charley either unable to oppose him at all or so deteriorated by various ailments as to be prevented from doing themselves anything like justice.

However that may have been, there was ample ground for the exultation of a 'compatriot' who has written:—

The 31st of May, 1865, will remain for ever memorable in the Turf annals of the two countries. For the first time their undisputed sceptre [not undisputed, however: let Dangu, Royallieu, and Hospodar bear witness] had been wrested from our neighbours' hands; for the first time a foreign horse had beaten the pick of the produce of the United Kingdom. The fact made a great noise: it was the culmination of the work undertaken by the Société d'Encouragement (French Jockey Club); it was the reward of the audacious efforts made by the Count de Lagrange. After the first moment of stupefaction the English themselves could not restrain their admiration for this wonderful animal. '*When Gladiateur gallops*,' wrote the English papers, '*the other horses seem to stand still.*' H.R.H. the Prince of Wales, wishing to give the Count de Lagrange a striking proof of his distinguished sympathy, invited to meet him at a large dinner party the greatest stars of English society. Lord Derby, a descendant of the nobleman who founded the great national race that Gladiateur had just won, congratulated the Count in a speech full of courtesy and good feeling towards France. A still more enthusiastic ovation awaited the great conqueror's fortunate owner on his return to France. The French thoroughbred ('pur sang') still had a rival, but no longer a master.

Gladiateur exhibited himself (in his 'war paint') for the first time to his 'compatriots' as a candidate for the international Grand Prix de Paris; and more than 150,000 persons (mostly 'compatriots') assembled to pay their respects to him and to impede his passage. His jockey (H. Grimshaw), with a 'coquetry' highly appreciated by the French, so handled his 'mount' as if he wished 'to show off on French soil the hero of the native breed in all his crushing superiority.' But it was not so easy; for, although the field for the Grand Prix comprised some excellent horses (there being but one 'Englishman,' however, among the six starters)—to wit, Vertugadin (second, winner of the Prix de l'Eté), Tourmalet (third, winner of the Poule des Produits), Gontran (fourth, winner of the French Derby), Todleben (English, fifth, very 'moderate'), and Le Mandarin (sixth, winner of the Prix de l'Empereur, now Grande Poule des Produits), they could not make Gladiateur gallop, and Grimshaw could only 'make a race of it' by pulling his horse back and keeping him seven or eight lengths behind Vertugadin until the last turn, so that the spectators thought for a moment that 'it would be too late.' Then suddenly Grimshaw let out his horse, which, in the words of a compatriot, 'coming like a torrent, passed all his competitors in three bounds, only to resume at their head his easy and tranquil stride. There was no struggle, no vestige of doubt: Gladiateur had put himself in motion, and all the rest were nowhere.'

At Ascot Gladiateur did not come out; but at Goodwood he won the Drawing-Room Stakes (beating Longdown, who had once run a dead heat with him at two years of age, by *forty lengths*) and walked over for the Bentinck Memorial; he won the St. Leger and the Doncaster Stakes; he won the Prix du Prince Impérial (now Prix Royal Oak) at Paris Autumn Meeting from his only opponent Vertugadin; he won the Newmarket Derby (again beating by *forty lengths* his old opponent Longdown, who alone faced him); and, lastly, as if to try whether he were really horse or demon, he was started for the Cambridgeshire with the impossible

weight for a three-year-old of 9 st. 12 lbs. Still he was
not without backers; indeed, he started equal first
favourite with Moldavia (three years, 6 st. 2 lbs.), and
a 'backer,' when remonstrated with by a friend for
backing a horse to do what no horse could be expected
to do, answered complacently, 'Ah! but he isn't a
horse; he's some sort of machine.' Gladiateur in 1865
had 'swept the board:' he had won 'the triple crown'
—the Two Thousand, the Derby, and the St. Leger—
as before him West Australian alone had done; and he
had also won the valuable Grand Prix (which was not
in existence for 'the West' to win), thus (with minor
things which he 'took in his stride') bringing to his
owner (in stakes alone) upwards of 26,000*l.*, a sum
unprecedented, unequalled, and probably never to be
attained again (though Ormonde might have done as
well, had he been entered and run for the Grand Prix)
by a single horse in a single year.

In 1866 Gladiateur scored six victories (having been
successful in every attempt he made)—at Newmarket
(w.o. for the Derby Trial Stakes and the Claret Stakes),
at Paris (won the Grand Prix de l'Impératrice, now Prix
Rainbow, by twenty lengths, from Fumée and Vertugadin, and La Coupe from Le Mandarin, Gontran, and
Ronce), at Ascot (won the Gold Cup by forty lengths
from Regalia, with Breadalbane 'trotting in' a long
way behind), and at Paris again (won the Grand Prix
de l'Empereur, now Prix Gladiateur, with Vertugadin
second). For this last race he was ridden by George
Pratt (brother of the more celebrated Charles Pratt),
for H. Grimshaw, who had hitherto always ridden
Gladiateur (save in his two-year-old races, for which
he was ridden by A. Edwards), had lately been thrown
from a dog-cart and killed on the Newmarket Road.

Gladiateur, whose fore legs, it was said, had for some time been shaky, was now sent to the stud. The shakiness is supposed to have been partly the reason for the gingerly fashion in which he seemed to be ridden for the Ascot Cup (one of his most wonderful performances), when he 'waited' so long upon Regalia and Breadalbane that spectators thought it was all over; and even Admiral Rous, it is said, expressed some anxiety to Count F. de Lagrange, who is reported to have replied quite coolly, 'Mais, monsieur l'amiral, c'est absolument certain.' And so it was. As soon as the dangers of descent were over, and Gladiateur was 'let out' just before the turn into the straight, he literally galloped over his two opponents and won in a canter by *forty lengths*.

Of course Gladiateur was not allowed to escape calumny any more than if he had been a maiden, 'cold as ice and pure as snow.' It was hospitably insinuated that he was 'four years old' in 1865, and the owner of Regalia (second to him for the St. Leger) is stated to have expressed a wish to have his mouth examined; but the wish, promptly acceded to by his owner, is understood to have been withdrawn. At any rate nothing came of it.

For a year Gladiateur was at the 'haras' of Dangu, having stood for two seasons in England; then at the time of the Franco-Prussian war, when Count F. de Lagrange sold almost all his horses in a lump to M. Lefèvre (of Chamant), Gladiateur was included in the sale, but, whether he became the property of M. Lefèvre first or not, he was soon purchased by Mr. Blenkiron (in 1870) for 5,800 guineas; and he cost Mr. Harcourt 7,000 guineas at the sale of the Middle Park stud in 1872. when Blair Athol fetched 12,500 guineas and

Breadalbane 6,000 guineas (paid by Count Lehndorf for the German Government). Gladiateur died in 1876 (of 'old age,' said the unconverted cynics, but 'of inflammation, at fourteen years of age,' say the more sober chronicles), having been a dead failure at the stud, if the progeny he begot be compared with himself and his achievements.

In appearance Gladiateur was, as nearly as one can remember, what his 'compatriots' term a 'bai zain,' or 'perfect bay' with black points. He is described as standing (at three years of age) 16 hands 1 inch; with a large and plain head, a 'beautifully arched neck,' powerful, sloping shoulders, very muscular arms and thighs, and deep girth. However that may be, it is a fact that, as so often happens, the learned judges of horseflesh 'did not like him' until *after* he had done wonders. But is it not a fact that the great physical phenomenon is very often—if not generally—anything but a 'model' as the authorities would draw it? Your 'Tipton Slasher' has legs like a 'K;' your Blacklock 'of the mighty stride' is a 'beauty' in the ironical sense. And how frequently is the 'strong man' square-shouldered? If he be not as frequently or more frequently round-shouldered, or sloping-shouldered, then let no man trust his eyesight. Heenan was more of a 'model' than either Tom Sayers or Tom King; but he did not beat them, not either of them decisively, and King did beat him decisively—very—if memory may be trusted.

What a marvel Gladiateur was may be inferred from some 'trials' recorded by Lord Suffolk and Berkshire in his half-volume of the 'Badminton Library.' Here is the account of them.

On April 19, 1865 (when the 'French wonder' was

three years old). Gladiateur was tried over a mile course, at Newmarket, carrying 9 st., against Argences (who had just run in the Newmarket Biennial and was consequently made the 'trial horse'), three years, 8 st., Le Mandarin (thought to be second only to Gladiateur, three years, 8 st. 7 lbs., and Le Béarnais (who had won the Queen's Plate at Ascot and the Grand Critérium at Paris the previous year), three years, 8 st.; and they 'finished' in the order given: 'Won as he liked' being the verdict.

On the 29th he was again tried over the same distance, still carrying 9 st., against Le Mandarin, three years, 7 st. 10 lbs., and Vivid (who had run third for the Oaks in 1863 and in 1864 had beaten Wingrave, Bathilde, and Moulsey at weight for age over Rowley's mile), five years, 8 st. 8 lbs.; and they finished in the order given: 'Won as he liked' being again the verdict.

Then came the Two Thousand, which he won, but apparently with so little in hand that he was again tried (for the Derby), still carrying 9 st., over a mile and a half course, against Fille de l'Air (herself a 'wonder,' who had won the Oaks the previous year), four years, 8 st. 6 lbs., Vivid, five years, 8 st. 6 lbs., and Soumise (a great performer in France the previous year), four years, 8 st. 6 lbs.; and they finished in the order given, the verdict being once more: 'Won as he liked.'

It only remains to be recorded that of Gladiateur's French 'æquales,' all equally unable to make him so much as gallop, Vertugadin (sire of Saltarelle, Stathouder, Saltéador, Mignonette, and Mondaine) did infinitely better than he at the stud, and Le Mandarin, Gontran, and Tourmalet not much, if any, worse.

CHAPTER IX.

FROM THE 'TURN OF THE TIDE' TO THE 'DÉCHÉANCE.'

AFTER the flood came the ebb. The year 1865 had been emphatically 'Gladiateur's year,' the year of French fulness and glory; the year 1866 (with the exception of Gladiateur's Ascot Cup) was as emphatically 'Lord Lyon's year,' the year of French poverty in horseflesh. So poor were the French three-year-olds, indeed, that the Duke of Beaufort had no difficulty in winning the Grand Prix de Paris with so moderate a horse as Ceylon, neither Lord Lyon (a member of the Sunday Observance Society) nor the Bribery colt (afterwards called Savernake, of the same persuasion) being entered. What made the matter more remarkable was that out of eleven runners four only were French, all the rest being English. Still, in England, some French two-year-olds did well—to wit, Trocadéro, Neméa, Dragon, Atalante (the very last 'mount' of the unfortunate Harry Grimshaw), and others.

Moreover there were other little consolations—in the Grand Prix de l'Empereur at Paris, for instance, the Marquis of Hastings's The Duke and Blue Riband and the Duke of Beaufort's Mr. Pitt were beaten by Vertugadin, Baïonnette, and Gontran. The other French 'cracks' were: La Fortune (four years, winner of the Prix du Cadran), Victorieuse (three years, winner of the Prix de Longchamps), Gladiateur (four years, winner of what is now the Prix Rainbow), Marengo (three years, winner of the Poule d'Essai and the Poule des Produits), and Lesbos (three years, winner of what is now the Grande Poule des Produits) at Paris Spring Meeting; at Chantilly Spring meeting Victorieuse (three years, winner of the French Oaks) and Florentin (three years, winner of the French Derby); at Baden Etoile Filante (three years, winner of the Continental Derby and of the Grand Prix); and at Paris Autumn Meeting Etoile Filante (winner of what is now the Prix Royal Oak) and Gladiateur (winner of what is now the Prix Gladiateur). Among the two-year-olds M. Delâtre's Finot (afterwards called Champ d'Oiseau) and Count F. de Lagrange's Atalante and Montgoubert had won the three principal 'Critériums.'

Of these animals there ran in England (where alone the proper measure of their qualities could be taken) La Fortune (third for the Goodwood Stakes and a bad third and last for the Bentinck Memorial Stakes at Goodwood); Gladiateur (already dealt with), who won all his six races that year, whether in France or in England; Florentin (unplaced for the Gold Vase at Ascot); Etoile Filante (unplaced for the Cambridgeshire and for a subscription handicap plate at Newmarket Houghton Meeting); Atalante (second for the Spring Stakes at Newmarket First Spring Meeting; unplaced to Hippia, &c., for the Two-year-old Plate; won the Harleston Nursery Plate at Northampton; unplaced to Viridis, &c., for a Nursery stakes at Newmarket Houghton; and second to that good horse Knight of the Garter for the Blankney Stakes at Lincoln); and Montgoubert (unplaced to Hermit, Vauban, Viridis, &c., for the Eighth Stockbridge Biennial, at the Bibury Club Meeting; and unplaced to Achievement, D'Estournel, Vauban, &c., for the July Stakes at Newmarket). Of other reputed French 'cracks' in this year, 1866, such as Gontran (four years), belonging to 'Major Fridolin,' and the three-year-olds—the once promising Y. Monarque (own brother to Hospodar and winner the year before of the Champagne Stakes at Bibury Club Meeting), Auguste (who was at one time a good favourite for our Derby in the teeth of Lord Lyon), Baïonnette (second by a head only for the One Thousand and second for the French Derby, and 'second for everything,' if not third), all belonging to Count F. de Lagrange, and *tutti quanti*, including La Favorite (unplaced for the Cambridgeshire)—none of them justified their 'crack'fulness either in France or in England. Y. Monarque, the hope of France, went amiss in 1865. Indeed, the measure of the French three-year-olds of 1866 may be taken through the Grand Prix de Paris, which (with Lord Lyon, Savernake, and other English horses not entered or not allowed to run on Sunday) was won, as has been said, by the Duke of Beaufort's moderate Ceylon, there being only four 'Frenchmen' (Auguste, Cinna, Maravedis, and Fernan Cortes) in a field of eleven. Howbeit Major Fridolin's Sultan won the Stewards' Cup at Goodwood. Count F. de Lagrange's Plutus (winner of the Great Eastern Handicap and a great French sire) was bred in England; but Auguste ('bred in France') won the Drawing-Room Stakes at Goodwood.

The French were better off the next year, 1867, though that was emphatically, so far as England was concerned, the year of Hermit and Achievement, both English from crest to coronet, from muzzle to 'frog.' The French 'cracks' in that year were Patricien (three years, winner of the French Derby, of the Prix de Longchamps, of the Prix Royal Oak, as it is now called, and loser by a 'nose' of the Grand Prix de Paris); Jeune Première (three years, winner of the French Oaks); Nicolet (three years, winner of the Poule d'Essai); Trocadéro (three years, winner of what is now the Grande Poule des Produits and of the Grand Saint-Léger de France); Cerf-Volant (three years, winner of the Poule des Produits); Fervacques (three years, winner of the Grand Prix de Paris); Auguste (four years, winner of the Prix du Cadran and of what is now the Prix Rainbow); Vertugadin (five years, winner of what is now the Prix Gladiateur); Ruy Blas (three years, winner of more than a dozen races); Montagnard (three years, winner of half a dozen or more), and Montgoubert, winner of the Deauville Cup, beating Ruy Blas); and among the two-year-olds Pompier (by Royal-quand-même), Virgule (by Saunterer), Le Sarrazin (by Monarque), and above all, for the sake of his later great fame, Mortemer (by Compiègne).

This was a very notable year in the history of French horse-racing, though their great horses did not do much good in England, and though they were no doubt very lucky in that circumstances or highly respectable prejudices prevented Hermit, Achievement, Hippia, and other English 'cracks' from trying conclusions with them in the Grand Prix. And a very memorable Grand Prix it was. Out of ten runners there were but two English horses, D'Estournel and Honolulu (this latter belonging, however, to a French owner, M. H. Delamarre, and appearing in our Stud Book simply as the brown colt by Trumpeter and Honduras). The race was extraordinary on many accounts. First of all Fervacques (by Underhand and

Slapdash) only very narrowly escaped being an Englishman, his dam (Slapdash) having him 'concealed about her person' when she was imported into France. Then Fervacques ran a dead heat for the Prix with Patricien, and on the 'run-off' very nearly ran another, being officially declared to have 'won by a *nose*,' a distance it must take a combination of a 'lynx' and an 'Argus' to 'spot.' Then, again, Patricien, the loser, was notoriously about a stone superior to Fervacques, the winner, which is one of those little puzzles so frequent in horse-racing and yet so incomprehensible to the ingenuous, something that 'no feller can understand.' Then, still further, the best horse in the race was probably Trocadéro, who was not 'in it.' However not only had both Patricien and Trocadéro a very severe race 'in them,' which they had run for the French Derby, but 'Troc' (as also Fervacques, as he had lately shown) was possessed of a 'devil of a temper,' which he had not hitherto displayed very badly, but which he kept up at the stud, making it difficult for anybody to shoe him, and showing a disposition to eat a gentleman named Carriès who went to 'tame' him (and did tame him, with some trouble, just long enough for 'shoeing' him) *à la* Rarey. Then, moreover, Fervacques was bred at the 'haras' of Fervacques, belonging to that Count de Montgomery who 'ought to have' won the very first of the Grands Prix with La Toucques, but postponed the achievement till he had a worse horse to perform it with. Lastly, Fervacques became a sojourner in that England of which he had so narrowly escaped being a native, and where he was running at the great age of nine years in 1873, having condescended (it would seem) to the 'jumping business,' which Patricien, his old 'dead-heater,' would never have 'bemeaned' himself to do.

Of these French 'cracks' just enumerated, many like Fervacques (winner of the Northumberland Plate— as became a son of his sire, Underhand—&c.), ran in England in 1867, but did not make much by their 'motion,' though in after years they made a great deal. Still Jeune Première did not hesitate to run for the Cambridgeshire (at odds of forty to one against her), or to oppose (in vain) such horses as Julius and The Palmer in a free handicap sweepstakes at Newmarket Houghton; Trocadéro went for the Two Thousand (unplaced), won two races at Brighton, and ran second for the Newmarket St. Leger (beating Hippia), second for the Newmarket October Handicap, and unplaced (in company with his 'compatriote' Jeune Première) for the Free Handicap Sweepstakes; Auguste won the Claret Stakes at Newmarket against a single nameless and fameless opponent, and had two other (unsuccessful) 'shies' (including the Alexandra Plate, won by Lecturer, at Ascot); Montagnard ran for the Lincolnshire Handicap (unplaced), for the Prince of Wales's Stakes (handicap) at Newmarket (unplaced), and for the Cambridgeshire (unplaced); Montgoubert ran (second to The Palmer) for the Ascot Derby and lost it by a head only, for the Gold Cup (unplaced), for the Biennial at Bibury Club Meeting (fourth to Vauban, Ailesbury, and Opoponax), for the Summer Stakes (handicap) at Newmarket July (unplaced to Julius, &c.), for the Cesarewitch (unplaced in company with his 'compatriote' Etoile Filante), for the Select Stakes at Newmarket Second October (beaten by his sole opponent Friponnier, with the significant comment 'No betting'), and (unplaced) for a handicap plate (won by Saccharometer) at Newmarket Houghton; Cerf-Volant 'took an easy polish' from Vauban at Goodwood, and from Verulam at Doncaster; and of the two-year-olds Pompier ran unsuccessfully for the Brocklesby Stakes at Lincoln, for the Ipswich Nursey Stakes (second to Contempt), for the Ryhall Stakes (second to Speculum) at Stamford, for two Two-year-old Sweepstakes (second to Victorine, and unplaced to Amour Propre) at Newmarket Second October, and (third and last) for the Blankney Stakes at Lincoln Autumn Meeting; Le Sarrazin began admirably by winning the Woodcote Stakes at Epsom (beating Speculum, Restitution, &c.), was fourth (to Lady Elizabeth, &c.) for the July Stakes, was unplaced (to Athena, &c.) for the Lavant Stakes, was third (to Banditto and Europa) for the Molecomb Stakes, and was unplaced (to Greensleeve, Rosicrucian, &c.) for the Middle Park Plate (for which he carried extra weight); and Mortemer seems to have run but once in England this year (1867), when he was unplaced for the Stockbridge Biennial (won by Europa, with Seesaw second and Ironmaster third). Some of these horses, however, as will appear hereafter, made a very strong mark upon the English Turf in subsequent years; but it is as sires that they have made the greatest impression in England. Especially notable have been Trocadéro (sire of almost innumerable French winners, some of them highly respected in this country), who, four years after his death (in 1881), stood second (in 1885) among the French 'winning sires;' Vertugadin (sire of Saltarelle, Stathouder, Saltéador, and Mondaine, all highly esteemed either by repute or from experience in England); Ruy Blas (who, however, did not visit England in person). sire of numerous winners (including Nubienne, who defeated Scapegrace, the only English horse [and perhaps the worst which ever ran for that race] among the runners for the Grand Prix of 1879);

Montagnard, who won the Newmarket Handicap in 1868, and 'settled' as a stud horse in England; Pompier (who was to be the sire of Inval, well known among us, and of other horses, better and worse); Le Sarrazin (who was to be the sire of Monsieur de Fligny, greatly distinguished as a two-year-old at Goodwood in 1875, of Milan, and of other 'cracks'); and, high above all, the famous Mortemer (who was to be the sire of St. Christophe, winner of the Grand Prix; of Chamant, winner of the Two Thousand, &c.; of Verneuil, winner of the Ascot Cup, &c., and whom the Americans were to purchase in 1880 for 5,200*l.*, or the equivalent in dollars). The accident to which Le Sarrazin owed his birth is singular enough to deserve notice, as a warning to owners and breeders (remembering that Marske, sire to Eclipse, was sold for a song, and Squirt, sire of Marske, was all but shot as worthless—before he begot Marske and Syphon and the dam of Pumpkin, Maiden, and Purity) to be careful how they make dogs' meat of well-bred horses and mares. Now the dam of Le Sarrazin was Constance (daughter of Gladiator and Lanterne, splendid breeding), an undersized little mare, so despised in her foalhood that it was thought useless to train her; and when, at the request of Mr. Henry Jennings, her astute trainer, she had been trained and tried on the racecourse, she broke her cannon bone and was to have been shot, when Mr. Jennings again begged her off, and she was sent to the stud, where she first produced (by Nuncio) a fine black foal, called Esteemed Friend (afterwards Le Monsieur), which developed (it is said) into the charger ridden by Marshal Macmahon in his Italian campaign, and then she gave birth to a very numerous progeny, including Fidélité, Monitor, La Favorite, and the aforesaid Le Sarrazin (all by

Monarque, and all more or less distinguished on the Turf). She died in 1872, aged twenty-four: breeders 'will be pleased to accept of this intimation.'

The year 1868 was memorable in the annals of French horse-racing, though the 'Frenchmen' had not a very brilliant campaign in England and were beaten (by the Marquis of Hastings with The Earl) in the Grand Prix de Paris. For the English it was—in France—the 'Earl's year;' for the French it was emphatically 'Suzerain's year.'

The principal French 'cracks' in that year were Suzerain (three years, winner of the French Derby and of what is now the Grande Poule des Produits, and second to The Earl for the Grand Prix); Jenny (three years, winner of the French Oaks); Gouvernail (three years, winner of the Poule d'Essai); Le Bosphore (three years, winner of the Prix de Longchamps); Longchamps (four years, winner of the Prix du Cadran and of what is now the Prix Rainbow); Nélusko (three years, winner of La Coupe at Paris and of what is now the Prix Royal Oak); Auguste (five years, winner of what is now the Prix Gladiateur); Mortemer (three years, rather on *ex post facto* grounds than on his three victories at Paris out of ten attempts at various meetings in France and in England); and, among the two-year-olds, Consul (by Monarque), Manette II. (by Pretty Boy), and Mademoiselle de Fligny (by Bois-Roussel), winners of the three principal 'Critériums,' of which triad Consul was destined to become very distinguished indeed at both post and paddock.

The year was memorable in France for the comparatively poor class of the horses that ran in the French Derby, and indeed of the French three-year-olds generally; for the fact that Baron A. Schickler,

whose father as well as himself had been racing from
the earliest days of the French Jockey Club, who had
imported into France The Nabob (one of the happiest
importations ever made), and had thus supplied M. H.
Delamarre with Vermout and Bois-Roussel (to win the
Grand Prix de Paris and the French Derby in 1864),
had hitherto been unable to win either Grand Prix or
Derby for himself, and even now had no joy of Suzerain,
because the horse never could be made fit to run again
after the Grand Prix; and for the complete collapse of
the promising Le Sarrazin, as well as for the cloud
which still obscured the splendid qualities of Mortemer,
to whom (in England) Blue Gown (of the same age)
presented two stone and any amount of beating. This
also is among the wonders of horse-racing.

To the 'cracks' already mentioned should perhaps
be added the name of Ouragan II. (three years, winner
of the Poule des Produits, son of Monarque and Sun-
rise, and therefore own brother to Hospodar and Y.
Monarque). He was imported into England in 1867
(at two years of age), was running there at eight years
of age (like Fervacques) in 1873, and settled there as a
stud horse.

Of the said French 'cracks' several ran in England
in 1868 with rather less than more success. Let us
begin with Ouragan II., because his career was so
singular. He commenced (in 1867) by running second
to The Earl for the Gimcrack Stakes, and then, after
running a dead heat with the same celebrated horse
(winner of the Grand Prix, be it remembered, and
thought to be superior to Blue Gown in 1868) for the
Bedford Stakes at Newmarket Second October, defeated
him fairly and squarely in the 'decider,' after which
he seems to have gone off colour, and in 1868 he did

nothing of note in England; in 1869 he confined his attentions to his own country, as also in 1870, and then he returned, not much like a giant refreshed, to his galloping on English turf, at Epsom, at Ascot, at Worcester (where he won the Worcestershire Stakes Handicap), and elsewhere, but not recalling to mind the young Ouragan 'what had bin upsides with The Earl.'

The rest that ran in England did not include Longchamps (who at three years of age had beaten the afterwards illustrious sire Hermit, in 1867, for the Newmarket Derby, with an advantage, however, of a stone in weight, after running unplaced behind Achievement and Hermit for the Doncaster St. Leger), or Suzerain (who ran but three times—in France—and was then 'horse de combat,' as the English turfite pronounces, or used to pronounce, before the days of School Boards), or Jenny, or Gouvernail, or Le Bosphore, or Auguste; but Nélusko ran moderately at Newmarket (fourth for the Biennial and third for the Cesarewitch) and at Ascot (second by half a length to Seesaw for the New Biennial); Mortemer ran at Ascot (unplaced to King Alfred, &c., for the Prince of Wales's Stakes), at Stockbridge (third to Seesaw and Parson for the Ninth Biennial), at Newmarket (second to Athena and beating Seesaw for the Grand Duke Michael Stakes, and unplaced to Blue Gown, &c., for the Free Handicap at the Houghton Meeting); little Consul ran at Lewes (unplaced to Melody, &c., for the Priory Stakes); and Mademoiselle de Fligny ran at Epsom (unplaced to De Vere, &c., for the Two-year-old Stakes, and to Masaniello, De Vere, &c., for the New Two-year-old Stakes).

The French 'stars' of 1869 were, in their own country, Consul (three years, winner of the French

Derby), Péripétie (three years, winner of the French Oaks), Cerdagne (three years, winner of what is now the Grande Poule des Produits), Pandour (three years, winner of the Prix de Longchamps, now called Prix Hocquart), Le Sarrazin 'redivivus' (four years, winner of the Prix du Cadran), Trocadéro (five years, winner of what is now the Prix Gladiateur and of what is now called the Prix Rainbow), Clotho (three years, winner of what is now called the Prix Royal Oak), Glaneur (winner of the Grand Prix de Paris), Mortemer (four years, winner of nine races or more out of eighteen on the Continent); and among the two-year-olds Florian (by Hospodar), Luisette (by Zouave, son of The Baron), and Sornette (by Light), winners of the principal 'Critériums,' and also Roquefort (by Hospodar), winner of the Prix de Morny (called Prix de Deux Ans since the 'déchéance,' since 1871 that is) at Deauville.

Of these 'stars' Consul (who won the Prix de Guiche, the Poule d'Essai, and the Prix de Seine-et-Marne, as well as the French Derby, in 1869) was a small but a remarkably good horse. How he lost the Grand Prix (for which he was a strong favourite) is one of the mysteries of horse-racing (especially when the winner was such a 'rogue' as Glaneur). He became an excellent sire (of Kilt, and of Albion, winners of the French Derby in 1876 and 1881, of Nougat, and of Archiduc, among others), and it was a pity, perhaps, that the French allowed him to be sold out of the country. He was purchased for Russia at Count de Lagrange's death in 1883 (sale in 1884) for 28,000 francs (about 1,120*l.*), very cheap.

The year 1869 was remarkable in France for the successes of quite a recent 'turfman,' M. Delâtre, who that year stood second among French winning owners to Count de Lagrange, with MM. Lupin, Delamarre, and 'Major Fridolin' next.

The event of 1869 for which the French had most reason to set up their horn on high was undoubtedly the Grand Prix de Paris, for which neither Pretender nor Pero Gomez, first and second in the English Derby, would or could run, but the third in the English Derby— to wit, Mr. E. Jones's The Drummer—went over to Paris and was accompanied by three other English horses, namely, Mr. H. Savile's Ryshworth, Mr. T. Parr's ('Fisherman' Parr's) Tim Bobbin, and the Duke of Hamilton's Wild Oats. Of course had this been the Wild Oats of the year before, the Wild Oats that won the Prendergast Stakes and ran a dead heat with Pero Gomez for the Criterion in 1868, it would or should have been all over but shouting. But it was Wild Oats on but three legs; therefore men betted 50 to 1 against him, degrading him to the level of Boulogne, and laid 6 to 4 against Consul, the favourite, 5 to 2 against The Drummer, 5 to 1 against Ryshworth, and 7 to 1 against Glaneur. It was thought that The Drummer, having been second and third so often (for the Lincolnshire Handicap, for the City and Suburban, and for the Derby), might this time work into first place (as he had done in the Great Metropolitan) : but his 'head was turned ;' instead of winning he lost by that portion of his conformation, and the winner was not Consul, but Glaneur. Καὶ τόδε Φωκυλίδου· this also is one of those things 'that no feller can understand.' For this Glaneur was a 'commoner' (with a magnificent stride, however), an 'uncertain customer,' very 'nasty' in temper, and so difficult to 'keep up to the mark' that he disappeared altogether from the racecourse at the end of his three-year-old season. So, but for a different reason, did

Consul; and, when it came to the stud and 'reproduction,' Consul was to Glaneur, in the capacity of sire, as Hyperion to a satyr. What made Glaneur's success the more notable was that he belonged to the same 'circonscription' as Souvenir, and was bred by the same breeder, M. Jules Robin.

Of the French 'stars' of 1869 there ran in England Count F. de Lagrange's Consul (fourth—out of five—to Martyrdom, Pero Gomez, and Typhon for the Prince of Wales's Stakes at Ascot, and second to Pero Gomez for the Ascot Derby); M. Delâtre's Cerdagne (second with 7 st. 8 lbs. to Vestminster, the same age, three years, with 6 st. 4 lbs., for the Cambridgeshire); Count F. de Lagrange's Le Sarrazin (beaten by his sole opponent, Typhöeus, for the Claret Stakes at Newmarket); Count F. de Lagrange's Trocadéro (won the Walton Manor Stakes at Epsom, with 9 st. 5 lbs.; unplaced with 9 st. 11 lbs. for the Six-mile Hill Handicap at Epsom; last, save 'disqualified' Thorwaldsen, for the Ascot Cup; and second, 10 st. 8 lbs., to Restitution, four years, 10 st., for the Alexandra Plate); Count F. de Lagrange's Florian (unplaced for the Brocklesby Stakes; second to St. Leonards for the Lincoln Club Cup; second to Frivolity for the Althorp Park Stakes; favourite, but unplaced to Hawthornden, &c., for the Hinchingbrook Stakes at Huntingdon; favourite, and third to Religieuse and Thunderstorm, for the Milton Stakes at the same place; and second, 8 st. 12 lbs., to Gamos, 9 st. 1 lb., for the Windsor Stakes, second heat, at Newmarket Second October); and Count F. de Lagrange's Roquefort (third to Pâté and Bonnie Katie for the Blankney Stakes at Lincoln; second by a neck to Guy Dayrell for the New Two-year-old Stakes at Epsom Spring; unplaced to Gamos, &c., for the Weston Stakes at Bath, though favourite; unplaced to Pâté, Frivolity, and Guy Dayrell for the Two-year-old Stakes at Epsom Summer, but won the Epsom Two-year-old Plate, 8 st. 4 lbs., against Pâté, 9 st., and eight others; unplaced for the New Stakes at Ascot; and unplaced for the Criterion Stakes at Newmarket, behind Hester, Sunlight, and Kingcraft). Boulogne too, though scarcely a 'crack,' defeated Pretender (who had 7 lbs. the worse in weight) for the Newmarket Derby.

We have now reached a very momentous period in the history both of France and of French horse-racing; we have come to the eve of what Frenchmen call euphemistically 'les évènements,' to the memorable year 1870, to the time of the march (which never 'came off') 'à Berlin,' to the gathering of the war cloud which was soon to burst and to cause the 'déchéance' of Napoleon III. We have already seen how, when the French were 'coming on nicely with their horse-racing,' both in the days when Philippe Egalité ran horses in England and imported English horses into France and when Charles X. and his son, the Dauphin, and Louis Philippe and his son, the Duke d'Orléans, were improving the breed of Franco-English or Anglo-French thoroughbreds by importation and the encouragement of horse-racing, there came a revolution or a war or both, which stopped the good work for a longer or shorter while; and so it was again. The Franco-Prussian war, with a revolution 'to follow' or to accompany it, once more threw the French back in their horse-breeding and horse-racing, but not nearly so much as heretofore; still quite enough. 'Les évènements,' or apprehension of them, led Count F. de Lagrange to offer his gigantic establishment for sale, so that he might be ready for action; produced what is called the 'emigration,' both of owners and especially of horses, from France to England or elsewhither; and brought about the 'déchéance' of Napoleon III., the temporary cessation of horse-racing in France, and the withdrawal of 'Imperial' from the titles of all French races on which the Emperor's sympathy and influence had been exercised, whether as 'godfather' or as procurer of subsidies, and which consequently underwent a change of appellation. Hence it is that in the records we find 'Pas couru' in 1870 and 1871 significantly printed in the place where the winner's name is inscribed in other years under names of certain races, and the names themselves altered. Thus we find that the French Derby was 'pas couru' in 1871, as well, of course, as the French Oaks, the Poule d'Essai, the Grande Poule des Produits, the Grand Prix de Paris, the Prix de Longchamps, the Prix du Cadran, and so on; and that in 1870 the Prix Gladiateur was 'pas couru,' and that the then principal 'Critériums,' as well as some other races, suffered the same stoppage. Some races, such as the Grand Saint-Léger de France, were run neither in 1870 nor in 1871. We learn too that, in consequence, no doubt, of 'les évènements,' the 'Prix de l'Empereur' at Paris became the 'Grande Poule des Produits,' the 'Prix Morny' at Deauville the 'Prix de Deux Ans,' the 'Grand Prix de l'Empereur' at Paris the 'Prix Gladiateur,' the 'Prix de l'Impératrice' the 'Prix Rainbow' (after a celebrated sire), and the 'Prix du Prince Impérial' the 'Prix Royal Oak' (after a still more celebrated sire, imported by Lord Henry Seymour). The inconvenience of giving anything like a dynastic title in a country so liable as France to shocks of revolution and violent changes of Government is illustrated in a remarkable manner by the 'péripéties' which the title of the Prix Gladiateur has undergone: the race dates from a comparatively very early period, and it was originally called 'Prix Royal,' then 'Prix National,' then 'Prix Impérial,' or 'Grand Prix de l'Empereur,' until it was at last named after a horse, a name which should be 'stable.'

So now we have come to 1870; and the most important question, so far as French horse-racing was concerned, was what would become of the horses which Count F. de Lagrange desired to sell, keeping to himself, however, most fortunately, at his 'haras' at Dangu, the great sire Monarque, certain 'youngsters,' and the 'galaxy' of brood mares whose sultan that sire was. The hour and the man both came: M. Joachim Lefèvre, a 'financial' gentleman settled (it was understood) in London (though afterwards of Chamant and Newmarket), having formerly had a small racing-stable at Chantilly or in the neighbourhood, was found equal to the occasion, becoming, either for himself or an association of which he was head, the purchaser—in a lump—of all the Count's horses in training or about to commence training, and taking over (*quod rerum omnium fuit primum*) the experienced Monsieur Thomas de Jennings, *Anglicè* Tom Jennings, to be trainer and manager. So it is said by a good French authority; but Général was certainly purchased, whether from the Count himself or from M. Lefèvre, by the Duke of Hamilton, and won the Criterion in his name.

M. Lefèvre forthwith began to race in England under the appropriate pseudonym of 'Mr. T. Lombard' (with a playful allusion, it was supposed, to Lombard Street), as well as in his own name, with the 'colours' of the Republic, red, white, and blue.

But this is outrunning the clock a little; let us

go back to the spring of 1870 ; before there was any stoppage of horse-racing in France, or any talk of 'déchéance.' M. Delâtre, be it remarked by the way, had won 200,000 francs before he had to put his horses in a place of security.

The French 'cracks,' then, that ran in France in 1870 were Bigarreau (three years, winner of the French Derby); Sornette (three years, winner of the French Oaks and of the Grand Prix de Paris, as well as of what is now the Grande Poule des Produits); Boulogne (four years, winner of the Prix du Cadran); Mortemer (five years, winner of the Coupe at Paris); Dutch Skater (four years, winner of the Grand Prix at Deauville); Bachelette (three years, winner of the Poule des Produits); Trocadéro (six years, winner of what is now the Prix Rainbow for the second year in succession); Valois (three years, winner of the Poule d'Essai); and, among the two-year-olds, Eole II. (winner of what is now the Prix de Deux Ans at Deauville). The very best of the French two-year-olds, Général (son of Monarque and Tolla, and prominent among the favourites for the English Derby of 1871), did not run at all in France.

Of these 'cracks' Boulogne, Trocadéro, Eole II., and Général ran in the name of Count F. de Lagrange, who was their owner up to the time of the sale of his horses, when Trocadéro, withdrawn from training, seemed likely to remain a fixture in England, but, fortunately for French horse-breeding, he was repurchased in 1871 by M. P. Aumont, of the Victot 'haras,' and domiciled in France. Of the said 'cracks' the following ran in England: Sornette (won the Fitzwilliam Stakes at Doncaster and the Doncaster Cup; third to Prince Henry and her 'compatriot' Nélusko for the Trial Stakes at Newmarket First October; second to Faraway for a free handicap at the Second October; won a sweepstakes from two 'compatriots,' her only opponents, Dutch Skater and Nélusko, at Newmarket Houghton; third to Agility and Falkland for the Free Handicap Sweepstakes at the same meeting; third to Musket and Dutch Skater for the Queen's Plate at Shrewsbury, where she was unplaced for another race); Boulogne (a bad second to Midsummer for the Newmarket Biennial for four-year-olds, and won, in grand style, the eighteenth Bentinck Memorial at Goodwood from Standard-Bearer and Ryshworth); Mortemer (won the Stockbridge Cup with consummate ease); Dutch Skater (won the Queen's Plate at Warwick, the Trial Stakes at Edinburgh, as well as the People's Plate, a Plate of 100 guineas at Perth, and ran about half a dozen times besides, unsuccessfully); Trocadéro (ran a bad second to Sabinus for the Ascot Cup, but won the Alexandra Plate from his sole opponent Siderolite); Eole II. (unplaced for a two-year-old plate at Newmarket First October, and third for a selling plate at the Houghton Meeting, as well as unplaced for the Second Nursery); and Général (who gained laurels by running second to Hannah for the July Stakes, and by winning the Lavant, the Molecomb, and the Criterion, though unplaced for the Middle Park Plate).

Of the animals mentioned Bigarreau, Sornette, Dutch Skater, and Eole II. deserve special notice (Mortemer and Trocadéro having already been dealt with).

But first let it be observed that the Grand Prix de Paris of 1870 was a great triumph for the French and a remarkable race in itself; for though the French were again lucky, as they had (for the usual reasons, whether highly respectable prejudices or other causes) no winner of the English Derby (Kingcraft), or of the English Oaks (Gamos), or of the Two Thousand (Macgregor, broken down), or of the One Thousand (Hester), to oppose them, yet out of a field of twelve there were four English horses—Coutts (son of the French sire Dollar by the way), Nobleman (winner of the Newmarket Stakes), Prince of Wales (a better favourite than Kingcraft for the English Derby), and The Recorder (half-bred)—and both Sornette and Bigarreau were better favourites than any one of them. Moreover Mr. C. Pratt, trainer and rider of Sornette, knowing her peculiar temper and seeing that the pace set was not likely to suit her, adopted the bold and even dangerous but completely justified tactics of making all the running, six or seven lengths ahead of her field, and she won in a canter; the field, no doubt, being 'no great shakes.'

And now a few words about Bigarreau and Sornette, who were both 'children of Light.' It will be remembered, perhaps, that when the 'Big Stable,' the confederacy of Nivière-Lagrange, split asunder, Baron Nivière took to himself as partner M. Charles Laffitte (who raced as 'Major Fridolin'). This latter gentleman became, in course of time, sole owner of the racing stable and the Villebon 'haras,' near Palaiseau, and consequently of Bigarreau and Sornette (the latter by Light and Surprise, and the former by Light and Battaglia), both foaled at Villebon. With these two 'cracks' the 'Major' won, in the same year (1870) the French Derby and Oaks, the Grand Prix de Paris, the Prix de Longchamps, the Prix de l'Empereur (Grande Poule des Produits), and other races, whether in England or France; a feat almost equal to that of M. Delamarre in 1864 with Vermout and Bois-Roussel; almost equal, for though M. Delamarre did not win the French Oaks as well as the French Derby, yet, on the other hand, he in the Grand Prix defeated the winner of the English Derby and the winner of both the French and the English Oaks (Fille de l'Air.) Of the distinguished pair, Bigarreau and Sornette, the former went into temporary retirement after the Grand Prix, emerged in 1872, did nothing noteworthy, and was told off to the stud, where he cannot be said to have 'illustrated himself' very greatly as a sire; the latter went on running, became quite a household word in England, or the 'horsey' parts thereof, and came to such a characteristic end when she was taken out of training at the end of 1871 that a short memoir of her may not be thrown away.

This 'child of Light,' well named Sornette (from her lightness, frivolity, fantasticalness), was a very interesting character. She was from the first as 'wild and wayward' as the 'Queen of the May' (and far more dangerous), and there was no more knowing 'where to have her' than there was in the famous case of 'Dame Quickly.' In the early days of her training, as a yearling or fifteen-months-ling, she escaped from the man who held her by the leading-rein, bolted into the forest at Villebon, and was sought in vain for two days, when she 'turned up,' it is said, 'permiscuous.' Like our own Caller Ou she had her fancies in running and would only 'go' when she had her own way (if anybody could discover what that was on any particular day); and when, upon being taken out of training, she was turned loose in the happy breeding-grounds of Villebon, she tore like a mad thing ('which,' as the late Mr. Robson would have said, 'she wor'), and a blind one to boot, down an alley where was a heap of stakes, and, being unable to stop herself (even had she desired to do so), ran herself through the vitals, and died almost immediately; a clear case of suicide committed in a state of temporary insanity. Had she lived she might have produced something wonderfully good, or, quite as probably, something execrably bad, a prodigy or a monstrosity: odds on the latter.

Dutch Skater (who became the property of the all-purchasing M. Lefèvre about the time that he bought Count de Lagrange's horses in training, at which time and afterwards he bought freely on all sides all manner of beasts, whether French or English) deserves special notice not only for his victories (which will be set forth in due course) in England, but because he became a popular stud horse among English owners and was the sire of Lord Falmouth's celebrated mare Dutch Oven (winner of the St. Leger in 1882), as well as of the good but unfortunate French horse Insulaire, not less well known and respected in England than in France; and Eole II., because from an insignificant two-year-old he developed into a sort of Fisherman in a small way, a very respectable if not a great 'stayer,' beating even Lilian on one occasion for a Queen's Plate (to say nothing of Shannon) and defeating Albert Victor at four years of age over the D. I. (2 miles 105 yards). But that was in 1872; and we are now only on the eve of the 'déchéance,' which followed the defeat of ' the Man of Sedan' on September 2, 1870.

On June 10 in that year, by the way, the famous Blue Gown (carrying 10 st. 8 lbs., however, and being ' off colour') was beaten in France for the Grand Prix de la Ville de Lyon by the 'Frenchmen' Massinissa, Minotaure, Gabier, and Capsule.

The last French meeting held that year was Deauville, August 6, 7, and 8, when M. A. Lupin's (or M. Delâtre's) Dutch Skater won the Cup (now called Grand Prix) in such grand style, beating Baron A. Schickler's Rafale and, belonging to various other owners, Don Carlos, Massinissa, Cerdagne, Paganini, Monseigneur, Trocadéro, and Mortemer.

Then came the 'emigration' and the dispersal of French horses.

It has been said, on good French authority, that M. C. J. Lefèvre (or an association headed by him under the assumed name of Mr. T. Lombard) purchased in a lump nearly all Count F. de Lagrange's horses in training; but, however that may be, it appears that the Duke of Hamilton became the owner of Général for 3,800*l*., of Boulogne for 300*l*., and of Orthodoxe for 500*l*.; M. Lefèvre of Alaric for 840*l*. and Henry for 1,350*l*. Mr. Blenkiron bought the famous Gladiateur (a bad bargain) for a stud-horse at the price of 5,800*l*.; and the Count's whole sale is said to have fetched no more than 23,760*l*.

About the earliest and most prudent of the 'emigrants' (anxious to avoid the attentions of the invading Germans) is said to have been Mr. Henry Jennings, who is stated to have left La Croix St. Ouen for the safer ground of Newmarket in the middle of August. About the same time M. Delamarre's Clotaire, Boréal, Bivouac, Véranda, Verdure, and others were sent to Newmarket (where the stud horses Vermout and Patricien seem to have found a temporary residence). Thither too, either earlier or later, came the horses of Baron Schickler and Mr. Gibson the trainer. M. A. Lupin's horses remained for some time at Chantilly, undisturbed but closely watched by the Germans, and only after much (more or less necessary) 'dodging' were got as far as Boulogne and thence to Ilsley in the month of December. The horses of 'Major Fridolin' left La Morlaye early in September, and, with Sornette and the youngsters Somno and Gantelet among them, were put up at Newmarket. The horses of the Duke of Hamilton, whose stable was under the protection of the British flag, partly remained at Chantilly (Gouvernail, Honesty, Sly Fox, &c., are said to have been among them) to the end of the war under the care of Mould, the head 'lad;' others, including Monseigneur, Eckmühl, and Barbillon, left France, under the charge of Mr. Planner, the trainer, and were installed at Lambourne. Some trainers took refuge in the western parts of France, some in Belgium; some, like Messrs. Cassidy and Thorp, remained—for a while, if not altogether—at Chantilly and La Morlaye. Count de Lagrange's unsold stud horses and brood mares stayed on at Dangu, where the little Flageolet (to say nothing of Combat and Tambour), foaled in 1870, remained with his dam till the armistice was signed, and he went to take his first lessons at Royallieu. Such, at least, is the account of the French authority.

With the stoppage of racing the sporting papers naturally stopped; 'Le Sport' ceased to appear and was not republished until June 27, 1871.

Probably a great deal more fuss was made than was necessary; there could not be any regular race meetings of course, but the fear of having their race horses 'requisitioned' and 'annexed' by the Germans was probably quite groundless, and Count Lehndorff himself proved how baseless were the charges made against him of 'harrying' a stud farm or stud farms within a hundred miles of which he had never been.

Still, for the sake of running their horses, picking up

stakes, and exercising the animals in peace, quietness, and freedom, owners and trainers were quite right to 'emigrate;' and England was about the only place open to them for the three purposes.

The French horses, then, that ran in England, from the close of the Deauville meeting to the end of the season, were chiefly (besides Général, Boulogne, and others that may have been mentioned already) Croisade, Chérubin, Matelot, La Verzée, Bismarck (by Cobnut), Ballerine, Frédéric-Charles, Masaniello, Satanstoë (formerly M. Delâtre's), Roquefort, Capsule, Jarnicoton II., Bellone, Turquoise, Messager, Fidélia; the Duke of Hamilton's Capitaliste and Monseigneur; Mr. 'Kennington's' Algérie, Myosotis, Jarnac, Pistache, and Canon; M. Delâtre's Dutch Skater, Eole II., Cerdagne, Luisette, and La Baronne; the 'Lombard' stable's (or Mr. T. Jennings's) Nélusko, Alaric, La Néva, Electeur, Manette II., Gascogne, and Manille (be it noted that out of thirteen runners for a selling sweepstakes won by Gascogne at Newmarket First October no fewer than six were 'bred in France'—to wit, Gascogne himself, Messager II., Satanstoë, Amber, Masaniello, and Malatesta); M. de la Charme's Royauté, Gouache, Mademoiselle de Saint-Igny, and Méléurge (winner of a Nursery handicap of 400*l*. at Newmarket Houghton, for which five starters out of fifteen were 'bred in France'—to wit, Manille, Gantelet, Clotaire, Pensée, and the winner); M. André's Don Carlos, Fervacques, and Chevreuse; M. Aumont's Miss Hervina, Pensée, Haydée, and Enéide (won a handicap plate of 200*l*. at Newarket Houghton against twenty opponents); M. de Montgomery's La Calonne, La Risle, Mademoiselle de Mailloc, and Toucques; M. Desvignes's Eckmühl; M. A. Lupin's Pythonisse, Hérault d'Armes, Cantate, Ermeline, Pistole, and Pos-

térité; M. H. Delamarre's Porphyre, La Tracone, Clos
Vougeot, Véranda, Verdure, Clotaire, and Congo;
'Major Fridolin's' Curieuse, Gaston, Suzanne, Gourbi,
Somno, and Gantelet; Baron A. Schickler's Evohé,
Rafale, Malatesta, Deva Daro, and Soteira. Some of
these changed hands, either by purchase or by 'claim-
ing' in selling races, and ran in various owners' names
and colours, sometimes French and sometimes English.

At the end of the season of 1870, it has been calculated by a 'compatriot,' there had been won by
French horses in England (before and after the 'emigration') some 300,000 francs (about 12,000*l*.) in
stakes.

CHAPTER X.

M. LEFÈVRE'S CAMPAIGN OF 1871 — THE LAGRANGE-LEFÈVRE 'FUSION' — LORD FALMOUTH'S HOWL FOR 'RECIPROCITY.'

LAMENTABLE as may have been the recklessness with which the French undertook to march at a moment's notice 'à Berlin,' equally admirable is the ease and readiness with which they raised their millions of ransom from their midst and themselves from disaster and despondency. Before 1871 had arrived at its latter end our neighbours were at their horse-racing again, almost as if nothing had happened. Only they had lost—'it might be for years and it might be for ever'—their chances at Baden-Baden, which had been a kind of 'Tom Tiddler's ground' to them, where they had picked up gold and silver, yellow mark pieces and white, every autumn for years: the Grand Prix de Bade had been as good as a gift to them since the establishment of the racecourse at Iffezheim (under the auspices of the astute M. Bénazet, who foresaw 'grist to his mill,' advantage to his 'hell' thereby) in 1858, since when the race had been won regularly every year by a Frenchman with a French horse—by M. A. Lupin with La Maladetta, Baron Nivière with Géologie, M. Benoist with Capucine, M. P. Aumont with Mon Etoile, Count F. de Lagrange with Stradella, M. A. de Montgomery with

La Toucques, M. H. Delamarre with Vermont and Vertugadin in two successive years, M. H. Lunel with Etoile Filante, M. L. André with Ruy Blas, Count F. de Lagrange with Trocadéro, and M. L. Delâtre with Cerdagne. The war had cost them or lost them a 'Goldpokal' (given by the Grand Duke) and about a thousand pounds a year. It was enough to make them turn their swords into ploughshares and their spears into some other agricultural implement, to call a spade a spade, and to refuse to learn war any more.

But what were the French 'cracks' of 1871?

Those that ran in France that year (in the autumn thereof) were Don Carlos (four years, winner of the newly-named Prix Gladiateur), La Périchole (four years, winner of the Grand Prix de Deauville, where the war 'didn't make no difference'), and the two-year-olds Revigny (winner of two of the three principal 'Critériums'), Little Agnes (winner of one 'Critérium'), and Seul (winner of the Prix de Deux Ans, lately called the Prix Morny, at Deauville).

The other 'cracks' remained in England with the 'emigrants' (owners, jockeys, and trainers), among whom M. Lefèvre might be counted (with his huge bi-national racing-stable), or with English owners, having bought them (pretty freely too) with money.

Of those specified there ran in England Don Carlos (son of Monarque and Noëlie, second to Lumley for the Queen's Plate at Newcastle-on-Tyne, unplaced for the Lambton Plate, 'beaten off' for the Cup Stakes at Huntingdon by Lady Masham and Prince Henry), Revigny (son of Orphelin and Woman in Red, second to Lighthouse for a two-year-old sweepstakes at Newmarket July), and Seul (son of West Australian and Mon Etoile, unplaced to Successful and Il Maestro for the Corporation Stakes at Brighton, where he won the Bevingdean Stakes). That Little Agnes, though belonging to the English Duke of Hamilton, should not run in England is a little curious, but the records seem to imply that she did not.

About Revigny there is a sad tale to tell, and it may as well be got over at once. His sire, it will have been observed, was the excellent Orphelin (so called because his dam, the much-esteemed Echelle, died at the very early age of ten in the very year (1859) of his birth). Now Orphelin (sire of Montargis and a lot of ' good uns ') died about 1869–70, being no older than his dam had been at her death; and Revigny, after proving himself a horse of great merit, died in 1876, being but seven years old. Surely this was ' rough ' on M. P. Aumont, owner of Echelle and breeder and owner of both Orphelin and Revigny.

Of course, in consequence of ' les évènements,' the number of French horses that ran in England in 1871, whether for French ' emigrants ' or for English owners, was legion ; and some of them ' illustrated ' the French nation and French horse-breeding most brilliantly. There were Acide Prussique (four years, sold in England), *Alaric* (four years), Algérie (four years, sold in England), Almenesches (two years), Anacréon (three years), Antalo (three years), Antiochus (three years), Arlésienne (two years, sold in England), Artilleur (two years), Assouan (two years), Ballerine (three years), Banderolle (three years), *Barbillon* (two years), Barbillonne (three years, formerly Mi-Voie), Bar-le-Duc (two years), Beaumanoir (three years), Belernia (two years), Belle Princesse (two years), Bellone (four years), Bernac (three years), Bilbao (four years), Bivouac (three years), Bloater (late La Superga, sold in England in

1870, two years), Boreas (four years), *Bourgogne* (four years), *Brick* (aged, sold into England in 1869), Brigadier (two years, sold in England in 1870), Brisbane (two years), Cabotin (five years), Calvados (three years), Cambronne (five years), Cantate (four years), Cap Horn (two years, sold in England in 1870), Capitaliste (six years), Capsule (four years), Cardigan (three years), *Chassepot* (three years, sold in England in 1870), Chérubin (four years), *Chevreuse* (four years), Claudia (two years), Clearsight (three years), Clos Vougeot (four years), Clotaire (three years), Comédienne (two years), Congo (three years), Conquérant (three years), Contrebande (five years), Corrégidor (three years), Coucou (six years), Cramoisi (three years), Croisade (three years), Curaçoa (three years), Curieuse (five years), Deauville (two years), *Dutch Skater* (five years), Demi-Soleil (four years), Derviche (four years), Diomed (three years, formerly called Electeur), Dominante (two years, ran for the Middle Park Plate), *Don Carlos* (four years), *Eckmühl* (five years), Ecossaise (two years), Ella (three years), Enéide (three years), *Eole II.* (three years), Ermeline (two years), Eurotas (two years), Evohé (five years), Fanfaron (three years, by The Ranger), Fanfaron (two years, by Young Monarque), Fantôme (three years), Favori (three years, sold in England in 1870), *Fervacques* (aged, sold into England), *Fidélia* (five years), *Finisterre* (by Tournament, four years), Firefly (late Boston, five years), *Fleur de Péché* (three years), Fleuriste (four years), Florizel (two years, sold in England), Folie (three years), Framboise (three years, sold in England), Galante (two years), Gantelet (three years), Garde Mobile (three years), Gascogne (three years, sold in England), Gaston (five years), *Géant des Batailles* (six years), *Général* (three years), Gentleman (two years),

Gilberte (three years, sold in England), Giselle (two years), *Glaïeul* (five years), Golos (three years), Gondolier (six years), Gouache (four years), Gourbi (five years, sold in England), Gourmette (two years), Gouvieux (two years, sold in England), Graziella (two years), Guzman (two years), Hamlet (late Géronte, two years, sold in England), Harriette (or Henriette, four years, by Scamandre and Scythia), Haydée (three years), *Henri IV.* (two years, son of the celebrated La Toucques), *Henry* (three years, by Monarque and Miss Ion), Héraut d'Armes (four years, sold in England), *Il Maestro* (two years, sold in England), Industry (late Eliza, three years, sold in England), *Jarnac* (four years, sold in England), Jarnicoton II. (three years), Jeannot (two years), Julien (three years), Kirghiz (three years, by Argonaut and No*r*a, not No*v*a), L'Ingénue (two years), La Baronne (three years), *La Calonne* (four years, daughter of the celebrated La Toucques), La Cocarde (three years), La Hague (two years), La Nuit (two years), La Quarantine (two years), La Risle (four years), La Verzée (three years), *Lady Henriette* (six years, sold in England), Laodice (three years), Le Batave (four years), Le Régent (two years), Le Ténor (three years), *Luisette* (four years), Mâcon (two years, sold in England), Mademoiselle de Birague (three years, sold in England), Mademoiselle de Magny (four years), Mademoiselle de Mailloc (three years), Mademoiselle de Saint-Igny (five years), Magdala (three years, sold in England in 1870), Manille (three years), Manlius (four years), Matelot (five years, sold in England), Mathilde (three years), Méléurge (three years, sold in England), Merlerault (two years, sold in England), *Miss Hervine* (four years), Moissonneuse (two years), Mons. le Prince (three years), Monseigneur (four years),

M. LEFÈVRE'S CAMPAIGN OF 1871

Mons. de Camors (three years, sold in England in 1870), Montabart (three years), *Mortemer* (six years), Napolitain (two years), *Nélusko* (six years), Némo (two years), Neptunus (four years), New York (three years), Nicanor (three years), Nita (six years), Oakley (late Procureur, three years, sold in England), Ophélia (afterwards Miss Frances, three years), Orthodoxe (three years), *Ouragan II.* (six years), Pamoison (three years, sold in England), Parmesan (by Ventre Saint-Gris and Dame d'Honneur, two years, sold in England in 1870), Paulus (three years, sold in 1871), Pensée (three years, sold in England in 1870), Pistole (four years) Postérité (three years), Premier Argonaut (three years, sold in England in 1870), Proserpine (four years), Régane (two years), *Reine* (two years), Reugny (three years), *Rerigny* (two years), *Roquefort* (two years), Sacripant (five years), Sans-Souci (three years), Satanstoë (four years), Satrape (three years), *Seul* (two years), Somno (three years), *Sornette* (four years), Soteira (four years), Spécifique (five years), Suzanne (five years, sold in England), Sylla (four years, sold in England), Talisman (three years), Tarantelle (four years), Tasman (half-brother to Dutch Skater, three years), Theodoros (three years, sold in England), Toucques (three years, daughter of the celebrated La Toucques), Tourbillon (by Fort-à-bras, three years, sold in England), *Turquoise* (three years), *Véranda* (three years), Vicksburg (two years), Victoire (two years, sold in England), Vigogne (three years), Wasp (three years), Yes (three years), and a host of others chiefly known in hurdle races and steeple-chases, such as Alcibiade, Astrolabe, Chantilly, Charleville, Colère, Cristal, Gertrude, Grisette, Guiscard, Honolulu, La Martinière, Le Mancenillier, Loustic, Manolo, Marin, Massinissa, Mons. Louis, Montgoubert, Montrachet, Navarette

Nonant, *Prétentaine II.*, Printanier, Pythonisse, *Réalité*, Souvenance, Turenne, and *Valentino*, some of which animals ran in the Liverpool Grand National of 1871.

The names of the horses that at some time or other distinguished themselves on the flat have been printed in italics; and of the French horses that ran and were sold in England in 1870 some have been noted, but it was impossible to specify every case of sale, whilst, on the other hand, many that were sold did not run, if at all, until later (as in the notable case of Salvanos—by Dollar and Sauvagine—who was sold to Mr. Joseph Radcliff in 1870, did not run in 1871, and won the Cesarewitch, worth 1,515*l.*, in a canter in 1872). The French, however, 'jumped off with the lead' in 1871, for they won the very first race of the year (at Lincoln) with Curaçoa; but the good omen was somewhat delusive.

It goes without saying that there was no Grand Prix de Paris to run for in 1871; and so it was in England alone that the best French and English horses could 'try conclusions.' That year the 'Frenchmen,' notwithstanding the unusually large number (nearly 200) that ran on the flat in England, were not very successful, not nearly so successful as they were to be the next year. The Duke of Hamilton was in a unique position; for, though his best horses were 'bred in France,' he was not, as an Englishman, prevented by his feelings from running them at Baden-Baden, and there, accordingly, he picked up the Prix de la Ville and the Grand Prix de Bade (which had been an annual income to the French) with Monseigneur, the Prix du Rhin with Orthodoxe, the Prix d'Eberstein with Barbillonne, the Prix des Dames with Wasp, and so on.

In England M. Lefèvre was as yet scarcely 'in the saddle;' but he had added to the horses he had purchased from Count F. de Lagrange certain others, English and French, notably among the latter Dutch Skater, Verdure, and Eole II., and with their help he did more than respectably. The horses, moreover, he had purchased from the Count included Henry (by Monarque and Miss Ion), a great horse, as well as Reine (by Monarque and Fille de l'Air), who was to win both the One Thousand and the Oaks the next year.

It has been calculated that (if flat races and hurdle races, &c., be combined) in 1871 'more than 220 French-bred horses ran in England and won more than 180 (out of some 1,200) events, amounting in value to more than 570,000 francs, or 22,800*l*.,' the lion's share of which, no doubt, fell to ' Mr. T. Lombard '—that is, M Lefèvre.

In the English 'classic' races of 1871 (the Two Thousand, One Thousand, Derby, Oaks, and St. Leger) the 'Frenchmen' were represented by M. H. Delamarre's Clotaire (by Vermout and Lady Clocklo), the Duke of Hamilton's Général (a great favourite at one time for both Two Thousand and Derby, by Monarque and Tolla), and Mr. H. Jennings's Enéide (by W. Australian and Tartarie), and of these none made a better show than Général, fourth for the St. Leger. But this was no more or less than was to be expected in what was called ' the Baron's year '—that is, the year in which the ' English ' Baron Rothschild won the Derby with Favonius, the One Thousand, Oaks, and Leger with Hannah, and the Cesarewitch with Corisande.

The ' Frenchmen ' that did best were as follows :—

1. M. Lefèvre's Mortemer (won the Ascot Gold Cup, worth 1,030*l*. ; second with 9 st. 3 lbs. to Glenlivat, four years, 6 st. 2 lbs., for the Chester Cup ; and third to Shannon and Favonius for the Goodwood Cup) ; Henry

(won the Ascot Derby of 925*l.*, the Newmarket Derby of 640*l.*, and was first favourite but unplaced for the Cambridgeshire); Verdure (won the Derby Trial Plate at Newmarket of 200*l.*; was second to Mortemer for the Ascot Cup; won the Queen's Plate of 105*l.* at Newmarket July; won the Newmarket Oaks of 690*l.*, beating Hannah at a difference of 7 lbs.; and won the Lincoln Autumn Handicap of 345*l.*); Dutch Skater (won the Queen's Plate of 105*l.* at Newmarket Craven; w.o. for 100*l.* at the First Spring; won the Queen's Plate of 105*l.* at Hampton, at Chelmsford, at Lewes, at Egham, and at York [w.o.]); Eole II. (w.o. for 150*l.* at Newmarket Craven; won a plate of 100*l.* at the First Spring; won the Queen's Plate of 105*l.* at Ipswich, at Newmarket First October, and at Lincoln); Alaric ('off colour,' but won a plate of 50*l.* at Newmarket First Spring, A.F.); Luisette (won a subscription selling plate of 50*l.* at Newmarket Craven; won a selling sweepstakes of 120*l.* at Newmarket First October, and 60*l.* for two other small events; won the Leicestershire Handicap of 96*l.* and the Queen's Plate at Leicester of 105*l.*), and Manille (won the Trial Handicap Plate of 100*l.* at Epsom Spring and the Queen's Plate at Windsor, beating Sornette) = 5,706*l.*

2. M. Delamarre's Véranda (ran a dead heat with Vulcan for the Lincolnshire Handicap and divided 1,240*l.*), Clotaire (won the Blankney Stakes of 340*l.*), Clos Vougeot (won two small races worth about 90*l.*), Cramoisi (won the Stewards' Cup of 80*l.* at Hampton), and Vigogne (won the Duke of Richmond's Plate of 100*l.* at Goodwood) = 1,230*l.*

3. M. Lupin's Héraut d'Armes (won the Champagne Stakes of 74*l.* at Ayr), Le Ténor (won the Egham Stakes of 35*l.* and the Duke of Edinburgh's Cup of 80*l.*

at Egham), Neptunus (won 70*l*. and 50*l*. at Edinburgh), Pistole (won the Hornby Handicap of 95*l*. at Catterick Bridge) = 404*l*.

4. M. C. Laffitte's (Major Fridolin's) Finisterre (won the Ascot Plate of 1,050*l*.), Gourbi (won a handicap plate of 50*l*. at Newmarket First Spring, the Windsor Handicap of 120*l*., and the Visitors' Plate (handicap) of 200*l*. at Goodwood), Somno (won the Select Stakes of 175*l*. at Newmarket Second October), Sornette (won the Trial Stakes of 150*l*. at Epsom and the Queen's Plate of 105*l*., after a dead heat with Inquisition) = 1,850*l*.

5. Count de Montgomery's Calvados (won the Burton Welter Handicap Plate of 50*l*. at Richmond, Yorks, and the Liverpool Hunt Club Autumn Handicap of 66*l*.), Jarnac (won the Liverpool Spring Cup of 405*l*., the Liverpool Hunt Club Spring Handicap of 82*l*., the Scarborough Spring Handicap of 65*l*., and the Caledonian Handicap, Kelso, of 184*l*.), La Calonne (won the Glasgow Plate at York of 100*l*. and the Lincoln Plate of 50*l*.). La Risle (won the Wilton Handicap of 70*l*. at Manchester, the Grimston Plate of 90*l*. at Beverley as well as the Londesborough Plate of 55*l*., the Wynyard Handicap of 92*l*. at Stockton, the Croxteth Flying Stakes of 125*l*. and the Huntroyde Handicap of 115*l*. at Liverpool, and the Battlefield Handicap of 225*l*. at Shrewsbury), Mademoiselle de Mailloc (ran a dead heat with Field Marshal at Stockton for the Great Northern Leger and divided 315*l*.), and Postérité (won the Craven Stakes of 70*l*. at York Spring and the Corby Castle Handicap of 115*l*. at Carlisle) = 2,116*l*.

6. The Duke of Hamilton's (a French owner's, though an English as well as French Duke's) Almeneschès (won 100*l*. Plate at Goodwood), Barbillonne (won

the Castle Handicap of 230*l.* at Windsor), Eckmühl (won the Eton Handicap of 360*l.* at Windsor, the Beaudesert Welter Plate of 90*l.* at Lichfield, and the Birmingham Plate Handicap of 80*l.* at Sutton Park), and Monseigneur (won the Manchester Tradesmen's Cup of 520*l.*) = 1,380*l.*

7. M. P. Aumont's Graziella (won the Hinchingbrook Stakes of 325*l.* at Huntingdon), and Miss Hervine (won the Newcastle Handicap of 249*l.*) = 574*l.*

8. M. L. André's Chevreuse (won the Norfolk and Suffolk Handicap of 80*l.* at Great Yarmouth and the Aintree Handicap Plate of 50*l.* at Liverpool) = 130*l.*

9. M. A. Fould's Sylla (won the Cromwell Handicap Plate of 100*l.* at Huntingdon and the Hawkstone Welter of 185*l.* at Shrewsbury) = 285*l.*

10. Baron A. Schickler's Acide Prussique (won a plate of 45*l.* at Newmarket), Monsieur Le Prince (won a plate of 100*l.* at Newmarket), and Premier Argonaut (won a plate of 100*l.* at Epsom) = 245*l.*

These were the chief of the French gentlemen whose horses ran in England in 1871, and these were the chief winners among their horses, the whole amount accounted for being 13,286*l.* for ten owners and about forty horses, won on the flat alone, so that the calculation of 22,800*l.* for the 220 French horses that ran altogether in England in 1871, whether in French or English names, for French or English owners, is very likely to be near the mark, as the remainder of the horses that won would have been winners on a smaller scale. Of course some of the horses named above did not belong to their French owners all through the season, or even at the beginning of the season; but the point is that they were 'bred in France' and belonged at some time previous to 1871 to those owners.

The year 1872 saw racing once more in full swing upon the French courses, and consequently there was a good reason why fewer French owners and French horses should be found running in England. In point of fact the French horses running in England were fewer by a hundred or so, but they acquitted themselves, whether they were 'settlers' or only temporary sojourners in England, most admirably.

The winners of the principal French races were M. P. Aumont's Revigny (three years, winner of the French Derby and of the Poule d'Essai), the Duke of Hamilton's Little Agnes (three years, winner of the French Oaks and the Grande Poule des Produits), M. A. Lupin's Néthou (three years, winner of the Poule des Produits), M. H. Delamarre's Véranda (four years, winner of the Prix du Cadran) and Faublas (three years, winner of the Prix de Longchamps), M. C. J. Lefèvre's Henry (four years, winner of the Prix Rainbow), the Duke of Hamilton's Barbillon (three years, winner of the Prix Royal Oak), M. C. J. Lefèvre's Dutch Skater (six years, winner of the Prix Gladiateur), M. H. Delamarre's Clotaire (four years, winner of La Coupe at Paris), and, among the two-year-olds, M. A. Fould's Hydromel, M. A. Desvignes's Demi-Lune, M. C. Laffitte's (Major Fridolin's) Franc-Tireur, winners of the three principal 'Critériums,' and, memorable above all, M. C. J. Lefèvre's Flageolet, winner of the Prix de Deux Ans at Deauville.

As for the Grand Prix de Paris of 1872, it was a foregone conclusion for the 'perfidious' English, though they had but one horse running; but that horse was Cremorne, winner of the English Derby, one in a thousand, and after him it was vain for Barbillon (though winner of the Prix de Satory), and Reine (though winner of the One Thousand and of the English Oaks), and Berryer (though his experienced owner, Mr. Henry Jennings, may have considered him—not without reason—the best French horse of his year), and Revigny (winner of the French Derby), and Little Agnes (winner of the French Oaks), and Faublas (winner of the Prix de Longchamps) to put their best foot foremost. The Grand Prix was curious in one respect—that on its resuscitation it was won by the same gentleman (Mr. Henry Savile) who had won it with The Ranger in its first year of institution.

Of the French horses already mentioned there ran in England neither Revigny (though he had run at Newmarket the year before), nor Little Agnes (though belonging to an English duke), nor Néthou, nor Véranda (though she had shared the Lincolnshire Handicap with Vulcan the year before), nor Faublas, nor Barbillon, nor Clotaire, nor Berryer, nor Hydromel, nor Demi-Lune, nor Franc-Tireur, but only Henry, Dutch Skater, Reine, and Flageolet, who all did worshipfully.

Henry ran only once, it is true; but then he won the Ascot Cup against Favonius (a winner of the English Derby) and Hannah (a winner of the English Oaks and St. Leger), with 5 to 2 *on* Favonius. This was 'bouleversing' the 'Baron's year' with a vengeance.

Dutch Skater won seven races out of eleven, carrying off the Great Metropolitan (1,065*l.*), the Warwick Cup (230*l.*), the Doncaster Cup (300*l.*), in which, by the way, he defeated *a* Fisherman, and taking 'the balance' in Queen's Plates, like *the* Fisherman, son of Heron.

Reine ran only three times, but 'realised the stakes' (3,150*l.*) in the One Thousand and (4,175*l.*) in the Oaks. Her performance for the Queen's Plate won by Favonius at Newmarket, however, was a decided *faux pas*.

Yet one would have thought a 'Reine,' and a daughter of a 'Monarque,' had a sort of indefeasible claim to a 'Queen's' Plate.

Flageolet was beaten twice only out of seven attempts —fourth for the Middle Park Plate and second, 9 st. 2 lbs., for the Prendergast Stakes by a head to Andred, 8 st. 10 lbs., three lengths in front of Surinam, 9 st. 2 lbs., the winner of the Middle Park Plate. He won the Hopeful Stakes (650*l.*) at Newmarket First October, as well as the Rutland Stakes (330*l.*) and the Forlorn Stakes (400*l.*); the Burwell (370*l.*) at the Second October; and the Criterion (960*l.*), beating Paladin, Kaiser, and Surinam at the Houghton Meeting.

Of the French horses resident or visiting in England, besides those already specified, the most distinguished were Mr. Joseph Radcliff's Salvanos (by Dollar and Sauvagine), who won the Cesarewitch of 1,575*l.*; Mr. Beadman's Messager (by Gladiateur and Nuncia), who won the Great Northamptonshire Stakes of 685*l.*; Lord Wilton's Napolitain (by Hospodar and Sérénade), who won the Chesterfield Cup of 945*l.* at Goodwood; M. C. J. Lefèvre's Alaric (by Monarque and Liouba), 100*l.* at Lincoln, 100*l.* at Goodwood, and 290*l.* at Ayr; Mr. Gerard Sturt's Theodoros (by Monarque and Magenta), the Visitors' Plate of 340*l.* at Goodwood; M. C. J. Lefèvre's Chancellor (by Monitor II. and Queen of Diamonds), 100*l.* and 190*l.* at Brighton; Count de Montgomery's Mademoiselle de Mailloc (by Muscovite and Slapdash), the Corporation Stakes of 270*l.* at Doncaster and 105*l.* at Newmarket Second October); M. C. J. Lefèvre's Manille (by Orphelin and Didon), the Trial Stakes of 120*l.* and the Brownlow Plate of 50*l.* at Lincoln, and 100*l.* and 50*l.* at Newmarket Houghton; Mr. Mumford's Matelot (by Pretty Boy and Batwing), 50*l.* at

Lincoln, 35*l.* at West Drayton, 50*l.* at Chelmsford, and 50*l.* at Gravesend; Col. Carleton's Hamlet (by Rémus and Gertrude), Earl Spencer's Plate of 460*l.* at Northampton and the Shobdon Cup of 215*l.* at Shrewsbury; Mr. H. R. Ray's Sylla (by Rémus and Ségréenne) the Hylton Cup of 175*l.* at Liverpool, a plate of 50*l.* at Newmarket Craven, and the Johnstone Plate of 100*l.* at Lincoln Autumn; Lord Eglinton's Suzanne (by Tournament and Susannah) the Carlisle Spring Handicap of 75*l.* and the Manchester and Knutsford Subscription Cup of 90*l.*; Captain Sandeman's Fervacques (by Underhand and Slapdash) the Visitors' Plate of 100*l.* at Ascot; Mr. Ranny's Gascogne (by Ventre Saint-Gris and Arcadia) the Bushy Park Stakes of 90*l.* at Hampton, the Members' Plate of 35*l.* at Dover, the Shirley Stakes of 52*l.* at Scarborough, and the County Handicap of 225*l.* at Warwick; Count de Montgomery's La Risle (by Vermout and Whirl) the Bentinck Welter Handicap of 80*l.* at Liverpool and 95*l.* at Leamington; M. C. J. Lefèvre's Régane (by Vertugadin and Reine Blanche) the FitzWilliam Stakes of 190*l.* at Doncaster; M. C. J. Lefèvre's Eole II. (by West Australian and Noëlie), who ran only twice, the Claret Stakes of 400*l.* and the Queen's Plate at Newmarket Craven; M. C. J. Lefèvre's Verdure (by West Australian and Vermeille) the Queen's Plates at Epsom, Bedford, Leicester, and Lincoln (420*l.*); and M. C. J. Lefèvre's Luisette (by Zouave [son of The Baron] and Sylvia) the (Alexandra) Park Autumn Handicap of 240*l.* and a free handicap sweepstakes of 325*l.* at Newmarket Houghton.

Altogether it has been calculated that in the season of 1872 M. C. J. Lefèvre with twenty-one French horses (Montfort, Il Maestro, John, Dutch Skater, Sator, Alaric, Chérubin, Crépuscule, Henry, Puritain, Reine

Chancellor, Belzébuth, Faust, Manille, Flageolet, Régane, Eole II., Verdure, Luisette, and Moissonneur) won 16,345*l.* in stakes in England, and with sixteen English horses (Lighthouse, Tourbillon, Ravenshoe, Trombone, Guimauve, La Méprisée, Fez, Badsworth, Blenheim, Mannington, Drummond, Fifi, Negro, Barford, Houghton, and the 'resurrectionist' Vulcan) 7,109*l.*, making in all 23,454*l.*, and putting him quite or very nearly at the head of all the 'winning owners' in England, before even Mr. H. Savile, who with Cremorne's Derby and Grand Prix could sum up no more than about 22,465*l.* in stakes.

This was a feather in the cap of the French and a triumph for the 'tricolour' of 'Mr. T. Lombard,' who moreover (having already purchased Regalia in 1871) made this year some capital purchases of brood mares— to wit, Isoline for 100 gs., Feu-de-joie for 800 gs., and Araucaria for 1,300 gs.—for these mares were to be the dams respectively of Braconnier and Saint-Christophe, of Allumette (second to Camélia for the One Thousand), and of Camélia and Chamant. It should be noted, however, that Braconnier (by Caterer), Allumette (by Caterer), and Camélia (by Macaroni), foaled in 1873, really (though unborn) left England with their dams in 1872 and were only technically 'bred in France.'

In 1873 the principal 'French' winners in France were M. H. Delamarre's Boïard (three years, winner of the French Derby, of the Grand Prix de Paris, of the Poule des Produits, and of the Prix Royal Oak), M. H. Delamarre's Campêche (three years, winner of the French Oaks), M. P. Aumont's Revigny (four years, winner of the Prix du Cadran), M. A. Lupin's Absalon (three years, winner of the Prix de Longchamps), M. C. Laffitte's (Major Fridolin's) Sire (three years, winner of the Poule d'Essai), M. C. Laffitte's Franc-Tireur (winner of the Grande Poule des Produits), the Duke of Hamilton's Barbillon (four years, winner of La Coupe at Paris, of the Prix Rainbow, and of the Prix Gladiateur), and, among the two-year-olds, Mr. Henry Jennings's Vincent (by Le Petit Caporal), the Duc de FitzJames's Aurore (by Plutus), M. A. Lupin's Fidéline (by Dollar), winners of the three principal 'Critériums,' and M. A. Lupin's Perla (by Dollar), winner of the Prix de Deux Ans at Deauville.

In France M. H. Delamarre of course stood *facile princeps* among French owners; he had outdone himself and his triumphs of 1864 (when he won the French Derby with Bois-Roussel and the Grand Prix with Vermout), for he had added in this year 1873 the French Oaks to the other two great races. Moreover he had won a very notable Grand Prix with a very notable horse; for it is a curious fact that, just as Mr. H. Savile had won the first Grand Prix (in 1863) and the first renewal of it (in 1872, after 'les évènements'), so M. H. Delamarre, who had won the second Grand Prix (in 1864) with Vermout, beating Blair Athol (winner of the English Derby), won the second renewal (in 1873) with Boïard, beating Doncaster (another winner of the English Derby); and what is more remarkable is that Boïard, who defeated the winner of the English Derby in 1873, was a son of that Vermout who had beaten the winner of the English Derby in 1864, that in both cases the beaten winner of the English Derby was a son of the great Stockwell, and that those two beaten winners of the English Derby commanded the biggest prices ever paid for a thoroughbred sire—namely, 12,500 guineas for Blair Athol in 1872 and 14,000*l.* for Doncaster in 1874. Nor was Doncaster even second for the Grand Prix: he was beaten by another French horse, M. Lefèvre's Flageolet, so that M. Delamarre, having beaten both Flageolet and Doncaster, may be considered to have been 'cock of the walk' both in England and in France. What is very remarkable, again, is that Boïard, Flageolet, and Doncaster all ran for the Two Thousand, and yet none of the three obtained so much as a place.

Boïard's history is altogether strange and interesting. His dam was called La Bossue (by De Clare and Canezou), and her very name bewrays her. She was a 'cast-off,' accordingly, from Lord Derby's stud, and is said to have been sold into Hanover first of all, whence she found her way into M. H. Delamarre's stud at Bois-Roussel. He thought, no doubt, that a daughter of Canezou ought to be at least good enough to breed from, and so it turned out. But she was not lucky with Boston, Bombance and Boréal, her first produce registered in France in 1866, 1867, 1868. Next came Boa (by Vermout), foaled in 1869, but he died in 1871, about the time of 'les évènements.' In 1870, however, she threw Boïard, the best horse of his year, one of the best horses ever known either in England or France; and thus she did enough at one 'throw' to 'illustrate' herself and to honour the memory of her illustrious dam, Canezou. At the beginning, nevertheless, it looked as if La Bossue was to be as unfortunate almost with her son Boïard as she had been with Boa, and as she was afterwards with her daughter Bossette (by Patricien) and her son Boïador (own brother—but 'quantum mutatus ab illo!'—to Boïard); for a plaguy venomous insect (as they relate) gat hold upon him and bit him badly at two years of age, so that he could only run once (unsuccessfully) in that year and was like to have been 'spoilt' for ever. A similar mishap, it may be remembered, befell M. Lefèvre's Versigny at the same age (in 1879) and retarded her at her outset in life. Such little accidents are by no means uncommon : it is on record that the very distinguished English sire, Snake by name (sire of Mr. Metcalfe's Old Snake mare, that was the dam of Squirt, that was the sire of Marske, that was the sire of Eclipse), was bitten, or supposed to have been bitten, so badly in early life by some venomous creature (reptile or insect, snake or fly) that he could not be trained.

Of the chief French winners on French soil besides Boïard (who, as we have seen, did not ' come off' in the Two Thousand, and who was a bad second to Kaiser for the Newmarket Derby, his only two English races that year) there ran in England Revigny (a bad third to Cremorne and Flageolet for the Ascot Cup), Barbillon (unplaced for the Jockey Club Cup at Newmarket Houghton), and Vincent (beaten by his only opponent, Couronne de Fer, for the Prince of Wales's Stakes at Alexandra Park, where he won the Alexandra Stakes of 230*l.* in July, and unplaced for the Hinchingbrook Stakes and for the Milton Stakes at Huntingdon).

Of the other French horses that ran in England, whether belonging to French or English owners, the principal were (independently of the many that prosecuted the 'jumping business') Mr. Houldsworth's Alaric ; M. C. J. Lefèvre's Arrogant, Artilleur, Blanchette, Borély, Brillant, Clairvoyant, Combat, Eole II., Exilé (foaled in England, as the English Prince Charlie in France), Feu d'Amour, Flageolet, Frondeur, Jeanne la Folle, John, La Revanche, Luisette, Maimbville, Manille, Moissonneur, Novateur, Pacha, Planète, Poudrière, Régane, Reine, Réquisition, Résistance, Roquefort, Succès, Tambour, and Tendresse ; various other owners,

Andalouse, Androclès, Ann, Arsinoë, Baby, Bataillon, Bismarck, Borny, Brisbane, Calvados, Chancellor (once M. Lefèvre's), Comédienne, Comtesse, Coq de Bruyère, Christiane, Crocodile, Croisade, Faust, Fervacques (*nine years old*), Florizel, Framboise, Gascogne, Général, Henry IV., Il Maestro, Jarnac, La Risle, Lopez, Mamelouk, Mardi Gras, Méléurge, Mélusine, Merlerault, Myosotis, Napolitain, Northiam, Pensée, Pharaide, Premier Argonaut, Révolver, Salvestro, Sarchedon (ex-Jovial), Sucre d'Orge, Theodoros—some eighty or so in number—and above all Count de Juigné's and Prince d'Arenberg's (late M. P. Aumont's) Montargis (own brother to the ill-starred Revigny and himself of too short a life), who won the Cambridgeshire of 2,270*l*. (with forty to one against him) on October 21, 1871, following in the footsteps of his 'compatriot' Palestro (who won the great handicap in 1861) and showing a bright example which was to be followed by his 'compatriots' Peut-être, Jongleur, and Plaisanterie, who were to go and do likewise (and more also in the case of Plaisanterie, winner of the Cesarewitch as well) in 1874, 1877, and 1885.

For M. Lefèvre, in England, the year 1873 was as the preceding year, and still more abundant; for though it was 'Mr. Merry's year' (with Doncaster and Marie Stuart) in one sense in England (as it certainly was 'M. Delamarre's year' in France with Boïard and Campêche), yet M. Lefèvre stood first among 'winning owners' in England, with 25,913*l*. set down to him as the amount he won in sheer stakes, next to him coming Mr. Merry and Mr. Savile with from a third to a half less money. This is not to be wondered at when it appears that M. Lefèvre had rather more than fewer than a hundred animals *entered* (which does not always mean that as many as half of them *run*) for the races of 1873, to say nothing of those that ran for races requiring no previous entry of more than a few days. It is true that he did not win (as he had won the year before) the One Thousand and the Oaks, but he is credited by one of his compatriots with having made (in France and England together), by picking up here a little and there a little, as much as 756,000 francs, or 30,240*l.*, in stakes. That, however, would be little more than a drop in the ocean to an owner with so many horses in training. M. Lefèvre's horses were, of course, not all 'bred in France;' the following lists will show how he fared with his French and English horses respectively, or at least with the most notable of them.

Among those 'bred in France' were—

1. Flageolet (three years: won the Goodwood Cup of 470*l.*, beating two winners of the English Derby— his only opponents, Favonius and Cremorne, but a Cremorne with 'the edge off'—in a canter; the Grand Duke Michael Stakes of 600*l.*, beating another winner of the English Derby—Doncaster—into 'another street;' a Free Handicap Sweepstakes of 600*l.*, beating the reputed 'stayer' Thorn, his only opponent, and the Jockey Club Cup of 580*l.*, in a canter, both at Newmarket Houghton Meeting) = 2,250*l.*

2. Feu d'Amour (two years, beaten by a neck for the Doncaster Champagne Stakes; won—like Gladiateur—the Clearwell Stakes of 790*l.*, and—unlike Gladiateur, who was beaten therefor—the Prendergast Stakes of 1,200*l.*) = 1,990*l.*

3. Reine (four years; won the Prince of Wales's Stakes of 150*l.* at Newmarket First Spring and the Ascot Plate of 695*l.*) = 845*l.*

4. Poudrière (two years; won the Mottisfont Stakes of 330*l*. at Stockbridge; w.o. for the Sussex Stakes of 50*l*. at Lewes; won the Aylesford Stakes of 380*l*. at Warwick; w.o. for a sweepstakes of 120*l*. at Newmarket First October; w.o. for a sweepstakes of 50*l*. and won the Troy Stakes of 200*l*., beating Mr. Winkle, at the Houghton Meeting) = 1,130*l*.

5. Novateur (two years; ran only once and won the Burwell Stakes of 200*l*. at Newmarket Second October Meeting) = 200*l*.

6. Exilé (foaled in England, as our Prince Charlie was in France; two years; won a sweepstakes of 100*l*. at Newmarket July Meeting and the Fifth Biennial Stakes of 175*l*. at Nottingham) = 275*l*.

7. Régane (four years; won a handicap sweepstakes of 89*l*. at Warwick, and w.o. for the Beaudesert Welter Cup of 90*l*. at Lichfield) = 179*l*.

8. Frondeur (two years; won the Chesterfield Stakes of 55*l*. at Derby, a maiden plate of 100*l*. at Warwick, the Nursery Plate Handicap of 40*l*. at Leicester; w.o. for Granby Stakes of 180*l*. at Newmarket First October, for a sweepstakes of 30*l*. at the Second October, and for a sweepstakes of 50*l*. at the Houghton Meeting) = 455*l*.

9. Planète (three years; won a sweepstakes of 100*l*. at Newmarket Craven Meeting and the Coffee Room Stakes of 150*l*. at the First Spring) = 250*l*.

10. Eole II. (w.o. for a sweepstakes of 100*l*. at Newmarket First Spring and won Queen's Plate at the First October, beating Shannon, Lilian, and Thunderer) = 205*l*.

11. Borély (three years; won a plate of 50*l*. at Newmarket Craven Meeting) = 50*l*.

12. Combat (three years; won the Saltram Stakes,

handicap of 55*l.*, and the Queen's Plate at Plymouth) = 160*l.*

13. Jeanne la Folle (two years; only ran twice and won the Gopsal Park Stakes of 97*l.* at Leicester) = 97*l.*

14. Roquefort (six years; won the Carholme Handicap of 180*l.* and the Brownlow Handicap of 125*l.* at Lincoln, the Newcastle Plate at Nottingham of 100*l.*, a handicap plate of 140*l.* and another of 130*l.* at Newmarket Craven, the Duke of Richmond's Plate of 195*l.* at Goodwood, and w.o. for the Sussex Cup of 85*l.* at Brighton) = 955*l.*

15. John (three years; won the City Handicap of 220*l.* at Lincoln, w.o. for a handicap sweepstakes of 20*l.* at Newmarket Craven, and won a selling sweepstakes of 70*l.* at the Second October) = 310*l.*

16. Tambour (three years; won a sweepstakes of 100*l.* at Newmarket Second Spring, won the Rous Stakes of 60*l.* and the Derby of 350*l.* and w.o. for the Queen's Plate at Goodwood, and w.o. for the Champagne Stakes of 90*l.* at Brighton) = 705*l.*

Total . . . . . 10,056*l.*

Bred in England and purchased there were—

1. Blenheim (five years; won the Newmarket Spring Handicap of 300*l.* and a welter handicap of 230*l.* at the First October) = 530*l.*

2. Drummond (four years; w.o. for the Claret Stakes at Newmarket Craven of 300*l.*, won the Windsor Handicap of 630*l.* at Ascot, won the Chesterfield Cup of 705*l.* at Goodwood and the Stewards' Welter Plate of 200*l.* at Brighton) = 1,835*l.*

3. Ecossais (two years; won the New Stakes of 820*l.* at Ascot and the July Stakes of 1,670*l.*, as well as the Chesterfield of 1,110*l.*, running three times only—and winning every time) = 3,600*l.*

4. Miss Toto (two years; ran five times altogether and was unbeaten; won the Two-year-old Plate of 220*l.* at Newmarket First Spring, w.o. for the Spring Two-year-old Stakes of 300*l.* at the Second Spring, won the Fern Hill Stakes of 225*l.* at Ascot, won the Bretby Stakes of 450*l.* at Newmarket Second October, and won the Criterion Stakes of 1,190*l.*—with George Frederick among the beaten—at Newmarket Houghton) = 2,385*l.*

5. Trombone (three years; won the Town Plate Handicap of 90*l.* at Newmarket July, the Berkshire Cup of 185*l.* at Windsor, and the Select Stakes of 175*l.* at Newmarket Second October, beating the crack German horse Hochstapler) = 450*l.*

6. Houghton (five years; won the Newmarket Handicap of 955*l.*, the Bibury Stakes of 140*l.*, the Third Welter Handicap of 180*l.* at Newmarket July as well as the Suffolk Stakes of 140*l.*, and the Andover Stakes of 90*l.* at Stockbridge) = 1,505*l.*

7. Lighthouse (four years; won a handicap sweepstakes of 60*l.* at Newmarket Craven, and of 115*l.* at the First Spring, and a Queen's Plate at Winchester) = 280*l.*

8. Negro (three years; won the Fifteenth Newmarket Biennial of 568*l.*) = 568*l.*

9. Minister (two years; won a two-year-old plate of 50*l.* at Newmarket First Spring, a sweepstakes of 125*l.* at Newmarket Second October, and the Glasgow Stakes of 450*l.* at the Houghton Meeting, beating Atlantic by a head) = 625*l.*

10. Miss Buckland (three years; won the Queen's Plate at Leicester) = 105*l.*

11. La Coureuse (English, like Ecossais, for all the Frenchiness of their names; two years; won the Lavant Stakes of 700*l.* and a maiden plate of 100*l.* at Good-

wood, the Corporation Stakes of 110*l.* and the Bevendean Stakes of 130*l.* at Brighton, and a sweepstakes of 600*l.* at Newmarket Second October, winning five times out of seven attempts) = 1,640*l.*

12. Laird of Holywell (three years; won the Twentieth Triennial of 259*l.* at Ascot) = 259*l.*

13. Tourbillon (three years, another ' Englishman ' with a French name; won the Fifteenth Sale Stakes of 300*l.* at Newmarket Craven, besides walking over for a sweepstakes of 250*l.*; won the Trial Selling Stakes of 80*l.* at the First October and also a handicap sweepstakes of 140*l.*) = 770*l.*

14. Régal (two years; won the Strafford Stakes of 180*l.* at Goodwood and [w.o.] the Forlorn Stakes of 200*l.* at Newmarket First October Meeting) = 380*l.*

15. La Jeunesse (two years, another of the English lot with French names; won a selling sweepstakes of 70*l.* at Newmarket First Spring, and was claimed by that excellent judge Mr. Matthew Dawson) = 70*l.*

16. Minette (two years, another of the French-named ' Englishers;' won a selling sweepstakes of 55*l.* at Newmarket July Meeting and another of 60*l.*, and another at Goodwood of 130*l.*, after which she left M. Lefèvre by sale) = 245*l.*

Total	15,247*l.*
Total for French horses . .	10,056*l.*
Grand total	25,303*l.*

Of course M. Lefèvre had other horses that ran and won occasionally, and their ' scores ' would soon bring this grand total up to the 25,913*l.* ascribed to him in the records of the day.

The year 1873, then, was a great year for France, with Boïard and Flageolet (the latter, however, never a match for the former, in their own country especially) at home, and with M. Lefèvre picking up English gold and silver abroad. France had beaten England in the Grand Prix, in the Goodwood Cup, and in the Cambridgeshire, and might reasonably claim to have the best horse (three-year-old) of the year, as well as two or three French horses (with Feu d'Amour 'coming on') as good as any two or three English. Among these, however, cannot be numbered Combat, though he is said to have been the best colt (at any rate up to his date) ever begotten by the great Gladiateur; he certainly ran third to Kaiser and Gang Forward for the Prince of Wales's Stakes at Ascot, but it was a bad third, and they both carried 9 st. 1 lb. to his 8 st. 4 lbs.

The year 1874 was a notable period in the history of French horse-racing, though it was not very glorious for French horse-breeding at home or abroad as regarded the three-year-olds (the specially remarked age in each year), or for French owners in England, whether with the French or English horses owned by France's indomitable representative M. Lefèvre. He was thoroughly unfortunate; Feu d'Amour went the way of Général, and Ecossais and Miss Toto did not 'come off.'

But let us commence, as usual, with a list of the French 'cracks' at home.

They were M. Edouard Fould's Saltarelle (three years, winner of the French Derby), M. P. Aumont's Destinée (three years, winner of the French Oaks after a dead heat with M. A. Lupin's Perla), M. C. J. Lefèvre's Novateur (three years, winner of the Poule d'Essai), Major Fridolin's (M. Charles Laffite's) Sabre (three years, winner of the Grande Poule des Produits), M.

C. J. Lefèvre's Succès (three years, winner of the Prix de Longchamps), M. Fould's Mignonette (three years, winner of the Prix Royal Oak), M. H. Delamarre's Boïard (four years, winner of the Prix du Cadran and of the Prix Rainbow), Count de Juigné's Christiania (four years, winner of the Prix Gladiateur), and among the two-year-olds M. P. Aumont's Soupçon, M. Delâtre's Dictature, Baron A. Schickler's Perplexe, winners of the three principal 'Critériums,' and Major Fridolin's Macaron (winner of the Prix de Deux Ans at Deauville).

As for the Grand Prix de Paris, the race for it was humiliating to the French, since, though George Frederick and Apology and Atlantic and Couronne de Fer were not in the way, any one of them, French owners could produce nothing able to beat Mr. R. Marshall's very moderate 'Englishman' Trent, to whom even Saltarelle could only get second. This looks very much as if the French three-year-olds of 1874 were decidedly poor; and the suspicion is confirmed by the significant fact that Destinée (who won both the French Oaks and the Poule des Produits, now called the Prix Daru, but did not run for the Grand Prix) was the only three-year-old that won more than one of the most important races assigned to her age. This equal distribution is generally, though not always, a sign of 'a weak year.'

Of these French 'cracks' there ran in England Saltarelle (unplaced for the Cesarewitch), Novateur (unplaced for the Stewards' Cup but won the Racing Stakes of 250*l.* from his only opponent, Volturno, at Goodwood; was a poor second to Modena for the Stewards' Cup, handicap, at Brighton; won the Grand Duke Michael Stakes of 650*l.* in great style from his only opponent, Leolinus, at Newmarket First October; was unplaced for the Cambridgeshire and for a free handicap sweepstakes at the Houghton Meeting, and there also was easily beaten by Prince Charlie with Montargis to make a third for the All-aged Stakes), Sabre (unplaced for the All-aged Trial Selling Stakes at Newmarket Houghton), Mignonette (unplaced for the Cambridgeshire), Boïard (set the seal to his fame by winning in splendid fashion the Ascot Cup, with Flageolet and Doncaster running a dead heat behind him in front of such ' cracks' as Gang Forward, Marie Stuart, and Kaiser, but was most unexpectedly beaten [four years, 9 st. 5 lbs.] by King Lud [five years, 9 st. 6 lbs.] for the Alexandra Plate), Christiania (an unsuccessful candidate for the Queen's Plate and for the Jockey Club Cup at Newmarket), and Perplexe (whose chance of the Middle Park Plate was correctly estimated at about 40 to 1).

Of the other French horses that ran in England it has already been stated that the promising Feu d'Amour (unplaced for the St. Leger) had gone all to pieces. Then there was Flageolet, M. Lefèvre's pride; if he went over to his own country (where he was always unfortunate—where at any rate he was often unsuccessful) it was only to be beaten by Boïard, and in England (though he won the Claret Stakes at Newmarket against Gang Forward and Negro) he could do no better than make a dead heat with Doncaster for second in the Ascot Cup, and ran a bad third for the Alexandra Plate, in both cases having the tail of the said Boïard to contemplate. Not a single genuine 'Frenchman' (out of the score or so that might have carried the colours of M. Lefèvre, and out of the few entered by other French owners) made a decent bid

P

for the Two Thousand (for which M. Adolphe Fould's Vincent ran), or for the One Thousand (for which not a single 'Frenchie' ran), or for the Derby (to which the same remark applies), or for the Oaks (same remark again), or for the St. Leger (for which both Feu d'Amour and Boulet ran, but could not see the way Apology went). English horses, indeed, M. Lefèvre did run for those races, and singularly unlucky he was with them: third—but a bad third—for the Two Thousand with Ecossais (a hot favourite, and supposed to be the 'moral'—which appears to be a corruption of 'model' in the general sense of 'image'—of his sire, Blair Athol); second by half a length with La Coureuse for the One Thousand, and second with Miss Toto for the Oaks. This was bad luck enough for tearing of hair. Nor was there much consolation for M. Lefèvre (save in his capacity of compatriot) in the victories won by M. de Caumont la Force's Aurore in the Great Eastern Handicap at Newmarket, and by M. P. Aumont's Peut-être in the Cambridgeshire, with the big field of forty-two runners, as well as by M. H. Delamarre's great horse Boïard in the race for the Ascot Cup, as already recorded. And, as Boïard succumbed to King Lud (not dishonourably, however) in the race for the Alexandra Plate, it may be said that the 'Frenchmen' did not make much of their English campaign of 1874, but narrowly escaped defeat all along the line. It is not wonderful, then, if we find that M. Lefèvre stood only third (but still with the respectable sum of 14,624*l.*) to Lord Falmouth (15,775*l.*) and the Rev. Mr. 'Launde' (15,275*l.*) among the 'winning owners' of 1874 in England, especially as the formidable Count F. de Lagrange had once more come upon the scene and already taken a 'place' among the winning owners (with 4,525*l*.)

That reappearance was one of the most notable events of the Turf in 1874, though its full effects were not to be seen till MM. de Lagrange and Lefèvre joined forces and formed what has been called 'the fusion'—another 'Big Stable' after the Nivière-Lagrange pattern. The 'fusion' was rendered easy, if not inevitable, by the arrangements which had been made at the time when (as already mentioned) M. Lefèvre took over Count de Lagrange's stable (but not breeding stud) bodily or nearly so on the eve or at the commencement of 'les évènements.' After that M. Lefèvre took the place which had been won by Count F. de Lagrange and held it until the Count's colours reappeared in 1874; and that reappearance, if there be no mistake, dated (at any rate in France) from the day upon which Frondeur carried the once familiar 'blue, red sleeves and cap' at Paris Autumn Meeting, though no doubt the 'Lagrange-Lefèvre' horses had become a little 'mixed,' so that it is in some cases difficult to distinguish 't'other from which' and assign every runner to the proper owner.'

And now, ere we pass on to 1875, attention must be drawn to a deed of daring on the part of the French: they matched their horse Peut-être (three years, 7 st. 11 lbs., car. 7 st. 12 lbs.) to run the celebrated Prince Charlie (foaled in France, by the way; five years, 8 st. 10 lbs.) over Rowley's mile. This was a match worthy of the intrepid French 'sapeur' to whom 'nothing is sacred.' Here was Prince Charlie, who, though only a prince in his own right, had won the title of 'King of the T.Y.C.,' whom Drummond, and Blenheim, and Chopette, and Tangible, and Vulcan, all the 'flyers' and 'resurrectionists' of the day, had been trying for two years (generally without success) to 'extend,' and who had lost only one event out of eighteen; and here were the dauntless descendants of Vercingétorix offering to match against him a horse that was contemptuously styled a (comparatively) very small 'pertater.' It is true the match was over Rowley's mile—1 mile 17 yards—instead of the T.Y.C., but that is the very course over which 'the Prince,' roarer though he was, had won the Two Thousand against such a 'clipper' as Cremorne. Let Clio—muse of history—relate what was the fate of 'Pertater:' he was beaten 'in a canter.'

We have now arrived at the year 1875, when 'the fusion' was a fully accomplished fact, when Lagrange and Lefèvre, as formerly Lagrange and Nivière, had united their hosts, when once more a 'Big Stable,' or even a 'Bigger Stable,' threatened to sweep off everything on the 'hippodromes' of fair France and on the racecourses of perfidious Albion.

But, once more, it was not to be. Neither in France nor in England was 'the fusion' irresistible in 1875.

In that year the French 'cracks' at home were M. Lupin's Salvator (three years, winner of the French Derby and of the Grand Prix de Paris), M. Delâtre's Tyrolienne (three years, winner of the French Oaks, after a dead heat with Almanza), M. Lupin's Saint-Cyr (three years, winner of the Poule d'Essai and of the Prix de Longchamps), M. Lupin's Almanza (three years; ran a dead heat with Tyrolienne for the French Oaks, and won the Poule des Produits, now called Prix Daru, and the Grande Poule des Produits), Mr. Davis's Perplexe (three years, winner of the Prix Royal Oak), M. H. Delamarre's Boïard (five years, winner of the Prix

Rainbow), M. Fould's Saltarelle (four years, winner of the Prix du Cadran), M. P. Aumont's Figaro II. (four years, winner of the Prix Gladiateur), and among the two-year-olds M. H. Delamarre's Marmot, M. de la Charme's Volage II., Count de Juigné's Jonquille, winners of the three principal 'Critériums,' and M. Staub's (Haras de Lonray's) Le Drôle, winner of the Prix de Deux Ans at Deauville.

Evidently, then, in France it was M. A. Lupin's year with his Salvator, Saint-Cyr, and Almanza—all three, be it remarked, boasting for their sire that excellent horse Dollar, son of The Flying Dutchman.

Of the Grand Prix, won by Salvator, it should be observed that the result was a triumph for the French, as Camballo (winner of the Two Thousand) and Claremont (second for the Derby) made up with Seymour the tale of the English horses that ran; and not one of them obtained a place. Had Galopin been there it might have been different; but, for one or other of the usual reasons (want of nomination or something else), he could not or did not run. And then, *en revanche*, Salvator was amiss and could not run for the Doncaster St. Leger, for which Galopin was not entered. And so it happened, as it so often happens, that Salvator and Galopin, the two best horses of their year, never 'tried conclusions;' and the Doncaster St. Leger fell to the very inferior Craig Millar. Howbeit Salvator did not start favourite for the international race; that post was occupied by the excellent little horse Nougat, belonging to the Lagrange-Lefèvre 'fusion;' and yet Nougat had but run a dead heat in the French Derby with Saint-Cyr for second place behind Salvator.

Of the French 'cracks' mentioned there ran in England Saint-Cyr (unplaced for the St. Leger), Per-

plexe (unplaced for the Prince of Wales's Stakes at
Ascot and a bad third for the Cesarewitch), Figaro II.
(unplaced for the Alexandra Plate at Ascot and for the
Cesarewitch, second by a head to Louise Victoria for
the Queen's Plate at Newmarket, unplaced for the
Cambridgeshire, and beaten—after a dead heat—by
Lily Agnes for the Queen's Plate at Lincoln), Nougat
(third to Doncaster and Aventurière for the Ascot Cup,
which was won, however, in a canter by six lengths; a
bad third to Louise-Victoria and Figaro II. for the
Queen's Plate at Newmarket; unplaced for the Cambridgeshire, third to Carnelion and Balfe for a free
handicap sweepstakes, and unplaced for the Jockey
Club Cup, also won by Carnelion, at the Houghton
Meeting), and that is all. So that neither the French
in general nor the Lagrange-Lefèvre 'fusion' in particular won much distinction in their English campaign;
although, but for his being 'amiss,' Salvator would
have been pretty sure of the St. Leger.

Opportunity may here be taken of remarking that
Salvator, so highly was he thought of, was hired for a
while to stand at the famous Neasham Hall stud in
England and became the sire of the Duke of Hamilton's
Ossian, winner of the St. Leger in 1883. Of course M.
Lupin stood *facile princeps* among French 'winning
owners.'

Howbeit the 'fusion' was not altogether unsuccessful in England, inasmuch as the partners are placed high
among the 'winning owners' of 1875, with nearly
10,000*l.* to their credit, a small amount however compared with the 21,152*l.* assigned to Lord Falmouth, who
was No. 1. The 'fusion' owed their position chiefly to
Allumette (two years; won the Stanley Stakes of 325*l.* at
Epsom, the Exeter Stakes of 560*l.* at Newmarket July,

and the Brighton Club Two-year-old Stakes of 125*l*. = 1,010*l*.), to Camélia (two years; won a sweepstakes of 1,400*l*. at Goodwood and the Corporation Stakes of 465*l*. at Brighton=1,865*l*.), and to Monsieur de Fligny (two years; won the Lavant Stakes of 830*l*., the Findon Stakes of 380*l*., and the Nursery Stakes of 260*l*. at Goodwood = 1,470*l*.) among their French-bred animals (though Allumette and Camélia were to all but technical intents and purposes as English as Caterer and Macaroni, their sires, or as Feu-de-joie and Araucaria, their dams), and among their English-bred animals, to Miss Toto (four years; won the Claret Stakes of 800*l*. at Newmarket Craven Meeting, and w.o. for a sweepstakes of 250*l*. at Goodwood=1,050*l*.)=5,395*l*. for the four.

About ninety other French-bred animals ran on the flat in England that year; the most noticeable were Artilleur (six years), *Augusta* (two years), Bernardet (three years), Bijou (two years), Brodick (two years), Boulet (four years), *Braconnier* (two years), Bragance (four years), Calvados (aged), *Camembert* (two years), Chancellor (five years), *Charivari* (two years), Chimène (two years), Christiane (four years), Colchique (three years), *Commandeur* (two years), *Confiance* (three years), *Conseil* (four years), *Damoiseau* (four years), *Dictature* (three years), Eclair (two years), Eclipse II. (two years), Empress Eugénie (four years), *Enchanteur II.* (five years), *Enguerrande* (two years), Fairfax (three years), Feu d'Amour (four years), *Figaro II.* (four years), Fleurange (three years), Fortunio (two years), Framboise (aged), Frondeur (four years), Garde Noble (two years), *Gavarni* (two years), Golden Pippin (two years), *Heurtebise* (two years, third for the Middle Park Plate), Jarnac (aged), John (five years), *Jonville* (two years), Kate II. (three years), Kermesse (two years), La Gelée (four years), *La Sauteuse* (three years), *La Seine* (two years), Laurier (three years), Le Champis (six years), Léonide (two years), *Lina* (two years), Locomotive (three years), *Lollipop* (two years), Macadam (three years), Maravilla (three years), Marigny (three years), *Marion Delorme* (two years), Mercury (two years), *Montargis* (five years), *Myosotis* (aged), *Papillon* (two years), *Parempuyre* (three years), Patagon (two years), *Peau d'Ane* (three years), *Peut-être* (four years), Pluton (two years), Poudrière (four years), *Premier Mai* (four years), *Punch* (three years), Puysaleine (four years), *Rabagas II.* (three years), Récalcitrant (three years), *Régalade* (three years), *Roquefort* (aged), Rosette (two years), Roussillon (two years), *Saint-Léger* (three years), Satisfaction (three years), Suzette (two years), Tamerlan II. (two years), Vaillance (two years), and *Wild Tommy* (two years), of which those that obtained more or less reputation at some time or other, whether for sound or unsound reasons, in their own country or in England, have their names printed in italics.

Let us now pass on to the year 1876, which is one of the most notable, if not the very notablest, in the whole history of horse-racing in France—partly for what was popularly known as 'the De Goncourt fraud,' and partly because in this year the long-smouldering discontent at the succession of French horses upon the English Turf flamed forth in earnest, accompanied by a loud roar for 'reciprocity.' Perhaps it was merely by a happy accident of involuntary prophecy and unintentional significance that the filly of Seesaw and Wild Cherry, foaled in 1873, had been named Reciprocity; but, whether or no, the claim had for some time been attracting attention, and the propriety of establishing it had been canvassed, as will be noticed hereafter.

CHAPTER XI.

FROM THE HOWL FOR 'RECIPROCITY' TO THE PRESENT DAY.

In 1876 the French 'cracks' at home were Baron de Rothschild's Kilt (three years, winner of the French Derby and of the Prix Royal Oak), M. Fould's Mondaine (three years, winner of the French Oaks), M. A. Lupin's Enguerrande (three years, winner of the Poule d'Essai), Count F. de Lagrange's Braconnier (three years, winner of the Poule des Produits—now Prix Daru —and of the Grande Poule des Produits), M. H. Delamarre's Filoselle (three years, winner of the Prix de Longchamps), M. A. Lupin's Saint-Cyr (four years, winner of the Prix du Cadran), Count F. de Lagrange's Nougat (four years, winner of the Prix Rainbow, of La Coupe at Paris, and of the Prix Gladiateur), and among the two-year-olds Count G. de Juigné's Charivari II. (by Capitaliste), M. J. Prat's Faisane and Count G. de Juigné's Jongleur, winners of the three principal 'Critériums,' and M. A. Lupin's Astrée, winner of the Prix de Deux Ans at Deauville.

The race for the Grand Prix was very remarkable. Neither French nor English could claim the winner, which nevertheless was a 'foreigner.' There was not a single competitor 'bred in England' among the eleven starters; and the winner, Kisbér, was 'bred in

Hungary.' Moreover Kisbér had won the English Derby; so that the British lion was very sore indeed and roared aloud for 'reciprocity' or something to save him from being skinned alive by these 'furriners.' Howbeit Kisbér was really not much more purely Hungarian than Braconnier and Camélia were purely French, for both his sire, Buccaneer, and his dam, Mineral, were importations from England, and the latter had been but a year or fifteen months in Hungary when her colt of 1873 was foaled. So that, as far as mere credit due to the breeder was concerned, the British lion could not consider that his tail had been trodden upon much.

Well, of the French 'cracks' mentioned there ran in England in 1876 Kilt (third—and a bad third—to Charon and to the nondescript Jester for the Brighton Cup), Enguerrande (ran a dead heat for the Oaks and divided with Count F. de Lagrange's Camélia, 2,150*l.* apiece), Braconnier (giving up, as it was thought, the substance of the French Derby for the shadow of the English, ran unplaced—like Petrarch!—for the great race at Epsom, unplaced for the Cesarewitch and the Cambridgeshire, and won the Jockey Club Cup of 650*l.*, beating Nougat), Filoselle (unplaced behind her 'compatriotes' for the Oaks), Nougat (unplaced for the Jockey Club Cup), and Jongleur (ran once and won the Criterion Stakes of 940*l.*, beating his 'compatriot' Verneuil, second, and the Hungarian 'Voltella colt,' a bad third, so that no English competitor—not even the high-priced Sidonia, for whom the ridiculous sum of 2,400 guineas was paid as a yearling—could get so much as a place behind three 'owdacious furriners' in the truly British Criterion Stakes at the home of British horse-racing).

No wonder the British lion gave another howl of anguish and another roar of indignation. And when, at the end of the season, he 'totted up' the insults he had been obliged to pocket and the money of his that had been pocketed by the foreigner, he found the account to stand somewhat as follows:

The Lagrange-Lefèvre 'fusion' were credited with 17,650*l*. and stood at the head of the 'winning owners' on the English Turf, the second place being assigned to Lord Rosebery with 13,190*l*., and only the third, instead of the former first, to my Lord Falmouth with his 21,152*l*. reduced to a paltry 10,000*l*., much the same as the 'fusion' had won the year before.

Entering a little more into particulars, the British lion observed that the French horses, 'cracks' or not, that had run in England were, as nearly as he could make out, between ninety and a hundred, as follows: Adrienne (two years), *Allumette* (three years), Artilleur (aged), Augusta (three years), *Babylas* (six years), Basquine (three years), *Bernardet* (four years), Biéville (five years), Blanchette (five years), *Braconnier* (three years), Bragance (five years), *Camélia* (three years), Camembert (three years), Chaffinch (two years), *Chamant* (two years), Commandeur (three years), *Conseil* (five years), Courtomer (four years), Crépuscule (six years), Damoiseau (five years), Docteur (three years), Dogskin (two years), Doucereuse (two years), Echanson (two years), Emma Jane (three years), *Enguerrande* (three years), Fileuse (two years), Filoselle (three years), Fleurange (four years), Framboise (aged), Frondeur (five years), Fumoux (two years), *Gavarni* (three years), Golden Drop (two years), Golden Pippin (three years), Guéménée (two years), Hallate (two years), Heurtebise (three years), Jeannette (two years), *Jongleur* (two years),

Jonquille (three years), *Jonville* (three years), Jujube (two years), Kilt (three years), La Sauteuse (four years), *La Seine* (three years), *Laurier* (four years), Le Duc (two years), Léontine (two years), *Léopold* (two years), Lina (three years), *Lollipop* (three years), *Macadam* (four years), Mademoiselle (two years), Margote (four years), Marguillier (two years), Merry Agnes (two years), Monsieur de Fligny (three years), Moulin (three years), *Myosotis* (aged), Muguet (two years), Napolitain (aged), Nougat (four years), Pagnotte (two years), Patagon (three years), *Paysanne* (three years), Pearl Drop (three years), Pensacola (four years), Pivonnet (two years), *Plaisante* (two years), *Pluton* (three years), Premier Mai (five years), *Prophète* (three years), Purple (two years), Rabagas II. (four years), *Régalade* (four years), Richmond (two years), Rigoletto (two years), Rivalité (two years), *Roquefort* (aged), Saint-Christophe (two years), *Satisfaction* (four years), *Sugarloaf* (two years), *Suzette* (three years), Talisman (late Figaro II. five years), Vaillance (three years), Vaucluse (two years), *Verneuil* (two years), Vésuve (two years), and *Wild Tommy* (three years), and that all those whose names are printed in italics had been money out of his pocket to the following tune :—

1. Allumette (won Town Three-year-old Plate of 90l. at Newmarket July and the Royal Stakes of 880l. at the Second October) = 970l.

2. Babylas (Railway Stakes, handicap, of 48l. at Londonderry) = 48l.

3. Bernardet (Westwood Handicap Selling Stakes of 61l.) = 61l.

4. Braconnier (Jockey Club Cup of 650l.) = 650l.

5. Camélia (the One Thousand of 3,100l. and ½ the Oaks of 4,300l.) = 5,250l.

6. Camembert (a post sweepstakes of 400*l*. at Newmarket First Spring) = 400*l*.

7. Chamant (the Priory Stakes of 500*l*. at Lewes, the Middle Park Plate of 3,860*l*., and the Dewhurst Plate of 1,570*l*.) = 5,930*l*.

8. Conseil (Manchester Cup, handicap, of 815*l*. = 815*l*.

9. Enguerrande ($\frac{1}{2}$ the Oaks of 4,300*l*.) = 2,150*l*.

10. Gavarni (a post sweepstakes of 350*l*. at Newmarket First Spring) = 350*l*.

11. Jongleur (the Criterion Stakes of 940*l*.) = 940*l*.

12. Jonville (Consolation Free Handicap at Newmarket Houghton of 160*l*.) = 160*l*.

13. La Seine (a free handicap of 140*l*. at Newmarket Craven from her only opponent, a 'compatriot,' Heurtebise) = 140*l*.

14. Laurier (the De Trafford Handicap of 105*l*. as well as the Stamford Handicap of 120*l*. at Manchester, a welter handicap of 150*l*. at Sandown Park, the Palace Handicap of 210*l*. at Alexandra Park and the Alexandra Handicap of 175*l*.) = 760*l*.

15. Léopold (the Rutland Stakes of 250*l*. at Newmarket First October) = 250*l*.

16. Lina (the Newmarket Oaks of 530*l*., and the Ancaster Welter Handicap Plate at Newmarket Houghton of 160*l*.) = 690*l*.

17. Lollipop (the Portland Plate of 425*l*. and the Prince of Wales's Plate of 200*l*. at Doncaster) = 625*l*.

18. Macadam (a selling welter plate of 50*l*. and the Acton Burnell Stakes of 100*l*. at Shrewsbury, and the Enville Stakes of 90*l*. at Warwick) = 240*l*.

19. Myosotis (the Paisley Licensed Victuallers' Selling Stakes of 50*l*.) = 50*l*.

20. Paysanne (a selling handicap of 80*l.* at Newmarket Second Spring) = 80*l.*

21. Plaisante (the Lincoln Cup of 150*l.*, the Blankney Nursery Handicap of 285*l.* and the Brownlow Nursery Plate Handicap of 200*l.* at Lincoln) = 635*l.*

22. Pluton (the Newmarket Spring Handicap of 275*l.*, the Royal Cup of 300*l.* at Windsor, and a sweepstakes of 290*l.* at Newmarket July) = 865*l.*

23. Prophète (the Crosby Welter Handicap of 100*l.* at Liverpool, the Delapré Welter Handicap of 65*l.* at Northampton, and the Second Welter Handicap Plate of 100*l.* at Newmarket First Spring) = 265*l.*

24. Régalade (a Triennial Produce Stakes of 391*l.* at Newmarket First October) = 391*l.*

25. Roquefort (the Middlesex Handicap of 27*l.* at Alexandra Park, the Hornsey Wood Welter Handicap of 65*l.* at the same place, a selling sweepstakes of 70*l.* at Wrexham, a selling stakes of 55*l.* and the Shorts Selling Stakes of 65*l.* at Worcester, and the Wrekin Stakes of 80*l.* at Shrewsbury) = 362*l.*

26. Satisfaction (the Wilton Handicap of 105*l.* at Chester, the Catterick Selling Plate of 50*l.*, and the Buckley Stakes of 95*l.* at Manchester) = 250*l.*

27. Sugarloaf (a maiden stakes of 130*l.* at Newmarket July, and the Houghton Plate of 375*l.*) = 505*l.*

28. Suzette (the Londesborough Plate of 55*l.* at Beverly) = 55*l.*

29. Verneuil (the Glasgow Stakes of 200*l.* at Doncaster, and the Buckenham Produce Stakes of 1,500*l.* at Newmarket First October, beating—*nota bene*—Silvio, 7 to 4 *on* the latter) = 1,700*l.*

30. Wild Tommy (a post sweepstakes of 450*l.* at Newmarket Craven, and *all but* won the St. Leger

from that princely horse Petrarch, beating Kisbér, the winner of the Derby, and the blinkered Julius Cæsar, second for the Two Thousand, and third for the Derby and Leger) = 450*l*.

Total won by 'Frenchmen' = 26,037*l*., all out of the British lion's pocket.

Surely this were enough to make any lion, let alone a 'shop-keeping' lion, put his tail between his legs and howl with anguish.

But that is not all. Not only does the British lion perceive that many 'Frenchmen' are come about him, but he is uncomfortably conscious that 'furriners' close him in on every side. He is beset by animals from Germany, from Austria-Hungary, from Russia (witness Neva, daughter of Morizet and Zoraide), from America (witness Mate, Preakness, Donna, &c.), and even from his own colony of Australia (witness Commodore, by Yattendon, and King of the West, by Imported Kingston); and some of them have won his best races and a lot of his money, as follows:—

1. Adélaïde (bred in Germany; the Haydock Plate of 60*l*. at Newton) = 60*l*.

2. Bayard (bred in Hungary; a selling handicap of 100*l*. at Newmarket Houghton) = 100*l*.

3. Bay Final. (bred in America; the Dullingham Handicap of 410*l*. at Newmarket Houghton) = 410*l*.

4. Eberhard (bred in Hungary; the First Welter Handicap of 260*l*. at Newmarket Houghton) = 260*l*.

5. Fanny Day (bred in Hungary; the Londesborough Stakes of 80*l*. and the Juvenile Plate of 100*l*. at Scarborough, the Park Hill Plate of 100*l*. at Pontefract, the Wilton Plate of 200*l*. at Redcar, the Elton Juvenile Stakes of 146*l*. at Stockton, the Londesborough Plate of 100*l*. at Scarborough Summer Meeting, the Chillington

Stakes of 120*l*. at Wolverhampton, and the Easby Plate of 50*l*. at Richmond, Yorks) = 896*l*.

6. King of the West (bred in Australia; the Harrow Plate of 50*l*. at Kingsbury July Meeting) = 50*l*.

7. Kisbér (bred in Hungary; the Derby of 5,575*l*.) = 5,575*l*.

8. Pirat (bred in Germany; a plate of 180*l*.) = 180*l*.

9. Preakness (bred in America; w.o. for the Brighton Cup of 100*l*.) = 100*l*.

10. Regimentstochter (bred in Germany; the Copeland Stakes of 230*l*. at Manchester, a dead heat with Kitty Sprightly, dividing the 540*l*., for the Exeter Stakes at Newmarket July, having already in the spring won the Prince of Wales's Stakes of 125*l*. at Pontefract) = 625*l*.

Total for 'foreigners' other than 'Frenchmen' = 8,256*l*.

Total for all the 'danged furriners' together = 34,293*l*.

This of course was 'very tolerable, not to be endured.' Why, it was almost as much as the 34,378*l*. in stakes that a single English owner, Lord Falmouth, was to win 'off his own bat' the very next year.

Wherefore the British lion, represented by Lord Falmouth and other members of the Jockey Club, Lords Hardwicke and Vivian in particular, and Admiral Rous in a half-hearted way, raised a loud roar for reciprocity, though how reciprocity was to mend things it was not easy to see.

The more the British lion examined the matter the less he liked the look of it; for not only had the foreigners, and especially the French, whose most prominent champions were, of course, the Lagrange-Lefèvre 'fusion,' won a pretty large sum of money in stakes, but there were some very ugly symptoms as regarded the English horses and their prospects for the future.

It made the business worse rather than better to point out that very many of the 'foreigners' belonged to English owners, and therefore could not be said to take English money out of the country; for these 'foreigners' were by no means the pick of the bunch, and it looked, therefore, as if—whilst the best 'foreigners' would be winning our most important and valuable races—the inferior would be purchased by native Englishmen to pick up a handicap now and then.

Anyhow this was the picture which presented itself to the British lion at the end of the season 1876. Not only had the Derby, the Oaks, and the One Thousand (to say nothing of the Grand Prix de Paris) been won—and the Doncaster St. Leger very nearly—by 'foreigners,' but in the One Thousand the first three (Camélia, Allumette, and La Seine), in the Oaks the first two (Camélia and Enguerrande, who ran a dead heat), in the Royal Stakes at Newmarket the first two (Allumette and Camembert, beating Farnese), in the Newmarket Oaks the first three (Lina, Augusta, and Basquine), were all foreigners, as if an English competitor or competitress could not get so much as a 'look in.' Then among the two-year-olds there was every indication of trouble in store for the Britisher. Just a glimpse of the cloven hoof was seen when Saint-Christophe (whose time, however, was to be next year) came out at the Epsom Summer Meeting and obtained a place (third) for the Two-year-old Plate, and then ran second to Rob Roy for the New Stakes at Ascot; more had been seen when Sugarloaf got second twice (to

Placida and to Warren Hastings) at Bibury Club Meeting; more still when Doucereuse ran second to Silvio for the Ham Stakes and Chamant to Shillelagh for the Lavant Stakes at Goodwood, and when the latter won the Priory Stakes at Lewes; but not until the autumn, not until the Doncaster Meeting, did the Englishmen begin to fully recognise the French demon that was upon them. No sooner was one French two-year-old defeated than another came on. Chamant is nowhere for the Champagne Stakes, and immediately his 'compatriot' Verneuil steps forward and wins the Glasgow Stakes, though he had been beaten at Goodwood and though he starts the least fancied of the first three; but he fails to get within three lengths of Lady Golightly for the Wentworth. After this, however, when the Newmarket Autumn Meetings begin, French victories in the great two-year-old races succeed one another so rapidly as to become almost monotonous. Verneuil wins the Buckenham Stakes (beating Silvio, *nota bene*), Léopold wins the Rutland Stakes (these at the First October); Chamant wins the Middle Park Plate (at the Second October); and at the Houghton Meeting Jongleur wins the Criterion (with two other 'foreigners,' Verneuil and the Voltella colt behind him), Chamant wins the Dewhurst Plate, and Sugarloaf wins the Houghton Plate. It appears, then, to the British lion that not only do these plaguy French win English races of the highest order, but that they sometimes occupy the first three places; that in Chamant, Jongleur, and Verneuil (Saint-Christophe not yet being quite revealed) they have probably the best two-year-olds of the year, about to be the best three-year-olds of the next; and that as the Derby of 1876 was won by a 'foreigner' so very probably will the Derby of 1877 be won (besides many other great races, so that 'the board' may be 'swept') by a Chamant, a Jongleur, a Verneuil, a Léopold, a Saint-Christophe, or any one of them that may be entered. Such an one was Chamant: he was undoubtedly the best horse of his year, and there is every reason to believe that, had he not met with a mishap, he would not have finished his career, begun so well in 1877 by winning the Two Thousand, without winning 'everything,' like his illustrious compatriot and predecessor Gladiateur; instead of which it was his sad fate to be sold into the hands of his country's deadly enemies, the Germans, in 1878. However he (with the help of other 'compatriots' and 'foreigners') fairly frightened the British lion and made him howl in earnest for reciprocity.

The question had already been mooted and played with, but now a serious appeal was made to the Société d'Encouragement for an open French Turf, such as the English had always been.

It is understood that Lord Falmouth, who was now the chief mover, had for some years kept the subject under consideration and had drawn attention to it, and that letters had passed between the English Jockey Club, represented by Admiral Rous (who died in 1877), and the French Jockey Club (Société d'Encouragement), represented by Count (or Viscount) Paul Daru (who died in Paris, April 18, 1877, just two months before Admiral Rous, and with whom the office of 'vice-president' or 'president of the Race Committee' of the French Jockey Club ceased), for the purpose of bringing about an arrangement, but to no purpose.

At the end of 1876 the affair was taken up with apparent vigour by Lord Falmouth and other members of the Jockey Club: either all French races were to be thrown open to English competition or reprisals were threatened.

Lord Falmouth, accordingly, gave notice of a motion—to come before the Jockey Club in 1877—which would exclude foreign horses from competition in 'certain weight for age races' on English racecourses. It is due to Lord Falmouth to note that he had for years been trying to impress his views upon the Club, and that he cannot be accused of acting under the influence of sudden panic or of a temporary smart and sense of injury: his cup of bitterness, rather, had been gradually filling up, and at last overflowed. He did not foresee, perhaps, that, notwithstanding the obtrusive foreigners, he would some day come to be credited with having cleared more than 150,000*l.* in stakes during his career on the Turf. However his notice of motion led to some remarks in the 'Daily Telegraph,' and he replied to those remarks in a letter dated January 23, 1877. That letter was especially worthy of notice as containing an expression of Lord Falmouth's opinion that there are no more cakes and ale, there is no more old-fashioned sport, but that the breeding and running of race horses are, in his own words, 'matters of hard business in which British interests are involved.' To some ears this sounded strange doctrine for an English nobleman to utter. However the motion was duly submitted, and still more stringent measures of protection were proposed by Lords Vivian and Hardwicke. Controversy ran high, articles appeared in nearly all the newspapers, and letters were published in the 'Daily Telegraph' and in the 'Times' during February from Lord Falmouth, Lord Ailesbury, Admiral Rous, and, on the part of the French, from M. Auguste Lupin, the representative of the French Jockey Club (though M. Ernest Leroy, one of the original 'fourteen,' including the hon. members, the Duke d'Orléans and the Duke de Nemours, was still living and the real 'doyen' of the Club). M. Lupin, of course, justified the French, with the usual arguments of 'non possumus,' as 'it is one of the fundamental rules of the French Club that all their races are confined to French horses;' of the wide difference between the great English and French races, the former being run by owners for one another's subscriptions and the latter for a prize consisting—mainly in the earliest days, and to a very considerable extent still —of 'added money' in the form of a 'dotation' from the Société d'Encouragement; of the difficulty that there would be in making, and certainly in carrying, a proposal for so great an alteration as was demanded, and even of the danger there would be of disheartening French owners by the alteration, and so checking the already wonderful development of French horse-racing, and so forth. Admiral Rous was not quite so outspoken and dictatorial as was usual with him, but he certainly inclined towards Lord Falmouth's views. Lord Ailesbury, on the contrary, was diametrically opposed to Lord Falmouth, expressing the most manly, noble-manly, liberal, and sensible opinions, and declaring that, for his part, he would 'breed from foreign horses if necessary; but exclude them—never.'

The question was naturally much discussed in France, and this is the place to give what was written at the time by one of the ablest and most experienced French authorities ('Le Sport').

When a man of Lord Falmouth's importance takes the trouble to occupy his mind with a proposal calculated to make so much stir as that which he intends to submit to the English Jockey Club, the question is: What is really in his thoughts?

Lord Falmouth has spoken, and other sportsmen, of no less weight, have followed his banner and enrolled themselves on his side. Lord Vivian, Lord Hardwicke, and Admiral Rous have declared that, exceptionally and for this once, England would do well to drop her liberal policy so as to exclude us from her horse races. What current of ideas has impelled the noble patrons of the English Turf to this course?

Undoubtedly, in London as well as in Paris, there is no lack of vulgar simpletons who, under a false idea of patriotism, cannot endure the notion of being beaten by a foreigner, even in a friendly contest. When Gladiateur won the Derby, the mob at Epsom was highly displeased; there was a ferment among the folks who get red in the nose at the slightest provocation, and a cry at once arose to the effect that for a French-bred colt to beat the English 'cracks' there must have been some sorcery or fraud employed. There was but one cry heard from the gorse at Tattenham corner, that Gladiateur was a four-year-old!

The same disappointment was displayed last year, and the same puerile accusations greeted the victory of Kisbér, bred at an Austrian stud.

I repeat that the mob raised an outcry, and could ill digest the defeat of the home-bred champions. But in the higher circles of the Turf, where people are gentlemen before everything, not the slightest sign of displeasure was allowed to appear. In both cases the exceptional victories of two friendly nations were received with applause. That was perfectly well understood in France and appreciated among the higher classes, of whom the English have certainly never had to complain when they have come over to win the Grand Prix de Paris from us. . . .

In these latter years, it is true, we have been rather more lucky, and some slight successes have given us the measure of our progress in horse-breeding.

Finally, last autumn we made a far more brilliant show, and the laurels gathered by Chamant and Jongleur have begun to rather trouble the peaceful slumbers of our friendly neighbours.

Now, what is the exact meaning of Lord Falmouth's proposal? Is it really reciprocity that he asks of us, and does he really wish to have English horses admitted to run in France with the same readiness with which ours are welcomed in England?

There is reason to doubt it. And we have the more cause to be surprised at such a pretence, seeing that to this very day English horses have shown far less alacrity in coming to run on our racecourses than we have shown in admitting them.

The conditions of all the great prizes, outside of the statutes of the Société d'Encouragement, were drawn up with a view of attracting them.

If, the Grand Prix de Paris notwithstanding, there was a fear that we might not offer sufficient attractions, we made a point of admitting them to the race for the Grand Prix de Deauville. At Dieppe too we tried to tempt them by conditions specially devised in their favour. In steeple-chases also we showed no less alacrity, of which the Grand International de Paris is proof. Nevertheless our pains were thrown away. . . . In the hope of obtaining a readier response to our invitations we sacrificed our customs, in order that the races to which we invited English horses should be run on a week day; but the invitations were nearly always declined.

Lord Falmouth is well aware that the Société d'Encouragement is precluded from acceding at once to his demand for reciprocity between the two countries; and that, perhaps, is why he makes a point of it as a ground for excluding us from English racecourses. . . .

Lord Ailesbury is not less an authority—quite the contrary—than Lord Falmouth; and the former refutes so cleverly and logically the proposition advanced by the latter that it seems to me useless to add a single word to his arguments. . . .

I cannot refrain, however, from telling Lord Falmouth that, if his proposal be carried, he will have done his country's horse-breeding a very ill turn. England will have great difficulty in maintaining her supremacy upon the Turf if she ceases to assert it by fresh successes against foreign produce. As for us, our position is excellent, should our neighbours warn us off their racecourses; for it will remain on record that we alarmed them so greatly by our victories as to make them desirous of retiring from the contest.

This proud boast marks the climax in the history of French horse-racing; our neighbours evidently did not like the idea of being excluded from our races, but they also evidently, and not without reason, believed that they had reached a period when their thoroughbred stock would be able to compete in the markets of the world on equal terms, to say the least of it, with the English. And it was not to be very long before a French horse, Flageolet, would have his services at the stud put at the 200 guineas charged for those of a Stockwell (during a very limited period) and for a Hermit (who afterwards, however, attained to 250 guineas).

Perhaps in England the majority of thoughtful persons agreed with Lord Ailesbury rather than with Lord Falmouth. They argued thus: You cannot eat your cake and have it; if you let the French buy your best blood (not for nothing, *bien entendu,* and sometimes they had very bad bargains) you cannot expect to beat them for ever and ever without a check. Nay, if you sow the wind you must not be surprised if you reap the whirlwind. And things are not nearly so bad as that. The foreigners, French, German, Austrian, Hungarian, Russian, American, and *tutti quanti,* have been excellent customers of ours for a hundred years or more (off and on); yet they have won only two Derbies (1865 and 1876), three 'Oakses' (1864, 1872, and 1876), one Two Thousand (1865), two One Thousands (ungrammatical as it sounds, in 1872 and 1876), and one St. Leger (1865) up to the end of this year 1876; and what is that among so many? Besides, nobody will contend that we opened our races to them because we thought they had a good chance of beating us; it was because we liked the colour of the money they paid for so many years both for subscription to our stakes, &c., which they had small chance of winning, and for the horses and mares we sold them (at great prices very often), and because by so liberally inviting them to come and be beaten we encouraged them to go on buying and persevering, at the same time that by continuing to beat them we raised our prestige and the value of our produce, if anybody should want to buy any. Furthermore the French had not asked us to open our racecourses to them; it had been quite voluntary (not without some *arrière-pensée*, not altogether unlike that with which the spider invites the fly) on our part, and they really had some reason when they said that they had already opened (partly only, because of that awkward Sunday) the Grand Prix (the most valuable of all races on the Continent and not less valuable than any in England, as a general rule), that we had taken considerable advantage of the chance, that there were almost insurmountable difficulties in the way of opening all their races just at present, that they would very likely, however, be all opened in good time, but that it was for them and not for us to say when that time had arrived. Moreover, if we did exclude their horses, just when they were beginning to show a general superiority to ours, it was evident to the meanest capacity that such a step would be very likely to endanger our prestige and to depreciate our thoroughbred produce. Lastly, what would be the good of reciprocity? For the owner of horses England was still and was pretty sure to be always a better sort of Tom Tiddler's ground than any Continental country; and, so far as the French were concerned (against whom the howl for reciprocity was chiefly directed, not only because they were sinners above all foreigners that 'tried conclusions' with us, but also because their racecourses were within easier reach), as their principal and most valuable races (with the exception of the already open Grand Prix) invariably take place a little earlier than ours corresponding, was it to be supposed that an English owner with a horse good enough to win the English Derby would send it over for the French? On the other hand a French horse good enough to win the English Derby might reasonably neglect the less for the more valuable engagement, and at the same time leave at home a 'compatriot' (compare the case of Rayon d'Or and Zut, though the former did *not* win the English Derby) good enough to beat an inferior English horse for the French; and as for the Oaks, Fille de l'Air showed (in 1864) how possible it is for an extraordinarily good French filly to win the Prix de Diane first and then come over and win the Oaks at Epsom, although it is very improbable that an English owner would run the risk of sending an extraordinarily good English filly to try for the less valuable event first. 'No,' said many an Englishman to his neighbour, 'reciprocity is of no use; if our horses are good in any given year we are not likely to trouble the French racecourses (unless for the Grand Prix) at all, and if our horses are bad the French are as likely as not to beat us at home first and then here, whether with the same horse (witness Insulaire, winner of the French and second for the English Derby in 1878) or with a "crack" and a "demi-crack." Lord Ailesbury's is the only plan; if we can no longer breed from our own stock a produce that shall beat the French, we must breed from French stock (it will only be getting back our own) and improve upon it: for the fact is that we can only maintain our supremacy by beating the very best

" foreigners," and no amount of reciprocity will enable us to do that with inferior animals. If we wish to win French races as well as English the right way is to have two studs, as the Duke of Hamilton, as Count de Lagrange, as M. Lefèvre, one in France and one in England; or, good faith, if the exclusion of "foreigners" is not carried, one in France (or " abroad ") alone will do.'

Well, in April 1877 Lord Falmouth's motion came on, and, very significantly, was adjourned to the Houghton Meeting, but eventually, it appears, was allowed to ' slide.' At any rate, as we all know, nothing has come of it, or of Lord Vivian's amendment, or of Lord Hardwicke's proposal (though Iroquois and Foxhall have carried everything before them since then, and they were ' foreigners ').

Now, what had happened in the meanwhile, between April and the Houghton Meeting (the end of October), 1877? Chamant, after winning the Two Thousand, had gone amiss; and Lord Falmouth, at the conclusion of the Houghton Meeting, with incredible luck had won the Derby and the St. Leger with Silvio; the Prendergast as well as the Chesterfield Stakes at Newmarket, the Prince of Wales's Stakes at Goodwood, and a sweepstakes of 440*l.* at Doncaster; the Richmond Stakes at Goodwood and the Clearwell and the Criterion at Newmarket with Jannette, as well as other races; ten events (including the Great Yorkshire Stakes and the Yorkshire Oaks) with Lady Golightly, &c. &c. ; and, in fact, stood at the head of ' winning owners ' with the enormous sum of 34,378*l.* in stakes, having the Lagrange-Lefèvre 'fusion' behind him, a 'bad second,' with 12,681*l*. Whether that had anything to do with the 'sliding' of his motion and with the ensuing silence about reciprocity matters little. The controversy had shown the English people that horse-racing was no longer regarded by English lords as a 'sport of kings,' to be carried on in the spirit of the 'grand seigneur,' as it was carried on in former days by Lord Fitzwilliam, Lord Egremont, and Lord Derby upon the English Turf, and by the Duke d'Orléans and Prince Marc de Beauvau on the French; it was henceforth to be included, in Lord Falmouth's own words, among 'matters of hard business.'

So be it. But if that is the case it can be proved by actual arithmetic that horse-racing and combined racehorse-breeding cannot possibly be a paying 'industry;' they are 'matters of hard business,' out of which a Lord Falmouth, a Chaplin, a Blenkiron, an I'Anson, or another or two may make good round sums (say, 200,000*l*. in twenty or twenty-five years); but the great bulk of owners (who are, of course, the paymasters of the breeders)—say, ninety-nine out of a hundred—must lose money, for the horses they breed and own and keep and run must lose most of their races. Racehorse-breeding, disconnected from owning (the former having been the branch preferred by the successful Mr. Tattersall, owner of Highflyer), may, no doubt, be very profitable indeed so long as there are 'gentlemen sportsmen' who do *not* agree with Lord Falmouth, but are prepared to pay for their 'hobby' (a queer name for a thoroughbred race horse).

One other affair there was (connected with horse-racing in France) which made the year 1876 very memorable, and which affords a good illustration of the way in which 'wheel within wheel' characterises the machinery of the world; so that the case known as the 'Great Turf Fraud' led to another known as the 'Great

Detective Case,' which brought to light the rotten moral condition of the most important and most trusted among the various branches of our police force.

Madame de Goncourt was a lady, a widow, living at Château de Goncourt, which is described with some vagueness as being 'about 100 miles distant from Paris.' There, in her rural retirement, she received a circular and other documents from a firm of English swindlers, living—or having a place of what they were pleased to term business—in London, and holding, no doubt, that, as the Claimant would have put it, some French widows 'has plenty money and no brains.' So impressed was she by the advantages set forth in those documents that at various times during the year 1876 she transmitted to the enterprising English firm of swindlers no less than 10,000*l.* to be invested in bets upon horse races. This shows how deeply the sport of horse-racing (especially as a medium of investment) had impressed the French mind by this time, and how widely spread among all circles of French society was the fancy for the Turf as a pecuniary speculation; else it could never have occurred even to the most enterprising English swindlers to propound their plan to a French widow a hundred miles from Paris, or to her to make them her agents. Some thirty years previously such a French widow would not have known what 'the Turf' meant, and the documents of the English swindlers would have been as incomprehensible as a cuneiform inscription to her. Even as it was Madame de Goncourt seems to have been a little 'fogged' and to have been imposed upon by the term used by the swindlers, who assumed the style and title of 'sworn bookmakers,' which she appears to have confounded in some way with 'sworn brokers.' However the firm evidently knew that French widows (whose husbands, perhaps, had been 'connected with the Turf') were ripe for swindling in the matter of bets upon horse races, and the lady evidently had some notion (whencesoever derived) that a profit was to be realised by judiciously 'throwing a commission into the market,' as the phrase is; and these two facts entitle the case of Madame de Goncourt to prominent mention in a history of horse-racing in France. It would be tedious, however, to enter into details: they may be found by anybody who cares to look for them in the newspapers of 1876-77, commencing with the autumn of the former year. It will be enough to remark here that Madame de Goncourt, getting no return for or of her money, and suspecting (most justly) that she was being swindled, had recourse to the law. The upshot was the 'Great Turf Fraud' case, which led to the conviction of the notorious Mr. Benson (the accomplished swindler, of good birth and education, who was much esteemed in the Isle of Wight) and of his accomplices. The trial lasted twelve days: Mr. Benson was sentenced to fifteen years' penal servitude, Messrs. William and Frederick Kerr (or Kurr) and Mr. Charles Bale to ten years', and Mr. Edwin Murray to eighteen months' hard labour. Then did Mr. Benson, in the hope of getting his sentence mitigated, volunteer some information which led to the celebrated trial of the detectives Messrs. Meiklejohn, Druscovitch, Palmer, and Clarke, and of the useful solicitor Mr. Edward Froggatt, and to a revelation which startled the English community.

To these memorable events of the year 1876 may be added the double success of Rosebery in the Cesarewitch and Cambridgeshire, which had never before been won by the same horse, either in the same year or in two years; for though the winner was neither a French horse nor any kind of foreigner, yet the precedent thus established was to be followed by two 'foreigners'— by the American Foxhall in 1881 and by the French Plaisanterie in 1885.

It is now full time to pass on to 1877, in which year the French 'cracks' at home were Count de Juigné's Jongleur (three years, winner of the French Derby, of the Grande Poule des Produits, and of the Prix Royal Oak), M. A. Lupin's La Jonchère (three years, winner of the French Oaks and the Prix Daru, as the old Poule des Produits had been renamed in memory of the lamented Count Paul Daru), M. A. Lupin's Fontainebleau (three years, winner of the Poule d'Essai), Baron de Rothschild's Stracchino (three years, winner of La Coupe at Paris), Count F. de Lagrange's Saint-Christophe (three years, winner of the Grand Prix de Paris) and Verneuil (three years), M. H. Delamarre's Vésuve (three years, winner of the Prix de Longchamps), M. A. Lupin's Enguerrande (four years, winner of the Prix du Cadran), Baron de Rothschild's Kilt (four years, winner of the Prix Rainbow), M. Fould's Mondaine (four years, winner of the Prix Gladiateur), and among the two-year-olds Count F. de Lagrange's Phénix and Count de Juigné's Roscoff and Mantille, winners of the three principal 'Critériums' and of the Prix de Deux Ans at Deauville.

The Grand Prix de Paris (for which, of course, Lord Falmouth's Silvio did not run) was a remarkable triumph for the French in one respect; for out of the seven runners there was but one English representative, K. G. (who might as well have stayed at home), to face the 'natives;' and these 'natives' included Saint-Christophe, Jongleur, Stracchino, and Verneuil, four such horses as the French might well be proud of.

Fontainebleau, of whom great hopes had been entertained, and who indeed had at one time been thought the best of his year, was amiss and did not start; and the same remark applies to Chamant. Else it had seemed at one time as if the French with six such animals as Chamant, Jongleur, Saint-Christophe, Stracchino, Verneuil, and Fontainebleau, to say nothing of La Jonchère (another absentee from the race for the Grand Prix) must 'clear the board' in England between them. But the glory of horse-racing is its uncertainty.

Of the French 'cracks' which distinguished themselves at home there ran in England Jongleur (won the Select Stakes of 410*l.* at Newmarket Second October, beating Placida, the winner of the Oaks, and the Cambridgeshire of 2,155*l.*, beating Belphœbe, winner of the One Thousand), La Jonchère (unplaced for the Oaks and for the Cleveland Handicap at Doncaster), Fontainebleau (unplaced for the St. Leger), Stracchino (unplaced for the Two Thousand, for which he was third favourite, and for the St. Leger), Saint-Christophe (won the Twenty-ninth Triennial at Newmarket First October of 466*l.*, and was beaten into third and last place by Verneuil and Belphœbe for the Jockey Club Cup at the Houghton Meeting), and Verneuil (w.o. for the Drawing-Room Stakes of 190*l.* at Goodwood, third to Jongleur and Placida for the Select Stakes at Newmarket Second October, unplaced for the Cambridgeshire, and won the Jockey Club Cup of 530*l.* easily from Belphœbe and Saint-Christophe).

Of these horses Jongleur, Saint-Christophe, and Verneuil deserve especial notice. Jongleur, after so greatly distinguishing himself, died from the results of an accident in September 1878 (tetanus from running a splinter into his pastern), at the early age of four years (like the Rev. Mr. 'Launde's' celebrated Holy Friar); he 'should have died hereafter,' for he might have been a great sire. Saint-Christophe (died at the Government Stud, Sées, in April 1883) ran a wonderful *double dead heat* with Mondaine (four years) for the Prix de Chantilly in September 1877; the distance was *two miles*, and twice the judge was unable to separate the determined pair, so that after the second heat the stakes were divided. And Verneuil (whose great year was to be the next, 1878) was so powerful an animal that Lord Suffolk (in the 'Badminton Library') gives the horse's measurement, as follows: height 16 hands $2\frac{3}{4}$ inches, girth 6 feet 6 inches, round the cannon bone $8\frac{3}{4}$ inches, fore feet 6 inches across. He was sold (says Lord Suffolk) for 8,000*l.* to the Austro-Hungarian Government by Count de Lagrange, who missed a telegram (from America) offering 10,000*l.* for the magnificent animal. M. E. Cavailhou ('Haras de France,' p. 215) says that Verneuil was sold for 360,000 fr., which would be more than the 14,000*l.* given for Doncaster!

Of the other French horses that ran in England on the flat the most noticeable, if not the whole of them, were Adrienne (three years, *Allumette* (four years, unplaced for the Bretby Handicap Plate at Newmarket Craven), Arlette (two years, ran 'all over the shop' to no purpose), Astrée (three years, unplaced for the Oaks), Augusta (four years, won the Twenty-eighth Triennial of 500*l.* at Newmarket First October; unplaced for the October Handicap, for the Cesarewitch, &c.), Bataille (three years, unplaced for the Great Eastern Railway Handicap at Newmarket First October), Bijou (four years, unplaced for the Cambridgeshire), Caen (three years), Camembert (four years, second to Trappist by

R

a head for the Autumn Handicap at Newmarket Second
October), *Chamant* (three years, won the Two Thousand
of 5,200*l.*, after walking over for the Bennington Stakes
of 100*l.* at the Craven Meeting), Chimère (four years,
unplaced for the Dullingham Handicap won by Bay
Final), *Clémentine* (two years, third for the Exeter
Stakes, third for the Ham Stakes, third for the Molecomb Stakes, won the Doncaster Champagne Stakes of
1,250*l.*, dead heat for second [and last] to Childeric for
a sweepstakes at Doncaster, a bad third for a post
sweepstakes at Newmarket Second October, unplaced
for the Middle Park Plate, second by a neck to Jannette
for the Criterion, and third to Pilgrimage and Redwing
for a post sweepstakes at the Houghton Meeting), Colifichet (two years), Créature (two years, won a couple
of selling stakes), D'Artagnan (three years, unplaced
for Dullingham Handicap), Dogskin (three years), Doucereuse (three years), Fauvette (two years), Fille de
Roland (two years), *Gavarni* (four years, unplaced for
the Newmarket Handicap), *Gladia* (three years, third
to Jongleur and Belphœbe for the Cambridgeshire).
Greenback (two years, won the Stetchworth Stakes of
385*l.*), Guémenée (three years, unplaced for the Great
Eastern Railway Handicap and for the Moulton Stakes
Handicap), Hollandais (two years), Hollandaise (two
years, won the Second Spring Two-year-old Stakes of
340*l.*), *Insulaire* (two years, unplaced for the July Stakes,
third for the Richmond Stakes at Goodwood, won the
Corporation Stakes of 620*l.* at Brighton, unplaced for
the Astley Stakes at Lewes, won the Rutland Stakes of
270*l.* at Newmarket First October, beaten by Jannette
by half a length for the Clearwell, unplaced for the
Middle Park Plate, and second by half a length to
Pilgrimage for the Dewhurst Plate), *Inval* (two years,

third for the Dewhurst Plate, a dead heat with Oasis for second and last to Childeric for the Prendergast), Isole (two years), Jeannine (two years), La Sauteuse (five years, won the Newmarket Spring Handicap of 330*l.*), La Tamise (four years), Laurier (five years, won the Stamford Handicap of 150*l.* at Manchester), Léoline (two years, unplaced for the Ham Stakes at Goodwood), *Léopold* (three years, second for the Summer Cup at Newmarket July to Norwich, and unplaced for the Newmarket Derby), *Lollipop* (four years, won three handicaps of 590*l.* together), Mab (two years), Mademoiselle de la Vallée (two years), Mantille (two years, by Pompier), *Marion Delorme* (four years, hurdle-racer), Messman (two years), *Miss Rovel* (two years, won the Weston Stakes at Bath of 280*l.* and a sweepstakes of 125*l.* at Newmarket Second October), *Mourle* (two years, won the Granby Handicap of 200*l.* at Newmarket First October), Muguet (three years), Opoponax (two years), *Pardon* (four years, won the May Stakes Handicap of 300*l.* at Newmarket First Spring, and a selling sweepstakes of 210*l.* at the July Meeting), Patagon (four years, won the Windsor Handicap of 480*l.*), Pearl Drop (four years, hurdle-racer), Piano (two years), Pivonnet (three years, unplaced for Royal Hunt Cup at Ascot, &c.), Pluton (four years, hurdle-racer, but won the Liverpool Stewards' Cup Handicap of 255*l.*, &c.), Pomme d'Api (three years), *Pornic* (three years, second to Hampton for the Queen's Plate at Newmarket, and won the Free Handicap Sweepstakes of 700*l.* at the Houghton Meeting), *Rabagas II.* (five years), *Roi de la Montagne* (three years), Roquefort (aged), Rubigant (two years), Satisfaction (five years), Scipion (two years), *Sugarloaf* (three years, won a plate of 120*l.* at Newmarket Craven and the Suffolk Handicap of 175*l*. at Ipswich), Sutler (two years), *Talisman* (six years), Triomphe (two years, by Consul), Vélocité (two years), Verdurette (three years), Wild Darell (two years), and *Wild Tommy* (four years), of which animals (some sixty or seventy in number) those whose names are printed in italics acquired more or less reputation at one time or another in their own country or in England.

We now come to the year 1878 : it was memorable in the history of French horse-racing for what has been called the 'scission,' which took place at the end of the racing season, when Messrs. Lagrange and Lefèvre parted asunder, and in consequence of which, instead of partnership, there was to be rivalry between Count de Lagrange with Dangu in France and Phantom Cottage in England, and M. Lefèvre with Chamant in France and Lowther House in England.

But to begin in the usual way.

The French 'cracks' at home in 1878 were Count F. de Lagrange's Insulaire (three years, winner of the French Derby), Baron de Rothschild's Brie (three years, winner of the French Oaks), Count F. de Lagrange's Clémentine (three years, winner of the Poule d'Essai and of the Grande Poule des Produits), M. Fould's Stathouder (three years, winner of the Prix de Longchamps and of the Prix Daru, formerly Poule des Produits), Count F. de Lagrange's Inval (three years, winner of the Prix Royal Oak), Count F. de Lagrange's Saint-Christophe (four years, winner of the Prix du Cadran and of the Prix Rainbow), Count F. de Lagrange's Verneuil (four years, winner of the Prix Gladiateur), Count F. de Lagrange's Balagny (four years, winner of La Coupe at Paris), and among the two-year-olds Baron de Rothschild's Commandant, M. A. Lupin's Mademoiselle

Clairon, and Count P. de Meeus's Swift, winners of three principal 'Critériums' and of the Prix de Deux Ans at Deauville.

The Grand Prix de Paris of 1878 was disastrous for the French, who had seven representatives out of the eight starters, including Insulaire, the favourite at 7 to 4 *on*; but the race was won by Prince Soltykoff with by no means a first-rate horse, Thurio, the only English candidate. Count F. de Lagrange was second, third, and fourth with Insulaire, Inval, and Clémentine; and altogether, in their contests with the English, the year 1878 was about the most unlucky, if not the most disastrous, the French had ever known. As will appear presently in more detail, they ran second for the Two Thousand, the Derby, and the Grand Prix, third for the One Thousand and the Oaks, and fourth for the St. Leger; else, as they won the Ascot Cup, the Alexandra Plate, and many other races for horses of all ages, they might have had the most splendid season that ever they had known on English ground, including even 'Gladiateur's year.'

Well, of the 'cracks' mentioned there ran in England Insulaire (three years, a very hardy but unfortunate horse, a worthy son of Dutch Skater, second to Pilgrimage and beating Sefton for the Two Thousand, second to Sefton for the Derby, won the Ascot Derby of 625*l*., beating Jannette; unplaced for the Rous Memorial, won by Petrarch, at Ascot; beaten by Clocher for the Sussex Stakes at Goodwood, unplaced for the St. Leger, walked over for the Don Stakes of 100*l*., second to Sefton for the Newmarket St. Leger, unplaced—like Sefton—for the Cesarewitch, second for the Free Handicap Sweepstakes at the Houghton Meeting, and second to Silvio for the Jockey Club Cup),

Brie (third for the Coronation Stakes at Ascot, second to Lord Clive for the Select Stakes at Newmarket, and unplaced for the Cambridgeshire), Clémentine (three years, third to Pilgrimage and Jannette for the One Thousand, third to Jannette and Pilgrimage for the Oaks, unplaced for the Prince of Wales's Stakes at Ascot, second to Lord Clive for the Goodwood Derby, second to Eau de Vie for the Nassau Stakes, second to Lord Clive for the Grand Duke Michael Stakes, beaten by Jannette for the Newmarket Oaks, unplaced for the Cambridgeshire, and unplaced for the Free Handicap Sweepstakes), Inval (three years, unplaced for the Two Thousand, won the Drawing-Room Stakes of 500*l.* at Goodwood, a bad third to Sefton and Insulaire for the Newmarket St. Leger, second by a head to Thurio for the Newmarket Derby, and second to Jagellon for the Dullingham Handicap), Saint-Christophe (four years; third for the Ascot Cup, but a 'bad second and third,' and beaten in a canter by Verneuil, with two others, for the Alexandra Plate), Verneuil (four years, the undoubted French hero of the year, beaten in a canter by Thunderstone for the Claret Stakes at Newmarket Craven, unplaced for the City and Suburban; second by a length to Hampton for the Epsom Gold Cup, beating Lord Clive and others: won the Queen's Vase and 80*l.*, beating Lady Golightly in a canter; the Gold Cup of 1,460*l.*, beating Silvio, Saint-Christophe, and Hampton in a canter; and the Alexandra Plate of 1,090*l.*, beating Saint-Christophe and two others in a canter—all at Ascot: unplaced for the Champion Stakes, won by Jannette; beaten in a canter by Hampton for the Queen's Plate at Newmarket, and unplaced for the Jockey Club Cup won by Silvio), Balagny (four years, beaten in a canter by Lady

Golightly for the Twenty-ninth Triennial at Newmarket First October); but of the two-year-olds, Commandant, Mademoiselle Clairon, and Swift, none ran in England.

The number of times that some of these French horses ran second or third in England must strike the most inadvertent reader; and sometimes—such was their ill luck—when 'on paper' it seemed a 'good thing' for them. Some of the animals mentioned deserve notice for other reasons. The magnificent proportions of Verneuil and his sale have already been spoken of; but it should be added that (according to Lord Suffolk) the cause why Count F. de Lagrange did not receive the telegram in time to close with the American's offer of 10,000*l.* for Verneuil was that the Count was ill—too ill to go to the Jockey Club (in Rue Scribe), to which the telegram had been sent—and that the sapient porter of that Club, after mature consideration, decided to keep the telegram till the Count put in an appearance, which was three or four months too late. That porter ought to have been sued for 2,000*l.* Balagny was remarkable as a 'savage,' like our Merlin (son of Castrel), General Chassé, and many others; he was sold some years after 1878 to a gentleman (an Italian at Milan, if memory may be depended upon) by whom he was occasionally ridden, and whom he one day dislodged, deposited upon the turnpike road, worried, and all but killed on the spot. Swift was remarkable for losing only once out of the ten races (no 'walk over') that she ran at two years of age (in France and Belgium)—and even then she was 'placed' (third to Phénix and Faisan, three years each, for the Prix de la Forêt at Chantilly)—and for being utterly unable at three and four years of age to win a single race (worth mentioning, if at all). It is easy to say that 'this comes of running or over-running at two years of age;' but Swift could run second to Nubienne for the French Oaks and to two other animals on two other occasions at three years of age, and could carry high weights at four years, which does not look like harm taken at two years. It is only extraordinary.

Of the other French horses that ran in England in 1878 the chief, if not the whole, that ran on the flat were Alsace (three years, won—by the disqualification of Arab—a selling handicap plate of 100*l*. at Alexandra Park), Anémone (two years), Arlette (three years), *Augusta* (five years), Barde (two years), Beauclair (two years), Bergère (two years), Bienvenu (three years), Bilboquet (four years), Boule de Neige (two years), *Boulouf* (three years, won the Town Plate of 200 gs. at Doncaster), Buridan (four years), *Camembert* (five years), Chalumeau (two years), *Charivari III.* (five years), *Clocher* (three years; won the Sussex Stakes of 1,895*l*. at Goodwood from his only opponent, Insulaire; unplaced for the Cambridgeshire, third for the Limited Free Handicap at Newmarket Houghton, and second for the Winding-up Handicap), Créature (three years, won the Stewards' Selling Plate Handicap of 125*l*. at Worcester and the Garrick Selling Handicap Plate of 100*l*. at Kempton Park), Cuisinière (two years), Etolia (three years), *Faisan* (three years, won the Hamilton Stakes of 257*l*. and the Rous Stakes of 245*l*. at Brighton, unplaced for the Cambridgeshire and for the Limited Free Handicap), *Faisane* (four years, unplaced for the Third Welter Handicap at Newmarket Houghton), *Fauvette* (three years, unplaced for the Coronation Stakes at Ascot), Fier-à-bras (four years), Gourmand (two years), Guémenée (four years), Hollandaise (three years), Ismael (two years), *Isolier* (two years), *Japonica* (two years; won the Milton Plate of 395*l*. at Huntingdon, the Nursery Selling Stakes of 255*l*. at Goodwood, the Clewer Plate of 395*l*. at Windsor, the First October Two-year-old Stakes of 252*l*. at Newmarket, and the New Nursery Stakes Handicap of 337*l*., with Monsieur Philippe second, at the Houghton Meeting), Laurier (six years; won the Middlesex Handicap of 206*l*. at Alexandra Park, the Duke of Edinburgh's Cup Handicap of 157*l*. at Egham, the County Cup Stakes of 100*l*. at Leicester, a selling welter stakes of 100*l*. at Alexandra Park, and the Mile Selling Stakes of 197*l*. at Manchester), Léoline (three years, won the Roodee Stakes of 165*l*. at Chester), *Léopold* (four years, won the Bibury Stakes Handicap of 205*l*., and the Summer Handicap of 235*l*. at Newmarket July), *Lina* (five years, won the Newmarket October Handicap of 342*l*.), *Lollipop* (five years; won the Whittlebury Cup of 290*l*. at Northampton, the Rous Stakes of 235*l*. at Newmarket Second Spring, the Queen's Stand Plate of 390*l*. at Ascot, the Chichester Stakes Handicap of 600*l*. at Goodwood, and the First Great Challenge Stakes of 1,327*l*. at Newmarket Second October, beating Placida, Phénix, and Trappist among others), Macadam (six years; won a scurry selling stakes of 100*l*. at Wolverhampton and the Greenock Handicap Selling Plate of 101*l*. at Paisley), Mademoiselle de la Vallée (three years), Mandolinata (two years), *Mantille*, by Florin (two years, unplaced for the Cambridgeshire), Méphisto (two years), Miss Rovel (three years, won the Second Welter Handicap of 190*l*. at Newmarket July), *Monsieur Philippe* (two years; won the Criterion Stakes of 1,070*l*., beating Lancastrian, Rayon d'Or, and Zut among others), Muguet (four years), Œillet (two years), Opoponax (three years; won the Palmer's Green Selling

Plate of 100*l.* at Alexandra Park, a selling welter stakes of 113*l.* at Chelmsford, besides two hurdle races), *Oulgouriska* (three years), Parabole (two years), *Pardon* (five years; won the Bretby Plate Handicap of 355*l.* at Newmarket Craven, the Stamford Plate Handicap of 100*l.* at Epsom Spring, the Stand Handicap of 170*l.* at Newmarket First Spring, the Bentinck Selling Welter Handicap at Epsom Summer of 255*l.*, and a handicap plate of 100*l.* at the same meeting), Patagon (five years; won the Suffolk Handicap of 170*l.* at Ipswich, the Derby Trial Handicap of 220*l.* at Newmarket Second Spring, the First Summer Handicap of 280*l.* at Sandown Park, and a hurdle race at Shrewsbury), Pearldrop (five years, won a hurdle race at Ipswich and a handicap of 102*l.* at Chelmsford), *Phénix* (three years, won the Moulton Stakes Handicap of 225*l.* at Newmarket First October), Piano (three years, won the Yarmouth Handicap of 100*l.*), *Pivonnet* (four years), Plaisante (four years, won a welter handicap of 265*l.* at Epsom Spring), Pluton (five years, won a hurdle race at Warwick and the Bognor Selling Stakes of 230*l.* at Goodwood), *Pontoise* (three years, won the Newmarket Biennial for three-year-olds of 568*l.* and a sweepstakes of 185*l.* at the same Craven Meeting), *Porcelaine* (three years, unplaced for the Great Eastern Railway Handicap at Newmarket First October and for a handicap sweepstakes at the same meeting), *Prologue* (two years, won a plate of 177*l.* at Newmarket Second October), Prophète (five years, won 45*l.* at Liverpool), *Rayon d'Or* (won the Lavant Stakes of 930*l.* at Goodwood, a sweepstakes of 500*l.* at Doncaster, the Clearwell Stakes —like Gladiateur—of 980*l.*, and the Glasgow Stakes of 300*l.* at the Houghton Meeting), Recruit, by Vedette (five years), Réveillon (four years), Rigolade (two years), Rossnaven (two years), Saucisse (two years, unplaced for the Hyde Park Plate at Epsom Spring), *Sugarloaf* (four years, hurdles), Sutler (three years, won the Ayr Gold Cup of 290*l.* and the First Welter Handicap of 237*l.* at Newmarket Houghton), Ultima (two years, won the Bedford Stakes of 300*l.* at Newmarket Second October), Verdurette (four years, unplaced for the Newmarket Handicap won by Thurio), Wild Darell (three years), and *Zut* (two years, divided a post sweepstakes of 400*l.* after a dead heat with Lancastrian at Newmarket Second October Meeting), making about seventy in number, of which those whose names are printed in italics acquired more or less reputation either at home or in England. Of the winners the majority of course belonged to the Lagrange-Lefèvre 'fusion' (compared with any other single or double ownership); all of them, in fact, but Alsace (Mr. Porter's), Boulouf and Clocher (M. Delâtre's), Créature (Mr. Cheese's), Faisan (M. J. Prat's), Greenback, Léoline, Lollipop, Pearldrop, and Sutler (the Duke of Hamilton's), Japonica, Mademoiselle de la Vallée, and Piano (Mr. T. Jennings's), Laurier (Mr. G. Trimmer's), Macadam (the Duke of Montrose's), Monsieur Philippe (M. L. André's), Opoponax (Mr. J. Nightingall's), Patagon (Mr. C. Rayner's), Plaisante (Mr. R. Peck's), Pluton (Capt. Stirling's), and Prophète (Lord Anglesey's). The most mysterious of them all was Monsieur Philippe, who, after his meteoric blaze in the Criterion, was thought a great deal of, but disappeared at the commencement of his three-year-old career in a cloud of rumour and scandal. Nor were the French much feared for the next campaign in England, notwithstanding Rayon d'Or, Zut, and Monsieur Philippe; for at the end of the season of 1878 Peter (to be disqualified by the death of General Peel) was favourite for the next year's English Derby; but Rayon d'Or was included in a bet of six (Peter, Gunnersbury, Victor Chief, Cadogan, Falmouth, and Rayon d'Or) against 'the field,' the name of Sir Bevys being as yet scarcely known. Although the French, unlucky as they were, cannot be said to have done badly in 1878 (especially with Verneuil, Monsieur Philippe, and Rayon d'Or) they were not encouraged to make a spontaneous offer of 'reciprocity,' for which Lord Falmouth (standing at the head of English 'winning owners,' with the prodigious sum of 37,681*l*. in stakes) probably no longer felt disposed to ask. Next to him came Mr. W. S. Crawfurd with 17,450*l*., Lord Lonsdale with 14,520*l*., the Duke of Hamilton (Anglo-French) with 10,880*l*., Mr. F. Gretton with 9,969*l*., and the Lagrange-Lefèvre 'fusion,' almost 'out of the hunt' comparatively, with (for them) a poor 9,872*l*.

This year the French themselves had suffered in a manner from the 'foreigner;' for their Grand Prix de Deauville, which they had for so long kept open to horses 'de toute espèce et de tout pays,' out of compliment and 'reciprocity' towards the disdainful, inappreciative, perfidious Albionites, and which was worth nearly 800*l*., was won by the celebrated Austro-Hungarian mare 'Kincsem,' the 'Darling,' the most interesting, if not the most illustrious, animal of the year. She had already won the Goodwood Cup (worth only 480*l*.), in very bad time, however, and beating only Pageant and Lady Golightly; but her owner made a more or less tenable excuse for refusing to match her against Silvio. She was a daughter of Cambuscan and Waternymph (English sire but Hungarian dam, bred by Prince Esterhazy). She won ten races at two years of age, seventeen at three, fifteen at four, and twelve at five (fifty-four in all, and about 20,000*l.* in stakes); and was never beaten, though she ran a dead heat with Prince Giles I. at Baden in 1878, and her owner, as already remarked, refused to run her against Silvio. After this, at six years of age, she received a severe kick from a horse and a brother, in consequence of which she had to be withdrawn from training. Contrary to experience with such distinguished mares, she soon had progeny that distinguished themselves in their own country: for instance, it was announced on May 21, 1884, that 'le premier produit de Kincsem, une pouliche de Buccaneer, vient de gagner à Vienne un prix de 5,000 fr. pour chevaux de deux ans.' If she was not, as Mr. Hannibal Chollop was, 'fever-proof and likewise agur,' it is reported of her that she was never either 'sick or sorry,' that no weather came amiss to her, and she ran equally well in heat and cold, upon adamantine 'going' and through 'dirt.' Such a 'Darling' of course had her 'little ways,' and she is said to have been so particular about her eating and drinking that oats, hay, and water had to be provided on purpose for her, and even carried about with her whithersoever she went (unless it was known that she would find there what she liked).

The year 1879, remarkable for the dearth of good English as well as good French horses (for Peter, in England, was rendered *hors de combat* by disqualification), was memorable in the history of French horse-racing for being the first year of antagonism between Lagrange and Lefèvre, Dangu and Chamant.

Of Dangu a 'poet' has already been permitted to discourse; of a visit to Chamant a very pleasant description was given in 'Le Figaro' by 'Robert Milton,' which is understood to have been the assumed name of

M. de Saint-Albin, proprietor and editor of 'Le Sport.' M. Lefèvre, said the writer, was the tenant of Prince Lucien Bonaparte. The château, a specimen of modern 'restoration,' was described as 'of no account,' but comfortably arranged and furnished in the interior and glittering with silver trophies won on English race-courses. The park and paddocks, the writer thought, were the best part of Chamant; with the splendid stud horses, the precious dams, and more than a hundred thoroughbreds of various ages, all much more carefully tended than many a human being even of the upper classes. Above all there were the friendly 'youngsters,' the yearlings, that came rubbing their noses by way of greeting (in the fashion of New Zealand) against the visitor's garments (instead of nose); and there was 'Mus,' abbreviated from 'Muscat,' the retriever dog that positively used to collect the yearlings together and start them—not by flag but by bark, and not from the front but from the rear—on a jockeyless, prizeless race, a mere friendly trial of speed. Then the visitor saw two-year-olds as well as yearlings, Versigny among them, and he ventured to make some complimentary prophetic remarks, which were only very feebly justified by their performances in 1880–81. Perhaps the greatest triumph ever won by Chamant was not on the race-course but on the show ground at the 'Exposition Universelle Chevaline' in September 1878, when Flageolet and Mortemer were placed first and third (with Salvator to 'split' them) among thoroughbred sires, and among thoroughbred mares Regalia, belonging to the Chamant stud, was placed first; but she, of course, reflected honour upon England, whereas Flageolet and Mortemer were native French. Then it was that the 'objet d'art' was awarded to M. C. J. Lefèvre, of the

Chamant stud, for exhibiting the best lot of thoroughbreds, comprising Flageolet, Mortemer, Camélia, Reine, and Regalia.

In 1879 the French 'cracks' at home were Count F. de Lagrange's Zut (three years, winner of the French Derby, of the Poule d'Essai, and of the Prix Royal Oak), M. E. Blanc's Nubienne (three years, winner of the French Oaks and of the Grand Prix de Paris), M. Fould's Saltéador (three years, winner of the Prix de Longchamps, of the Prix Daru, and of the Grande Poule des Produits), M. Delâtre's Clocher (four years, winner of the Prix du Cadran and of the Prix Rainbow), Count F. de Lagrange's Clémentine (four years, winner of the Prix Gladiateur), Baron de Rothschild's Brie (four years, winner of La Coupe at Paris), and among the two-year-olds Baron Finot's Chiffon, Mr. H. Jennings's Basilique, and Baron Rothschild's Louis d'Or, winners of the three principal 'Critériums' (of which Basilique won two, after a dead heat with Louis d'Or in one of them) and of the Prix de Deux Ans at Deauville.

The Grand Prix de Paris this year was a signal success for the French, especially for M. E. Blanc, elder son and co-heir of him who was sometimes called the 'Old Gentleman' in consequence of his presiding over what is not very euphemistically termed the 'hell' at Monte Carlo. M. E. Blanc, a young aspirant for the honours of the Turf, came, saw, and conquered, for at the first time of asking (if there be no mistake) he won, as we have seen, both French Oaks and Grand Prix with Nubienne, though Zut was a strong favourite at seven to four, whilst six to one was offered against the filly. Rayon d'Or did not run, as no doubt Zut was considered good enough to win against his ten opponents, among whom there was but a single 'Englishman,' the incapable Scapegrace. As it was Count F. de Lagrange ran three candidates—Zut, Flavio II., and Ismaël—and could only get third with Flavio II. and a bad fourth and fifth with Zut and Ismaël. Of course Lord Falmouth, as usual, had nothing entered; else it goes without saying that his Wheel of Fortune would have galloped over the whole lot.

Of the French 'cracks' specified there ran in England Zut (won a post sweepstakes of 250*l*. at Newmarket Craven, unplaced for the Two Thousand, unplaced for the Derby, unplaced for the Ascot Derby, won the Racing Stakes of 460*l*. at Goodwood, unplaced for the St. Leger, like Sir Bevys, unplaced for the Select Stakes at Newmarket Second October, a bad third to Westbourne and Lancastrian for the Newmarket Derby, and unplaced for the Jockey Club Cup won by Jannette), Nubienne (unplaced for the Cambridgeshire), Saltéador (unplaced for the St. Leger), Clémentine (unplaced for the Newmarket International Handicap, a bad third and last to Inval and Lord Clive for the Prince of Wales's Stakes at Newmarket First Spring, unplaced for the Ascot Plate, unplaced for the Second Great Challenge Stakes at Newmarket Second October, unplaced for the Great Tom Stakes and for the Autumn Handicap at Lincoln), and that is all.

The chief, if not the whole, of the other 'Frenchmen' that ran on the flat in England in 1879 were Afghanistan (? late Dur-à-Cuire, four years), Aigrette (three years), Ascot (two years), Aurélie (two years), *Barde* (three years, unplaced for the Cesarewitch), The Bear (hurdle-racer and steeple-chaser, six years, unplaced for the Cesarewitch), Beauclair (three years), Bergère II. (three years), Boutade (two years, third for the Snailwell Stakes at Newmarket First October), Caleçon (three years), *Camembert* (six years, won a welter handicap of 137*l.* at Newmarket Second Spring), *Castillon* (two years), *Conquête* (two years, won the Brocklesby Stakes), *Clélie* (two years, unplaced for the Dewhurst Plate), Création (two years), Créature (four years, won the Trial Selling Stakes of 100*l.* at Southampton and also the All-aged Selling Plate of 100*l.*), Diane (two years), Distinguo (three years, beaten easily by Lipscombe for the Drawing-Room Stakes at Goodwood, &c.), *Dora* (two years, unplaced for the July Stakes, third to Bend Or and Petal for the Chesterfield, a bad third for the Richmond Stakes won by Bend Or at Goodwood, second to Robert the Devil for the Rous Memorial at Goodwood, third to Bend Or and Cannie Chiel for the Rous Memorial at Newmarket First October, third to Beaudesert and Grace Cup for the Middle Park Plate, third to Strathardle and Poulet for the Prendergast, second by a head to Prestonpans for the Criterion, and third—beating her 'compatriot' Milan—to Grace Cup and Ambassadress for the Dewhurst Plate : surely a very unlucky, almost ' uncanny ' sort of filly), Emilia (two years), *FitzPlutus* (four years, unplaced for the Cambridgeshire, &c.), Fleuret (two years, unplaced for the Clearwell Stakes and for the Glasgow Stakes at Newmarket), Frondeuse (two years, unplaced for the Findon Stakes, &c.), Gourmand (three years, unplaced for the Great Eastern Railway Handicap at Newmarket First October), Innocent (two years ; won the Maiden Stakes of 150*l.* at Newmarket July, the Chelmsford Two-year-old Plate of 114*l.*, and the Burwell Stakes of 170*l.* at Newmarket Second October), *Insulaire* (four years, won the Claret Stakes of 300*l.* at Newmarket Craven, second to Isonomy for the Ascot Cup, won the Alexandra Plate of 1,095*l.*, and

s

unplaced for the Jockey Club Cup), *Inval* (four years; won the Prince of Wales's Stakes of 527*l.*, beating Lord Clive and Clémentine, at Newmarket First Spring), *Ismaël* (three years), *Japonica* (three years, won the Singleton Stakes of 467*l.* at Goodwood and the Rous Stakes of 245*l.* at Brighton), La Française (two years, unplaced for the Thirty-second Triennial won by Bend Or at Newmarket First October), Landrail II. (two years), Laurier (aged), *Lina* (six years), *Lollipop* (six years; won the Whittlebury Cup of 287*l.* at Northampton, beating Placida; w.o. for the Rous Stakes of 70*l.* at Newmarket Second Spring; won the Lennox Stakes of 295*l.* at Goodwood, beating Placida; second by half a length to Rayon d'Or for the Second Great Challenge Stakes at Newmarket Second October, again beating Placida; won in a canter the Subscription Stakes of 600*l.* at Newmarket Houghton against Kaleidoscope, and won the All-aged Stakes of 682*l.* at the same meeting against Hackthorpe), *Milan* (two years, by Le Sarrazin; third to Brotherhood and Pappoose for the Molecomb Stakes at Goodwood, and unplaced for the Dewhurst Plate), *Milan II.* (two years, by Don Carlos; unplaced for the Twenty-second Ascot Biennial, won by Sabella), Nature (two years), *Océanie* (two years; a regular 'flyer,' whose career was spoilt by an accident; ran only three times and won every time—the Newmarket Two-year-old Plate of 422*l.* at the Second Spring, the Two-year-old Stakes of 305*l.* at Epsom Summer, and the New Stakes of 1,304*l.* at Ascot), Palatin (three years, unplaced for a handicap sweepstakes at Newmarket First Spring), *Pardon* (six years; won the Rufford Abbey Plate of 150*l.* at Nottingham, the Rous Course Handicap Plate of 137*l.* at Newmarket Craven, second to Bondsman for a handicap, and won

the Two Thousand Guineas Trial Stakes of 117*l.* at
Newmarket First Spring, and was sold to Lord Rosebery for 1,050 guineas), Patagon (six years, won over
hurdles), *Phénix* (four years; won the Prince of Wales's
Stakes Handicap of 377*l.* at Newmarket First Spring;
beaten by Paul's Cray for the Rosebery Stakes at Epsom
Summer; won the Rous Memorial of 970*l.* at Ascot;
won the July Cup of 280*l.* at Newmarket, and also the
Bunbury Stakes of 230*l.*, beating Silvio), Plaisante (five
years; won the Warwick Welter Cup of 200*l.*, the Mile
Selling Plate of 100*l.* at Brighton, and the Stewards'
Welter Cup of 100*l.* at Alexandra Park), Pontoise (four
years), *Poulet* (two years; unplaced for the Middle Park
Plate; second to Strathardle, beating Dora, for the
Prendergast), *Prologue* (three years), *Prudhomme* (two
years; third for the Walton Two-year-old Plate at
Sandown Park; third for a maiden plate for two-year-
olds at Ascot, won by Orchid, and for another won by
Lancaster Bowman; unplaced for the Princess of Wales's
Cup at Newmarket July, unplaced for the Glasgow
Plate at Doncaster, and unplaced for the Juvenile
Handicap at Newmarket Second October), *Rayon d'Or*
(three years; third to Charibert and Cadogan for the
Two Thousand; unplaced, like Charibert and Cadogan,
for the Derby; third to Wheel of Fortune and Adventure for the Prince of Wales's Stakes at Ascot, won by
Wheel of Fortune in a canter; won the St. James's
Palace Stakes of 1,500*l.* at Ascot; won the Sussex Stakes
of 1,522*l.* at Goodwood; won the Doncaster St. Leger
of 6,525*l.*; w.o. for the Zetland Stakes of 250*l.* at
Doncaster; won the Great Foal Stakes of 4,042*l.* at Newmarket First October; beaten by Bay Archer, who had
7 lbs. less weight, for the Newmarket St. Leger; won
the Select Stakes of 495*l.* at Newmarket Second October,

also the Champion Stakes of 2,496*l.* and the Second Great Challenge Stakes of 1,117*l.*, and third with 9 st. to Out of Bounds, 7 st. 12 lbs., and Knight of Burley, 7 st. 2 lbs., for a free handicap sweepstakes at Newmarket Houghton, winning altogether 17,947*l.* in a little over *four months*), Saint-Jean (three years), *Saltéador* (three years, unplaced for the St. Leger), Séville (two years, by Don Carlos; unplaced for the Middle Park Plate and for the Criterion), Sirène (two years; beaten by her only opponent, Petal, for the Stetchworth Stakes at Newmarket July, &c.), Sutler (four years, won the Rufford Abbey Stakes Handicap of 145*l.* at Doncaster and the Stewards' Cup Handicap of 116*l.* at Liverpool), *Tafna* (two years, won ½ the Lincoln Cup of 222*l.* by running a dead heat with Macaria, unplaced for the Brocklesby Stakes at Lincoln, third to Prestonpans and Illuminata for the Alexandra Stakes at Harpenden, and unplaced for the Cheveley Stakes at Newmarket Houghton), Ultima (three years, unplaced for the Coronation Stakes at Ascot), *Verneuil* (five years, unplaced for the Ascot Cup), Volte-face (two years), and Venise (three years)—some threescore, or thereabouts, in number, whereof those whose names are printed in italics won more or less reputation at some time or other in their own country or in England.

Rayon d'Or of course stands out conspicuously beyond all his compatriots, with his brilliant series of successes in the latter half of the season, after losing the Derby and Two Thousand, which he certainly ought to have won. But he and his owner, Count F. de Lagrange, were undoubtedly indebted for their very material triumph to the misfortune of Lord Falmouth's Wheel of Fortune, who broke down, or something very like it, in the Great Yorkshire Stakes, having been hitherto unbeaten both at two and at three years of age. But for this misadventure there can be little doubt that Rayon d'Or would no more have won the St. Leger than he had won the Derby, though he might have been somewhat nearer winning the former than the latter; and but for this misadventure there can be little doubt again that Rayon d'Or's value as a stud horse (when he came to be sold at his owner's death) would not have been rated so high as it was.

Well, then, on the whole the French horses of 1879, though they had not performed so brilliantly as on some former occasions in their English campaign, had done exceedingly well on the whole, thanks chiefly to Rayon d'Or, Insulaire, and Océanie, so that Count F. de Lagrange once more stood at the head of 'winning owners' in England with the handsome sum of 26,366*l*., with Lord Falmouth beaten into second place and 23,528*l*. There might have been another howl for 'reciprocity,' but there wasn't. As for M. C. J. Lefèvre, he took a very back seat indeed with 828*l*. only to pay for the cost of his English stud. And so in the first year of rivalry Dangu had beaten Chamant in a canter. But Chamant was in a comparatively unprepared condition; in three years' time it would beat Dangu into a cocked hat, with the 15,687*l*. of 1882 against Dangu's 3,175*l*. For Chamant had Mortemer and Flageolet—a host in themselves—for stud horses, and of brood mares quite a 'galaxy,' including Regalia, Green Sleeve, Feu-de-joie, Isoline, Araucaria, Contempt, and *tutte quante*.

A word must be said about Phénix, one of the most noteworthy French horses of 1879—not so much because of his performances (though they were very good) as because of the disgraceful riot that took place at Epsom when he was beaten by Paul's Cray (a hurdle-racer) for the Rosebery Stakes, the odds having very significantly varied from 6 to 4 *on* Phénix to 2 to 1 *against*; whereupon two or three thousand ruffians, belonging to what has been called by a describer of the scene ' the worst scum of the earth,' showed an unmistakable intention of tasting blood and of forthwith 'lynching' Mr. T. Jennings (owner and trainer of Paul's Cray and trainer of Phénix) and Mr. James Goater (rider of Phénix). Howbeit Mr. Jennings (being about sixty years of age or more) promptly knocked over one or two of his more aggressive enemies and made good his retreat into the paddock, whilst the police took charge of horse and jockey, and so imminent murder was prevented (*v.* Lord Suffolk's account in the 'Badminton Library.')

In 1880 the French were altogether in a bad way. Their 'cracks' at home were M. C. J. Lefèvre's (that is, the Haras de Chamant's) Beauminet (three years; winner of the French Derby, of the Grande Poule des Produits, and of the Prix Royal Oak), M. C. J. Lefèvre's Versigny (three years, winner of the French Oaks and of the Prix de Longchamps), M. A. Lupin's Voilette (three years, winner of the Prix Daru), M. A. Staub's Le Destrier (three years, winner of the Poule d'Essai), Count F. de Lagrange's Rayon d'Or (four years, winner of the Prix du Cadran and of the Prix Rainbow), Count F. de Lagrange's Courtois (four years, winner of the Prix Gladiateur), Count F. de Lagrange's Castillon (three years) and M. E. Blanc's FitzPlutus (five years), who ran a dead heat for La Coupe at Paris; and among the two-year-olds Count F. de Lagrange's Gourgandin and Tontine, Baron A. Schickler's (that is, the Haras de Martinvast's) Perplexité, and Baron de

Rothschild's Strelitz, winners of the three principal 'Critériums' and of the Prix de Deux Ans at Deauville.

The Grand Prix de Paris of 1880 was a great blow for the 'Frenchmen;' for though there were ten runners and only one 'Englishman' among them, that single exception was 'Robert the Devil;' and 'the Devil among the tailors' was nothing to the English horse among his French opponents, comprising Le Destrier, the two Milans, Beauminet, Pacific, Poulet, Boum, Versigny, and Arbitre.

In England, besides, the year turned out to be Bend Or's and Robert the Devil's. The former horse, belonging to the Duke of Westminster, of course was not even entered for the Grand Prix.

Yet, strange so say, at the outset of the season the French were supposed to have an unusually strong lot and to be very dangerous. Versigny had quite recovered from the 'venomous bite' of which mention has already been made, and was to be an Enguerrande and a Camélia all in one, and make a dead heat with herself only for the Epsom Oaks. Beauminet was to be a second Chamant, and much more triumphant, in the Two Thousand, and it seemed a thousand pities—a dead loss—that there was something wrong about his nomination for the Epsom Derby. There was Castillon too, whose name had unfortunately been omitted from the great races both in France and in England, but he would, no doubt, make his mark; and as for Le Destrier, he was bound to find a way of astonishing both the natives and the foreigners. But nothing of all this happened, as will quickly appear ; and at the end of the season neither Dangu nor Chamant, Lagrange nor Lefèvre, had done much on English soil to boast of: the former with 6,722*l.* to his credit, and the latter with a 'pittance' of 2,914*l*., which, by the way, would be reduced still further the next year—to a miserable 1,500*l*.

Well, then, of the French 'cracks' mentioned there ran in England: Beauminet (unplaced—though actually fourth—for the Two Thousand and for the St. Leger), Versigny (started favourite, but was only second to Elizabeth for the One Thousand, and favourite again but unplaced for the Oaks), Le Destrier (unplaced for the Cesarewitch, and won the Queen's Plate of 315*l*. at Newmarket against Ridotto, Star, Reveller, and Bracken), Rayon d'Or (w.o. for the Post Stakes of 150*l*. at Newmarket Craven, w.o. for the Prince of Wales's Stakes of 207*l*. at Newmarket First Spring, won the Rous Memorial of 920*l*. at Ascot, and second to Exeter—though it was 13 to 8 *on* Rayon d'Or for the Hardwicke Stakes at Ascot), Castillon (unplaced for the Cambridgeshire, for which he was third in favouritism), and Strelitz (unplaced for the Prendergast Stakes).

The other French horses that ran in England were, for the most part if not altogether: *Albion* (two years, unplaced for the Breeders' Plate at Newmarket Second Spring, unplaced for the July Stakes, third to Wandering Nun and Iroquois for the Findon Stakes, unplaced for the Middle Park Plate, and unplaced for the Criterion Stakes), *Basilique* (three years, unplaced for the Cambridgeshire), Beauclair (four years), *Belliqueux* (two years, third for the Great Sapling Plate at Sandown Park, unplaced for the Tuesday Nursery Handicap, and unplaced for the New Nursery Stakes Handicap at Newmarket Houghton, having won the Exning Two-year-old Plate of 218*l*. at the Second Spring), Bretonne II. (two years), Camériste (two years), *Clémentine* (five years, third for the International Handicap at Newmarket), Conquête (three years), Cotonnade (two years), Création (three years, unplaced for the Ascot Derby), Déesse (five years, a hurdle-racer), *Dora* (three years, unplaced for the Second Great Foal Stakes behind Robert the Devil and Bend Or at Newmarket First October), *Eliacin* (two years), Euphrasie (two years; won several selling plates, amounting to 1,068*l*.), *Fleuret* (three years), unplaced for the Two Thousand and for the Newmarket St. Leger), Folie (three years, won two selling handicaps of 100*l*. each at Alexandra Park), Gourmand (four years, won the South Down Gold Cup of 117*l*. at Lewes), Héristal (two years), *Herman* (two years, won St. George's Plate of 197*l*. at Windsor), *Innocent* (three years), *Inval* (five years, won the Derby Trial Handicap of 227*l*. at Newmarket Second Spring and the Queen's Plate of 210*l*. at Winchester), Isolina (four years; won several selling plates, amounting to 533*l*.), *Japonica* (four years), *La Bultée* (two years), *La Scala* (four years, by Dollar, unplaced for the Cambridgeshire), *Laurier* (aged ; won a welter handicap of 100*l*. at Alexandra Park and the Alexandra Handicap of 177*l*., the Mile Selling Highweight Plate of 102*l*. at Sandown Park, the Mile Selling Plate of 100*l*. at Brighton, the Kimbolton Welter Handicap of 213*l*. at Huntingdon, the De Trafford Handicap of 225*l*. at Manchester, and the Haughmond Plate of 150*l*. at Shrewsbury), *Léon* (two years, third to Bal Gal and Josyan for the Clearwell Stakes, &c.), Lord Marion (three years, a hurdle-racer), Loyalty (two years), *Macadam* (aged, won the Blankney Plate of 150*l*. at Lincoln, won the Town Welter Handicap Plate of 146*l*. at Newcastle, won the Lowther Handicap of 115*l*. at Carlisle, and won the Hamilton Welter Handicap Plate of 102*l*. at Lanark), Marie Thérèse (two years, un-

placed for the Lavant Stakes at Goodwood and for
the Prendergast at Newmarket), *Milan* (three years, by
Le Sarrazin ; unplaced for the Two Thousand, unplaced
for the Payne Stakes, second to Abbot for the Grand
Duke Michael, second to Sportsman for the Newmarket
St. Leger, won the Newmarket Derby of 695*l.*, won the
First Welter Handicap of 232*l.* at Newmarket Houghton,
unplaced for one three-year-old handicap and for the
Coffee-room Handicap), Montdidier (two years), Montgomme (two years), Muguet (six years), Natte (three
years, unplaced for the Cambridgeshire), Nessus (two
years), *Océanie* (three years, won the All-aged Stakes of
475*l.* at Newmarket Houghton), *Panique* (two years ;
second to Iroquois, running a dead heat for second
place with Voluptuary, for the Chesterfield Stakes, and
won the Stetchworth Stakes of 247*l.* at Newmarket
July), *Pardon* (aged, won the Borough Members'
Selling Welter Handicap Plate of 100*l.* a Shrewsbury),
Patagon (aged), *Phénix* (five years ; second to Charibert
for the Queen's Stand Plate at Ascot ; second, 10 st. 2 lbs.,
to Elfe, two years, 6 st. 2 lbs., for the Stockbridge Cup ;
second to Charibert for the July Cup at Newmarket ;
won the Bunbury Stakes of 160*l.* at the same meeting ;
won the Lennox Stakes of 315*l.* at Goodwood, but unplaced for the Stewards' Cup and a bad second to
Peter and a neck only in front of the other runner, the
' American ' Parole, for the Singleton Stakes), Picador
(two years, won the Tankerville Nursery Handicap of
203*l.* at Shrewsbury, and the Kempton [Park] Nursery
Handicap of 197*l.*), *Plaisante* (six years ; won the St.
Liz Handicap of 240*l.* at Northampton, won the Manor
Plate Handicap of 124*l.* at Hampton, and won the
Kempton Park July Handicap of 755*l.*), *Poulet* (three
years ; unplaced for the Select Stakes at Newmarket

Second October and second to Milan for the Newmarket Derby, and won the Free Handicap of 750*l.* at the Houghton Meeting), *Prologue* (four years; unplaced for the Newmarket Handicap, &c.), Quarteronne (two years; won the Wakefield Lawn Selling Stakes of 145*l.* at Northampton, the Nursery Plate Handicap of 102*l.* at Leicester as well as the Curzon Nursery Handicap of 102*l.*, and the Chesterfield Nursery Handicap Plate of 195*l.* at Derby), Régine (two years), Réglisse (three years), *Regrettée* (two years, won the Two-year-old Stakes of 227*l.* at Newmarket First Spring), Rita (two years), *Saint-Firmin* (two years), Saint-Laurent (two years, won a Two-year-old Selling Plate of 127*l.* at Newmarket First Spring), *Sutler* (five years; won the Datchet Handicap Plate of 147*l.* at Windsor; won the Ditch Mile Handicap Plate of 102*l.* at Newmarket Second Spring; won the Stewards' Cup of 188*l.* at Sandown Park, the Sandown Autumn Cup of 190*l.*, and the Oatlands Midweight Handicap of 227*l.*), *Tafna* (three years, won the Fern Hill Stakes at Ascot of 380*l.*), Tototte (two years), and *Zut* (third and last behind Isonomy and Chippendale for the Ascot Cup)—about fifty in number, those whose names are printed in italics having acquired more or less reputation at some time or other either in their own country or in England.

Flageolet, it should be observed, was the sire of the chief 'cracks,' except Castillon, Courtois, Océanie, and Voilette; he was the sire of Beauminet, Rayon d'Or, Regrettée, Versigny, Le Destrier, Zut, and he stood at the head of the French 'winning sires' in 1880 with some 530,000 francs, or 21,200*l.*, in Stakes to the credit of his produce.

As regards Beauminet, it should be added that his 'compatriots' were not at all pleased at his not being 'placed' at Newmarket by the judge, Mr. Clark. They even appear to have thought that M. Lefèvre's horse won the Two Thousand, if there be anything in the remarks printed in 'Le Sport' on April 24, 1886. 'M. Lefèvre,' we are told, ' won a race one day with a colt named John [by Dollar]. The horse had taken a lead of a length on the post beyond the three competitors that finished with him. Mr. Clark did not even place him in the first three. The same owner's Negro [by Saccharometer?] won a Biennial [not specified] by half a length and was not placed. *It was the same with Beauminet* in the Two Thousand.' All this really looks as if there were something in the famous remark attributed to a 'leg' (who was 'in the know' and had backed 'Running Rein' for the Derby of 1844) when he observed bitterly, 'What's the use of winning the Derby if they won't let you have it?' Still there certainly was something said at the time about Beauminet's treatment, though it is doubtful whether any impartial spectator really thought or contended that he had actually won. On the other hand, no doubt, there were many people ready to maintain to their latest breath that Daniel O'Rourke did not really win the Derby of 1852, and that Lord Clifden did win that of 1863; but some of us saw with our own eyes either both or one of them and know better.

The year 1881 was to be no more favourable for the 'Frenchmen' than 1880 had been. True the 'foreigner' was to have it all his own way in England and in the Grand Prix de Paris; but the 'foreigner' was to be American, not French, and the year was to be Iroquois's year and Foxhall's year.

Let us first of all record the melancholy fate of M. H. Delamarre's Vizir (three years, son of Vermout and Virgule), who was supposed by many of his friends to be the 'coming horse,' though in the previous year he was always running second (when he got a place at all) instead of first; second to Serpolette II. for the Prix Calenge at Cabourg, second to Gourgandin for the First Critérium at Fontainebleau, second to La Bultée for the Prix de Condé (run at Paris instead of Chantilly that year, in consequence of the repairs at the latter place), and unplaced behind Strelitz for the Prix de Deux Ans at Deauville and behind Perplexité, Strelitz, and Dublin for the Grand Critérium at Paris. But no sooner was the racing season of 1881 open than Vizir showed how much he had improved during the winter, for he came out at Rheims, beating Gourgandin and Prométhée for the Derby de l'Est. This was on March 28. The next time he came out was on the third day (April 18) of the Paris Spring Meeting, when he won the twenty-fourth Prix Biennal, beating Regrettée, Serpolette II., Gourgandin, Strelitz, and others; and his friends swore, 'Parbleu! this is good enough form to win the French Derby.' But on April 27, as Vizir, ridden by Rolfe, was taking a friendly gallop in company with M. H. Delamarre's very eccentric Viveur (four years, son of Vermout and Vipère), ridden by Musgrove, the four-year-old, without any explanation, with great suddenness, and unlike a horse and a brother, fell savagely upon the three-year-old and broke one of his legs in two places, so badly that, though he was taken home and had his leg put into 'suspenders' at first, he had to be destroyed in the course of two or three days. Such was the end of Vizir, who was to have been the 'coming horse.'

The French 'cracks' of 1881, then, in France were Count F. de Lagrange's Albion (three years, winner of the French Derby and of the Prix Daru), M. Ephrussi's Serpolette II. (three years, winner of the French Oaks and of the Prix de Longchamps), Count F. de Lagrange's Léon (three years, winner of the Grande Poule des Produits), Count F. de Lagrange's Milan (four years, winner of the Prix du Cadran and of the Prix Rainbow), M. A. Lupin's Prométhée (three years, winner of the Poule d'Essai), Baron A. Schickler's (Haras de Martinvast's) Perplexité (three years, winner of the Prix Royal Oak), Baron Roger's Pourquoi? (five years, winner of the Prix Gladiateur), M. Staub's (Haras de Lonray's) Le Destrier (four years, winner of La Coupe at Paris), and among the two-year-olds Mr. H. Jennings's Pythagore II., M. Ephrussi's Fleur de Mai, M. H. Delamarre's Vigilant, and Mr. H. Jennings's Favorite, winners of the three principal 'Critériums' and of the Prix de Deux Ans at Deauville. And to these may be added M. C. J. Lefèvre's (Haras de Chamant's) Comte Alfred, winner of the Prix de la Salamandre at Chantilly, though after all his promise he turned out a 'grand deception,' having developed a temper and taken—at three years of age—to kicking his stable to pieces.

The Grand Prix de Paris of 1881 was a bad business both for Gallia and for Albion, for the descendants of Vercingétorix and for the children of Brut. An American, Mr. James R. Keene, gave both Frenchmen and Englishmen 'pepper' and 'mustard' with Foxhall; and though the Haras de Chamant ran second with Tristan, this son of Hermit and Thrift was bred in England and not in France. Albion, winner of the French Derby, was only a moderate third. Of the English horses, bred in England and owned by Englishmen, there were but two—Scobell and Fiddler—out of the ten runners, and neither could obtain so much as a place.

Of the French 'cracks' mentioned, to the number whereof should no doubt be added Baron Rothschild's Forum (three years, winner of the Prix du Nabob), there ran in England: Albion (unplaced for the Champion Stakes won by Bend Or, with Scobell second and Iroquois third, at Newmarket Second October), Léon (third to Scobell and Ishmael for the Epsom Grand Prize; unplaced for the Ascot Derby, won by his owner with the English Maskelyne, and beaten by Iroquois by a neck for the St. James's Palace Stakes), Milan (won the Prince of Wales's Stakes of 297*l*. at Newmarket First Spring), Prométhée (unplaced for the Cambridgeshire, won by Foxall), and Perplexité (unplaced for the Oaks, and won the Newmarket Oaks, beating Corrie Roy, Josyan, and Bal Gal).

Of the other French horses that ran in England the principal, if not the whole, were: Ambassade (two years; ran often, and won the All-aged Plate of 101*l*. at Great Yarmouth), Armand (two years, toiled a deal and took nothing), *Barbe Bleue* (two years, won a maiden plate of 217*l*. at Newmarket Second October), *Bariolet* (three years, ran three times to no purpose), *Belliqueux* (three years, ran often and won the Norfolk and Suffolk Handicap Plate of 171*l*. at Great Yarmouth), Billy Pepper (two years, ran four times for nothing), Borest (three years, ran once for nothing), *Boum* (four years, ran three times for nothing), *Bras de Fer* (two years; ran three times for nothing, but was second for the Lincoln Cup), Chablis (two years, ran twice for nothing), *Commandant* (five years; won the Great Northamptonshire Stakes of 531*l*., but, like the gentleman who 'came over with the Conqueror,' did nothing else),

Créancier (three years, won the Trial Stakes of 118*l.* at Epsom and the South Denes All-aged Selling Plate of 101*l.* at Great Yarmouth), Culloden (three years; ran four times for nothing—in the Derby, the Prince of Wales's Stakes at Ascot, the Chetwynd Plate at Windsor, and the Mile Selling Plate at Brighton), *Dandin* (two years; unplaced for the July Stakes, for the Rous Memorial at Newmarket First October, for the Clearwell Stakes at the Second October, and for the Criterion Stakes at the Houghton), *Eliacin* (three years; ran a deal, but only won a sweepstakes of 157*l.* at Newmarket Second October), Euphrasie (three years, won the Surly Hall Welter Handicap Plate of 102*l.* at Windsor, and ran thirteen times besides for nothing), *Fénelon* (two years, ran twice for nothing), *Innocent* (four years; ran six times for nothing, but several times was 'placed'), Le Basque (two years, ran twice for nothing), Loyalty (three years, ran three times for nothing), *Macadam* (aged, ran 'a vast' and only won the Members' Handicap Plate of 150*l.* at Ripon and the 'Silver Bells' of 102*l.* at Paisley), Marie Thérèse (three years, unplaced for the One Thousand), Merise (two years, ran four times for nothing), Montlevêque (three years, ran seven times for nothing), Moqueur (two years, ran seven times for nothing), *Muguet* (aged, ran three times for nothing), Natal (two years; ran once, to no purpose). Nestor (two years; ran once, to no purpose), Nickel (two years; won the Ramsay Abbey Plate of 102*l.* at Huntingdon, and ran three times besides), *Océanie* (four years; the shadow of herself, beaten by her only opponent, Charibert, for the All-aged Stakes at Ascot), *Panique* (three years; ran once, unplaced for the Coronation Stakes at Ascot), *Pardon* (aged, won two poor things worth 263*l.* between them, i.e. both together), Patagon (aged, had four 'goes' for nothing), Picador (three years, won the Salford Welter Handicap of 253*l.* at Manchester), Pompette (three years, ran four times for nothing), *Poulet* (four years, ran a deal and won the Rous Memorial of 990*l.* at Ascot and the Lincoln Autumn Handicap of 231*l.*), Première Duchesse (two years, ran once only and made a *faux pas* at Alexandra Park), *Prudhomme* (four years, ran a deal and won the Ayrshire Handicap of 556*l.*), Quarteronne (three years; won the Town Welter Plate of 102*l.* at Newcastle, and then ran nine times for nothing), Raphaël (two years, ran four times to no purpose), Raray (three years; ran twice, unplaced), Réglisse (four years; ran once to no purpose at Newmarket First Spring, and then kicked—the bucket), Rémoulade (two years, ran twice to no purpose), Retriever (two years, third and last for the Exning Two-year-old Plate at Newmarket Second Spring), *Réussi* (two years; ran twice, unplaced), Rita (three years; ran three times, unplaced), Rouge-Gorge (two years; ran seventeen mortal times, and won two poor things worth some 212*l.* between them), *Royaumont* (three years, third to Exeter and Prudhomme for the Rosebery Plate at Newmarket First Spring), Saint-Laurent (three years, won once 110*l.* out of ten attempts), *Sutler* (six years; won the Bretby Plate of 212*l.* at Newmarket Craven, the Crown Welter Handicap of 180*l.* at Windsor, the Ditch Mile Plate of 102*l.* at Newmarket Second Spring, the St. James's Stakes Handicap of 216*l.* at Sandown Park, the Kempton Park July Handicap of 835*l.*, the Visitors' Plate Handicap of 345*l.* at Goodwood, the All-aged Trial Stakes of 227*l.* at Newmarket First October, and the Trial Stakes of 257*l.* at the Houghton—eight races 'right off the reel,' after beginning the season with two defeats at Liverpool), *Tafna* (four years; won a sweepstakes of 197*l.*

at Newmarket Second October and lost ten times), Talmouse (three years; won two selling events of 227*l.* between them out of twelve attempts), and Valseuse (two years; ran twice and did nothing)—about fifty altogether, whereof those whose names are printed in italics obtained more or less reputation at some time or other in their own country or in England.

On the whole, then, the year 1881 was not a brilliant one for the French; their horses bred at home were of little use in England, and, though Dangu had beaten Chamant 'in a trot,' as regards the contest between the two former confederates, Count F. de Lagrange himself stood only tenth among the 'winning owners' in England, and M. Lefèvre was very near the bottom of 'his class.' Still the French could lay to their souls the flattering unction that not the Union Jack but the Stars and Stripes had been covered with glory; for the Derby, the St. Leger, the Grand Prix de Paris, the Cesarewitch, the Cambridgeshire, the Prince of Wales's Stakes at Ascot, &c. &c., had been won by 'Americans,' Iroquois and Foxhall. Howbeit neither Mr. Lorillard, owner of Iroquois, nor Mr. J. R. Keene, owner of Foxhall, stood first among 'winning owners' in England; the former was second to Mr. W. S. Crawfurd, with 17,913*l.* to 17,919*l.*, beaten by a 'short head,' and the latter (if the value of the Grand Prix, which is not an English race, be deducted) stood below Count F. de Lagrange with 4,966*l.* to the Count's 5,829*l.* Thus might the French find balm in Gilead; and they might have found more by observing how 'foreigners' were beginning to over-run John Bull's racecourses, swarming like grasshoppers over the English 'turf,' and giving a hint that before long John Bull would have to make up his mind to see his valuable Derby and St. Leger, and other races, won not only by 'Frenchmen,' like Gladiateur, and 'Austro-Hungarians,' like Kisbér, and 'Americans,' like Iroquois and Foxhall, but by all people, nations, and languages. Perhaps it was this consideration which prevented Lord Falmouth and his friends from raising another howl for 'reciprocity,' seeing that the French as well as the English appeared likely to be beaten on English ground, that it would consequently be unreasonable to demand from France a 'reciprocity' which was not to be applied to all the world, and that it would be a mere farce to ask—if asking were even necessary—for such a 'white elephant' from dwellers in the uttermost parts of the earth. That they should think it worth while to visit England was intelligible, for it was only by beating English horses on English ground that they could gain the credit they wanted. But would they be likely to continue the expensive practice when once they had established their own prestige by 'annexing' England's? When they had done that, and not before, it might be for English owners to consider whether the time had come for England to no longer consider her soil as the central arena of international horse-racing—the arena on which she would hold her own against all comers—and to sue for 'reciprocity,' wherever it was not already accorded without any suing, in order that she might pick up a few prizes in foreign lands and learn of the foreigner, whom she used to teach, how to rear and train and race the thoroughbred. But though the Frenchman may have chuckled at the 'rod in pickle' for 'perfidious Albion' in 1881, when he saw Americans victorious and other 'foreigners' among the runners on English soil, he may also have felt a qualm (when he thought of his Grand Prix de Paris and of the additional competitors he would have to encounter on the 'Tom Tiddler's ground' of England) as he read—in his English Calendar of 1881—about the perfect swarm of animals bred elsewhere than in England or France: about Aranza, Aristocrat, Barrett, Bookmaker, Boreas, Brakespeare, Bran Dance, Don Fulano, El Capitan, Fine, Forget-me-not, Gemsbok, General Scott, Gerald, Golden Gate, Idea, Lord Murphy, Marshal Macdonald, Meteor, Mirth, Mistake, North Star, Nuncio, Passaic, Queenfisher, Ranchero, Romeo, Seminole, Seneca, Susquehanna, Useful, Wallenstein, and Wilbert, all 'bred in America;' about Alma, Der Wucherer, Donna Christine, Rawcliffe Ings, bred in Germany; about Bajtars, Berzencze, Coquine, La Gondola, Merry Heart, bred in Austria-Hungary; about Cæsar (by Billesdon), Mowerina (by Scottish Chief), Sheila (by The Palmer), bred in Denmark; about Ciarlatano and Ofanto (both by Heir-at-Law), Speranza and Sukey (both by Pirate King), bred in Italy; and about Darley (by Vadim), Lady Lyon (by Lord Lyon), and Stchaistia (by Vadim), bred in Russia; especially if he remembered that animals 'bred in Australia' had already left the Antipodes and run in the Podes, whether at Newcastle or elsewhere in England, and if his prophetic soul or a 'Calendar of Races to Come' supplied him with a vision of candidates 'bred in Poland,' or 'bred in Spain,' or 'bred in Roumania.' Of course 'bred in Belgium' would have been common enough to him.

But neither for the Frenchmen nor for John Bull himself has there been anything much to fear hitherto; for the former lest any other foreigner should interfere with his 'little pickings' on the English Turf, and for the latter lest Frenchman, German, Austro-Hungarian, Russian, Pole, Italian, Spaniard, Roumanian, Australian, or 'New Zealander' should do him any permanent harm or wrest from him—for more than a moment—his supremacy and his prestige. There has been no Gladiateur since 1865, no Kisbér since 1876, no Chamant since 1877, no Rayon d'Or since 1879, no Iroquois since 1881; and, whatever John Bull may think, it is not for Frenchmen to regret that the deeds of Foxhall in 1881 in England were almost paralleled in 1885 by those of Plaisanterie, or if the Fille de l'Air of 1864 had her example followed by the Reine of 1872, the Camélia and the Enguerrande of 1876. At any rate the swarm of 'Americans' and other 'strange' cattle that threatened the English Turf in 1881 and the following years have either disappeared altogether or have done no permanent damage in any case to Englishmen or Frenchmen. But that as long as England supplies the world with her own 'crack' thoroughbreds one or two of their descendants should swoop down from time to time upon her racecourses and 'clear the board' is only what might be expected and is no more than fair, considering that she offers the rod for her own back—for a 'consideration' of course, and a mighty remunerative one too. There is no great chance, however, to judge from all appearances, that the foreigners' occasional superiority will become chronic. More will be said upon this point hereafter.

To return to the strayed sheep, or rather to make the strayed sheep return.

In 1882 the French nose was still very much out of joint, although M. Lefèvre, with the help of his English horses chiefly, managed to stand second among 'winning owners' in England with 15,087*l.* against Mr. W. S. Crawfurd's 25,797*l.* Count F. de Lagrange was very low down, with 3,175*l.* among 'winning owners' in England (the redoubtable Mr. P. Lorillard having dropped to the bottom of his class with 1,018*l*.). Thus on English soil Chamant had turned the tables completely on Dangu. But meanwhile the famous Dangu stud had come to the hammer, as will appear in the proper place.

In 1882, then, the French 'cracks' at home were M. Michel Ephrussi's St. James and Count F. de Lagrange's Dandin (three years, who ran a dead heat for the French Derby and 'divided'), M. P. Aumont's Mademoiselle de Senlis (three years, winner of the Prix Daru and of the French Oaks), Baron de Rothschild's Barbe-Bleue (three years, winner of the Poule d'Essai), M. H. Delamarre's Vigilant (three years, winner of the Grande Poule des Produits), M. Michel Ephrussi's Dictateur II. (three years, winner of the Prix de Longchamps), M. H. Delamarre's Clio (three years, winner of the Prix Royal Oak and previously of the newly instituted Prix Greffulhe), Count F. de Lagrange's Poulet (five years, winner of the Prix Rainbow), M. Maurice Ephrussi's, Bariolet, four years (winner of the Prix du Cadran, of La Coupe at Paris, and of the Prix Gladiateur), M. A. Lupin's Cimier (three years, winner of the Prix du Nabob); and among the two-year-olds M. A. Lupin's Ontario, Count de Juigné's Madame II., and M. H. Delamarre's Vernet, winners of the three principal 'Critériums,' and M. P. Aumont's Chitré (not engaged in the great races of 1883), winner of the Prix de Deux Ans at Deauville, beating Vernet and Madame II.

Of these 'cracks' there ran in England St. James (unplaced for the Cambridgeshire), Barbe-Bleue (won the Newmarket International Handicap of 405*l*. at the Craven Meeting), Poulet (winner of the Lincolnshire Handicap of 1,614*l*., and third to Tristan and Sweetbread for the valuable Hardwicke Stakes at Ascot), and Bariolet (unplaced for the Goodwood Cup).

The inferior quality of the French three-year-olds of 1882 might be inferred from the manner in which they would beat one another, without rhyme or reason, as seldom happens when there is a really good lot of three-year-olds running, and also from the result of the Grand Prix, in which Bruce, not by any means the best English horse of his year (horse including mare), 'had reason' easily of the seven French competitors brought against him, though they certainly did not include Mademoiselle de Senlis, Clio, Barbe-Bleue, or Comte Alfred.

As for this last, the hope of Chamant so far as 'French' horses were concerned, how he took to humours and tantrums and violence and caused 'grand deceptions' has already been noticed. In his own country, at three years of age, he was of very little use (though he ran second to Barbe-Bleue for the Poule d'Essai and won the Prix de Meautry at Deauville from some moderate opponents), but in England, after being unplaced for the Two Thousand, he won the Sussex Stakes (with odds of 20 to 1 against him) of 1,042*l*. at Goodwood, beating Dutch Oven, the favourite at evens, but she afterwards galloped out of his sight at Newmarket.

Of the other French horses that ran in England the chief, if not the whole, were Alcindor (two years, unplaced for the July Stakes and for the Rous Memorial at Goodwood), Athalie (two years; ran 'all over the shop,' but won nothing beyond a selling handicap of 101*l*. at Alexandra Park), Azor (two years, did nothing but ran much), Azur (two years; unplaced for the Halnaker Stakes at Goodwood, and did no more), *Castillon* (five years, unplaced for the Visitors' Plate at Newmarket and for the Stewards' Cup at Goodwood), Conquérant (two years, unplaced for the Hopeful Stakes at Newmarket First October), Crédo (three years, second for the Burwell Stakes and unplaced for the Payne Stakes at Newmarket Second Spring), Déesse (two years, ran thrice to no purpose), *Eliacin* (four years, won the Visitors' Plate of 194*l.* at Newmarket First Spring, won the Beaudesert Welter Plate of 101*l.* at Lichfield, won a selling sweepstakes of 102*l.* at Newmarket Second October, and won the All-aged Selling Plate of 102*l.* at Newmarket Houghton), Etincelle (two years; ran once—unsuccessfully—for a selling plate at Newmarket July), *Fénelon* (unplaced for the Derby and for the Royal Hunt Cup at Ascot; won the Brighton Cup of 438*l.*, beating Petronel in a canter; unplaced for the St. Leger), Feuille de Frêne (four years, unplaced for the Visitors' Plate at Newmarket July, unplaced for the Prince of Wales's Cup Handicap at Kempton Park, unplaced for the Surbiton Handicap at Sandown Park, fourth and last for the Forest Handicap at Windsor), Fusain (three years, third for the Batthyany Stakes at Lincoln), Ganimède (two years, unplaced for a Scurry Nursery at Newmarket Second October), *Innocent* (five years, unplaced for the Craven Stakes at Epsom, &c.), *Jasmin* (three years; unplaced for the Cesarewitch, for the Queen's Plate at Newmarket, and for the Cambridgeshire), *Macadam* (aged; ran once—at Hampton—unplaced), *Malibran* (two years; unplaced for the Acorn Stakes at Epsom, unplaced for the Chesterfield Stakes at Newmarket July, and unplaced for the Clearwell Stakes), Michel (five years; won a welter handicap of 177*l.* at Newmarket Craven; unplaced for the City and Suburban, &c.), Newmarket (two years; ran twice, unplaced), *Panique* (four years; unplaced for the Lincolnshire Handicap, won by her 'compatriot' Poulet, &c.),

Prudhomme (five years, won the Chester Cup of 947*l*., and 170*l*. at Newmarket), Picador (four years, did no good), Prolixe (three years, did no good), *Regain* (two years, unplaced for the Dewhurst Plate), *Risette* (two years; unplaced for the July Stakes, &c.), Salade (two years, did no good), *Sutler* (aged, won the Royal Stakes of 316*l*. at Sandown Park and the Alexandra Plate of 370*l*. at Doncaster), Talmouse (four years, won two selling plates amounting to 202*l*.), Uranie (two years, unplaced twice), and Villers (two years; ran four times, unplaced)—about thirty in number, those whose names are printed in italics having acquired some sort of reputation at some time or other either at home or in England.

The French horses of 1882, then, whether belonging to French or English owners, did not do much to 'illustrate' either themselves or their 'blood;' and the front shown among 'winning owners' in England by M. Lefèvre was due to the prowess of his horses 'bred in England'—to Tristan (with whom, as a yearling, so good a judge as Lord Rosslyn was very surprisingly induced to part at a moderate price), to Hauteur, to Ladislas, and so on, the first-named having won (counting a dead heat) nine events and 6,641*l*. in England (besides the Grand Prix de Deauville of 960*l*.), and the other two having won the Doncaster Champagne Stakes of 1,030*l*., the Clearwell Stakes of 1,067*l*., and the Dewhurst Plate of 1,557*l*. between them, besides smaller stakes.

Undoubtedly, however, the great event of the French Turf in 1882 was the break-up of the 'Lagrange' confederacy and the consequent sale of the Dangu stud, of which Count F. de Lagrange had been either the owner or the director (after a confederacy had been formed) ever since the 'split' with Baron Nivière.

The sale was announced for the 5th, 6th, and 7th of September, and was accompanied by a great flourish of trumpets. Mr. Edmund Tattersall was engaged to wield the hammer, or to assist the representative of 'Le Tattersall Français' in wielding it; and they were backed up by the legal co-operation of M. Hemet, of Chantilly, and M. Foullon, notary, of Gisors.

There were thirty-two brood mares, forty-five mares with foals, forty-six suckers, twenty-nine yearlings, and eleven stallions.

After all the fuss that had been made about it the sale was a bit of a failure, a case of 'parturiunt montes, &c.'

The stallions Peut-être, Prologue, Fleuret, and Albion were withdrawn at reserve prices of 1,680*l.*, 200*l.*, 260*l.*, and 700*l.* respectively. Of the other seven stallions Rayon d'Or was sold to an American (for Mr. W. Scott's stud, Pennsylvania) for 150,000 francs (6,000*l.*), Isolier was sold to M. Aveline for 6,200 francs (248*l.*), Léon to the Duke de Feltre for 8,500 francs (340*l.*), Inval to MM. Coppée and Buisseret for 10,100 francs (404*l.*), Milan to the Haras de Villebon (Count de Meëus) for 33,000 francs (1,320*l.*), Nougat to M. Malapert (of the Haras d'Albian, Vienne) for 41,000 francs (1,640*l.*), and Flavio to M. Joubert for 20,000 francs (800*l.*).

The noted mare Clémentine was withdrawn at a reserve price of 38,000 francs (1,520*l.*).

Of the most famous mares sold Tafna went to M. Crombez for only 4,700 francs (188*l.*), Fauvette to Mr. T. Jennings (who resold her to M. Fould) for 14,600 francs (584*l.*), Printanière to M. A. Lupin for 25,000 francs (1,000*l.*), Océanie to M. C. J. Lefèvre for

29,500 francs (1,180*l*.), Dotation to M. Joubert for 10,000 francs (400*l*.), La Farandole to Count Lehndorf for 8,000 francs (320*l*.), Laure to Count Lehndorf for 7,000 francs (280*l*.), Aigrette to M. de la Charme for 8,000 francs (320*l*.), Caroline to Count de Robien for 8,000 francs (320*l*.), Silencieuse to M. Joubert for 7,000 francs (280*l*.), Ultima to M. Joubert for 10,000 francs (400*l*.), Vengeance to Baron A. Schickler for 8,400 francs (336*l*.), Verdurette to Count Lehndorf for 22,000 francs (880*l*.), Japonica to Baron A. Schickler for 13,000 francs (520*l*.), Doucereuse to Mr. Kronenberg for 9,600 francs (384*l*.), Hallate to Count de Robien for 6,000 francs (240*l*.), and Isole to Mr. H. Hawes for 6,000 francs (240*l*.), &c.

The highest price fetched for a yearling was given for Diplomate (by Saint Christophe and Dotation), purchased by Count A. de Montgomery for 30,000 francs (1,200*l*.), a price which even Mr. Henry Chaplin (who would be much amused at the other prices) would not altogether despise. Diplomate, however, went the way of most high-priced yearlings: at two years of age (having come into the hands of Baron de Rothschild) he ran once, and that once in England, but could do nothing better than a 'bad third' to Fantail and Votary for the Round Tower Plate at Windsor; and at three years of age he did not run at all in England, but ran ten times in his own country, where he did not 'illustrate himself' at all, winning just one (selling) race and being sold for 181 sovs. This may have been 'diplomacy,' but it was not a paying description of it.

Altogether (twenty lots being withdrawn) the sale fetched 895,000 francs (35,800*l*.).

This sale was naturally followed by another (of horses in training and others), which took place on

November 11 and was not more successful than the former.

Meanwhile, be it premised, some of the horses belonging to the 'Lagrange' stable had been sold at Newmarket, including Dandin (to Count Lehndorf for 600 guineas), Déjanire (to Mr. Cocksworth for 20 guineas), Executor (to Mr. Barnard for 130 guineas), Psycho (to Mr. Sheriff for 60 guineas), Nuremberg (to Mr. Baker for 25 guineas), and Lady May (to Mr. A. Cooper for 190 guineas).

For Farfadet (then two years old) there was some disputation, and Mr. F. Robinson went as high as 108,000 francs (4,320*l*.), but he was bought in for 109,000 francs (4,360*l*.), and Veston (three years) and Octave (five years) were bought in for 62,000 francs (2,480*l*.) and 23,500 francs (940*l*.) respectively. Withdrawn also were Hollandaise, Albion, Castillon, Fleuret, Bengale, Bombivore, Cléopâtre, D'Argental, Derviche, Duc, Florida, Fortunée, Futée, Péruvienne, Turnus, Valère, Danois, Ducat, Intègre, Natal, Gourgandin, and Pâtre. Ultimately Count de Lagrange himself secured Farfadet.

The sold, then, were the following, at the prices given:—

Florence, by Consul and Flaub, Baron van Loo, 2,750 francs (110*l*.).

Maîtresse, by Flageolet and Cerdagne, M. Guyon, 1,800 francs (72*l*.).

Sirène, by Boïard and Sérénade, Baron van Loo, 2,100 francs (84*l*.).

Ballade, by Beau Merle and Blanche, M. Guyon, 1,425 francs (57*l*.).

Flambant, by Insulaire or Peut-être and Florence, M. Moreau-Chaslon, 1,275 francs (51*l*.).

Lieutenant, by Insulaire or Peut-être and Lumineuse, the same, 1,475 francs (59*l*.).

Maximum, by Rayon d'Or and Mademoiselle de Mello, Duke de Feltre, 2,100 francs (84*l.*).

Opérette, by Saint-Christophe or Peut-être and Lumineuse, M. Guyon, 1,175 francs (47*l.*).

Prélude, by Flavio and Piquette, M. Moreau-Chaslon, 1,325 francs (53*l.*).

Scintillant, by Nougat and Sirène, M. Balensi, 1,700 francs (68*l.*).

Perdrix, by Nougat and Printanière, Baron van Loo, 3,000 francs (120*l.*).

Touffe, by Nougat and Tulipe, Mr. H. Gibson, 1,475 francs (59*l.*).

Prologue, by Dollar and Planète, M. Delamarre, 5,000 francs (200*l.*).

Arabelle, by Beau Merle and Angleterre, Mr. Hawes, 11,500 francs (460*l.*).

Benoiton, by Beau Merle and Batterie, M. Boulanger, 1,000 francs (40*l.*).

Brune, by Consul and Bombarde, M. Mosselman, 4,000 francs (160*l.*).

Fanal, by Consul and Faribole, M. Maurice W., 10,100 francs (404*l.*).

Hidalgo, by Consul and Hallate, M. Olery, 1,000 francs (40*l.*).

Iliade, by Beau Merle and Inconnue, Duke de Fezensac, 1,300 francs (52*l.*).

Ménade, by Saint-Christophe and Moissonneuse, M. de la Charme, 1,500 francs (60*l.*).

Pandore, by Consul and Pie Grièche, Colonel de Blaramberg, 1,000 francs (40*l.*).

Rhéteur, by Beau Merle and La Reine Elisabeth, M. Riondel, 1,000 francs (40*l.*).

Sabine, by Beau Merle and Silencieuse, M. Maurice W., 35,000 francs (1,400*l.*).

Talisman, by Nougat and Tulipe, Count de Nicolay, 8,000 francs (320*l.*).

Tartare, by Saint-Christophe and Tolla, M. Fould, 6,200 francs (248*l.*).

Valois, by Consul and Verdurette, M. Balensi, 50,000 francs (2,000*l.*).

Alhambra, by Consul and The Abbess, M. Sureau, 6,000 francs (240*l*.).

Anglais, by Beau Merle and Angleterre, M. Balensi, 10,000 francs (400*l*.).

Cydalise, by Gabier and Chimène, M. Abeille, 2,000 francs (80*l*.).

Javeline, by Wellingtonia and Jeanne Hachette, M. Marais, 1,250 francs (50*l*.).

Merise, by Consul and Mark Over, Baron van Loo, 4,600 francs (184*l*.).

Montaigu, by Beau Merle and Marion, Mr. H. Gibson, 8,000 francs (320*l*.).

Nathalie, by Beau Merle and Noisette, M. Saulty, 2,750 francs (110*l*.).

Pistache, by Nougat and Printanière, M. Pariche, 3,400 francs (136*l*.).

Royallieu, by Nougat and La Reine Berthe, M. de Reverschoot, 12,000 francs (480*l*.).

Templier, by Consul and Teacher, M. Orsetti, 3,100 francs (124*l*.).

Turbulent, by Gabier and Tendresse, M. Maurice W., 19,300 francs (772*l*.).

Dublin, by Gabier and Dordogne, M. de Nieuil, 10,000 francs (400*l*.).

Lectrice, by Consul and La Reine Berthe, M. de Gernon, 8,000 francs (320*l*.).

Panique, by Gabier and Princesse, Mr. Wigginton, 7,800 francs (312*l*.).

Abîme, by Insulaire and Active, M. Marais, 2,000 francs (80*l*.).

Capitole, by Saint-Christophe or Rayon d'Or and Californie, M. Provost, 2,100 francs (84*l*.).

Total 260,500 francs (10,420*l*.).

Total for the two sales 1,155,500 francs (46,220*l*.).

This, though it looks very well in francs, is a very poor result in pounds sterling for the property of a 'confederacy' with the famous Count de Lagrange at its head. It is true that many 'lots' were withdrawn, but even then the grand total looks very shabby beside Mr. Blenkiron's 124,620*l.* (which did not include any horses in training) in 1872 and Lord Falmouth's 147,720*l.* (which does not include 7,000*l.* paid privately for Silvio) at Newmarket First Spring and July Meetings in 1884. The 'break-up' of the Lagrange confederacy was ominous of another 'break-up,' that of Count Lagrange himself, whose health had for some time been in an unsatisfactory state, and who was destined to 'go over to the majority' at the end of the next year (November 21, 1883).

In 1883 the French 'cracks' at home were the Duke de Castries's Frontin (three years, winner of the French Derby and of the Grand Prix de Paris), M. H. Delamarre's Verte-Bonne (three years, winner of the French Oaks), Count F. de Lagrange's Farfadet (three years, winner of the Prix de Longchamps and of the Prix Greffulhe), M. Lefèvre's (Haras de Chamant's) Regain (three years, winner of the Poule d'Essai des Poulains), M. A. Staub's (Haras de Lonray's) Stockholm (three years, winner of the Poule d'Essai des Pouliches and of the Prix Royal Oak), M. H. Delamarre's Vernet (three years, winner of the Prix du Nabob), M. Michel Ephrussi's Rubens (three years, winner of the Prix Daru), M. E. Blanc's Soukaras (three years, winner of the Grande Poule des Produits), the Duke de Castries's Seigneur II. (four years, winner of the Prix du Cadran), M. P. Aumont's Mademoiselle de Senlis (four years, winner of La Coupe at Paris and of the Prix Gladiateur), M. Maurice Ephrussi's Bariolet (five years, winner of the Prix Rainbow); and among the two-year-olds Count de Berteux's Sansonnet, (?) Mr. H. Jennings's Infidèle, M. P. Aumont's Fra Diavolo, and Viscount de Trédern's

Directrice, winners of the three principal Critériums and of the Prix de Deux Ans at Deauville.

It should be mentioned here that the old Poule d'Essai for colts and fillies was this year, 1883, split, as it were, into two, and run in two 'bits,' one called the Poule d'Essai des Poulains (for colts only) and the other the Poule d'Essai des Pouliches (for fillies only). The opportunity may be taken also of remarking that the Prix du Nabob (a Produce Stakes for three-year-olds) at Paris Spring Meeting was first run for in 1878 (when it was won by Clémentine, whose success was followed by that of Zut in 1879, Pacific in 1880, and Forum in 1881), and that the Prix Greffulhe (also a Produce Stakes for three-year-olds) at Paris Spring Meeting dates only from 1882, when it was won by Clio.

It will be convenient also to speak here of what befell Rubens and Fra Diavolo. In June 1883 poor Rubens, having met with an injury to his leg, went nearly mad with pain, and was ultimately found dead in his stable. As for Fra Diavolo, when he came out as a three-year-old in 1884 to win the Prix de Longchamps with 'odds *on* him' he was not 'in it,' and it was commonly stated that he had been 'got at,' 'nobbled,' 'hocussed,' and so on. Whether it was so or not he ran 'rabbit-like'—that is, 'in and out'—all his career.

But to return to the French 'cracks' of 1883 that won the chief races at home; of these there ran in England Regain (twice, unplaced) only. Of the other French horses that ran in England the chief, if not the whole, were M. C. J. Lefèvre's Arbalète (three years, ran a great deal and won one handicap of 187*l*. at Newmarket Houghton), Count F. de Lagrange's *Archi-*

duc (two years, second by a head to Queen Adelaide for the July Stakes and won the Criterion Stakes of 936*l*.), M. Michel Ephrussi's Bathilde (two years, unplaced for the Lincoln Spring Cup), M. C. J. Lefèvre's Bric-à-brac (three years, ran once and won 192*l*. at Newmarket Craven), M. C. J. Lefèvre's Carton (two years, unplaced at Newmarket July), Mr. W. Wright's Conquérant (three years, unplaced at Newmarket Second October), M. C. J. Lefèvre's Couvre-chef (two years, unplaced at Newmarket July), M. C. J. Lefèvre's Crédo (four years; won the Queen's Plate of 210*l*. at Salisbury, and ran six times besides to no purpose, for the Gold Vase and Alexandra Plate at Ascot, &c.), Baron de Rothschild's Diplomate (two years, third for the Round Tower Plate at Windsor), Baron de Rothschild's Egérie (two years, won the FitzWilliam Stakes of 245*l*. at Doncaster, but made six other attempts without success), Mr. Peck's *Eliacin* (five years; won the Prince of Wales's Cup of 295*l*. at Liverpool Spring, the Datchet Handicap Plate of 194*l*. at Windsor Spring, as well as the Winkfield Welter Handicap Plate of 102*l*. and the Londesborough Plate Handicap of 101*l*. at Doncaster Spring), Baron de Rothschild's Fée (two years, unplaced for the Portland Nursery Plate at Four Oaks Park), the Duke of Hamilton's *Fénelon* (four years; unplaced for the Royal Hunt Cup at Ascot; won the Goodwood Corinthian Plate Handicap of 437*l*.; unplaced for the Chichester Stakes Handicap at Goodwood, and broke down, but was second to Border Minstrel for the Caledonian Cup at Ayr), Count F. de Lagrange's Flandrin (two years, unplaced for the Chesterfield Stakes at Newmarket July), M. C. J. Lefèvre's Formalité (three years; unplaced for the Coronation Stakes at Ascot and for the Cambridgeshire, as well as the Newmarket October Handicap), M. Michel Ephrussi's Ganimède (three years, unplaced for the Two Thousand), Mr. F. Robinson's *Innocent* (six years, unplaced for the Lincolnshire Handicap and for the Craven Stakes at Goodwood), Baron de Rothschild's *Louis d'Or* (six years; won the Suffolk Plate of 154*l*. at Newmarket July, the July Handicap of 256*l*. at Windsor, and the Queen's Plate of 210*l*. at Huntingdon), Mr. E. Hunter's *Macadam* (aged, unplaced at Edinburgh), Count F. de Lagrange's *Malibran* (three years; a most unfortunate animal both at home and in England; second to Hauteur for the One Thousand by a head, unplaced for the Epsom Grand Prize, second to Bonny Jean for the Oaks, and twice unplaced, and in her own country second by a head to Stockholm at Paris and third by a 'short neck' and a head to Verte Bonne and Stockholm for the French Oaks at Chantilly), Baron de Rothschild's colt by Mars and My Wonder (two years, unplaced for the Brocklesby Stakes at Lincoln Spring), Baron de Rothschild's Merlin II. (three years, unplaced at Four Oaks Park), Baron de Rothschild's Monsieur (three years, ran once and won a plate of 102*l*. at Newmarket Craven), M. Michel Ephrussi's *Newmarket* (three years, ran once and won the Yarborough Plate Handicap of 146*l*. at Lincoln Spring), M. C. J. Lefèvre's Octave (six years, unplaced for the Lincolnshire Handicap), Mr. T. Cannon's Picador (five years, ran a great deal and won only the Liverpool Spring Cup of 651*l*.), M. C. J. Lefèvre's Piccolo II. (two years; second for the Brocklesby Stakes, second for the Althorp Park Stakes, and unplaced twice besides), Lord Rosebery's *Prudhomme* (six years; ran twice only and won two Queen's Plates, 420*l*.), M. Michel Ephrussi's *Richelieu* (two years; unplaced for the Fern Hill Stakes at Ascot, second for the Halnaker Stakes—*longo intervallo*—to the redoubtable St. Simon at Goodwood, second and last to Eastern Empress for the Lennox Stakes, second to The Lambkin for the Rous Plate at Doncaster, and unplaced twice besides), M. C. J. Lefèvre's Rosny (two years, fourth and last for the Granby Stakes at Newmarket First October), M. Michel Ephrussi's *St. James* (four years, unplaced for the Lincolnshire Handicap and for the Babraham Stakes at Newmarket Craven), Baron de Rothschild's *Serge II.* (two years, won the Stetchworth Stakes of 190*l.* at Newmarket July, third for the Midsummer Plate at Windsor July, third for the Richmond Stakes and for the Findon Stakes at Goodwood), M. C. J. Lefèvre's Serquigny (two years, unplaced at Newmarket Craven), Baron de Rothschild's *Skye* (three years; ran many times, and won 194*l.* at Brighton August and 101*l.* at Sandown Park), the American 'plunger' Mr. Walton's *Sutler* (aged, ran several times and won the Lewes Autumn Handicap of 199*l.*), Baron de Rothschild's Valence II. (three years; ran twice, unplaced), Baron de Rothschild's Vestris II. (unplaced for the Althorp Park Stakes), and Mr. H. N. Smith's Voisine (two years; third for a maiden plate at Ascot, fourth for the Stetchworth Stakes, and unplaced for a Nursery handicap at Newmarket First October)—about forty in number, and of them those whose names are printed in italics obtained some reputation at some time either at home or in England.

The Grand Prix de Paris was a great triumph for the French, recalling memories of 'Vermout's year' and 'Boïard's year,' for once more a winner of the English Derby (St. Blaise) was beaten (as Blair Athol and Doncaster had been) by a horse 'bred in France' (Frontin), though the 'Englishman' was second, beating all the other candidates—every one 'bred in France'—Farfadet, Satory, Regain, Attendez-moi sous l'Orme, Derviche, and Rêveuse. Virtually, however, it was a victory for John Bull, a testimonial to John Bull's thoroughbreds at any rate; for Frontin (by George Frederick and Frolicsome, English sire and English dam) had his 'foundations laid' in England, before his dam was imported into France. This was a fact for Lord Falmouth and his co-howlers for 'reciprocity' to ponder upon; for it seemed that France could not yet quite 'walk alone,' had still to rely upon England's thoroughbreds for something to win her own Derby at Chantilly and her Grand Prix de Paris. And this fact was to be further emphasised by what would take place the next year.

By the end of April 1883 the best French horses of the year (three-year-olds) were supposed to be Frontin, Farfadet, Florestan (did not run for the Grand Prix and was not seen in England, but he was a beauty to look at, it was said, and not a bad one to go), Chitré (not engaged in any of the great races), Regain, Satory, Skye, Garrick, Vernet, Dard, Soukaras, Stockholm, Malibran, and Rubens; but few of them, as we have seen, appeared in England, and none of them did anything particular there that year.

The Frenchmen's campaign of 1883, then, in England was not to their very great 'illustration;' for though M. C. J. Lefèvre once more headed the list of 'winning owners' in England with 20,536*l.*, giving Lord Falmouth (18,434*l.*) more than a '2,000*l.* beating,' it was to his English horses, especially to Tristan (7,628*l.* in England alone), that he was indebted for his score, to Hauteur (won the One Thousand of 2,900*l.*), to Wild Thyme (won the Woodcote Stakes of 897*l.*, the

New Stakes of 1,151*l*., the Exeter Stakes of 420*l*., the Lavant Stakes of 1,000*l*., and the Hopeful Stakes of 807*l*. = 4,275*l*. altogether), to Ladislas (winner of the Ascot Derby of 1,375*l*., beating Ossian and St. Blaise; ran a dead heat and divided 382*l*. for the Midsummer Stakes with Henley at Newmarket; won the Newmarket St. Leger of 797*l*., the Newmarket Derby of 767*l*., and the Jockey Club Cup of 520*l*., beating Corrie Roy, Faugh-a-Ballagh, and Dutch Oven = 3,841*l*.), and to one or two others. As for poor Count F. de Lagrange, he was 'nowhere,' with a paltry 936*l*. (though second with 320,000 francs or 12,800*l*. in his own country); and Chamant had beaten Dangu out of sight.

The most memorable event of 1883 for the French Turf was undoubtedly the death of Count F. de Lagrange, who had received a 'warning,' as it were, in the August of that year (from an affection of the heart); and on November 21 he died at his house in Rue du Cirque, Paris. The following sketches of the man and his career are taken from the English 'Standard,' and the French journals 'Le Sport' and 'Le Figaro.' Between them a full portrait will be obtained of the Frenchman who, though not among the earliest 'fathers of the French Turf,' was assuredly chief among its 'second fathers,' and did more than they all to make it celebrated throughout the world. Said the 'Standard'—

Count Frédéric de Lagrange, born in 1816, was the son of a distinguished French soldier, General Lagrange, who encountered the English on bloodier fields than those of Newmarket and Epsom, and who, having been created a Count of the Empire in 1806, was made a Peer of France by Louis Philippe in 1831, and died in 1836, leaving a large property and four children, Count Frédéric and three daughters. With the fortunes of the three daughters we need not here concern ourselves. They married among the French nobility, and their brother, Count

Frédéric, married twice, without issue. But the Count Frédéric was a considerable man of business and of fashion from his earliest days, taking great interest in mines, canals, railroads, and glass factories, and occupying a brilliant social position in Paris. He became noted for his dress and his equipages in the Bois, and as a patron of art and literature, music, and the drama. He (as well as his father) had been a member of the French Jockey Club almost from its origin in 1833, when he was but a boy; but it was not until 1857 that he took seriously to horse-racing. He had long before, however, in 1836, started his stag hounds at his Château of Dangu, which he inherited in right of his mother, a De Talhouët, and he had for huntsman the celebrated Latrace, whose services were borrowed by the Emperor Napoleon III.; for between the Emperor and the Count there was a close bond of friendship—so close, indeed, that rumours were current, and currently believed, concerning a confederacy formed between the two for the purposes of horse-racing. However that may be, the intimacy probably began or was cemented at a later date than 1848, when the Count is stated to have headed a battalion of the National Guards for the sake of preserving order.

When he had once fairly entered upon the business as well as pleasure of horse-racing, he soon became as well known both by sight and by name on the English turf as on the French, at Newmarket as at Chantilly; there is some tradition of his having acted as steward at one or more of our race meetings; and certainly in 1865 or 1866 he was elected an honorary member of our Jockey Club. From that date he was, as an owner and runner of race horses, almost more English than French. On the other hand, with him may be said to have originated the vast improvement which reached such rapid development among the French thoroughbreds that we in the course of a dozen years became alarmed for the supremacy we had so long enjoyed as the breeders and runners of the best horses in the world. The first foal ever dropped at the Count's own stud farm at Dangu is said to have been Marignan, by Womersley, foaled in 1859, who won races at two years of age in England, and was purchased for 1,000*l*. by the French Government at the break-up of the Lagrange-Nivière confederacy after the season of 1862. For Count de Lagrange, having begun his racing career by purchasing the excellent stud of the celebrated MM. Aumont, and retaining the services of Tom Jennings as trainer, in 1857, had soon afterwards entered into partnership with Baron Nivière, who had struck a similar bargain with Prince Marc de Beauvau for the stud of La Morlaye and the services of Henry Jennings, the elder brother of Tom; and the united owners set up an establishment at Newmarket, and, with the assistance of 'the great twin brethren' as trainers, Tom at Newmarket and Henry at Chantilly, Royallieu, La Morlaye, and wherever else the Count trained in France, did so well in England that the 'Big Stable,' as the fraternity was called, stood fifth on the English list of winning owners in 1861, the first year of asking. But at the end of another year the partnership was dissolved, and the Count carried on the campaign in England single-handed, and single-handed he carried the triumphs of French blood stock to a climax that astounded both countries. It was whispered, no doubt, that the Count had an Imperial partner in the place of the retired Baron, and the sale of the Count's stud on the eve of 'the event of 1870' has been held to give colour to the tale, but the whole story has also been denounced as an invention of the enemy, and at any rate it has never been substantiated.

The Count, then, has to be accepted as the sole head of the stable which raised the reputation of the French Turf to the highest possible pitch by meeting us and beating us on our own ground with such 'clippers' as Fille de l'Air and Gladiateur, after he had threatened us and made us quake for a while at the two-year-old doings of Hospodar. The Count too it was who bred the majority of French horses with which his successor and quasi-partner, M. Lefèvre, whether racing as 'Mr. Lombard' or as the 'Tricolour' personified, kept up the *prestige* of the French thoroughbreds. Chamant had not then made itself a name in the history of studs; it was from Dangu that M. Lefèvre received Mortemer, by Compiègne, whom the Americans purchased at a great price, and the high-priced sire Flageolet, by Plutus. The Count's familiar colours began to reappear upon the racecourse in 1874, but it was not until the next year that the Lagrange-Lefèvre 'fusion,' as it has been called, represented by the 'colours' of the Count, came out in such style that he seemed to have returned like a giant refreshed with sleep, and began to show a more formidable front than ever. None of the great races is set down to the credit of his name for that season, but at the end of it he stood third upon the list of 'winning owners' with upwards of 9,000*l*., though at a long interval certainly from Lord Falmouth, with more than 20,000*l*. The next year, however, was to show a different score, when the Count headed the list with more than 17,000*l*. to the 10,000*l*. of Lord Falmouth. The Count's Camélia and Allumette, though only technically French bred, were first and second for the One Thousand; his Camélia ran a dead heat with the French Enguerrande for the Oaks; his Braconnier won the Jockey Club Cup, and his two-year-olds Verneuil, Chamant, and Léopold did so valiantly that, Kisbér and other 'foreigners' having won the Derby and other races, the British lion fairly roared for 'reciprocity.' In 1877 the Count did very well with Saint-Christophe, Chamant, and Verneuil, and would have done wonderfully well if Chamant had not met with misfortune. In 1878 he—having left the 'fusion' and headed a partnership, or rather company—did not do so well. In 1879 he did magnificently, chiefly by means of Rayon d'Or, for he stood at the top of the list, with winnings that amounted to more than 26,000*l*.—about 3,000*l*. more than Lord Falmouth won. After this the glory departed from Dangu; the Count and his Company won less and less, and at last, in 1882, there was a dissolution of partnership and a sale of the stud. The sale, unfortunately, was a failure; for though the Americans gave 6,000*l*. for Rayon d'Or, the other horses, the brood mares, and the colts and fillies fetched but sorry prices.

To enumerate all the events won by the Count in his own country and in England would be to enumerate nearly all but the most insignificant provincial races of both countries, and of course he won both great and small races at the various meetings, not once or twice, but year after year. In England he began, to mention only the greater races, by winning the Goodwood Cup with Monarque, in his 'first year,' 1857; he won the Newmarket Handicap with Monarque in 1858; he won the Cambridgeshire with Palestro in 1861, a horse that had cost only sixteen guineas as a yearling; and he had already won the

Fern Hill Stakes at Ascot with Marignan, beating Brown Duchess, winner of the Oaks, by a head. In 1862 he made quite a temporary sensation with Hospodar, who won both the Clearwell and the Criterion, and so gave promise which, however, was not fulfilled. In 1863 he made even a greater, and certainly a more lasting, sensation with Fille de l'Air, who, distinguished as she was at two years of age, was far more distinguished at three. In 1864 he won the Lincolnshire Handicap with Benjamin, the Oaks and several other good things with Fille de l'Air, and the Clearwell with Gladiateur; in 1865 he simply swept the board both in England and France with Gladiateur, who won the Derby, for which Count de Lagrange had already made several gallant bids, but in vain, with Dangu and Royallieu and Hospodar and Jarnicoton. There was then a lull—though the Count won the Woodcote with Le Sarrazin in 1867, and some other races—until, after his stud was transferred to 'Mr. Lombard,' and Mortemer and Trocadéro had shed glory on the 'Tricolour' at Ascot and elsewhere, he returned in 1874 to the Turf, and ran horses, whether single-handed or in conjunction with M. Lefèvre. In 1875 the Count's colours were 'illustrated' generally rather than specially, so that he, representing the 'fusion,' stood second on the English list of 'winning owners;' but in 1876 he won the Middle Park Plate and the Dewhurst Plate with Chamant, and the One Thousand and half the Oaks with Camélia, as well as other races. In the three next years he won all manner of races, notably the Two Thousand and the St. Leger—with Chamant, Verneuil, Clémentine, the unlucky Yellow-Jack-like Insulaire, and the somewhat fortunate Rayon d'Or, with whom the tide may be said to have reached the flood and begun to ebb. Monarque, Gladiateur, Ventre Saint-Gris, Trocadéro, Mortemer, Consul, Le Sarrazin, Peut-être, Nougat, Flageolet, and Rayon d'Or have all at various times found a home, and Monarque has found a grave, at Dangu. These are names that must be remembered as long as the 'sport of kings' remains in vogue, and as often as they are mentioned they will recall the memory of Count F. de Lagrange. The best horses he had in these last days were Farfadet—and Farfadet was a disappointment—and Archiduc, with whom he won the Criterion at the late Houghton Meeting.

Said ' Le Sport '—

Ce nom évoque immédiatement à l'esprit celui de Gladiateur, dont les éclatants succès ont tant contribué à rendre populaire la casaque bleue et rouge. Il en est un autre cependant qui se trouve lié, sinon plus directement, au moins d'une façon plus constante, au souvenir de M. le comte de Lagrange : nous voulons parler de Monarque. C'est à lui que la célèbre casaque doit ses premières victoires, et c'est avec ses descendants, dont Gladiateur fut le plus illustre, qu'elle a remporté la plupart de ses triomphes ; c'est avec Farfadet, petit-fils (? arrière-petit-fils) de Monarque, qu'elle a obtenu ses plus récents succès et qu'elle a failli gagner le prix du Jockey Club pour la dernière fois.

La haute compétence de M. le comte de Lagrange en matière hippique n'a jamais été discutée et s'est révélée dès le premier jour par l'acquisition de ce cheval célèbre. Il avait, en outre, le don du commandement et les qualités nécessaires pour l'exercer. Il a su choisir les hommes qu'il employait et leur imposer son autorité. C'est une condition essentielle, on ne saurait le dire trop haut, pour bien conduire une grande écurie de courses : il y a sans contredit des chances heureuses, mais les succès obtenus pendant une longue période ne peuvent être le résultat du hasard.

L'histoire de la Grande Ecurie, dont le comte de Lagrange a été l'organisateur et le chef, comprend au moins sept périodes distinctes ; plusieurs associations ont été formées par lui et se sont ensuite dissoutes, mais les deux phases les plus brillantes de cette longue série de luttes toujours glorieuses ont été de 1864 à 1866 et de 1876 à 1879. Gladiateur et Fille de l'Air sont de la première époque. Chamant, Verneuil, Camélia, Saint-Christophe, Clémentine, Insulaire et Rayon d'Or appartiennent à la seconde.

On sait quels furent les débuts de cette écurie célèbre. En 1856 on apprit un jour que M. Aumont allait vendre ses chevaux. L'adjudication devait être publique et promettait d'être émouvante, mais elle n'eut pas lieu, car le comte de Lagrange, attiré vers le turf par les difficultés mêmes qu'on lui faisait pressentir, acheta directement Monarque, Peu d'Espoir, Mademoiselle de Chantilly, plusieurs autres chevaux à l'entraînement et treize yearlings avec cinq poulains et pouliches de l'année.

Ce fut une déconvenue pour quelques-uns, mais c'était une véritable fortune pour l'élevage. A partir de ce moment les tentatives un peu timides qui avaient été faites jusqu'alors pour entamer la lutte avec les chevaux anglais sur leur propre terrain furent renouvelées avec plus d'audace et de persévérance. Dès l'année suivante, c'est-à-dire en 1857, Monarque remportait dans la Coupe de Goodwood une victoire assez inattendue, puisqu'il partit à 16/1.

En 1858 il enleva le Newmarket Handicap, tandis que Mademoiselle de Chantilly, à la surprise générale, gagnait le City et Suburban. Puis, il fallut attendre jusqu'en 1861 pour remporter de nouveaux succès de quelque importance sur le turf anglais ; mais la lutte continuait, et cette ténacité trouva sa récompense avec Palestro dans le Cambridgeshire, avec Hospodar dans les Criterion et Clearwell Stakes, avec Stradella dans deux épreuves où elle battait les meilleurs chevaux de son âge, enfin avec Fille de l'Air et Gladiateur.

En France le prix de Diane fut gagné en 1857 et 1858 par Mademoiselle de Chantilly et Etoile du Nord ; le prix du Jockey Club, en 1858 et 1859, par Ventre Saint-Gris et Black Prince ; Monarque remporta le Grand Prix impérial (aujourd'hui prix Gladiateur) en 1857 ; Zouave et Nuncio enlevèrent successivement l'Omnium en 1858 et 1859.

Une seule écurie tenait tête à celle du comte Lagrange : M. le baron Nivière, à l'exemple de ce dernier, avait acheté en 1857 tous les chevaux du prince de Beauvau et gardé son entraîneur H. Jennings, comme M. de Lagrange avait conservé T. Jennings, l'entraîneur de Monarque.

Bientôt les deux écuries rivales s'associèrent : il y eut seulement deux centres d'entraînement, l'un à Newmarket sous la direction de T. Jennings, l'autre en France, où Henry Jennings était l'entraîneur. Cette fusion, dont le résultat immédiat était de diminuer considérablement l'intérêt des courses en France, n'était pas du goût du public, et l'association elle-même ne fut pas de longue durée. Les succès de la Grande Ecurie atteignirent leur apogée en 1861, où elle mit en ligne Prétendant, Compiègne, Finlande, Marignan, Gabrielle d'Estrées, qui fut victorieuse dans le prix du Jockey Club, Surprise, qui enleva l'Epsom Cup, et Palestro, vainqueur du Cambridgeshire. Cette année-là 118 prix, montant à 497,000 fr., furent gagnés en France et la Grande Ecurie occupait avec 186,000 fr. le cinquième rang sur la liste des propriétaires gagnants en Angleterre.

L'association fut dissoute en 1862 : tous les chevaux furent mis en vente à la fin d'octobre ; le comte de Lagrange n'hésita pas à dépenser des sommes importantes pour conserver ses favoris. Il paya Hospodar 125,000 fr., Stradella 38,750 fr., Jarnicoton, 46,000 fr., Fille de l'Air 8,500 francs, &c.

On n'a pas oublié les victoires et les défaites à sensation de Fille de l'Air en 1864, son éclatant succès dans les Oaks, qu'aucune pouliche française n'avait jamais gagnés, et les résultats divers de ses luttes contre Vermout. On connaît mieux encore la carrière de Gladiateur, qui enleva les Clearwell Stakes deux ans après Hospodar, et surtout sa magnifique campagne de 1865, où il gagna successivement les 2,000 Guinées, le Derby, le Saint-Léger et le Grand Prix de Paris. Ce n'était pas la première fois que le comte de Lagrange essayait de gagner le Derby : déjà il y avait fait courir plusieurs chevaux et non sans honneur. Dangu est le premier poulain français qui soit entré en lice dans cette grande épreuve ; l'audace parut si grande qu'il partit à 200/1 dans le Derby de 1860, gagné par Thormanby ; cependant il arriva quatrième. L'année suivante Royallieu était sixième dans le Derby de Kettledrum ; ces deux noms, Dangu et Royallieu, convenaient bien aux deux poulains qui portèrent les premiers dans le Derby les couleurs de la France et du comte de Lagrange.

On n'a pas oublié l'ovation qui fut faite à ce dernier en pleine Chambre des Députés après la victoire de Gladiateur. En 1866 celui-ci remporta la Coupe d'Ascot, qu'aucun cheval français n'avait encore gagnée, donnant ainsi un exemple qui, depuis cette époque, a été plusieurs fois suivi.

Il faut citer ensuite les noms de Trocadéro, Mortemer, de Rabican, aujourd'hui presque oublié, mais qui donnait à deux ans de magnifiques espérances ; enfin, de Sarrazin et de Consul. C'est avec ce dernier que le comte de Lagrange a remporté pour la quatrième fois le prix du Jockey Club en 1869. Ses chevaux y avaient été placés plusieurs fois, mais aucun d'eux n'avait pu gagner cette épreuve depuis 1861.

Lorsque la guerre éclata tous les chevaux à l'entraînement furent vendus : Gladiateur, dont le comte de Lagrange avait refusé, dit-on, 400,000 fr., s'en alla chez M. Blenkiron au prix de 145,000 fr. ; Général, sur lequel on comptait beaucoup, fut payé 95,000 fr. par le duc de Hamilton, et la meilleure acquisition fut assurément celle de Trocadéro, qui passa moyennant 35,000 fr. entre les mains de M. Aumont.

Le comte de Lagrange, qui avait conservé ses poulinières, ses produits de l'année et ses yearlings, les laissa sans inconvénient à Dangu pendant toute la durée de l'invasion. Il fit mine, tout d'abord, de se consacrer exclusivement à l'élevage, et fit même en ce sens un traité avec M. Lefèvre. Mais quand on a goûté du turf, de ses déceptions et de ses joies, de ses luttes et de ses fièvres, il est bien difficile, surtout avec une nature aussi active et aussi militante que celle de M. le comte de Lagrange, de se condamner longtemps à cette espèce de retraite.

Dès qu'il eut repris sa liberté, c'est-à-dire à l'automne de 1874, la casaque bleue et rouge reparut portée par Carver, qui montait Frondeur : lorsqu'on la revit, il y eut dans l'enceinte du pesage une réelle émotion. Carver et Frondeur rentrèrent victorieux. C'était d'un heureux présage.

La période qui commence alors est marquée par l'alliance de M. Lefèvre avec le comte de Lagrange. Les résultats furent des plus brillants : il suffit de rappeler la victoire de Camélia dans les Mille Guinées en 1876, son dead heat avec Enguerrande dans les Oaks, les succès de Chamant dans le Middle Park et le Dewhurst Plate, et sa victoire dans les Deux Mille Guinées l'année suivante. Il allait remporter le Derby, tout y présageait sa victoire, lorsqu'il fut victime d'un malheureux accident et ne prit part à la course que pour montrer qu'il était devenu incapable de la gagner.

Comme pour consoler ses propriétaires de cette perte irréparable, Saint-Christophe remporta, peu de temps après, un succès tout à fait inattendu dans le Grand Prix de Paris : c'est la seule grande course française que le comte de Lagrange n'ait gagnée que deux fois.

Insulaire y portait ses couleurs en 1878, lorsqu'il dut céder la première place à Thurio ; ce cheval malheureux était déjà arrivé second dans le Derby et les Deux Mille Guinées. Il parvint seulement à gagner le prix du Jockey Club, que son écurie remporta encore en 1879 avec Zut et en 1881 avec Albion. L'année dernière Dandin a partagé le prix avec Saint-James, et peu s'en est fallu cette année que Farfadet y triomphât de l'invincible Frontin. Pendant les six dernières années les couleurs du comte de Lagrange ont donc été représentées de la manière la plus brillante dans le Derby français.

Les derniers grands succès qu'elles aient remportés en Angleterre sont ceux de Poulet dans le Lincolnshire Handicap en 1882 et d'Archiduc dans les Criterium Stakes ; mais dans cette longue énumération de chevaux illustres, élevés et conduits à la victoire par M. le comte de Lagrange, il ne faut pas oublier Rayon d'Or, qui fut sans contredit, avec Gladiateur, celui dont la carrière fut la plus fructueuse et la plus brillante. En trois ans il a gagné 600,000 fr. de prix, dont 450,000 fr. à l'âge de trois ans. Le malheur a voulu qu'il ne fût pas prêt au moment du Derby, qui fut d'ailleurs couru par un temps épouvantable et sur un terrain complètement détrempé : mais il a du moins remporté le Saint-Léger de Doncaster, les Great Foal et Champion Stakes, etc.

On sait quel parti M. de Lagrange savait tirer de tous ses chevaux et comment il a su, par exemple, utiliser Castillon, qui n'avait pas de beaux engagements. Cette année encore il arrive en seconde ligne sur la liste des propriétaires gagnants en France et dépasse le chiffre de 320,000 fr., avec un petit nombre de chevaux, parmi lesquels se trouvent Archiduc, Azur et Farfadet.

Le hasard a voulu qu'avant la mort même du célèbre propriétaire les plus illustres de ses élèves eussent disparu ou quitté la France : Gladiateur, Monarque, Fille de l'Air et Trocadéro sont morts ; Rayon d'Or est allé rejoindre Mortemer en Amérique ; Chamant est en Allemagne et Verneuil en Autriche. Quelle que soit la gravité de ces pertes pour notre pays, l'écurie de M. le comte de Lagrange était si considérable qu'elle ne peut manquer de laisser en France des traces durables, et parmi les vainqueurs de l'avenir beaucoup naîtront de ces étalons ou de ces poulinières qui ont naguère illustré ses couleurs sur tant d'hippodromes de France et d'Angleterre.

In the 'supplement' to the journal 'Le Figaro' of 1879 a contributor, writing under the name of 'Robert

Milton' (understood to be the assumed name of M. de Saint-Albin, proprietor and editor of 'Le Sport'), gave the following lively sketch of Count de Lagrange:—

As he walks leaning on the arm of one of his nephews, and rounding his hips after the manner of waltzers, you would say that he was about to turn to the orchestra and call out, 'Now, M. Waldteufel, when you please!' The Count runs his horses without regard for the public, who 'know' no more than his own partners. He is determined to make it quite clear that a man does not keep two hundred horses in training simply to amuse the gallery. The Lagrange stable is a conjurer's box. Most frequently the horse that carries the first colours does not carry the money. The followers of the stable experience the most cruel 'sells;' the Count's partners tear their hair. But the Count himself remains impassible and preserves his Mephistophelian smile. The partner who has just burnt his fingers by backing the beaten horse of the stable dares not even complain. The Count would reply, 'Lost, have you, my dear fellow? Have you lost much? I'm sorry you didn't lose more. That will teach you to try and win money all by yourself, *without papa's permission.*' A little story will give an idea of the Count's discreetness and of the frequently clever way in which he escapes the reproaches of his friends when he omits—more or less intentionally—to make them sharers in his good things. During the Middle Park Plate week (when Chamant won) he had taken away with him for a visit at Phantom Cottage a rich and amiable sportsman with whom he was on very intimate terms. He had specially invited him to take him behind the scenes of a big stable and initiate him into all the mysteries of the Turf. One evening after an excellent dinner they remained chatting —with their feet on the fender—to a late hour; but the name of Chamant was never mentioned. Next day the horse won the Middle Park Plate in wonderfully easy style. 'But I rather think,' said the Count in reply to his friend's congratulations, 'I told you to back him?' 'No,' replied the friend, 'but, as I am pretty free with my money, I put a hundred pounds on him —on the off chance—at 20 to 1.' 'Then you win two thousand!' rejoined the Count, somewhat astonished. 'Two thousand pounds?' 'I'm quite delighted; but, you know, whenever you win a great deal on a race it is usual to make a present to the jockey that rode the winner.' 'Really?' 'Yes; so if I were in your place I should undoubtedly give Goater a hundred pounds.' And the friend did so, thinking it little to pay for apprenticeship in so good a school.

Finally, Count F. de Lagrange was stated by so good a judge as Count Paul Daru to have been ' un homme qui a toujours su se faire obéir ' ('a man who could always enforce his orders'): such a man was made to succeed on the Turf.

Of course the Count's death necessitated another sale, which took place on January 24 and 25, 1884. The most notable purchases were made by M. Marix for the Russian Administration des Haras, by whom Consul was bought for 28,000 francs (1,120*l.*), and the yearling Conscrit (by Rayon d'Or and Chimène) for 'le prix fabuleux' (as the French newspapers called it; but what would Mr. Henry Chaplin say?) of 25,500 francs (1,020*l.*) Here are the details:—

FIRST DAY—BROOD MARES.

Amourette, by Monarque and Courtoisie, sold to M. de Pavant, 1,800 francs (72*l.*).

Bombarde, by Ventre Saint-Gris and Arcadia, M. de Luetkens, 1,150 francs (46*l.*).

Championnette, by Partisan and Little Fawn, M. Gaston de Montesquieu, 550 francs (22*l.*).

Chimène, by Monarque and Championnette, M. Pierre Donon, 21,000 francs (840*l.*).

Dordogne, by Hospodar and Emma Bowes, M. Minoret, 1,000 francs (40*l.*).

Dulce Domum, by Cambuscan and Sweet Home, M. Michel Ephrussi, 3,450 francs (138*l.*).

Faveur, by Pompier and La Favorite, Baron de Blondel, 1,000 francs (160*l.*).

Finance, by Consul and Fille de l'Air, M. Léon André, 3,100 francs (124*l.*).

Fleurette, by Ventre Saint-Gris and Lady Nelson, M. Crombez, 3,100 francs (124*l*.).

Iphigénie, by Hospodar and Isabella, M. J. Prat, 4,100 francs (164*l*.).

La Favorite, by Monarque and Constance, M. Cossart d'Espiès, 1,050 francs (42*l*.).

La Reine Elisabeth, by Monarque and Miss Gladiator, M. Balensi, 1,200 francs (48*l*.).

Mandarine, by Le Mandarin and Ladybird, Viscount d'Hauterives, 2,100 francs (84*l*.).

Marion, by Marignan and Aphrodite, M. de Tracy, 800 francs (32*l*.).

Tendresse, by Monarque and Tolla, M. Fould, 4,600 francs (184*l*.).

STALLIONS.

Consul, by Monarque and Lady Lift, M. Marix, 28,000 francs (1,120*l*.).

Beau Merle, by Victorious and Merlette, M. Ouzile, 3,100 francs (124*l*.).

FOALED IN 1883.

Algarade, by Prologue and Amourette, M. Moreau-Chaslon, 750 francs (30*l*.).

Boréas, by Flavio and Bombarde, Duke de Castries, 2,600 francs (104*l*.).

Conscrit, by Rayon d'Or and Chimène, M. Marix, 25,500 francs (1,020*l*.).

Cuirassier, by Nougat and Championnette, M. J. Prat, 1,900 francs (76*l*.).

Diction, by Rayon d'Or and Dordogne, M. de Bray, 300 francs (12*l*.).

Dignitaire, by Beau Merle and Dulce Domum, M. Moreau-Chaslon, 250 francs (10*l*.).

Fabius, by Beau Merle and Finance, M. May, 1,050 francs (42*l*.).

Feuillet, by Flavio and Fleurette, M. J. Prat, 3,100 francs (124*l*.).

Forlane, by Beau Merle and La Favorite, Baron de Blondel, 1,000 francs (40*l*.).

Frasque, by Beau Merle and Faribole, M. Castel, 110 francs (4*l*.).

Germandrée, by Consul and Glycère, M. de Tracy, 300 francs (12*l*.).

Méduse, by Nougat and Mandarine, M. Baron, 1,000 francs (40*l*.).

Muscade, by Nougat and Marion, Mr. R. Carter, 5,000 francs (200*l*.).

Pétulant, by Peut-être and Percaline, Mr. Hawes, 3,100 francs (124*l*.).

Rotonde, by Beau Merle and La Reine Elisabeth, M. J. Prat, 1,600 francs (64*l*.).

Triomphant, by Beau Merle and Tendresse, M. Oppenheim, 10,700 francs (428*l*.).

SECOND DAY—17 THREE-YEAR-OLDS.

Adulte, by Beau Merle and Angleterre, M. Morterol, 3,200 francs (128*l*.).

Chansonnette, by Saint-Christophe and Chimène, Mr. Hopkinson, 1,800 francs (72*l*.).

Dagne, by Consul and Dulce Domum, M. Sieber, 6,300 francs (252*l*.).

Ebène, by Beau Merle and Esther, Mr. Stripp, 2,800 francs (112*l*.).

Fantassin, by Beau Merle and Fleurette, M. Sieber, 2,300 francs (92*l*.).

Finesse, by Beau Merle and Faveur, Mr. Walter, 3,200 francs (128*l*.).

Flandrin, by Saint-Christophe and La Favorite, M. Sieber, 18,100 francs (724*l*.).

Flick, by Beau Merle and Faribole, M. J. Prat, 22,000 francs (880*l*.).

Imposant, by Beau Merle and Iphigénie, Mr. R. Carter, 15,700 francs (628*l*.).

Marraine, by Beau Merle and Marion, M. de Fayolle, 2,050 francs (82*l*.).

Matador, by Beau Merle and Mandarine, Mr. Stripp, 7,000 francs (280*l*.).

Mauresque, by Consul and Mark Over, Mr. Wigginton, 8,000 francs (320*l*.).

Rameur, by Saint-Christophe and La Reine Elisabeth, Mr. Stripp, 6,000 francs (240*l*.).

Reflet, by Nougat and La Reine Berthe, M. Morterol, 5,000 francs (200*l*.).

Tablette, by Saint-Christophe and Tendresse, M. Rémond Balensi, 1,700 francs (68*l*.).

Taverne, by Saint-Christophe and Tolla, M. de Kronenberg, 7,000 francs (280*l*.).

Thémis, by Consul and Teacher, Mr. R. Carter, 16,700 francs (668*l*.).

13 TWO-YEAR-OLDS.

Adversaire, by Saint-Christophe or Beau Merle and Amourette, M. de Kronenberg, 5,400 francs (216*l*.).

Alto, by Flavio and Angleterre, M. Yehé, 1,050 francs (42*l*.).

Combattant, by Nougat and Championnette, Mr. R. Carter, 8,800 francs (352*l*.).

Dominante, by Nougat and Dulce Domum, M. R. Balensi, 500 francs (20*l*.).

Escapade, by Consul and Esther, M. Leproux, 3,000 francs (120*l*.).

Féerie, by Beau Merle and Faveur, Mr. Walter, 2,800 francs (112*l*.).

Fontana, by Nougat and Faribole, M. Michel Ephrussi, 1,200 francs (48*l*.).

Influent, by Insulaire and Iphigénie, M. J. Prat, 28,500 francs (1,140*l*.).

Mariquita, by Beau Merle and Mandarine, Mr. Hawes, 12,000 francs (480*l*.).

Pensif, by Saint-Christophe and Percaline, Mr. Hopkinson, 1,300 francs (52*l*.).

Rival, by Beau Merle and La Reine Elisabeth, Mr. Hurst, 4,000 francs (160*l*.).

Thames, by Peut-être and Tendresse, Mr. Stripp, 2,100 francs (84*l*.).

Tirailleur, by Rayon d'Or and Tolla, M. Baresse, 1,600 francs (64*l.*).

Total : 343,460 francs (13,738*l.*).

After this, commencing on Monday, February 26, there was a sale of 'objets d'art' won by Count de Lagrange's horses and of various sporting pictures. The 'Lion de Barye,' won by Fille de l'Air (silver-chased), went for 6,905 francs (277*l.*); but, on the whole, the 'objets d'art' had apparently lost about four-fifths of what was their estimated value at the time they were won. Mr. Harry Hall's great picture of Gladiateur was bought by Baron A. Schickler for the Jockey Club (French) at the price of 2,420 francs (about 96*l.*). The bridle in which the great horse won the Derby went for 625 francs (25*l.*), and the portrait of Fille de l'Air for 655 francs (about 26*l.*).

In this same year 1884 (August) died Mr. Flatman (brother of 'Nat'), the 'doyen' of English jockeys at Chantilly ; he was seventy-seven years of age. He rode Lion in the dead heat with Diamant for the French Derby of 1856.

In 1884 the 'cracks' among the French horses at home were the Duke de Castries's Little Duck (three years, winner of the French Derby and of the Grand Prix de Paris), M. L. André's Frégate (winner of the French Oaks), M. C. J. Lefèvre's Archiduc (three years ; winner of the Poule d'Essai des Poulains, of the Prix Daru, of the Grande Poule des Produits, and of the Prix Royal Oak), Count de Berteux's Silex (three years ; winner of the Prix de Longchamps, for which M. P. Aumont's Fra Diavolo started a great favourite at odds *on*, but was not placed, and was supposed to have been 'got at'), M. A. Lupin's Yvrande (three years, winner of the Poule d'Essai des Pouliches), M. A. Staub's (Haras de

Lonray's) Pi-Ouit II. (three years, winner of the Prix du Nabob), Baron de Rothschild's Serge (three years, winner of the Prix Greffulhe), M. C. J. Lefèvre's Formalité (four years, winner of La Coupe at Paris), M. C. J. Lefèvre's Regain (four years, winner of the Prix du Cadran), M. L. André's Satory (four years, winner of the Prix Rainbow and of the Prix Gladiateur); and among the two-year-olds Viscount de Fayolle's Valentin, M. J. Prat's Martingale, M. Martin's The Condor, and M. C. J. Lefèvre's Present Times, winners of the three principal Critériums and of the Prix de Deux Ans at Deauville.

Of these 'cracks' there ran in England Archiduc (third to Saint-Gatien and Polemic for the Cesarewitch, a bad fourth to Florence, Bendigo, and [a bad third] Pizarro for the Cambridgeshire, and beaten by Saint-Gatien, a distance of ten lengths, for the Jockey Club Cup), Serge (ran several times, to no purpose, generally a 'bad third'), Regain (unplaced for the Ascot Stakes), and Present Times (made ten attempts, and won once, the Royal Plate of 488*l.* at Windsor; unplaced for the Brocklesby Stakes at Lincoln; second to Lady Gladys for the Althorp Park Stakes; third to Hampton and Vacillation when they ran their dead heat for the Ascott Plate at Northampton; second by a head to Empress Queen for the Westminster Stakes at Epsom Spring; third and last to Luminary and Grecian Bride for the Hurstbourne Stakes at Stockbridge; a bad third to Luminary and Melton for the July Stakes; unplaced for the Chesterfield, at Newmarket July, and second to Kingwood by a neck for the Berkshire Plate at Windsor July).

Of the other French horses that ran in England in 1884 the chief, if not the whole, were M. C. J. Lefèvre's

Arbalète (four years, second to Whipper-in for the
Babraham Stakes at Newmarket Craven, unplaced for
the City and Suburban, third to Whipper-in and
Clochette for the Prince of Wales's Stakes Handicap at
Newmarket First Spring, and unplaced for the New-
market Spring Handicap), M. C. J. Lefèvre's Confiseur
(two years, second to Pegasus for the Tathwell Plate at
Lincoln), Mr. A. Yates's *Crédo* (five years, unplaced for
a selling welter plate at Brighton Autumn), Mr. H.
Jennings's Disqualifié (two years, twice unplaced at
Leicester Autumn), Baron de Rothschild's Egérie (three
years, twice ran third at Windsor Summer), Baron
Soubeyran's Faille (four years, ran twice to no purpose),
Mr. T. Jennings, junior's, La Puce (two years, unplaced
for the Paddock Plate at Windsor July), Mr. T. Jen
nings, junior's, Nonant (two years, ran five times and did
nothing better than one second), Mr. Macevoy's *Robert
Macaire* (four years, second to Penguin for the
Wynnstay Handicap at Chester and unplaced for the
Northumberland Plate), M. A. Staub's *Stockholm* (four
years; unplaced for the July Handicap at Newmarket;
unplaced for the Leicestershire Cup; won the Goodwood
Stakes of 645*l*., beating Florence; won the Goodwood
Corinthian Plate of 342*l*.; won the Queen's Plate of 210*l*.
at Lichfield; unplaced for the Cesarewitch, the Cam-
bridgeshire, and the Manchester November Handicap),
Mr. 'Plunger' Walton's *Sutler* (aged, ran four times to
no purpose, was third just once), Mr. A. C. Barclay's
Vautour (two years, unplaced for the Wakefield Lawn
Stakes at Northampton), Mr. M. Dawson's Voisine (three
years, ran three times to no purpose), and M. A. Lupin's
Xaintrailles (two years; second to Melton for the Middle
Park Plate, beating Paradox—then called the Casuistry
colt—and Royal Hampton, who ran a dead heat for

third; won the Prendergast Stakes of 872*l.*, and with 4 lbs. the worse of the weights was third to Paradox for the Dewhurst Plate)—some fourteen in number, of which only Stockholm and Xaintrailles were of much account. The latter, indeed, commonly called 'Entrails' for convenience, was thought at one time to be a second Gladiateur; but he was scarcely so much as a second Général or Feu d'Amour.

The campaign of the 'Frenchmen' in England, then, was a mighty poor one in 1884; and Count F. de Lagrange became very conspicuous by absence, his memory consequently very forcibly recalled. France seemed to have retrograded, to have gone back to the old times when a Nivière and a Lagrange came to the front and set seriously to work to make French horses respected in England. M. Lefèvre no longer seemed to be equal to the work; he stood second among French 'winning owners' (with 19,708*l.*) to the Duke de Castries (with 20,207*l.*), but among the English, with French and English horses combined, he had dropped into fifth place with a comparatively shabby 9,789*l.*, less than half of his previous year's 20,563*l.*

As for the Grand Prix de Paris, it had again been a great triumph for the Frenchmen, in a certain sense: the three English candidates—namely, Mr. Vyner's The Lambkin, M. Lefèvre's Brest, and the Duke of Hamilton's Loch Ranza—were beaten in a canter by the Duke de Castries's Little Duck, and The Lambkin was to win the Doncaster St. Leger. So far so good; but The Lambkin was by no means a star among winners of the St. Leger; Saint-Gatien, Busybody, Harvester, and other English 'cracks' could not, or at any rate did not, run for the Grand Prix, and the winner, Little Duck (a good name for a horse something under seventeen hands high), was, like Frontin the year before, to all intents and purposes (so far as breeding is concerned) an English horse (sire Seesaw, dam Light Drum), whose 'foundations had been laid' in England before his dam was imported into France in 1880. The honours of the season, then, as regards 'breeding,' clearly belonged to John Bull both in England and in France, and there was no reason to complain that 'foreigners' were beating the English horses or to howl for 'reciprocity.'

Of course the great surprise of the year in France was the singular collapse of M. Lefèvre's Archiduc, who, having become disqualified (by his late owner's death) for the English Derby, and having beaten Little Duck in the Poule d'Essai des Poulains, was supposed to have the French Derby at his mercy; but though, in the language of the 'Ring,' 'Archy Duck' and Little Duck finished first and second for the Derby at Chantilly, the 'little un bet Archy, instead of t'other way about:' the 'little un' standing, as has been said, something under seventeen hands.

The year 1885 saw the last of M. Balensi (the well-known financier) and of Baron d'Etreillis (the well-known rider, writer—under the assumed name of 'Ned Pearson' sometimes—and sometime starter at the Paris races). M. Balensi (who died at his country seat, Château de Gravelles, or Gravelle) was a comparatively new comer; but he won the Prix de Honfleur at Deauville for two-year-olds three years running, in 1882, 1883, and 1884, with Odette II., Bluette, and Chamarande, and he had just founded a promising 'haras' at Gravelles when he was called away. As for Baron Sainte-Aure d'Etreillis (who died rather suddenly on July 22, aged sixty-five), he had been kicked by a horse in the previous March, and was supposed to have never quite recovered from the effects. He was for many years a contributor to 'Le Sport,' and was the author of many works, among which the 'Dictionnaire du Sport Français' is a real κτῆμα ἐς ἀεί.

In 1885 the French 'cracks' at home were the Marquis de Bouthillier's Reluisant (three years, winner of the French Derby), M. Michel Ephrussi's Barberine (three years, winner of the French Oaks and of the Poule d'Essai des Pouliches), M. A. Lupin's Xaintrailles (three years, winner of the Poule d'Essai des Poulains and of the Grande Poule des Produits), Mr. T. Cunnington's Extra (three years; winner of the Prix Hocquart, formerly Prix de Longchamps, and of the Prix Daru), Baron de Rothschild's Aïda (three years, winner of the Prix du Nabob), M. C. J. Lefèvre's Archiduc (four years, winner of the Prix du Cadran and of the Prix Rainbow), M. P. Aumont's Fra Diavolo (four years, winner of La Coupe at Paris), M. H. Delamarre's Palamède (three years, winner of the Prix Greffulhe), Baron de Rothschild's Lavaret (four years, winner of the Prix Gladiateur), Baron A. Schickler's Escarboucle (three years, winner of the Prix Royal Oak); and among the two-year-olds the Duke de Castries's Viennois and Aïda II. and M. P. Aumont's Alger, winners of the three principal 'Critériums' and of the Prix de Deux Ans at Deauville (Alger won the Grand Critérium at Paris and the Prix de Deux Ans).

Of these 'cracks' there ran in England Barberine (won the Newmarket October Handicap of 1,500*l*., unplaced for the Cambridgeshire), Xaintrailles (unplaced for the Derby), and Lavaret (unplaced for the Great Northamptonshire, second to Borneo for the Visitors' Plate at Ascot, won the Suffolk Plate of 147*l*. at Newmarket July, won the Midsummer Welter Handicap of

450*l*. at Manchester July, won the Goodwood Plate of 295*l*., and won the Newmarket Whip and 200*l*. against the Duke of Hamilton's Cosmos).

Of the other French horses that ran in England the chief, if not the whole, were M. L. de Francisco Martin's *The Condor* (three years, unplaced for the Cesarewitch, unplaced for the Cambridgeshire, and unplaced for the Houghton Handicap Plate at Newmarket), M. C. J. Lefèvre's *Consigne* (two years, ran The Bard to half a length for the Westminster Stakes at Epsom Spring, unplaced for the Stanley Stakes at Epsom Summer, unplaced for the Midsummer Plate at Windsor, won the Findon Stakes of 330*l*. at Goodwood, won the Priory Stakes of 561*l*. at Pontefract, unplaced for the Dewhurst Plate, &c.), M. P. Donon's (Haras de Lonray's) *Diaprée* (three years, unplaced for the Oaks), M. Lefèvre's Feuillage (two years, unplaced for the Brocklesby, third for the First Spring Two-year-old Stakes at Newmarket as well as for the Second Spring Two-year-old Stakes, and second to The Beau for a maiden two-year-old plate at Newmarket July), M. A. de Montgomery's Flores (three years, unplaced for the One Thousand and twice second for small plates), M. Michel Ephrussi's Gargouille (two years, second to Twinkle for the New Nursery Handicap Plate at Newmarket Houghton), M. C. J. Lefèvre's Gédéon (three years; ran once, unplaced, at Newmarket Craven), Baron de Rothschild's Henri (two years; ran once, unplaced, at Derby September), Baron de Rothschild's Lagny (two years; ran once, unplaced, at Newmarket July), Baron de Rothschild's *Louis d'Or* (aged; beaten by Cosmos for the Newmarket Whip at the First Spring Meeting, unplaced for the Ascot Stakes, third and last for the Summer Cup at Newmarket July, and unplaced for the Doncaster Cup), M. Lefèvre's *Luc* (two years; won the Abergavenny Stakes of 300*l*. at Lewes Spring, second for a two-year-old plate at Newmarket Craven and won a plate of 200*l*., third for the Second Nursery Stakes at Newmarket First October and third for the Double Trial Plate of which the first heat was run at the Craven, and second for the Second October Nursery Stakes), M. H. Bouy's Madrid (three years, unplaced at Newmarket Houghton), Mr. T. Jennings's *Mariquita* (three years; second to Bedouin for the Batthyany Stakes at Lincoln, fourth for Earl Spencer's Plate at Northampton, won a selling plate of 102*l*. at Newmarket First Spring, and was bought for 630 guineas, and ran several times afterwards to no purpose), Mr. H. Macksey's Monsieur (five years, had nine 'goes' and won a welter plate of 102*l*. at Manchester July, the Hamsey Welter Handicap Plate of 194*l*. at Lewes Summer, a welter plate of 102*l*. at Windsor August, and the Milton Plate of 102*l*. at Huntingdon), Mr. W. R. Marshall's Niagara, late Monsieur Maxime (two years, ran four times and won the Southgate Nursery Handicap of 101*l*. at Alexandra Park Autumn), Mr. T. Jennings, junior's, Nonant (three years; ran twice, won nothing, but was second to Cymbalaria by a short head for a maiden plate at Newmarket Craven), M. A. Lupin's *Phœbus* (two years; fourth and last for the Exeter Stakes at Newmarket July, third to Gay Hermit and Modwena when they ran their dead heat for the Hopeful Stakes at the First October, unplaced for the Clearwell Stakes won by Miss Jummy, and second to Loved One by a length for the Cheveley Stakes at the Houghton Meeting), M. H. Bouy's *Plaisanterie* (three years; ran twice only, and won both the Cesarewitch, 1,130*l*., and the Cambridgeshire, 1,470*l*.), Baron de

Rothschild's *Prudence* (two years; won the Scurry Nursery Stakes Handicap of 247*l*. at Newmarket First October, the Monday Nursery Handicap Plate of 196*l*. at the Houghton, as well as a plate of 195*l*., and was second by a short neck, 9 st., to Yule Tide, 6 st. 8 lbs., for the Chesterfield Nursery Handicap at Derby Autumn), M. C. J. Lefèvre's Trident (two years, unplaced for the Rous Memorial at Newmarket First October and for the Cheveley Stakes at the Houghton Meeting), M. Lefèvre's Venette (two years; unplaced for the Stud Produce Stakes at Newmarket First Spring, unplaced for the Ascot Biennial won by Saraband, a bad third to Saraband and Lorgnette for the Astley Stakes at Lewes, and unplaced for the Bretby Nursery Handicap Plate at Newmarket Houghton), and M. Lefèvre's (afterwards Mr. F. Robinson's) Villeneuve (two years; ran several times, being sometimes honoured by the company of The Bard—a long way in front of her, so that she made 'a very bad third' to him and Bread Knife in the race for the John O'Gaunt Plate at Manchester, but she won nothing)—about a score, or a few more, in number, of which those whose names are printed in italics acquired some reputation at some time either at home or abroad.

As for the Grand Prix de Paris, the French nose was put very much out of joint this year, 1885; for the international race was won by an Englishman with an English horse, Mr. Brodrick-Cloete with Paradox (winner—by a head—of the Two Thousand and second—by a head—for the Derby), the only English horse among the seven runners. The six 'Frenchmen,' Reluisant, Present Times, Lapin, Barberine, The Condor, and Extra, were beaten with the greatest ease.

Surely, if we look at the performances of the
'Frenchmen' generally in England and in the Grand
Prix de Paris, the 'form' shown was not that which
they seemed at one time to have attained; it was not the
form of Fille de l'Air's day, of Vermout's, of Gladiateur's,
of Mortemer's and Henry's, of Boïard's and Flageolet's, of
Chamant's, Verneuil's, and Rayon d'Or's: it was not, in
a word, 'reciprocity form.' Yet something very like
the 'reciprocity spirit' was aroused by the achievement
of Plaisanterie, who, by winning both Cesarewitch and
Cambridgeshire (beating Bendigo, who was afterwards
to win the great Eclipse Stakes), seemed to have placed
herself on a level with Rosebery and even with the
great Foxhall. No doubt Plaisanterie was the wonder
of the year so far as French horseflesh was concerned.
She had been purchased for about 32*l.* as a yearling or
two-year-old, recalling the case which has already been
mentioned of the 'Frenchman' Palestro, who was purchased as a yearling for sixteen guineas and afterwards
won the Cambridgeshire in 1861; and she suddenly
came out and took nearly everything by storm. At
two years of age she won the Prix du Premier Pas
(776*l.*) at Caen, beating Martingale, won the Grand
Prix de Dieppe (876*l.*), beating Barberine, and was
second by a short head to The Condor for the Grand
Critérium at Paris. That was her 'record' at two
years of age, in 1884. In 1885 she won twelve events
out of thirteen in France and the two great handicaps
of Newmarket; she won the Prix de la Seine (536*l.*),
the Prix des Cars (345*l.*), the Prix Saint-James (w.o.,
140*l.*), the Prix Fould (174*l.*, w.o.), all at Paris Spring
Meeting; the Prix d'Apremont (428*l.*, beating Fra
Diavolo) at Chantilly; the Prix du Cèdre (433*l.*) and
the Prix Seymour (470*l.*, beating Barberine) at Paris

Summer Meeting; the Jubilee Prize (2,050*l.* and a gold 'Pokal,' beating The Condor), at Baden; the Prix de Chantilly (466*l.*), the Prix de Villebon (420*l.*, beating The Condor and Reluisant), the Prix d'Octobre (884*l.*), and the Prix du Prince d'Orange (497*l.*), all at Paris Autumn Meeting; and was only beaten once, and that by a short head, by Martin Pêcheur II. for the Prix du Prince de Galles at Paris Spring Meeting. Of course she was not in the 'classic' races, but she defeated opponents that were. No doubt such a career is astounding, beating English Crucifix's and Hungarian Kincsem's in some respects. But there does not seem to be in it anything that should have revived the old feeling as to 'reciprocity.' However the prowess of Plaisanterie in the Cesarewitch and Cambridgeshire was evidently at the bottom of a motion that was brought before the Jockey Club by Mr. W. G. Craven, a most experienced gentleman and sportsman, at the beginning of the season 1886, to the effect that foreign horses (such as Plaisanterie) should not be allowed to run in handicaps on English racecourses until they had been in training in England or had run races in England sufficiently long or sufficiently often to let their qualities be shown to the English handicapper; and Plaisanterie did not fulfil these conditions. Yet it is absurd to pretend even—in the face of the close connection established between the English and the French 'Turf'—to suppose that any French horse's performances and capabilities could escape the knowledge of any moderately observant handicapper if, as was the case with Plaisanterie, no dust had been thrown into French eyes, and the animal had run, as was the case with Plaisanterie, frequently in public, at Baden as well as in France. Nor is it easy to see how, if Plaisanterie had run once a week during the whole season before the very eyes of the English handicapper, he could have given her, being a filly and a three-year-old, with due regard for her sex and age, much more weight than the 7 st. 8 lbs. (4 lbs. only less than Foxhall, winner of the Grand Prix de Paris) and the 8 st. 12 lbs. (2 lbs. only less than Foxhall) she carried for the Cesarewitch and Cambridgeshire respectively.

One cannot help sympathising with a French writer who expressed his feelings about Mr. W. G. Craven's motion in the following bitter language :—

Les Anglais de 1886 ne sont décidément pas ce qu'on pourrait appeler de beaux joueurs. La double victoire de Plaisanterie dans le Cesarewitch et dans le Cambridgeshire a fait revivre les idées de lord Falmouth, qui ne voulait admettre la concurrence des chevaux français qu'à la condition que ceux-ci ne seraient jamais vainqueurs. Ce noble lord était particulièrement impressionnable ; le nom de Fille de l'Air le rendait épileptique et le nom de Gladiateur lui donnait la danse de Saint-Guy.

Quand il fit au Jockey Club ses propositions d'éviction, il ne fut pas écouté. Mais voici que M. Craven, profitant de la fermentation causée par nos succès de l'automne dernier, vient de faire voter *en première lecture* une mesure hypocrite qui nous ferme les grands handicaps d'Angleterre.

On exige des chevaux étrangers, pour qu'ils puissent courir dans un handicap, des conditions tellement absurdes, qu'il eût bien mieux valu déclarer qu'ils n'étaient plus qualifiés.

On veut que nos chevaux aient un séjour d'entraînement ou se soient montrés dans des courses publiques.

Est-ce à dire qu'on craint que nous ne songions à employer les ruses de nos voisins dans la préparation d'un coup ? S'il s'agissait de masquer, je crois qu'ils pourraient nous donner des leçons.

Avons-nous masqué Plaisanterie ? . . . Le handicapeur l'a-t-il lâchée ? Assurément non. Nous y avons été bon jeu, bon argent, avec si peu d'enthousiasme que nous avons failli même n'y pas aller du tout.

Ces excellents fils d'Albion nous ont empoché plus de [1] neuf millions à nous, en neuf Grands Prix de Paris. Nous sommes loin du compte.

Si le Jockey Club vote en seconde lecture la motion Craven, il aura bien tort, car tout le monde alors ferait naturellement cette remarque : Les petits-fils des Anglais de Fontenoy sont devenus des Anglais d'*Old England.*

In case anybody should be a little 'fogged' about the allusion to 'Old England,' it may be well to mention that the notorious Mr. Gully, ex-prize-fighter, ex-publican, and M.P. for Pontefract, had (in partnership with 'honest' John Day) a horse called Old England in 1844, that period when there was so much villany 'in the air' (of the Turf); that Old England was much fancied for the Derby of 1845 (for which he eventually ran third to Merry Monarch and Annandale); and that an attempt or proposition to 'nobble' him was made, creating so much scandal that the matter was brought before the Stewards of the Jockey Club, who, after enquiry, ordered that Messrs. 'J. F. Bloodsworth, William Stebbings, and William Day,' who were held to have conspired together for some more or less nefarious purpose, 'be warned off the course at Newmarket,' &c. It is said in the 'judgment' to have been ' positively stated by William Day and William Barrett that Stebbings did at Bloodsworth's house recommend that the horse's foot should be bruised by striking it with a hard stone or by tying a handkerchief round the leg and striking the sinew with a stick, and if that was not sufficient that he (Stebbings) could easily get a powder which, being mixed with the corn, would stop him. They added that Bloodsworth was averse to the

---

[1] This seems to be a slight mistake for 900,000. Unless in French 100,000 stands for a million, as 1,000 millions make a billion (according to French notation).

last part of this proposal.' Why? Because 'it was a lagging affair,' which means that it was an affair for which Mr. Bloodsworth and his confederates were liable to be 'lagged': or 'transported.' Such is the treatment to which the 'noble animal,' if he be a favourite for the Derby or some similar big race, is liable at the hands of ignoble man.

But to return to Plaisanterie: What was her breeding? She was a daughter of Wellingtonia and Poetess. Wellingtonia was an English sire, not imported into France permanently until 1885, but leased in 1878. Poetess was pure French, a daughter of the 'savage' Trocadéro and La Dorette; she was foaled at M. Aumont's celebrated 'Haras de Victot.' La Dorette's dam was Mon Etoile, daughter of Hervine, daughter of Lord Henry Seymour's famous Poetess (dam of Monarque), winner of the French Derby (Prix de Diane) in 1841. Now here is a puzzle for breeders: from which side, maternal (from Poetess, dam of both Hervine and Monarque) or paternal (from Wellingtonia and his progenitors) did Plaisanterie derive her excellence? For her dam, Poetess II., suffered (it has been said, but also denied) from 'paralysie dans les reins'; at any rate she appears to have been cast off at an early age from the famous Victot stud, to have been declined by the 'remount commission,' and to have never run. Not a very promising dam, one would think; but she was purchased by Viscount de Dauger, who has flatly denied the imputations against her soundness. As for Wellingtonia (son of Chattanooga, son of Orlando, son of Touchstone), he came of excellent descent, and by means of his progeny (Plaisanterie Prudence, Printemps, &c.) took the first place among 'winning sires' of French-bred animals (victories in

England included) in 1885, with 307,000 francs (12,280*l.*) against Flageolet's 272,000 francs (10,880*l.*), the defunct Trocadéro's 265,000 francs (10,600*l.*), and Dollar's 230,000 francs (9,200*l.*). We have seen, moreover, that the French horses of the year (three-year-olds) were of 'no account' compared with the English (the sole exception being Plaisanterie), and that the French 'cracks' (three-year-olds) of the two preceding seasons, Frontin and Little Duck, were virtually—though not technically—English-bred. So that an English scare and an English howl for 'reciprocity' appear to have been totally uncalled for and absurd; indeed it would have been more to the point to draw attention to the fact that the French had small ground for their proud boast (already mentioned) at the time of Lord Falmouth's outcry, and that they could not even yet do without John Bull's sires and dams (and as for John Bull's trainers and jockeys, what the French would do without *them* only a very imaginative person can conceive).

Indeed French writers themselves grew melancholy over the 'pertes sensibles,' or 'serious losses,' their breeding had sustained through the 'death or exportation of Trocadéro, Faublas, Androclès, Flageolet (sold to the Germans, of all people in the world, in 1885), Mortemer, Verneuil, Chamant, Rayon d'Or, Consul, Boïard, &c.,' and over the old age of Vermout and Dollar (whose services could not be counted upon much longer), but consoled themselves with the hope of filling the voids (already caused or to be soon caused) by means of Silvio and Wellingtonia (English sires) and others of like origin, and paid compliments to French owners who, like Count de Berteux and the Duke de Castries especially, spared no expense in still importing

English sires and dams to recruit failing French resources.

If the French had done badly as a rule in their campaign of 1885 in England, their principal representative, M. C. J. Lefèvre, 'took a back seat' both at home and abroad. In England he occupied among 'winning owners' the twenty-first place with 5,400*l.*, and in France the seventh with 208,594 francs (about 8,343*l.*), instead of the 492,724 francs (about 19,708*l.*) of the year before, behind the Duke de Castries, M. A. Lupin, the Count de Juigné, M. Michel Ephrussi, M. H. Delamarre, and the Marquis de Bouthillier, giving just '944 pounds' to the comparatively 'new-comer,' M. H. Bouy, owner of Plaisanterie.

To this year, lastly, belongs an announcement which shall be quoted for the sake of those very superior persons who think that anybody who has anything— however remote—to do with horse-racing, the turf, and the affairs thereof must necessarily be an ignoramus or something worse. Be it premised that the extract is from 'Le Sport':—

> Nous apprenons avec plaisir que notre confrère, Madame Grossmann (en littérature Blanche de Géry), femme du directeur du Tattersall français, a été nommée officier d'Académie, en reconnaissance des services qu'elle a rendus à l'instruction publique par ses travaux littéraires.

The year 1886, before the racing season commenced, was notable for an announcement which appeared in the English papers of February 27, from one of which the following extract is taken :—

> The Paris Civil Tribunal on Thursday last pronounced the civil interdiction of Baron Raymond Seillière, a well-known owner of racehorses, and a banker. Baron Raymond Seillière was the owner of Roi de la Montagne, Doublon, Fin-Picard, and

other horses which made names for themselves in the annals of the turf. The civil interdiction implies that the person who has been ornamented with a *conseil judiciaire* cannot contract any valid engagement or liability, and becomes at the same time freed from all the irksome procedure to which creditors are apt to resort when they find that their debtors find 'parting' too sweet a sorrow. The petition on which the ruling of the Court was founded was presented by Baron Frank Seillière, who based his prayer on the fact that during the last twelve years his brother had spent 40,000*l.* a year, besides incurring debts and liabilities to the extent of 200,000*l.* Opposition was offered by a large creditor, who asked the tribunal not to assent to such a method of wiping off old scores, but the Court thought that the expenditure amounted to prodigality, and gave judgment in favour of the petitioner.

This was a grievous ending of what had once promised to be a very brilliant career: it shows, nevertheless, how faithfully the traditions of the English turf (where so many noblemen, young, middle-aged, or old, have 'come to grief') are reproduced upon the French. Baron Raymond Seillière (who was well known in England, in flat-racing and steeplechasing, at Newmarket, Sandown Park, and elsewhere and everywhere) did not run horses in his own name until about the year 1877, but he was connected somehow with the stable whose horses ran in the name of Mr. Henry or Count Henry or Henri (Count Henri de Breteuil), in 1874 (Flamen, Peau d'Âne, Soupçon, &c.), in 1875 (Rabagas II. &c.), in 1876 (Vellon, Lord Seymour, Bibletto, &c.), and in 1877 (Roi de la Montagne, &c.). Mr. H. Gibson was the trainer; and the stable would win in stakes during a year (1877 and 1878, for instance) some 55,000 francs (about 2,200*l.*). But it was not for stakes that the Baron ran his horses: according to 'Robert Milton' (writing in 1879), he would 'risk a thousand louis like nothing at all,' he shared with M. E. Blanc the reputation of being 'the greatest punter in the Ring,' he had a 'private secretary always at his heels to put down his bets,' he was the sort of man to whom 'the bookmakers flocked like flies to honey,' he had been known to 'bet 100,000fr. (4,000*l*.) on a pigeon-shooting match at Deauville,' he bore his losses without moving a muscle (unless he bit his moustache a good deal), and he would back his own horses when they had not a chance. Such a gentleman was pretty sure to find the turf too much for him before long; and so in 1881, having been 'hard hit,' it was said, by the result of the Grand Steeple-chase de Paris (for which his horse Fin-Picard was first favourite, and for the loss of which the rider was supposed by some folks to have been responsible), he determined to sell his horses and confine himself to breeding at his magnificent place at Cirès-les-Mello, where his castle looks down from the heights over the branch railway between Creil and Beauvais, and where he had already founded a *haras* (such as the fine 'prairies' were, of course, intended for by Nature), with Roi de la Montagne (who had won a great race for the Prix du Lac and a great reputation in 1878) for stud-horse-in-chief.

The sale of the horses-in-training (steeple-chasers, three-year-olds, and two-year-olds) fetched 299,550fr. (11,982*l*.), of which 46,100fr. (1,844*l*.) were given by M. E. Blanc for the fateful Fin-Picard (whose name, of course, recalls the legendary Franc-Picard). The breeding does not seem to have been much more profitable hitherto to Baron Raymond than his horse-racing and steeple-chasing were; but, no-doubt, the horse of the future may yet come from Mello. The Baron is a good illustration of the truth that there is in the saying about 'birds of a feather'; for his sister (it is stated) married the Prince de Sagan (President of the Société des Steeplechases), and his brother, Baron Frank, a granddaughter (Mademoiselle de Gallifet) of the famous 'Major Fridolin' (M. Ch. Laffitte) whose daughter married the Marquis de Gallifet. Other illustrations are M. Maurice Ephrussi (who married a Rothschild), the Duke de Gramont (who also married a Rothschild), and Count de Clermont-Tonnerre (who married a niece of M. Auguste Lupin), &c., &c., the 'lien' being apparently a love of horse-racing, though, no doubt, there is also 'financing' in some cases, especially in the cases of the Rothschild and Ephrussi families.

Apropos of financing here is an exquisite specimen of the view which the French (and probably English) female mind took in 1886 of the turf and its operations, and the unhesitating manner in which that mind is prepared to take advantage of them, if at least the following letter were really received (as it is said to have been) by a correspondent of 'Le Sport.'

> Sir,—Having met with great misfortune, I should like to win a little money to get me out of my difficulties. I apply to you—swearing to keep everything perfectly secret—to tell me of some certainty, one of those things that are arranged on racecourses between owners and stewards, and where the result is known beforehand.
>
> I am, Sir, etc.
> (signed) Pauline Z.

It were a pity to doubt the genuineness of this letter; but it certainly seems to have been 'writ sarcastic' by somebody who had lost money when there appeared to be a certainty of winning, and is probably what certain members of Parliament would call 'an 'oax.'

The French 'cracks' of 1886 were (up to the time of writing this account): Count de Berteux's Upas, by

Dollar, and Baron A. Schickler's Sycomore, by Perplexe (both three years, ran a dead heat for the French Derby); M. A. Lupin's Presta, by Petrarch (three years, winner of the French Oaks); the Duke de Castries' Lapin, by Salvator (four years, winner of the Prix du Cadran); M. J. L. de F. Martin's The Condor, by Dollar (four years, winner of the Prix Rainbow, and of La Coupe at Paris), M. H. Delamarre's Verdière, by Idus (three years, winner of the Prix du Nabob); M. P. Aumont's Sauterelle, by Saxifrage (three years, winner of the Prix Greffulhe); Baron Schickler's Sakountala, by Perplexe (three years, winner of the Poule d'Essai des Pouliches), M. Michel Ephrussi's Gamin, by Hermit (three years, winner 'of the Poule d'Essai des Poulains); Mr. T. Carter's (the late Duke de Castries') Jupin, by Silvio (three years, winner of the Prix Daru and of the Grande Poule des Produits); M. A. Lupin's St. Honoré, by Dollar (three years, winner of the Prix Reiset, beating Sauterelle); and Comte de Berteux's Upas again (three years, who had won the Prix de Longchamps at Paris, beating Sycomore, before they ran their dead heat at Chantilly). Be it noted, therefore, that Presta, Verdière, Gamin, and Jupin are the produce of English sires, quite 'like old times.'

The Grand Prix de Paris of 1886 was a very bad job for the French. It was something like the 'Bruce' year (1882), when Mr. Rymill's English horse Bruce (for a long while and at the very start first favourite for the Derby) was unable to get a place for the great race at Epsom, and yet was too good in the race for the Grand Prix for the other seven competitors (all French). This year Mr. Vyner's Minting (English) had been for a long while first favourite for the Derby, until he was beaten by Ormonde for the Two Thousand, when he was promptly withdrawn (as a 'hopeless case') from the Derby, but was good enough to beat all the French horses (as well as Miss Jummy, winner of the English Oaks) for the Grand Prix de Paris, for which there was exactly the same number of French runners (seven) as in 'Bruce's year.' It was a pity, perhaps, that the late Duke de Castries' Jupin was disqualified (by the Duke's death), as, although he was beaten for the French Derby, he was considered by some good judges to be the best of the French horses.

The season of 1886 was memorable for the many losses the French turf sustained by the death of various owners of horses and promoters of horse-racing, especially at the beginning of the year. In January died (suddenly) M. Vincent (at Tarbes), son of 'the Man of the Mountain,' and a great agent in the transactions between the horse-breeders of the South and the horse-owners of the North; Mr. T. Wigginton, the trainer, nephew of Mr. Henry Jennings; in March M. Richard Hennessy (after two days' illness), of 'Cognac' celebrity (at Cognac), who had some success on the turf with Prétentaine and Entraîneur; in April the Duke de Castries; in May M. Bony (part owner of Plaisanterie) and M. René Denneticr, one of the two brothers (Alphonse, predeceased, was the other) who were regarded as the 'Fathers of Suburban Racing,' and had the management of the meetings at Nice.

The Duke de Castries, who was the head of the confederacy that took the place of the late M. E. Fould (with their 'haras' at Saint Georges and their stable at Avermes), died on the 19th of April of heart disease, from which he had suffered for a long while, though there was thought to be no immediate danger.

He was Edmond Charles Auguste de la Croix, born

in 1838. He entered the army, but had to leave
through ill-health in 1864 ; in which year he married a
daughter of Baron Sina. She brought him an immense
fortune, and gave him the Princesses Ypsilanti and
Mavrocordato and the Countess Zichy (who were her
sisters) for his near connections by marriage. His sister
married the Marshal Duke de MacMahon, and his
mother was the Countess de Castries, a d'Harcourt by
birth. He became Duke on the death of his uncle, who
married Mlle. Henriette de Maillé, but left no issue, and
he himself died without issue, so that his title became
extinct, unless his cousin were authorised to adopt it.
The house of la Croix de Castries is said to be originally of Languedoc, and to have numbered among its
members Guillaume de la Croix, President of the Cour
des Aides of Montpellier, who was in great favour at
the courts of Louis XI., Charles VIII., and Louis XII.
The de Castries property was made a marquisate in
1645 ; at the Revolution in 1789 the head of the family
was the Marquis de Castries (Marshal of France and
Knight of the King's Orders), who died in 1801. His
son Armand is said to have received the title of duke
by patent in 1784, and to have been summoned to the
peerage in 1814 with the title and rank of hereditary
duke. He was appointed governor of the Château of
Meudon (where the great 'haras' was) in 1822, was
created a Knight of the King's Orders at the coronation
of Charles X., and died in 1842. He left two sons, of
whom the elder, Edmond, Duke de Castries, died without issue, and the younger having predeceased him, the
title devolved upon the last Duke.

The Duke's colours (white, cherry cap, gold tassel)
had been barely four years known upon the turf, and
already he had won nearly everything (in France) with

Frontin, Little Duck, Seigneur II., Lapin, Roi-Fou, Jupin, Aïda II., Viennois, Sourire, &c. Never before had anybody (not even Count de Lagrange) done so much in so short a time: three years in succession he had stood at the head of French winning owners, and at the time of his death his stable had won in stakes over 1,500,000 francs, which looks enormous in that form, but is not so imposing in the shape of 60,000*l*., though even that is something more than respectable. For him M. Malapert bought—as his first two purchases—Frolicsome and Light Drum (who already had Frontin and Little Duck concealed about their persons, respectively); and at the time of Lord Falmouth's famous sale he went over to Newmarket, where he by private arrangement gave 175,000 francs (7,000*l*.), it is said, for Silvio (whose progeny, as we have partly seen, have been doing wonderfully well). At Saint-Georges his energy made a fine 'haras' out of a wilderness, and forty broodmares were soon in clover there; whilst at Avermes he had at his decease more than sixty horses in training, under the care of one of the many Messrs. Carter.

But, successful as the Duke de Castries was, he was not altogether lucky. For instance, in the summer of 1883 he lost six yearlings in a very extraordinary fashion during a storm. The stud-groom had been serving out the oats to the youngsters, standing by twos in each box, an iron-lined manger running from end to end of the whole building, and supplying all the boxes. When he reached the last box, having served out the oats, he was all of a sudden thrown down underneath a colt which fell—struck with lightning—atop of him, and which he discovered (when he got the better of his natural fright) to be stone-dead, whilst his stable-companion was safe and sound. And, strange to say, it was so in every compartment; one (the one with its muzzle in the manger) had been struck dead by the lightning, the other had escaped. If both had been able to feed at the same time, the whole twelve—instead of six— would assuredly have been killed. The names of five of the killed are given: Czarda (by Salvator and Czarina), Gargantua (by Stracchino and The Garry), Mic-Mac (by Gilbert and Merry May), Tape-à-l'Œil (by Salvator or Saladin and a dam not mentioned), and Vis-à-Vis (by (Uhlan and Vigogne).

It is by no means an uncommon thing for thorough-bred youngsters to be killed by lightning, but that it should happen on so wholesale a scale, and under such interesting circumstances, as regards the alternation, is very unusual indeed.

M. H. Bouy (the half-owner of Plaisanterie), who died at the early age of thirty-nine, was a 'chimiste' (a scientific chemist, not a chemist and druggist); but the word recalls the case of Mr. A. Nichol (of New-castle, the owner of Newminster, The Wizard, &c.), who was a merchant 'chemist' ('pharmacien'), but as favourable as M. Bouy to racehorses and horse-racing. M. Bouy (born at Senlis, near Chantilly, and so inhaling 'horse' with his native air) first began the business he loved best (which was not 'scientific chemistry') in 1877. In 1878 he ran two horses, Pompée II. (by Le Mandarin and Picciola) and Vermisseau (by Hospodar and Volatile), the latter having belonged first of all to the Haras de Lonray (Messrs. Staub and Donon), and then to the Viscount E. Gouy-d'Arsy, but does not seem to have seen much besides other horses' tails (though he did run third now and then): at last (by a 'fluke,' of course) he was lucky enough to purchase Plaisanterie (for some 32*l.*), of Viscount Dauger, and so his name remains 'illustrated' for ever in the annals of the French turf. At his death there was a sale of seven horses in training (Macquinez, Gibellin, Trouvère, Eolien, Flâneur, Otage, Qui Vive), two brood mares (Illusion and Algarade), and one stallion (Problème, who won in his day 1,000*l.* in stakes), belonging to the deceased gentleman alone, and of ten other animals in training (La Louve, Beaumontel, Formigny, Richepance, Solitaire, Hidalgo, Clarabide, Sans Marque, Sénégal, and Plaisanterie), which belonged to him and to Mr. T. Carter jointly. The sale produced less than 2,000*l.*, with the exception of Plaisanterie, for whom the deceased gentleman's partner, Mr. T. Carter, gave 150,000 francs (6,000*l.*). Mr. Carter also bought most of the other 'lots,' including Beaumontel (the highest-priced of all at 13,500 francs, or 540*l.*). There was not, apparently, the expected struggle between England and America for the possession of Plaisanterie; at any rate they did not outbid Mr. T. Carter's 6,000*l.* (which is more than anybody would give at Lord Falmouth's sale for Jannette, or Spinaway, or Dutch Oven, or Wheel of Fortune, or Cantinière, but considerably less than the 8,800*l.* given for Busybody at three years of age; and, of course Plaisanterie, being but four years of age, might run again, although rumour spoke ill of her chances).

CHAPTER XII.

A SUMMARY.

LET us now imagine a boy at a Board School being examined by his teacher (after a long course of the 'Racing Calendar,' duly expounded and commented upon by a competent lecturer) in the orthodox manner. The examination would run as follows, with question (*Q.*) and answer (*A.*):—

Q. How long have Frenchmen been purchasing English thoroughbred horses?

A. For more than a hundred years, off and on.

Q. What do you mean by 'off and on'?

A. With interruptions caused by the many Revolutions to which that favoured land is liable by nature.

Q. Very well. When would you date the first purchase?

A. About 1765, in Louis XV.'s reign, when Count de Lauraguais purchased the celebrated Gimcrack, took him over to France, and ran him twenty-two and a half miles within the hour, for a big bet.

Q. Very well indeed. And the next purchases?

A. A little later, in the reign of Louis XVI., when the Count d'Artois (afterwards Charles X.) and Philippe Egalité (Duke de Chartres and Duke d'Orléans, who was beheaded at the Revolution) imported, by means of the Marquis de Conflans and others, the celebrated horses King Pepin (by Turf), Comus (by Otho), Glowworm (by Eclipse), Pyroïs (by Match'em), and Teucer (by Northumberland), all sold about 1776.

Q. Did any of their progeny run in England?

A. Oh yes, Philippe Egalité's Rouge, Vert, Petit-Gris, and Glowworm (by Glowworm) especially; it seemed as if the French were coming on nicely with their horse-racing, when the first Revolution came and stopped it all, else they might have won lots of English races, and caused a howl for 'reciprocity' long before Lord Falmouth's time.

Q. Moderate your enthusiasm and your language! How long did the interruption last?

A. Well, you may say, almost till the foundation of the French Jockey Club in 1833.

Q. And how would you measure the progress the French have made since that time?

A. By the number of the important races they have won at the principal English race-meetings.

Q. And what meetings are these?

A. I should say Newmarket, Epsom, Ascot, Goodwood, and Doncaster. A horse that does not win some notable event at one of those meetings is not likely to be of much account.

Q. What have been the principal achievements of French horses run by French owners at those five meetings, since the days of Philippe Egalité?

A. They have won the Two Thousand twice (with Gladiateur and Chamant, in 1865 and 1877), the One Thousand twice (with Reine and Camélia, in 1872 and 1876), the Great Foal Stakes once (with Rayon d'Or, in 1872), the Great Challenge Stakes once (with Rayon d'Or, in 1879), the Champion Stakes once (with Rayon d'Or, in 1879), the Cesarewitch once (with Plaisanterie, in 1885; for Salvanos, the winner in 1873, though a French horse, belonged to an English owner), the Cambridgeshire five times (with Palestro, Montargis, Peutêtre, Jongleur, and Plaisanterie, in 1861, 1873, 1874, 1877, and 1885), and, of the chief two-year-old events, the Middle Park Plate once (with Chamant, in 1876), the Dewhurst Plate once (with Chamant, in 1876), the Criterion Stakes six times (with Hospodar, Fille de l'Air, Flageolet, Jongleur, Monsieur Philippe, and Archiduc, in 1862, 1863, 1872, 1876, 1878, and 1883; for Général, the winner in 1870, though a French horse, belonged at the time to the Duke of Hamilton), and the Clearwell Stakes four times (with Hospodar, Gladiateur, Feu d'Amour, and Rayon d'Or, in 1862, 1864, 1873, and 1878; for M. Lefèvre's Negro, the winner in 1872, was bred in England), all at Newmarket (where, of course, they won a legion of other races of less celebrity); the Derby once (with Gladiateur, in 1865), the Oaks thrice (with Fille de l'Air in 1864, with Reine in 1872, and with Enguerrande and Camélia, running a dead heat for first and second, in 1876), the City and Suburban once (with Mademoiselle de Chantilly, in 1858), the Great Metropolitan once (with Dutch Skater, in 1872), and the Woodcote Stakes twice (with Fille de l'Air and Le Sarrazin, in 1863 and 1867), all at Epsom (where, of course, they won a great many other races of less importance); the Ascot Cup five times (with Gladiateur, Mortemer, Henry, Boïard, and Verneuil, in 1866, 1871, 1872, 1874, and 1878), the Queen's Vase once (with Verneuil, in 1878), the Rous Memorial Stakes three times (with Phénix, Rayon d'Or, and Poulet, in 1879, 1880, and 1881), the Alexandra Plate four times (with Fille de l'Air, Trocadéro, Verneuil, and Insulaire, in 1865, 1870, 1878, and 1879), and the New Stakes once (in 1879, with Océanie), all at Ascot (where, of course, they won many other races of less note); the Stewards' Cup once (with Sultan, in 1866), the Goodwood Stakes twice (with Stockholm, in 1884, and, transferred for lack of acceptances into the Goodwood Plate, with Lavaret in 1885), the Goodwood Cup five times (with Jouvence, Baroncino, and Monarque, in 1853, 1855, and 1857, when the 'Frenchmen' received a liberal discount of weight, and with Dollar and Flageolet, at full weight, in 1864 and 1873), and other less renowned races at Goodwood (where in 1872 the Chesterfield Cup was won by a French horse indeed, Napolitain, but his owner was Lord Wilton, an Englishman); and the St. Leger twice (with Gladiateur and Rayon d'Or, in 1865 and 1879), the Doncaster Cup three times (with Sornette, Dutch Skater, and Louis d'Or, in 1870, 1872, and 1884), and the Champagne Stakes once (with Clémentine in 1877); but, what was most remarkable, was the number of Queen's Plates (which were certainly meant to encourage 'native' merit alone) snapped up by the French: six in 1872 for instance (by Dutch Skater, Eole II., and Verdure), after that—in 1871—Dutch Skater had carried off no fewer than seven, Eole II. three, and Verdure one; and in 1884, when the number had been decreased, and the value increased, Louis d'Or snaps up four and Stockholm one. Another remarkable fact must be mentioned, that the once famous Newmarket 'Whip' was won in 1885, by a 'Frenchman,' for the first time within the memory of man: to wit, Baron de Rothschild's very moderate Lavaret, whose only opponent was the still more moderate Cosmos, who was again beaten (and 'broke down') for the Whip by the 'Frenchman' Serge II. in the spring of 1886. Such are the successors, sir, of

Match'em, Trajan, Dumplin, Bay Malton, Gimcrack, Cripple, Sweet William, Shark, and, above all, Pot8os.

Q. What would you say, then, of the successes of the French, who seem to have had some brilliant triumphs, and of the occasion for any concession on their part to English horses, by way of 'reciprocity'?

A. Brilliant as the successes have sometimes been, I would say that they are small compared with the lavish sums which the French have paid at intervals, during more than a hundred years, for English sires and English mares, to the great profit of English owners and breeders (like Lord Falmouth, to whom they gave 4,000*l.* for Atlantic and 7,000*l.* for Silvio, a very excellent 'deal' for the lord), and even compared with their expenditure of time, money, and pains since they took to horse-racing in real earnest, in 1833. I would say that the sums they have gained in stakes do not represent even an appreciable interest upon the capital they have invested. I would say that the chief successes and the most money have been won by two Frenchmen only (Messrs. de Lagrange and Lefèvre), who, having had costly establishments at Newmarket (where they employed a number of English men and boys), and having owed a great deal to horses 'bred in England,' have been really as much Englishmen as Frenchmen, so far as the turf is concerned; and that to grudge them, or any Frenchman, their victories and to howl for 'reciprocity' is both undignified and absurd. I would say it is absurd, because no good could possibly come of 'reciprocity.' If the French horses are better than the English (as the English used to be better than the French), it is surely of no use for English owners to go over to France to be beaten as well as being beaten in England; and if they do not intend to go over, what is the meaning of 'reciprocity'? In the former case, the condition of the English owners is hopeless; for the French horses are virtually the produce of the English, and all the French know about breeding and horse-racing is what they have learnt from the English. If, then, the latter have lost their old skill and knowledge, it is difficult to see how 'reciprocity' can help them. If, however, the claimants of 'reciprocity,' feeling that English horses are still (as there is good reason to believe) superior to the French nine years out of ten (or even more), desire 'reciprocity' in order that they may avenge themselves of their adversaries (who may be successful one year out of ten in England) by going over to France and making a clean sweep of everything valuable for nine consecutive years on the French race-courses, the idea is not magnanimous, and, moreover, is likely to defeat itself, as it would very soon create a distaste for horse-racing in France and would break up the turf there. I would say, further, that the outcry for 'reciprocity' is absurd on another ground: as long as the English stakes are more valuable than the French, it is not likely that a sane English owner would endanger his prospects at home by going for a smaller stake abroad, and if, from the quality of his horses, he should have no prospects at all at home, what would be his prospects in France, where (by the hypothesis on which the claim for reciprocity rests) the native horses would be at least as good as his own, if not better? The English, in fact, would be in the position in which the French formerly were, when these latter used to send their horses over to England to be beaten, as almost a foregone conclusion, but with the express purpose of learning and profiting by defeat, breeding from the blood of the victors, hiring the men who trained them or knew the method of training, watching to see in what their own race horses seemed to be deficient, and so on. If English owners are ready to accept that position, then they do well to ask for reciprocity. Otherwise they seem to have about as much 'reciprocity' as they need care for. The Frenchmen have opened their own Grand Prix, the most valuable race in the world (bar the fitful and quite recent Eclipse Stakes, &c.), to all peoples, nations, and languages; it has been run for twenty-three times, inclusive of this year (run June 6, 1886), and the French have won it only eleven times; the English have won it ten times, the Americans once, the Hungarians once. What ever would John Bull say if he were to win his own Derby, Oaks, Leger, Two Thousand, and One Thousand not oftener than once out of twice on an average? 'Reciprocity' would be nothing to express his feelings, he would almost certainly leave off subscribing to those races (which would collapse) and would turn his attention to something that would 'pay better.' The Grand Prix has paid him very well; he has won it ten times (to the tune of 55,000*l.*), whilst the French have had out of him one Derby (6,825*l.*), three 'Oakses' (5,025*l.*, 4,175*l.*, and 4,300*l.*), two Two Thousands (5,100*l.* and 5,200*l.*), two One Thousands (3,150*l.* and 3,100*l.*), and two St. Legers (5,950*l.* and 6,525*l.*), or about 49,350*l.* in all. The French certainly have won many valuable stakes besides; but they have paid a multitude of heavy 'subscriptions,' with no 'four sovs. forfeit' (such as the Grand Prix has), and have 'subscribed' (with 'fifty sovs. forfeit' and 'twenty-five sovs. forfeit') hundreds of times in vain.

Q. Have you said all you have to say? You see you are not an owner, a breeder, or a runner of horses, or you might take a different view, my boy, might you not?

A. I don't know, sir. I can only see quite plainly that, whatever may be the case with breeding, it is impossible for more than two or three owners of race horses to make much out of running for stakes. And to the breeders I would point out that the French 'crack' horses have lately been almost 'bred in England,' as in the 'good old times.' We have already spoken of Frontin and Little Duck and Plaisanterie; and of the chief French 'cracks' of this year (1886) —*Lapin* (four years), The Condor (four years), *Upas* (three years), *Verdière* (three years), Sauterelle (three years), *Sakountala* (three years), *Gamin* (three years), *Jupin* (three years), Saint-Honoré (three years), *Presta* (three years), *Sycomore* (three years)—up to the date of the Grand Prix de Paris—we find that the eight whose names are printed in italics are either of English sire or English dam, or both—that is, eight out of eleven. And, if we take the winners of the thirty-six races run at the Paris Summer Meeting of this year (1886), we find that the principal event (the most valuable—save the Eclipse Stakes—in the world, at any rate in Europe), which is the Grand Prix de Paris, was won by Minting (an English horse), and that the other thirty-five races were won by twenty-eight different animals—namely, *Indien* (by Silvio, Vertugadin, or Saltéador and Miss Ida), Hubic (by Salvator and La Jonchère), *Estelle* (by Pellegrino and Ethel Blair), Kroumir (by Androclès and Vénitienne), Sauterelle (by Saxifrage and Solliciteuse), Messagère II. (by Saxifrage and Miss Capucine), *Clarinette* (by Plutus and Convent), *Jupin* (by Silvio and Juliana), *Plaisance* (by Saxifrage and The Princess), Albany (by Salvator and Bariolette),

Viennois (by *Silvio* and Vigogne), *Le Nôtre* (by Idus and Versailles), *Parlement* (by Perplexe and War Queen), Rajah (by Pellegrino and Indiana), *Escogriffe* (by Caterer and Ella), *Polyeucte* (by Boïard and Polly Perkins), *Firmament* (by Silvio and Astrée), *Kara Koul* (by Perplexe and a brother to Strafford mare), *Fagotin II.* (by Mandrake and Fanny), *Udine* (by Vermout and Suttee), La Bultée (by Flageolet and Lady Henriette), Cormeilles (by Fleuret and Cornélie), Président (by Salvator and Mademoiselle de Juvigny), *Beaumesnil* (by Blenheim and Brown Rosalind), Fils d'Artois (by Beauminet and Fille de l'Oise), *Sigurd* (by Guy Dayrell and La Dauphine), *Escarboucle* (by Doncaster and Gem of Gems), and Aréthuse (by Gabier and Cascatelle), of which number the seventeen whose names are printed in italics are the progeny either of an English sire or of an English dam, or of both. I would further draw your attention, sir, and that of the School Board, to the last volume (vol. xv.) of the English Stud Book, from which it appears that during the four years (or thereabouts) accounted for in that volume France has purchased from England or imported from England (permanently or temporarily) no fewer than a hundred (or more) thoroughbred horses and two hundred and fifty (or more) thoroughbred mares, all 'bred in England.'

Q. What do you infer from this?

A. That however France may have come on with her horse-racing and horse-breeding, she cannot yet quite go alone; that she must constantly replenish her stock from England; and that England has as yet no reason to go a-begging for 'reciprocity' or to become alarmed whenever a French horse or mare (probably of English sire or English dam, or both) carries off a big

English sweepstakes or handicap, or two or three of them in succession.

Q. Can you enumerate briefly the chief breeders, owners, and racers of horses to whom you consider the French Turf to have been principally indebted from the first foundation of the Société d'Encouragement to the present day?

A. I will endeavour to do so. First of all I should put the State (Administration des Haras), because (notwithstanding its open or secret opposition—at various times—to the views of the Société) it has always done good service from the days of Colbert by the introduction of English and other (that is, Eastern) thoroughbreds (at Le Pin, Pompadour, and Rosières especially), and because to it was due the importation of Gladiator (in 1846). Then, just glancing at the intermediate services of Charles X. and the Dauphin (with the Meudon stud and Rowlston, imported in 1827), I would halt at the Duke d'Orléans (who took over the Meudon stud, bred Romulus, Nautilus, Gigès, Quoniam, &c., employed George Edwards as trainer-in-chief, and Edward Pavis as jockey-in-chief, and formed the racecourse at Chantilly), Lord Henry Seymour (who had his stud at Sablonville, introduced Royal Oak and bred Poetess, employed T. Carter as trainer-in-chief, and through him gave to the French Turf the inestimable services of H. and T. Jennings), M. Rieussec (with his stud at Viroflay, where Rainbow stood), and M. Eugène Aumont (who, though he got into trouble about Tontine, founded the great horse-breeding and horse-racing establishment which his brother, M. Alexandre Aumont, brought into celebrity by the purchase of Lord H. Seymour's Poetess—dam of Monarque—and by founding the stud at Victot, and by securing the services of Tom Hurst as trainer-in-chief). Then I would speak of M. Fasquel (with his stud at Courteuil), M. A. Lupin (with his two studs at Vaucresson and Viroflay, where he has had so many expensive English mares, winners of the Oaks or One Thousand, or both, from Wings, imported in 1837, to Songstress, imported in 1859, though he has done better with Currency and Payment, and others, who did not win the great races), and Prince Marc de Beauvau (with his stud at La Morlaye). Then I would show how some of these early breeders and runners threw out branches, as it were, so that from Lord Henry Seymour's stud, which had supplied Prince Marc de Beauvau's and MM. Aumont's with 'material' (such as Jenny and Poetess, both by Royal Oak, not to mention any more), may be said to have branched out the studs and stables associated with the names of Baron Nivière, 'Major Fridolin,' Count F. de Lagrange, and M. C. J. Lefèvre. For Prince Marc de Beauvau's establishment at La Morlaye, having become the property of a 'confederacy,' was sold, on the dissolution of that body, to Baron Nivière, with whom Count F. de Lagrange (having purchased meanwhile the stud of M. Alexandre Aumont) formed a partnership for a while, and then, on the breaking up of that partnership, Baron Nivière became the associate of 'Major Fridolin' (with the 'haras' which the Baron had formed at Villebon, near Palaiseau), whilst Count F. de Lagrange, after breeding and racing single-handed for many years, sold most of his horses to M. C. J. Lefèvre (who formed a stud at Chamant), then 'fused' with the proprietor of Chamant, and ultimately separated, leaving Dangu and Chamant in France, Phantom Cottage and Lowther House in England (at Newmarket) to represent two distinct French

breeding and racing establishments, both grown from
the same root. I would also mention M. Achille Fould,
the celebrated Minister of Finance, a great breeder (like
Baron de Nexon) in the South, whose family continued
his traditions, both in the South and in the North, until
at last, on the death of the Minister's nephew, M.
Edouard Fould, in April 1881, the breach made was
promptly filled up by a 'confederacy' composed of
Baron Soubeyran, Count Hallez-Claparède, and the late
Duke de Castries (in whose name and colours the horses
ran), two of the three (Baron Soubeyran and Count
Hallez-Claparède) having been associated with M. Fould.
The confederacy (with their establishment at Avermes,
near Moulins, and the 'haras' of Saint-Georges, in the
South) have kept up the Fould tradition splendidly;
and as M. E. Fould himself was for a while associated
with M. Henri Delamarre (of Vermout memory and of
the Bois-Roussel 'haras,' belonging to Count P. Roederer
originally) it is easy to see how the tale of ramification
is fulfilled. The Third Empire gave a great impetus to
horse-racing and the breeding of thoroughbreds, and
is a convenient line of demarcation to take; up to that
date I should say that the chief and most useful patrons
of the French Turf, and promoters of French horse-
breeding, besides those just mentioned, bore the names
of Des Cars, Crémieux, De Vanteaux, De Coux, De la
Bastide, Latache de Fay (both Monsieur and Madame),
Gaston de Blangy, Marion, Boutton-Levêque, F. and H.
Cutler, Laroque, De Croix, Petit de Sérans, Calenge
(the founder of Caen races, established in 1837), De
Prado, Sabatier, De Baracé, Durand (Baron and Madame
veuve), De la Rochette (a name to conjure with in the
Société d'Encouragement), Jules Rivière, Hippolyte
Mosselman (of the Verberie 'haras,' near Compiègne),

Finot, Célestin de Pontalba, N. de Rothschild (who won the French Derby with Mendon in 1846), Benoît, De Greffulhe, De Tocqueville (given over rather to the Arab heresy), and Prat (originally given to the same heresy); and after the accomplishment of the Empire I should put foremost (though some of them were well known— only less well known—before as 'hommes de cheval') MM. the Duke de FitzJames, the Count G. de Juigné and his 'frequent pardner' the Prince A. d'Arenberg, Th. Régis, the Viscount P. de Daru (president of the Société d'Encouragement, died in 1876), the Count de Berteux (importer of Taffrail, dam of Miss Gladiator, and a wonderfully good customer in the English market, with a 'haras' at Cheffreville, in Normandy), the Duke de Morny (founder of the Grand Prix de Paris and creator of Deauville), Mr. Mackenzie Grieves (constructor-general of racecourses to the French nation), the Baron A. Schickler (of the Martinvast stud, importer of The Nabob in 1857), Delâtre (of the 'haras' of Celle-Saint-Cloud, purchased in 1883 by M. E. Blanc, whose Nubienne, winner of the Grand Prix of 1879, was foaled there), the Count A. de Montgomery (who 'belonged to' La Toucques and Fervacques, the latter being named after his 'haras,' in Normandy), Jacques Reiset, Baron de Bray (died in August 1885; he was proprietor of the famous Montgeroult 'haras,' whence he supplied Count F. de Lagrange with 'produce' during several years, such as Nougat, Pardon, Phénix, Laurier, &c.), Desvignes (who died in January 1883, proprietor of the 'haras' of La Massellière, near La Flèche), Viscount de Dauger (breeder of Plaisanterie), E. de la Charme, Moreau-Chaslons (of the Haras du Bois de Boulogne), Laillier (importer of Woman in Red, dam of Revigny and Montargis), Malapert (of the

Haras d'Albian, Vienne), the brothers Ephrussi (Maurice and Michel, *par nobile fratrum*), Barons de Rothschild (of the Meautry stud), Alphonse Staub (died in April 1885), and his brother-in-law Pierre Donon (both being identified with the Lonray stud and with the victories of Stockholm, Le Destrier, Escogriffe, &c.), the Count Hocquart de Turtot (died December 1884), the Marquis de Saint-Sauveur (died January 1884), M. Bouy (owner or part owner of Plaisanterie; he died about May 7, 1886); and, please sir, I can't recollect any more at present.

Q. That will be quite enough, I should say, for the time being, unless you have anything further to add. Have you?

A. I should just like to say that though the importations of horseflesh had no doubt a great deal to do with the successes the French have achieved and the progress they have made, yet the real 'father' of their turf appears to me to have been Mr. Thomas Carter, the trainer, who is said to have trained the celebrated Miss Annette, Franck, Lydia, Vendredi, Poetess, and, in fact, nearly all the best horses of the day in France for Lord Henry Seymour, after whose retirement he trained for Baron Nathaniel de Rothschild and others (himself included), training such winners as Baron de Rothschild's Annetta (winner of the Prix du Cadran in Mr. Carter's name) and Meudon (winner of the French Derby), Expérience (winner of the French Derby for Mr. Carter himself), Celebrity (winner of the French Derby, in 1854, for M. Jacques Reiset, to whom Mr. Carter had sold him), and so on. But, what is more than all this, he was instrumental in bringing the brothers Jennings, those princes of trainers, into France and to the notice of Prince Marc de Beauvau and M.

Alexandre Aumont. Other excellent English trainers followed the example of these three, or even set them the example; but these three, or their relatives or apprentices, have undoubtedly trained between them all the most noted horses on the French turf from the days of Lord Henry Seymour to the days of Flageolet and Rayon d'Or; and that can hardly have been by mere accident. Mr. Carter died, full of years and honours, at Chantilly in September 1879. He was buried on September 28, leaving behind him many of his name and vocation, whether sons or nephews or others, to keep up his traditions—to wit, Messrs. T. Carter, T. R. Carter, R. Carter, F. Carter, &c. It was said of him at the time that he was a man 'dont toute la vie a été irréprochable' ('whose whole life was without reproach'); and that is a wonderful saying about a man who had been for half a century or thereabouts 'upon the Turf.' And, if I were asked to sum up briefly the history of horse-racing in France, I should say that it is a history of English trainers and English jockeys quite as much as of English thoroughbreds.

CHAPTER XIII.

CONCLUSION.

BEFORE author and reader part there are two or three matters which it may be worth while to handle separately.

First of all it is interesting to observe with what different purposes and in what different styles the English Jockey Club and the French Jockey Club (though the latter was in some respects an imitation of the former) seem to have been founded. The English Jockey Club, so far as there is any evidence to be obtained, was at its origin (in 1751 or thereabouts) an association of noblemen and gentlemen, who had nothing but private, selfish, exclusive ends in view, who wished to separate themselves from the vulgar herd or at any rate to keep it under and at a respectful distance, who instituted plates of their own, to be run for solely by horses of their own, ridden by the owners themselves or their friends and equals, and who certainly do not seem to have issued any public manifesto proclaiming any patriotic views or any serious intentions of devoting themselves to amelioration of the English breed of horses. It was not so with the French Jockey Club or Société d'Encouragement; their object was professedly patriotic and wholly free from private, selfish considerations; they even bound themselves not to reap any pecuniary profit, however successful their enterprise might be; and they published in December 1833 a manifesto (signed by the 'founders'), of which the following is the most important portion:—

The undersigned, impressed by the continually increasing degeneracy among the breeds of horses in France, and anxious to contribute by the improvement of them towards the creation of a new source of wealth in this beautiful country, met together to consult upon the means of doing so. They had no difficulty in ascertaining the causes of the evil. There is no need to enumerate them here in detail, but there was among them one which particularly claimed their serious attention. The want of encouragement given to the breeding of 'thoroughbreds' has for a long time past reduced this line of business to inactivity and sterility; yet nothing could be more important than to assist it and promote its development in every imaginable way, for it is the sole means (and the fact can no longer be disputed in these days) of providing France with those lighter species (saddle horses, as distinguished from heavy draught horses) in which she is so deficient, and of delivering her some day or other from that annual tax which she has to pay to foreigners. The propagation of thoroughbreds, then, at home in France is the object to which the undersigned had to direct their efforts chiefly; and, with the view of helping on that propagation to the best of their ability, they have founded the Société d'Encouragement pour l'Amélioration des Races de Chevaux en France.

For a long while arbitrary theories served in this country as the sole guide of our trainers; all sorts of experiments, combinations, and 'crosses' were tried without success in the hope of improving our breeds; nor was the Government more fortunate than private individuals in their attempts. Meanwhile the peace, by rendering our communications with England more frequent, permitted us to study more attentively the principles she adopts in her production and breeding of horses; and certain observant spirits, unshackled by time-honoured routine or narrow-minded considerations, were not long before they acquired the conviction that the immense superiority displayed by our neighbours across the Channel in this branch of business was due above all to the influence of the races, which, kept up by supplies of thoroughbred horses, caused a constant flow and circulation of *pure blood*, and thus more and more, year by year, tended to improve the stock of horses by the agency of these useful 'crosses.' The course to be followed, then, was very simple: it was to profit by observations made during a period of 300 years in England, to take advantage of ready-made experience by adopting approved methods, without losing time in looking about for some better solution of the question than the English had obtained; for there was no reasonable hope of surpassing them in that. Nevertheless, as cannot be denied, it is a very difficult matter to uproot certain prejudices in France; and we are unfortunately obliged to acknowledge that all the old objections to processes employed in England, and especially to horse-racing, have not yet disappeared. In fact, it is easy to see, from the very moderate amount of the prizes allotted to horse races by the Government, how small is the importance attributed to them by the Administration des Haras. And yet it is impossible not to admit that public opinion appears to be making sensible progress in that respect. There is a general desire to give the races further development; this desire makes itself felt more and more every day, and the Société is but the mouthpiece of all enlightened persons in declaring that it regards these contests as the best means that can be employed for purposes of improvement, and therefore thinks itself bound to employ its power to the utmost in multiplying their numbers more and more throughout France.

By admitting only *French thoroughbreds*, entire horses and mares, to compete for the prizes given at the races, the efficaciousness of such encouragements, as aids towards improvement, will be discerned before long: here, as in England, the 'thoroughbred' will be propagated, and its influence upon the whole stock of horses will soon be perceptible. France requires, too, a 'half-bred' supply: well, by the crossing of our strong native mares with thoroughbred stallions this result can be readily brought about. Let us offer, then, a sufficient reward for the production of thoroughbred colts and fillies; and that such encouragement may be both sensible and advantageous, let it be given only to a horse that has won a heat in which he carried off the palm for vigour, bottom, and speed.

A subscription for this purpose has been opened by the Société; it already amounts to 15,000 francs (600*l.*), which will be expended upon the prizes run for at the races in the first fortnight of May 1834.

Such were the serious, business-like, patriotic intentions which the French Jockey Club professed at its foundation; and such was the modest 'caisse' or 'race fund' with which it commenced; yet such was the success of its efforts that in 1881 (to take the nearest accounts within reach at the moment of writing this) it gave away in 'prix' no less than 1,308,000 francs (about 52,320*l.*), and in 1883 about 2,000,000 francs, or some 80,000*l*. Certain expressions which occur in the 'manifesto' foreshadow the disputes which would take place between the Société d'Encouragement and the Administration des Haras, and which were not settled until —after M. Gayot, the most determined member of the Administration des Haras in 1848, had retired, and General Fleury, as head of the Administration, had in his turn battled against the Société d'Encouragement —a compromise was effected and it was decreed that from 1866 flat racing (which had been under two sets of 'Rules,' the Administration's for their 'prix' and the Société's for theirs) should be under the rules of the Société d'Encouragement solely, steeple-chasing under the rules of the Société Générale des Steeple-chases, and trotting under the rules of the Société pour l'Amélioration du Cheval Français de Demi-sang.

To this compromise was probably due the rule (which first appears, if there be no mistake, in the new code drawn up by the Société in 1866-67) whereby a horse is disqualified for having run a public race in

France, at two years of age, before the first of August. It was perhaps a concession to the views of the Administration, which in the days of 'daggers drawn' used to have its races chiefly, if not entirely, in the autumn, leaving the spring to the Société, and which has quite lately endeavoured to stop two-year-old racing altogether. Now in the first set of rules published by the Société (about 1839) there is no restriction whatever placed upon two-year-old racing. On the contrary, there was a two-year-old stakes specially established at Chantilly Spring Meeting (May) in 1838, and (with other two-year-old races, such as the Prix du Premier Pas and the Prix de Chantilly, run in May) it was continued up to the very year 1866, when it was won by La Rochelle (who by the way never did anything else, though she ran often); it had been won, moreover, by the famous Poetess (dam of Monarque). The Prix du Premier Pas had been won by the celebrated Lanterne (who in the autumn of the same year, 1843, also won the Omnium 'for all ages'); and in 1850 and 1851 the Prix de Chantilly had been won by Madame Latache de Fay's Firstborn (winner of the Poule d'Essai) and Trust (winner of the Prix du Cadran, at four years of age, in 1853), much the same feats having been performed at two years of age by other horses, both male and female, that afterwards did well. So that it seems quite reasonable to set down the Société's new rule (new in 1867) to their desire 'to oblige' rather than to a conviction (forced upon them by experience) of the injurious effects produced by two-year-old racing (if not carried to excess) as early in the season as May.

And now, the vicissitudes of Chantilly may well come in for a few words of comment and reminder. There is no need to go back to the Montmorencys, from whom the estate passed to the Condés; it will be enough to refer to the last representative of these latter, who was found one morning, stark dead, hanging by a cord to one of the windows of the château. He had bequeathed this noble property to the Duke d'Aumale, a younger brother of the Duke d'Orléans (patron of the French Jockey Club). The Duke and Duchess d'Orléans (after the establishment of the racecourse in 1833–34) did the honours of the Château of Chantilly, whither, in consequence, it soon became 'the thing' to repair from Paris for the race week. Chantilly is about thirty miles from Paris, and in the days of the Duke and Duchess d'Orléans it was 'the thing' to go 'post,' with the usual blue-jacketed and yellow-breeched postilions, to do the journey 'in two,' stopping one night at some wayside inn; to take a train of servants, a service of plate, and other furniture; to be as expensive and luxurious as possible, in fact—insomuch that Lord Henry Seymour, the head of the 'viveurs,' is said to have paid 1,000 francs (or 40*l.*) for a tent (or 'pavilion') which he only used once—just to breakfast in.

So things went on until the railway came to destroy the 'outing' in some respects, but to greatly facilitate the means of locomotion, to increase the attendance on the course, and so to make the meeting more prosperous, and until in 1852, by decree of Napoleon III., dated June 22, the estate of Chantilly was sold. It was bought, if there be no mistake, by Messrs. Coutts, the bankers (possibly acting for the Duke d'Aumale), for 11,000,000 francs (440,000*l.*), and was let on lease, being occupied, wholly or in part, at one time or another, by Lord Cowley, M. Duchâtel (a former minister of Louis Philippe's), and the Duke de la Trémouille. Still the racing went on; and the gaieties went on in Chantilly itself, though there was no royal duchess to hold court at the Château, at the 'Versailles of the Condés.' These were the days of that 'Bohemianism' to which somehow—one cannot tell how—the Empire seemed to tend so naturally; the days when the line of demarcation between the 'monde' and what is incorrectly called the 'demi-monde' appeared to be almost effaced; the days when the chief of the 'gommeux' was the reckless young Duke de Gramont-Caderousse. The names of other 'viveurs' of the Empire, who were among the chief patrons of Chantilly, have been preserved by an admiring 'compatriot,' who especially mentions 'les Lauriston, les Saint-Romain, Saint-Germain, De Gouy, Gallifet, Dupin, Reiset, Friant, Fasquel, Mosselman, Delamarre, Daru, Finot, Chabrillan, Caillard, Demidoff, De Périgord, De Mouchy, Fould, FitzJames, De Poilly, De Greffulhe, Nivière, Lagrange, De Komar, Blount, D'Arenberg, Tolstoï, De Montreuil, Delangle,' &c. These are names of which several will recall to the reader services rendered to the cause which the Société d'Encouragement had at heart rather than the follies and gallantries for which the Duke de Gramont-Caderousse is understood to have been chiefly distinguished; but no doubt the 'compatriot' did not mean to tar all the personages with the same brush. The 'compatriot' also commemorates with much apparent pride and tender regard the most notorious courtesans of the period, assuring us that they had a great deal more 'chic' than their successors at the present time, although 'the 3,000 francs a month that would be given them represented the 20,000 of nowadays.' The 'compatriot' even records the names, real or assumed or 'nick,' of a few among the 'elegancies,' and a 'good thing' that was said by one of them. We read of Chouchou-Gautier, of a certain 'Doigt-de-pied' (so called 'because her nose resembled a "big toe"'), of Hortense Schneider (could that be the Grande Duchesse de Gérolstein?), of Constance and Armande Résuchs, of Adèle Courtois, Barucci, Judith Ferreyra, Lucile Mangin, Anna Deslion, Esther Guimont, Crénisse, Manvoy, Catinette, &c., who mixed (at Chantilly) in the highest circles (so far as men were concerned) and added the charm of their presence and their frailty to the week of 'distractions les plus échevelées,' which seems to mean in English 'the wildest debauchery.' The tone of those fair creatures is reflected in the remark attributed to one of them who said of her 'friend' (male) to her friend (female), 'My dear, he was an adorable fellow; I was quite eighteen months before I left him.' This is supposed by the 'compatriot' to show indisputably how 'polis, spirituels et bien vivants' the men of that day must have been.

Well, the 'déchéance' came and the Château of Chantilly came once more into the hands of the Duke d'Aumale. He has now had to quit both it and France again: but he has not been robbed again—as yet; and the newspapers have lately been occupied with his will, by which he leaves the magnificent property to the French Institute.

This work cannot be considered complete without a few pages concerning certain institutions which are parasites, or, to use a less offensive expression, offshoots or outcomes of horse-racing. The chief of these are betting, betting-rooms, and the specialties of breeding and selling thoroughbred stock. In England, as everybody knows, the headquarters of betting are and have been for about a century at the establishment of Messrs. Tattersall, who have also for about the same time—or longer—practically held the monoply as regards the sale of thoroughbred stock (though Mr. Pain, Mr. Rymill, and others have had a 'cut in'). This is the more extraordinary inasmuch as it is well known that Mr. Richard Tattersall (grandson of 'Old Tat,' the founder of the two concerns, or the double concern), who did more than any of the family to develop their betting business (as well as the auctioneering), personally hated betting, seldom made a bet himself (unless he was pressed by a 'patron'), and warned young men against belonging to his rooms; but somehow he does not appear to have had quite the courage of his opinions (courage enough to run the risk of ruining himself for principle's sake), so, instead of forbidding his premises to be used at all for the purposes of betting, he built his 'patrons' a place in which they could bet more commodiously than in the little room in which the practice had commenced.

It has already been seen that, if the French were long before they took to horse-racing in earnest, they took very soon and very kindly to betting on such horse races as they had, insomuch that Louis XV. prohibited horse-racing at one time for that reason, and Louis XVI. would bet his 'petit écu' for the sake of setting his courtiers an economical example and giving them a gentle hint. It is scarcely necessary to say, then, that, under the auspices of Lord Henry Seymour and his colleagues of 1833, there was plenty of betting, though there was as yet no 'Ring' and no 'Tattersall's.' Of course 'anglomanie' alone would have brought a French 'ring' and a French 'Tattersall's' into vogue in due time quite naturally; but there were special incidents which helped to hasten matters. We have seen that almost as soon as the French Jockey Club was instituted (if

not before) there was established an institution called
'Palmer's New Betting Rooms' (at Paris), whereof the
moving and owning spirit is supposed to have been
identical with the Mr. Palmer who filled the office of stud
groom (or something of the kind) to M. Rieussec and
used to exhibit the stud horse Rainbow (for a 'consideration') to admiring Parisians and provincials on the
festive Sundays. But in 1849 or thereabouts there was
founded by M. Chéri-Salvador (related by marriage to
the celebrated breeders MM. Crémieux) an establishment for the transaction of sales by auction such as had
taken place in England for generations at 'the Corner,'
which is 'Tattersall's.' Whether M. Chéri-Salvador
offered facilities for the betting which has become the
chief feature of the English 'Tattersall's' is not quite
clear, but it is certain that the success of his enterprise
(which was developed and is still in lively existence at
49 Rue de Ponthieu) led to speedy rivalry and to the
institution of what is titularly called 'Le Tattersall
Français' (at 24 Rue Beaujon, Champs Elysées), which
has flourished for many years and still flourishes under
the fostering care of M. Ch. Grossmann. But the
French is not a complete 'Tattersall's,' inasmuch as the
headquarters of betting are not there, but at what is
called the 'Salon des Courses' (established under the
auspices of the late Viscount P. Daru), which the development of regular and professional betting in France
rendered necessary and to which the annual subscription
was originally 40 francs (increased to 50 francs from
May 1, 1872, and perhaps to a higher sum since
then). It seems to have had various sites (in Rue
Basse du Rempart and elsewhere) before it was settled
at its present situation, 20 Boulevard des Capucines.
How England contributed to the formation of a per-

manent 'betting ring' in France, to which a 'Salon des Courses' became by degrees a necessity, is easily shown. England, in fact, turned France into a sort of Botany Bay for 'book-makers' and 'list-holders.' The Betting Act of 1853 (for the suppression of betting-houses), which has since been extended, led in the first instance to the emigration of 'parasites of the Ring' to 'Boulong,' to Paris (with 'betting agencies' all over the Rue de Choiseuil), and to other nice places in France, whither England—not of set purpose—transferred some of the 'nuisances,' just as she had transmitted many among the advantages, of the Turf. The more disreputable emigrants' example was followed by their more reputable brethren, who liked the climate, or the language, or the society, or the cookery of France, or more probably the facilities that country afforded, as comparatively virgin soil with unsophisticated inhabitants and legislators, for their favourite operations. And so the French Ring, otherwise 'le Ring,' otherwise (by a figure for which grammarians have a learned name) 'le Betting,' and the 'Salon des Courses' became the favourite haunts of many English 'book-makers' known to fame or notoriety. Such was Mr. J. B. Morris (who died at Paris, July 18, 1880; ran horses, won the St. Leger with Knight of St. George, and was noted in France for living 'like a fighting cock' at the Grand Hôtel and at Bignon's, where he won quite a reputation by eating—not four-and-twenty blackbirds baked in a pie, but four-and-twenty ortolans at a sitting). Such is or was Mr. H. Saffery (dubbed the 'cock of the book-makers,' who was never known to recoil at the amount of a bet, and who would answer a French nobleman's cry of 'A thousand louis on such and such a horse' with a ready 'Right you are, Count; will you lay it twice—four times

—six times over?'). Such is or was Mr. W. Wright (called 'the boy,' in playful allusion to a smooth face and plump cheeks, whose difference with Lord Royston over Alpenstock's City and Suburban is said to have led to the suppression of 'list betting)'; such Mr. Valentine (partner of Hardaway and Topping); such Mr. Haughton (called 'Groseille,' or 'Gooseberry'—*groseille à maquereau*—from a story concerning effervescing wines); such Mr. Marks (renowned as 'Antidote' Marks, by reason, it is stated, of some very sharp proceedings in connection with an animal called Antidote); such Mr. Burch (said to resemble a clergyman in appearance, as was also said of the celebrated 'old John Day,' the trainer), and many another. Of these 'book-makers' some have had careers almost as remarkable as those of the first 'Leviathan,' Mr. W. Davis (originally a workman at Cubitt's, where he is said to have begun by winning a half-crown in 1840), or of Mr. John Jackson, known as 'Jock o' Fairfield.'

Take, for instance, Messrs. Valentine, Hardaway, and Topping, of whom the senior partner was originally Mr. George Hardaway (who died October 15, 1882). They (as well as Mr. Wright, who was one of the 'firm' of Valentine and Wright) belonged to the regular 'betting-house agencies,' which were driven out of England in 1853 (the law having been further extended to Scotland in course of time). To 'Boulong' they went, and so flourished that, according to their biographer and panegyrist, writing in 1882, Mr. George Hardaway 'was associated with some very heavy pecuniary transactions,' and had a 'lot of folks' more or less 'dependent upon his almost princely charity;' and of the firm itself it is declared that 'few of our leading commercial houses in the great city of London have more clients and correspondents on their books, and each morning's post brings scores and hundreds of letters from all parts of England, Scotland, and Ireland,' which ' all contain money.' This is, no doubt, a truly awful revelation, this gigantic betting business, with its 'staff of clerks,' this unproductive industry, this alchemical institution for the extraction of money (without ' value received') from English, Scottish, and Irish pockets. Still it is mentioned by his biographer as a 'rise' for Mr. Robert Topping when he was admitted by that acute gentleman the late Mr. George Hardaway to be the very man the firm of Valentine and Hardaway wanted. Mr. Topping's 'rise' is said to have come about in this way: He was born at Manchester about the year 1845, and had to 'rise from the ranks,' insomuch that his first bet is said to have been even unmentionably more modest than the legendary half-crown of the 'Leviathan.' But Mr. Topping, 'being of the Lancashire school'—which appears to mean that he always 'preferred the nimble ninepence to the slow shilling' (in other words, money obtained by speculation rather than by equally hard work in the way of 'productive industry')—became at a very early age 'identified with the betting ring,' left Manchester for London, was engaged as 'clerk' to Mr. Shee, a 'bookmaker,' from 1865 (or thereabouts) to 1873 (or thereabouts), did so well for his employer as to think himself justified in demanding no longer a mere 'weekly wage,' but a 'share of the book,' was promptly refused, took the refusal cheerfully, but relinquished his post for the purpose of 'bettering himself,' was snapped up by Messrs. Valentine and Hardaway, became the life and soul of the 'Boulogne agency,' and 'rose' to 'wealth and affluence,' with a 'comfortable and substantial residence in one of the prettiest suburbs of London.' The prototype of this lucky race of men was the celebrated Mr. Hutchinson, of Shipton, near York, who, at fifteen years of age, being then a stable boy, won a bet (in 1751, more than a hundred and thirty years ago), which 'set him up,' until he became ' a squire,' the owner of many a celebrated race horse of the 'good old times,' and a friend and rival of the Reverend Mr. Goodricke, Prebendary of York Minster, who was supposed to be the best judge of race horses (of which he possessed a famous stud) at that epoch. It is sad, perhaps, to think that such examples of success in a very questionable line of 'industry' may exercise a strong fascination over the young and lead to the ruin of thousands.

The French, having ' le Turf,' and ' le Tattersall,' and ' le Ring,' could not, of course, go without their ' organ' or ' organs' (more ' special' than the old ' Journal des Haras ') in the way of ' sporting papers.' The first of these was ' Le Sport,' founded by M. Eugène Chapus, in the early days of the French Jockey Club, and by him it was afterwards made over to M. de Saint-Albin (Lagayère), who died in August 1878, and whose son, the present M. Albert de Saint-Albin (the ' Robert Milton' of ' Le Figaro ') continues it to this day. By degrees the number of sporting papers of course increased and multiplied. After ' Le Sport' came ' Le Jockey,' ' Le Derby,' and ' Le Journal des Courses,' and now ' the races' are made a special feature in all the following papers: ' Le Sport,' ' Le Jockey,' ' L'Entraîneur,' ' Vie Sportive,' ' Paris-Sport,' ' Echo du Sport,' ' Revue des Sports,' ' Chronique du Turf,' ' France Chevaline,' 'Journal des Haras,' ' Le Figaro,' ' Le Gaulois,' ' Le Gil-Blas,' ' Le Voltaire,' ' L'Echo de Paris,' ' Le Soir,' 'La République Française,' ' Le Matin,' ' Le Temps,' ' Le Siècle,' ' La France,' ' La Liberté,' ' Le

Télégraphe,' 'L'Evénement,' 'Le Petit Moniteur,' 'Le XIXe Siècle,' 'Le National,' 'Paris,' 'Le Triboulet,' 'Vie Moderne,' 'Petit Caporal,' 'L'Intransigeant,' 'L'Echo Agricole,' 'Tam-Tam,' 'L'Autorité,' 'Le Succès,' 'La Justice.'

As in England so in France, the practice of horse-racing has led sometimes to detestable acts of cruelty, and the practice of breeding from 'pur sang' (the 'pure blood of the Desert,' whether Arab, Barb, Turk, or any other that there may be to which the term 'thoroughbred' applies) has led to much difference of opinion.

As regards cruelty, it would be difficult to find a worse case than that of the two 'trotters' Verny and Mauvaise-Tête, matched (for 15,000 francs, or 600*l.*) to trot *thirty* (*French*) *leagues* (120 kilomètres) without stopping, in the neighbourhood of Paris. The affair 'came off' on July 5, 1879. The route was from the Arc de Triomphe de l'Etoile, through the Bois de Boulogne, St. Cloud, La Marche, Rocquencourt, St. Germain, Mantes, and Rosny, returning by the same road as far as St. Cloud, along the bank of the Seine to Boulogne, at the back of Baron de Rothschild's château, ending at the cascade on the racecourse. Poor Mauvaise-Tête was pulled up at St. Germain on the return journey, and died then and there. The winner, Verny, arrived at the goal, but was not in much better plight than the other, dropped down on entering the stable, and never got up again. The veterinary surgeon who tried to bleed the poor creature could get nothing but 'a sort of currant jelly.' The French papers, it should be mentioned, expressed nothing but disgust at the proceedings; it is only a pity the disgust was not expressed before the match, which was well advertised, took place.

This cruel race came soon after and may have been suggested by a different and much more humane match which had lately taken place (June 10, 1879) between M. Khan's Tambour-Battant (half-bred trotting pony) and Triboulet (a thoroughbred steeple-chaser, belonging to Baron Raymond de Seillère and backed by him and by Baron Finot), and which will give an opportunity of referring further to the difference of opinion already alluded to.

The 'trotter' was driven in a 'spider' by M. Plaizel; the 'chaser' was ridden by the jockey Gardener. The former was allowed to adopt the 'go as you please' style; the latter was bound to gallop all the way. The distance was 40 kilomètres (about 25 miles) on the macadamised road round the Longchamps racecourse; the stakes were 10,000 francs (about 400*l.*). The 'chaser,' galloping so regularly that he finished each of the 'rounds' (of which there were eleven) in something under eight minutes, won the match easily in 1 hour 20 minutes 3 seconds; whilst the 'trotter,' notwithstanding the application of the whip, was still seven kilomètres (about four miles) behind. 'Who will say now,' was the remark in one of the newspapers, 'that the thoroughbred has more speed but less bottom than the half-bred,' especially as Triboulet had not 'turned a hair,' or at any rate seemed 'less fatigued than his rider'?

But then, some one may say, Tambour-Battant was only a 'pony.' However that may be, the match is a convenient peg whereon to hang a few remarks about the aforesaid 'difference of opinion,' to which horse-racing in France has given rise, and which is not even yet quite settled. In England horse-racing has given rise to a difference of opinion about the respective merits of the native or 'natural' Arab (or 'son of the Desert') and of the English thoroughbred, and there are still Englishmen (and especially Englishwomen, thinking the Arab 'arch' so 'pretty') who, whether openly or secretly (notwithstanding Iambic and Asil, Avowal and the Prince of Wales's up to that time unbeaten Alep in 1877, &c. &c.), believe in the former rather than in the latter. In France (where the Arab has always been cultivated, and whence, as we have seen, England obtained some of her best early Arabs or Eastern sires, such as Saint-Victor's Barb, the Thoulouse Barb, the Belgrade Turk, the superexcellent bay Barb of Mr. Curwen, and the legendary Arabian of Lord Godolphin) the 'Arabian heresy' has apparently not been so prevalent, has even been exploded almost entirely at 'head-quarters'; but, on the other hand, the 'half-bred heresy,' the belief in the superior staying powers of the 'cock-tail,' has always been encouraged by the Administration des Haras (and its officers for the most part), and appears likely to be never wholly eradicated from every French bosom. Yet proof positive has constantly been forthcoming against the soundness of it, from the days of the Viscount Guy de Montécot and his friend and co-champion of 'pur sang' Viscount Guy du Bouëxie. The former riding a light 'weedy' bay thoroughbred mare (called Pateen, it is said, but probably Poteen) and the latter a thoroughbred (called Grey Hercules, by Sir Hercules), rode eight turns round the Champ de Mars (that is, about 16,000 mètres, or 10 miles) against Count Lancosme-Brèves on his half-bred hunter (called Roi des Bohémiens and much esteemed); and the two 'thoroughbreds' finished their journey, weighed in, and came out to see how the other was getting on. This was something like half a century before the days of Tambour-Battant and Triboulet.

In a history of horse-racing the hateful and vexed question of betting cannot be altogether ignored, but as little as possible has been said about it. What tremendous influence, however, it has upon the affairs of the Turf may be inferred from the following little narrative, which is specially interesting at the end of this year, 1886, when for the first time within the recollection of man there have been obstacles placed in the way of French candidates for the Cesarewitch and Cambridgeshire. 'That Plaisanterie put in an appearance [in 1885] for the Cesarewitch,' says the editor of 'L' Entraîneur,' 'is owing to two "bookmakers," MM. T. Wilde and Jack Moore. It was they who made it worth the while of the famous filly's owners, to whom they guaranteed 33 to 1, having themselves obtained no more than 20 to 1 in England. . . . Jack Moore paid nearly 600,000 francs (24,000*l.*) in five-franc, ten-franc, twenty-franc, and [if there are any] fifty-franc pieces at the highest, to backers of Plaisanterie. . . . T. Wilde was the "agent de change"—I can find no better term —who brought over from England to France the greater part of the *five millions* [of francs] that we won by backing Plaisanterie.' Five millions of francs! That is, 200,000*l.*; confessedly extracted from perfidious Albion. *Hinc illæ lacrymæ*, no doubt: hence that exclusive edict issued by the English Jockey Club. It was the prodigious amount of money won in bets by the 'French contingent' that produced so great an effect; Plaisanterie might have won the two handicaps and welcome otherwise. Especially as, being a daughter of Wellingtonia, she was no less English than most French winners were in the good old times, when nobody grudged our neighbours an occasional Goodwood Cup in return for their outlay in our markets and for their contributions or subscriptions to our stakes.

'Francia farà da se,' perhaps in the long run. But meanwhile, until that consummation is attained, until most of her winners are born of French sire and French dam, trained by French trainers, fed on French oats, ridden by native French Jockeys (who have learned at last 'se faire maigrir'), with French saddles to sit (as much as they can) upon, with French 'leathers,' French stirrups, French top-boots, French 'persuaders' attached to those boots, and French whalebone wherewith to administer 'rib-benders,' there does not seem to be much reason why any English body should sigh 'Ichabod' or babble of 'exclusion,' or why the British lion should roar for 'RECIPROCITY.'

INDEX.

AAR

AARON, 56
    Abbé de Pradt, M. l', 15, 101
Abbeville, 120
Aboukir, 108
Absalon, 197
Absinthe 124
Achères, 6, 96
Achievement, 158, 159, 166
Acide Prussique, 192
Adelaïde (German), 223
Administration des Haras, 3, 4, 14, 27, 43, 47, 50, 55, 61, 109, 117, 351, and *passim*; (the Russian), 304
Agile, 87
Agility, 174
Aguado, Viscount Onésime, 107
Aguila, 69
Aïda, 313
Aïda II., 313, 330
Ailesbury (horse), 161
Ailesbury, Lord, 228, 229, 231, 234
Alaric, 178, 190, 195, 196
Alba, 127
Albert Victor, 177
Albian, the Haras d', 282
Albion (horse), 167, 264, 269, 270, 282
Albion, the 'perfidious,' *passim*
Alcibiade, 136, 187
Alep (the Prince of Wales's, 'Arab'), 364
Alerte, 116, 126, 129, 136
Alfred the Great, 2
Algarade, 332
Alger, 313
Allez-y-gaîment, 72
Allez-y-rondement, 115, 123, 126
Allier, Haras de l', 101
Allumette, 197, 214, 220, 225
Almanza, 212
Almenesches, 191
Alpenstock, 359
Alteruter, 63, 64
Amalfi, 65, 82

ATT

America, 67, 223
'Americans,' 79, 277
Amour Propre, 162
André, M. E., 98
André, M. Léon, 183, 192, 251
André, M. Louis, 98
Andred, 195
Androclès, 322
Angell, Mr., 124
Angélo, 115, 116
Anglesey, Lord, 251
Anglomanie, 4, 8, 43, 356
Angora, 64
Annandale (horse), 320
Anne (of Luxembourg, of Bohemia), 13
Annetta, 63
Antoine, M., 55
Antoinette, 119
Antonia, 119, 120
Apology, 208, 210
Arabian, the Godolphin, 2, 58
Araucaria, 197, 215, 261
Araunah, 6, 7
Arbitre, 263
Archbishop of Malines, 15, 101
Archer, Mr. F. (jockey), ix
Archiduc, 167, 308, 312, 335
Archimedes, 149
Arenberg, Prince A. d', 201, 345, 354
Argences, 148, 155
Armagnac, 127, 130, 136, 138
Arthur, 129
Artois, The Count d', 9–11, 14, 97
Asil (the 'Arab'), 364
Asteroid, 117
Astrée, 217
Astrolabe, 187
Atalante, 156
Athelstan, 2
Athena, 162
Atherstone, 122
Atlantic (horse), 208, 337
Atom, 101
Attendez-moi sous l'Orme, 292
Attila (by Colwick), 63–5, 120

INDEX

ATT

Attrape-qui-peut, 123, 124
Aubenay, Buisson d', 5
Augusta, 215, 225
Auguste, 83, 166
Aumale, the Duke d', 22, 102, 353, 355
Aumont, MM. 23, 52, 53, 56, 62, 66, 69, 71, 109, 129, 146, and *passim*
Aurelian, 122
Auriol, Baron d', 130
Aurore, 198, 210
Australia, 124, 223, 276
Austria-Hungary, 144, 223, 276
Aveline, M., 282
Avenante, 87
Aventurière, 214
Avermes, 344
Avocat, 87
Avowal, 364

BABIÉGA, 64
Babouino (afterwards Franc Picard), 88, 89
Babylas, 219
Bachelette, 173
Baden-Baden, 109, 182, 188
'Badminton Library,' the, 154, 241
Badsworth, 197
Bailly, M., 103
Baïonnette, 158
Bakaloum, 108
Balaclava, 108, 120
Balagny (elder and younger), 81, 244, 247
Bale, Mr. (convict), 238
Balensi, M. E., 312
Balfe, 214
Baliverne, 116, 126, 127, 136
Balzac, 28
Baracé, M. de, 53, 344
Baragah, 143
Barb, Lord Godolphin's Arabian or, 2, 364
Barb, Mr. Curwen's bay, 2, 364
Barb, St. Victor's, 2, 364
Barb, the T(h)oulouse, 2, 364
Barbary, 10
Barbary horses, 13
Barbe Bleue, 271, 278, 279
Barberine, 313, 316, 317
Barbillon, 179, 193, 198, 200
Barbillonne, 184, 191
Bard, the, 314, 316
Barford, 197
Bariolet, 271, 278
Baron, The, 57, 58, 71, 75, 137
Baroncino, 49, 74, 112, 336
Baronello, 144
Barrett, MM. (jockeys), ix
Barrett, Mr. W., 320

BLA

Bartholomew, Mr. J., 54
Bartlett's Childers, 95
Basilique, 255, 264
Basquine, 219, 225
Bastide, M. de la, 98, 344
Bathilde, 130, 155
Battersea, the Red House at, 20
Bayard (Hungarian), 223
Bay Final (American), 223
Bay Middleton, 74, 83, 149
Beadsman, vi
Béatrix, 83, 136
Beaumesnil, 341
Beauminet, 262, 264, 267
Beaumont-Vassy, Viscount de, 28
Beaumontel, 332
Beauvais, 110
Beauvau, Prince Etienne de, 107
Beauvau, Prince Marc de, 49, 53, 107, 236
Bedford, 62, 73
Bedminster, 148
Beggarman, 23, 38, 62, 66
Béhague, M. de, 53
Belgium, 66
Bellerophon, 67
Belliqueux, 264, 271
Belzébuth, 197
Bénazet, M., 182
Bendigo (horse), 317
Bend Or, 82, 134, 263, 271
Benjamin, 115, 123, 125, 128
Benoît, M., 98, 111, 345
Benson, Mr. (convict), 238
Benvenuto, 68
Bernardet, 219, 220
Berryer, 194
Berteux, Count de, 322, 345, and *passim*
'Betting Rooms,' Palmer's New, 34, 357; other, 356, 357
Bibletto, 324
Biche, 11
Bigarreau, 35, 121, 174, 175
'Big Stable,' the, 107, 113; sale of horses belonging to the, 130, 131
'Bigger Stable,' the, 212
'Bignon's,' 358
Birmingham (Grand Steeple-chase), 92
Biron, the Duke de, 8
Biron, the Duke de Gontaut-, 9
Bissextil, 108
Bivouac, 178
Bizarre, 64
Blacklock, 154
Black Prince, 108, 109
Blair Athol, 39, 54, 58, 75, 82, 153, 198
Blanc, M. Edmond, 97, 255, 325

INDEX

BLA

'Blanche de Géry,' 323
Blangy, the Count Gaston de, 98, 344
Blenheim, 197, 204
Blenkiron, Mr., 153, 178, 236
Blois, 120
Bloodsworth, Mr., 320
Blount, Mr., 354
Blue Mantle, 127
Boa, 199
Boast, Mr., 54
Bohemia (horse), 128
Boïador, 199
Boïard, vi, 197, 198, 208, 209, 212, 335
Bois-Roussel, Haras de, 344
Bois-Roussel (horse), 49, 141, 144, 164
Boldrick, Mr., 53
Bombance, 199
Bonaparte, Prince Louis Napoleon, 23
Bordeaux, 90
Boréal, 199
Borély, 203
Boston, 199
Bouëxie, Viscount Guy de, 364
'Bouillons Duval,' the, 96
Boulet, 210
Boulogne (horse), 83, 168, 173, 178
Boulogne (town), 66, 76, 120
Boulogne (village), Bois de, 5, 8, 29, 96
Boum, 263, 271
Boute-feu, 127
Bouthillier, the Marquis de, 313, 323
Boutton-Levêque, M., 344
Bouy, M. H., 323, 331, 346
Bowes, Mr. J., 98, 99
Boyce, Mr. R., 30
Brabant, 62
Bracken, 264
Braconnier, 197, 217, 219
Bras de Fer, 271
Bray, the Baron de, 345
Breadalbane, 148, 152, 154
Brest (horse), 311
Breteuil, Count Henri de, 324
Brewer, The, 112
Bribery colt, the, vi, 156
Brick, 126, 130, 136
Brie, 244, 255
Brighton, 9 (the stakes), 69
Brighton Cup, the, 54
British Yeoman, 91
Brodick, 215
Brodrick-Cloete, Mr., 316
Brown Duchess, 119
Bruce, 279, 327
Brut, 270

CAS

Brutus, 76
Bryon, Mr. T., 19, 106
Buc, 15, 33, 100
Buccaneer, 111, 218
Buckstone, vi
Buisseret, M., 282
Buisson d'Aubenay, 5
Burch, Mr. (bookmaker), 359
Busybody, 311

CACCIA, Count Maximilian, 36
Caderousse, the Duke de Gramont-, 354
Cadland, 26, 63
Cadogan (horse), 252
Cadran, Prix du, 55
Caen (horse), 241
Caen (place), 49, 66, 80, 112, 120, 344
Caillard, M., 354
Caillé, M. D., 126
Caillotin, M. Zachary, 55
Calendar, the English, 68, 83
Calenge, M. Charles, 49, 344
Caller On, 119, 144
Calvados, 191
Camballo, 213
Cambis, Count de, 23, 37, 65
Cambis, the Marquis de (d'Orsan), 38
Cambridgeshire, the, 68, 69, 73, 238, 319
Cambuscan (sire of Kincsem), 252
Caméléon, 65
Camélia, 197, 215, 220, 225, 263, 334, 335
Camembert, 219, 221, 225, 257
Camillus, 3
Campêche, 197, 201
Cannon, Mr. T. (jockey), ix.
Cantator, 10, 111
Canterbury, 62
Cantinière, 332
Capri, 64
Capsule, 137, 177
Capucine, 111
Capucine II., 131
Caravan, 57, 64
Carlisle, Lord, 9
Carnelion, 214
Carriès, M. (horse-tamer), 160
Cars, Duke (Count) des, 15, 53, 98, 344
Carter, Messrs., 30, 53, 62, 146, 346, 347
Carter, Mr. T. (the ' doyen '), 312, 346, 347
Cassidy, Mr., 179
Cassique, 68
Castellane, the Count de, 98

CAS

Castillon, 262, 264, 267
Castor, 67
Castries, the Duke de, 308, 311, 328, 344
Caterer, 197, 215
Catton, 30, 102
Cauchemar, 24, 64
Caumont-la-Force, the Marquis de, 210
Cavailhon, M. E., ix, 241
Cavatine, 63
Cazalot, Monsieur and Madame, 33, 98
Celebrity, 69
Celle-Saint-Cloud, Haras de, 345
Cerdagne, 169, 178, 183
Cerf-Volant, 159, 161
Cesarewitch, the, 72, 238, 319
Ceylon, 156, 158
Chabrillan, M., 354
Chabrol, M. Pierre, 55
Chaloner, Mr. T., 54
Chamant, Haras de, 172, 253, 343, and *passim*
Chamant (horse), vi, 163, 197, 221, 226, 235, 263, 335
Champ de Mars, 22, 50, 96, 102
Champ d'Oiseau (ex-Finot), 157
Chancellor, 195, 197
Chantilly, 22, 40, 49, 50, 54, *passim*
Chantilly (horse), 187
Chantilly, Château of, 352-355
Chapelle-en-Serval, 97
Chaplin, Mr. H., 134, 236
Chapus, M. Eugène, 361
Charivari II., 217
Charlemagne, the Emperor, 146
Charles le Bel, 1, 5
Charles le Sage, 5
Charles VIII., 329
Charles X., 3, 4, 9, 32, 170, 342
Charles XII. (horse), 23
Charleville (horse), 187
Charme, M. E. de la, 213, 345
Charon, 218
Chartres, the Duke de ('Egalité'), 9, 10, 333
Chattanooga, 148, 321
Chédeville, M., 98, 117
Cheese, Mr., 251
Cheffreville, Haras de, 345
Chéri-Salvador, M., 34, 98, 357
Chérubin, 196
Chevrette, 78
Chevreuse, 192
Chiffon, 255
Chifney, Mr., 54
Chimène, 87
Chippendale, 267

CON

Chitré, 278, 292
Choisy-le-Roi, 125
Christiania, 208, 209
Christmas Carol, 149
Cimier, 278
Cinna, 158
'Circonscription de l'Ouest,' 53
'Circonscriptions,' the three, 125
Cirès-les-Mello, the estate of, 325
'Citizen King,' the, 15
City and Suburban, the, 68
'Claimant,' the, 237
Clarabide, 332
Claremont, 213
Clarinette, 340
Clark, Mr. (the English 'judge'), 268
Clarke, Mr. (detective), 238
Clearwell Stakes, 83, 128, 147
Clélie, 257
Clémentine, 242, 245, 264, 282, 336
Clérino, 37
Clermont-Tonnerre, the Count de, 326
Clift, Mr. W., 14
Clio, 278, 279
Clio (muse), 212
Clocher, 248, 251
Cloete, Mr. Brodrick, 316
Clos Vougeot, 190
Clotaire, 190, 193, 194
Clotho, 167
Clôture, La, 64, 66
Coastguard, 139
Colbert, 3, 14, 342
Cole, the Rev. W., 8
Colère, 187
Colombine or Columbine, 128
Colonel, The (steeple-chaser), 93
Combat, 179, 203
Comité des Courses, 36, 44
Commandant, 271
Commandeur, 119
Commodore (Australian), 223
Commodore Napier, 64
Commotion, 79
Compiègne (horse), 120, 124, 130
Compiègne (place), 344
Comte Alfred, 270, 279
Comus, 10, 14, 334
Condé, the last Prince de, 353
Condés, the, 353
Condor, The (M. Martin's), 309, 314, 316, 327
Conductor, 11
Confiance, 87
Conflans, the Marquis de, 9, 10, 97
Conqueror, 10

INDEX 371

CON

Conquête, 257
Conscrit, 305
Conseil, 221
Consigne, 314
Constance (by Gladiator), 163
Consul, 83, 85, 86, 124, 166, 167, 304
Contempt, 162, 261
Continental Derby, the, 72
Coppée, M., 282
Coquet (afterwards Palestro), 117
Cornelier, M. (jockey), 55
'Corner, The,' 357
Coronation Stakes (at Ascot), 86
Corrie Roy, 271, 293
Corringham, Mr., 3, 53
Corysandre, 18, 55
Cosmopolite, 111, 112, 116, 123
Cosmos, 314
Cossack horses, 60
Côte d'Or, 5
Cotherstone, 99, 149
Courteuil, 40
Courtois, 262, 267
Coutts (horse), 175
Coutts, Messrs. (bankers), 353
Coux, Count de, 53, 344
Coventry, 91
Coventry, Mr. Arthur, 43
Cowley, Lord, 353
Cramoisi, 190
Craon, 89
Craven, Mr. W. G., 318, 319
Crédo, 310
Crémieux, Madame veuve, 34
Crémieux, MM., 15, 30, 38, 98, 101, 344, 357
Cremorne, 193
Crépuscule, 196
Creusa, 62
Crimea, the, 39
Cripple, 337
Cristal, 187
Criterion Stakes, 83, 128, 335
Croix, MM. de, 344
Croix-de-Berny, 50, 90
Cromwell Road, 81
Crucifix (filly), 318
Crucifix, the French (filly), 142
Cruel Match, a, 362
Cubitt, Messrs., 359
Cumberland, the 'Culloden' Duke of, 44
Cunningham(e), Miss Fairlie, 35
Cunningham(e), Mr. Fairlie, 35
Cunningham, Mr. R. (trainer), 53
Cunnington, Mr. T., 313
Currency, 68, 313
Curwen Bay Barb, the, 2, 364
Cutler, MM., 344

DES

Cyprienne, 65
Czarda, 331

'D'S,' the three, 121
'Daily Telegraph,' the, 228
Damier, 136
Dandin, 272, 278, 284
Dangerous, 26
Dangu, Haras de, 84, 143, 146, 343, and *passim*
Dangu (horse), 111, 150
Daniel O'Rourke, 99, 268
Dard, 292
Daru, Viscount (Count) P., 20, 49, 122, 129, 132, 227, 345, 354, and *passim*
Dauger, Viscount de, 321, 345
Dauphin, the, 3, 7, 14, 21, 23, 170, 342
Davioud, M., 103
Davis, Mr. 'Leviathan' (bookmaker), 359
Day, Mr. (Honest) John, 320
Day, Mr. (Old) John, 359
Day, Mr. William, 320
Deauville, 103
Déception, 63
'Déchéance,' the, 177
D'Estournel, 159
Delamarre, Count Achille, 38
Delamarre, M. Casimir, 38
Delamarre, M. H., 39, 53, 75, 95, 129, 130, 190, 344, 354, and *passim*
Delangle, M., 354
Delarroque, M., 98
Delâtre, M., 167, 173, 345
Demidoff, Count Anatole, 39, 40, 354
Demi-Lune, 193, 194
'Demi-sang,' 47, 61
Démon, 136
Dennetier, MM. (fathers of suburban racing'), 328
Denormandie, M., 43
Derby, the Continental, 72
Derby, the English, 26, 39, 83, and *passim*
Derby, the French, 22, 31, 32, 47, 53, 55; (scandal connected with), 56; 61, 66, 102, and *passim*
Derby, a memorable French, 77
Derby, Lord, v, 150, 236
Derby du Midi, the, 126
Derviche, 292
Des Cars, the Duke (Count), 15, 53, 98, 344
'Descente de la Courtille,' the, 28
Desgrands, M., 98

B B 2

Desmaisons, 98
Destinée, 207, 208
Desvignes, M., 345
Diamant, 74, 94
Diane, the Prix de (or French Oaks), 22, 32, 37, 52, 102, and *passim*
Diaprée, 314
Dictateur II., 278
Dictator, 121
Dictature, 208
'Dictionnaire du Sport Français,' vii, 313
Didier, M. Martin, 38
Dieppe, 15, 50, 90, 92, 94
Diomed, 149
Diophantus, 121, 122
Diplomate, 283
Directrice, 288
Djali, 64
Dollar, vi, 54, 85, 127, 138, 145, 322, 336
Domenichino, 101
Don Carlos, 83, 178
Doncaster (horse), 58, 198, 209
Doncaster Stakes, 65
Donjon, 130
Donna (American), 223
Donon, M. P., 314, 346
Dora, 257 265
Dorade, 64
Dorette (La), 321
Doublon, 323
Doucereuse, 226
Doyle, Mr. (jockey), 123
Dragon, 156
Drummer, The (English), 54, 168
Drummer (French), 63, 65
Drummond, 197, 204
Druscovitch, Mr. (detective), 238
Dublin (horse), 269
Duchâtel. M., 353
Duchess(e), 77
Duke, The, 150
Dulcamara, 63, 65
Dulcinea, 11
Dumplin, 337
Dundee, 121, 122
Dupin, M., 354
Durand, the Baron, 344
Durand, Madame veuve, 344
Durdans Stakes, the, 62
Dutch Oven, 177, 293, 332
Dutch Skater, 174, 177, 189, 190, 194, 335, 336

EARL, The, 164, 165
Eberhard (Hungarian), 223
Echelle, 69, 184
Eckmühl, 179, 192
Eclaireur, 103
Eclipse, 83
Ecole d'Equitation, 37
Economist, 91
Ecossais, 204, 210
Edwards, A., 144, 152
Edwards, George, 23, 342
Edwards, Messrs., 54, 144
Edwin, 63
Egalité, Philippe, 9–11, 22, 62, 111, 170, 333
Egham, 68
Egremont, Lord, 236
Elchingen, the Dukes d', 31, 32
Eliacin, 265, 272
Elizabeth, 264
Elizondo, 62
Eltham (horse), 149
Elthiron, 57
Ely (the 'beautiful'), vi, 130, 143
Emblem, 95
Emblematic, 95
'Emigration' in 1870, the, 178
Emilius ('demi-sang'), 89, 90
Emperor, The, 58, 71
Emperor of the French, the, 113, 132
Empire, the First, 3, 14
Empire, the Third, 344, 354
Enéide, 189
English thoroughbreds imported, lists of, 10, 16–18, 24–26, 41, 57
Enguerrande, 217, 221, 225, 263, 335
Entraîneur (horse), 328
Eole (Fille de l'Air's first foal), 144
Eole II., 174, 189, 190, 196, 203, 336
Eolien, 332
Epernay, 101
Ephrussi, M. Maurice, 326, 346, and *passim*
Ephrussi, M. Michel, 346 and *passim*
Epsom, 11, 70
Eremos, 57
Escarboucle, 313, 341
Escogriffe, 341
Esméralda, 23
Esteemed Friend, 163
Estelle, 340
Etoile du Nord, 81
Etoile Filante, 157
Etreillis, the Baron Saint-Aure d', vii, 312
Eugène Sue, 2, 99
Europa, 162
'Evènements, Les,' 170 *et seq.*
Exactitude, 116, 124
Exilé, 200, 203

INDEX

EXP

Expérience, 64
Extra, 313
Extraordinary death of six yearlings, 331
Eylau, 55

FAGNIANI, Maria, 19
Fagotin II., 341
Fair Helen, 75
Faisane, 217
Falendre (ex-Magenta, afterwards L'Africain), 130
Falkland, 174
Falmouth (horse), 252
Falmouth, Lord, 133, 134, 210, 214, 219, 224, 227, 235, and *passim*
Fanny Day (Hungarian), 223
Faraway, 174
Farfadet, 284, 292
Farnese, 225
Fasquel (of Courteuil), M., 40, 53, 354
Fasquel, M. Alcibiade, 40
Fathers of the French Turf, 19-49
Faublas, 193, 194, 322
Fauconberg, 138
Faugh-a-Ballagh, 146
Faugh-a-Ballagh (the younger), 293
Faust, 201
Favonius, 189, 194
Favorite, 270
Fay, Madame Latache de, 110, 113, 344
Fay, M. Latache de, 110, 344
Fayolle, Viscount de, 309
Félix, 18, 33
Feltre, Duke de, 282
Fénelon, 272
Fernan Cortez, 158
Fervacques, Haras de, 137, 160, 345
Fervacques (horse), 159, 160, 196, 201, 345
Feu d'Amour, 202, 207, 209, 335
Feu-de-joie, 197, 215, 261
Fez, 197
Fiammetta, 64
Fiddler, 270
Fidélia, 180, 185
Fidéline, 198
Fidélité, 130, 163
Fieschi, 33
Fin, 197
Figaro II., 213, 214
'Figaro, Le' (journal), 253, 302, 361
Fille-de-l'Air, vi, 86, 127, 131, 136, 139, 146, 155, 234, 308, 335

FRA

Filoselle, 217
Finisterre, 191
Finlande, 123, 130
Finot, the Baron, 255, 345, 354, 363
Finot (horse), 157
Fin Picard, 325
Firmament, 341
Firstborn, 64, 352
Fisherman, 79, 194
FitzEmilius, 63, 65
FitzGladiator, 69, 111
Fitzjames, the Duke de, 9, 345, 354
Fitzjames, Marquis de, 9
FitzPlutus, 257, 262
Fitzwilliam, Lord, 236
Flageolet, 59, 179, 193, 194, 197, 202, 209, 232, 261, 267, 322, 335, 336
Flamen, 324
Flâneur, 332
Flatman, Mr. (brother of 'Nat'), 54, 308
Flavio II., 256, 282
Fleet, 64
Fleur de Mai, 270
Fleur de Marie, 65
Fleuret, 265, 282
Fleury, General, 117, 351
Flibustier, 138
Florence (city), 39
Florentin, 157
Florestan, 292
Florian, 137
Florin, 77
Flying Buck (steeple-chaser), 91
Flying Dutchman, The, 83, 109, 145
Fobert, Mr., 137
Folie, 265
Fontainebleau (horse), 130, 239
Fontainebleau (place), 9, 50, 96
Fontenoy, 127, 128, 136
Forbes, Lord, 8
Fordham, Mr. G., 54
Forest du Lys, 86
Formalité, 309
Formigny, 332
Fornarina, 83, 128
Fort-à-bras, 40, 108, 112
Fortitude, 10
Fortune, 109
Fortune, La, 156
Forum, 271
Fould, MM., 49, 53, 69, 73, 344, 354, and *passim*
Foullon, M., 282
Fourches, the Marquis de, 8
Foxhall, 235, 239, 268, 270, 317
Fra Diavolo (the elder), 38

FRA

Fra Diavolo (the younger), 287, 288, 313
Franck, 18, 30
Franc Picard (steeple-chaser), 54, 88, 89, 94
Franc-Tireur, 35, 193, 194
'Frank Pickard,' 88
Frégate, 308
French sporting papers, 361, 362
French successes in England, 334 *et seq.*
Friant, M., 354
'Fridolin,' Major (Colonel), 35, 98, and *passim*
Froggatt, Mr. Edward, 238
Frolicsome, 330
Froudeur, 203
Frontin, 292, 312, 322, 330, 340
Fumée, 152

GABIER, 177
Gabrielle d'Estrées, 67, 112, 116, 119, 136
Gallifet, Mademoiselle de, 326
Gallifet, the Marquis de, 326, 354
Gambetti, 64
Gamin, 340
Gamos, 175
Gang Forward, 207, 209
Gantelet, 181
Gardener, Mr. (jockey), 360
Gargantua, 331
Garrick (horse), 292
Garry Owen, 69, 73
Gascogne, 196
Gaspard, 109
Gate-money meetings, 47
Gaulois, 124
Gavarni, 219, 221
Gayot, M. E., 351
Gédéon, 83, 144
Gédéon (the younger), 314
Gemma, 128, 130
Gemma di Vergy, 79
Généalogie, 125
Général, 178, 335
General Peel, v, 251
General Peel (horse), vi, 143
Gentilhomme, 126, 128
Géologie, 108, 109
George Frederick, 208
Germany, 59, 62, 63, 223
Gertrude, 187
Ghent, 72
Gibellin, 332
Gibson, Mr. H., 178, 324
Gigès, 23, 63
Gillie, The, 137
Gimcrack, 8, 333, 337
Gimcrack Stakes, 128

GRE

Girardin, Madame de, 51
Gladiateur, 83, 123, 131, 145, 146, 154, 178, 308, 335
Gladiateurs, 85
Gladiator, 26, 58
Gland, 64
Glaneur, 54
Glatigny, 29
Glenbuck, 108
Glenlivat, 189
Glowworm (elder and younger), 10, 334
Goater, Mr. J., ix, 262
Godolphin Arabian, the, 2, 58, 95, 100
Goëlette, 81, 108, 109, 111
Goncourt, Madame de, 237, 238
'Goncourt case,' the, 216, 236, 237
Gontran, 35, 145, 151, 152, 155
Good-bye, 114
Goodricke the Rev. Mr., 361
Goodwood, 62, 63, 70
Goodwood Cup, the, 23, 38, 54, 57, 62, 66, 68, 69, and *passim*
Gourbi, 191
Gourgandin, 262
Gouvernail, 166, 179
Gouvieux, 82, 108, 130
Gouy, M. de, 354
Gouy-d'Arsy (Viscount E.), 331
Governor, 64
Governor (steeple-chaser), 93
Gramont (Grammont), the Duke de (ancien régime), 7
Gramont, the Duke de (modern), 326
Gramont-Caderousse, the Duke de, 354
Grand, M. le, 7
Grand Ecuyer, the, 7
Grande Dame, 138
'Grande Ecurie,' the, 35, 85, 107, 113
Grandhomme, MM., 106
Grand Monarque, the, 6, 147
Grand National (Liverpool), 91
Grand Prix at Paris, the, 18, 23, 30, 33, 55
Grand Prix de Paris, the, 33, 36, 55, 132, 159 (dead heat for, 159–160), 239, 339
Grand St. Léger, the, 72
Grand Steeplechase de Paris, 231 325
Gravelles, 312
Graziella, 192
'Great Detective Case,' the, 236
Great Ebor Handicap, the, 69
Great Metropolitan, the, 81
'Great Turf Fraud,' the, 236, 237
Great Yorkshire Handicap, 69

Green Sleeve, 162, 261
Greffülhe, MM. de, 98, 345, 354
Gretton. Mr. F., 252
Grey, Hercules, 364
Grieves, Mackenzie, Mr., 49, and *passim*
Grimshaw, Mr. H., 123, 151, 152, 156
Grisette, 187
Grossley, M. or Mr., 11
Grossmann, Madame, 323
Grossmann, M. C., 357
Groszos, M., 106
Guéménée, the Prince de, 97
Guerchy, M. de (the Count), 9
Guiche, the Duke de, 3, 15, 18, 23, 98
Guillaume-le-Taciturne, 144
Guimauve, 197
Guiscard, 187
Gully, Mr. (prize-fighter), 320
Gunboat, 79
Gunnersbury (horse), 252
Gustave, 110, 112

HAHN, Count, 63
Hall, Mr. (jockey), 54
Hall, Mr. (painter), 308
Hallez-Claparède, the Count, 344
Hamilton. the Duke of, 178, 235, 252, and *passim*
Hamlet, 196
Hannah, 174, 194
Haras, Administration des, 3, 4, 14, 43, 47, and *passim*
Haras, Journal des, 14
Harcourt, Mr., 153
Harcourt, the Prince d', 5, 6
Hardwicke, Lord, 224, 228, 235
Hartneitstein, 129
Harvester, 311
Hastings, the Marquis of, 149, 164
Haughton, Mr. ('Groseille'), 359
Hauteur, 292
Hawke, Mr. J. B., 127
Hawley, Sir Joseph, vi, 39, 134
Hédouville, Viscount (Count) de, 43, 49, 69, 102, and *passim*
Heenan (prize-fighter), 154
Helen, 11
Héliopolis, 112, 115
Hémart, MM, 101
Hemet, M., 282
Henckel of Donnersmarck, the Count, 118, 129
Hennessy, M. Richard (of Cognac), 328
Henry (horse), 83, 178, 189, 194, 196, 335
Henry, Mr. (or Count Henry or Henri), 324

Henry IV. (or Henri IV.), 138
Henry the Eighth, 13
Héraut d'Armes, 190
Hercule, 64
Hereford, 'Le Grand Steeplechase d',' 112
Herman, 265
Hermit, The, 59, 158, 166, 232
Hernandez, 67
Herod (King), 87
Herodia, 56
Hertford, the Marquis of, 19
Hervine, 27, 52, 64, 66, 68, 102, 321
Hester, 175
Hetman Platoff, 23
Hidalgo, 332
Highflyer, 236
High Treason, 111
Hippia, 159
'Hippodromes,' the French, 96, 97, 102, 105
Hippolytus, 22
Hocks, 10
Hocquart (de Turtot), the Count, 346
Holbein (horse), 18
Holy Friar, 241
Honduras (mare), 159
Honesty, 55, 69
Honesty (the younger), 179
Honolulu, 159, 187
Horace (Roman poet), 145
Hospoder, vi, 83, 128-130, 132, 136, 148, 150, 335
Houghton, 197, 205
Howard, the Hon. Bernard, 7
Hugh Capet, 2
Hugh the Great, 1
Humpty-Dumpty, 14
Hurst, Mr. T., 343
Husson, M., 98
Hutchinson, Mr. John (of Shipton, Yorks), 361
Hydromel, 193, 194

IAGO, 58
Iambic, 364
I-am-not-aware, v
I'Anson, Mr. W., 236
Ibos, 49
Ibrahim, 26, 30, 31
Iffezheim, 182
Illusion, 332
Illustration, 64
Il Maestro, 196
Ilsley, 179
Indien, 340
Infante, 83, 127, 128
Infidèle, 287

INN

Innocent, 257, 265, 272
Insulaire, vi, 242, 244, 257, 261, 335
Inval, 242, 244, 246, 256, 265, 282
Inverness, 138
Ion, 57, 59, 65
Ironmaster, 162
Iroquois, vi, 235, 268, 271
Isabella, 112
Ismaël, 248, 256
Isolier, 282
Isoline, 138, 197, 261
Isonomy, 267
Italy, 13, 39

JACKSON, Mr. John, 359
Jacob (the patriarch), 146, 147
Jannette (the elder), 101
Jannette (the younger), 235, 332
Jarnac, 191
Jarnicoton, 131, 136
Jarnicoton II, 180
Jean Duquesne (steeple-chaser), 91
Jeanne la Folle, 204
Jennings, Mr. Henry, 30, 53, 130, 163, 178, 194, 328, and *passim*
Jennings, Mr. Thomas, 30, 53, 85, 172, 251, and *passim*
Jennings, Mr. T., junr., 310
Jenny (the elder), 56, 63, 343
Jenny (the younger), 166
Jessie or Jessy, 65
Jester, 218
Jeune Première, 161
Jockey Club and Pigeon-shooting Club (English at Paris), 19
Jockey Club, the English, 20, 45, 46, 227, 228, 348, and *passim*
Jockey Club, the French, 2, 4, 16, 18, 19, 31, 33, 35, 44, 46–48, 50, and *passim*
Jockey Club, the French (manifesto of), 349
Jockey Club, the Prix du (or French Derby), 22, 47, 55, 102, and *passim*
Jockeys, Early English and French, 54, 55
'Jock o' Fairfield,' 359
John, 196, 204, 268
Johnstone, Mr. H., 134
Jongleur, 217, 221, 226, 240, 335
Jonquille, 213
Jonville, 220
Joseph, M. (jockey), 55
Josyan, 271
Joubert, M., 282
'Journal des Haras,' 14, 361
Jouvence, 57, 68, 144, 336
Jouy, the commune of, 43

LAC

Joyeuse, the Duke de, 5, 6
Judex, 137
Juigné, the Count G. de, 201, 213, 345, and *passim*
Julius, 161
Julius Cæsar, 223
July (mare), 101
Jumbo, 18
Jupin, 327, 340

'K'S,' the three, 121
Kaiser, 195, 207, 209
Kangaroo, 148
Kara Koul, 341
Keene, Mr. J. R. (American), 270, 274
'Kennington,' Mr., 180
Kent, Mr. F., 40
Kermesse, 56
Kerr (or Kurr), Messrs. (convicts), 238
Kertangui, M. de, 101
Kettledrum, 121, 122
'K. G.,' 239
Khan, M., 363
Kildonan, 121
Kilt, 167, 217
Kincsem, 252, 318
King, Tom (prize-fighter), 154
Kingcraft, 134, 175
King Herod (horse), 87
King Lud (horse), 209, 210
King of the Vale (horse), 137
King of the West (Australian horse), 223, 224
King Pepin (horse), 10, 14, 334
Kingston, 67, 68
Kingston or Kingstown (imported Australian), 223
King Tom (horse), 23
Kisbér (horse), 217, 224
Kisbér (stud), 144
Kitchener, Mr. (jockey), (bodily weight 2 st. 12 lbs.), 54, 77, 145
Klarikoff, 121, 122
Knave of Clubs (*alias* Prince Regent, *alias* Zoroaster), 101
Knight of St George, 358
Komar, Count Wladimir de, 107, 354
Kurr (or Kerr), Messrs. (convicts), 238

LA BOSSUE, 199
La Bultée, 269, 341
La Calonne, 138, 191
La Charmoye, Haras de, 101
La Clôture, 64, 66
La Coureuse, 205
La Croix de Berny, 50, 90

INDEX 377

LAC

La Croix (de Castries), 329
La Croix Saint-Onen, 140, 178
La Diva, 114
La Dorette, 321
La Favorite, 158, 163
La Fortune, 156, 157
La Jeunesse, 206
La Jonchère, 239, 240
La Louve, 332
La Maladetta, 81
La Marche, 50, 89, 90, 92, 93
La Martinière, 187
La Méprisée, 197
La Meute, 6
La Morlaye, 35, 49
La Mothe, M. de, 89
La Muette, 5, 6
'La Patrie' (journal), 38
La Périchole, 183
La Reine Berthe, 86, 131
La Risle, 191, 196
La Roche, Château de, 100
La Rochelle (horse), 352
La Rochette, the Baron de, 49, 344
La Seine, 138, 221, 225
La Toucques, vi, 132, 136–138, 345
La Vigne, M., 98
Laban, 146
Labanoff (or Lobanoff), Prince, 43, 102
Lacydes, 128
Ladislas, 293
Lady Arthur (steeplechaser), 91
Lady Elizabeth, 162
Lady Golightly, 226, 235
Lady Saddler, 117
Laffitte, M. C. ('Major Fridolin'), 35, 98, and *passim*
Laffitte, M. J. ('Prince du Rabot'), 32, 34
Laforce, the Marquis de Caumont, 210
Lagrange, the Count (General) de, 98
Lagrange, the Count Frédéric de, 49, 52, 71, 76, 107, 153, 210, 235, and *passim*; (death of), 293; (biographical sketch of), 293
'Lagrange Stud,' sales of the, 172, 282, 304
Lagrange-Lefèvre, the 'fusion' of, 211, 219, 224, 235; the 'scission' of, 244
Lagrange-Lefèvre, MM., 337
Lagrange-Nivière, the confederacy of, 35 and *passim*
'Lagrange-Nivière Stud,' sale of the, 130, 131
Laillier, M., 345
Laird of Holywell, 206

LIF

ambinos, 10
Lambkin, the, 311
Lamplugh, Mr. H., 54, 89
Lancosme-Brèves, Count, 364
Lanercost, 23, 58, 59
Lanterne, 64, 352
Lanterne (afterwards Nativa), 63, 102
Lapin, 316, 330, 340
Laroque or Larroque (or Delarroque), 344
Lastborn, 77
Latache de Fay, Madame, 53, 74, 110, 113, 344
Latache de Fay, M., 52, 110, 344
'Launde,' the Rev. Mr., 210, 241
Lauragnais, the Count de, 8, 333
Laurier, 221
Lauriston, the Count de, 354
Lauzun, the Duke de, 8, 9, 97
Lavaret, 313, 336
Le Béarnais, 145, 155
'Le Betting,' 358
Le Bosphore, 164
Le Cantal, 101
Le Destrier, 262, 263, 267, 270
Le Drôle, 213
'Le Figaro' (journal), 253, 302, 361
Le Mancenillier, 187
Le Mandarin, 83, 145, 148, 151, 152, 155
Le Mans, 120
Le Maréchal, 83, 127, 128, 130, 136
Le Monsieur (ex Esteemed Friend), 163
Le Nôtre, 341
Le Pecq, 7, 96
Le Pin, 14, 15, 50, 55, 89, 93, 100, 120, 342, and *passim*
'Le Ring,' 358
Le Roy (or Leroy), M. E., 41, 43, 228
Le Sarrazin, 83, 86, 162, 163, 165, 335
'Le Sport' (journal), 8, 179, 229, and *passim*
'Le Tattersall (Français),' 357
Le Ténor, 190
Le Vésinet, 7, 96
Leconte, M., 98
Lefèvre, M. C. J., 153, 172, 178, 209, 235, and *passim*
Lehndorf, Count, 130, 154, 179
Leolinus, 209
Léon, 265, 270, 282
Léopold, 221, 226
Lesbos, 157
Lichtwald, MM., 63
Liddington, 148–150
Lifeboat, 109

378 INDEX

LIG

Light, 108, 112, 116, 120
Light Drum, 312, 330
Lighthouse, 197, 205
Lilian, 177
Limosina, 130
Lina, 221, 225
Lion, 74, 76, 77
Liouba, 147
Lioubliou, 64
List of early members of the French Jockey Club, 98, 99
List of 'elegancies' at Chantilly under the Third Empire, 354, 355
List of 'foreign' horses in 1881, 276
List of 'great events' won by French horses in England, 334–336
List of the principal French horses expatriated through 'les évènements' in 1870, 179, 180, 184, 186
List of the principal 'haras' up to 1833, 100–102
Lists of French horses that have run in England at various times, 10, 62, 78–81, 108, 111, 115, 123, 124, 126, 127, 136, 157, 158, 161, 165, 166, 169, 173, 180, 183, 184–188, 195, 200, 201, 208, 210, 213, 215, 216, 219–226, 241–244, 248–251, 256–260, 264–267, 271–274, 278–281, 288–291, 309, 313–316
Lists of French race-courses (hippodromes), 96, 97, 105
Lists of noted French owners and breeders, 97, 98, 188–193, 342–346
Lists of the chief English thoroughbred sires imported by the French up to 1853, 10, 16–18, 24–26, 41, 57
Lists of the most noted French 'cracks,' 63–65, 84–86, 114, 125, 130, 131, 135, 136, 141, 142, 156–159, 164, 167, 173, 183, 189–193, 195–197, 200, 207–209, 212, 214, 217, 218, 225, 239, 240, 244, 245, 255, 256, 262–264, 269–271, 278, 287, 288, 308, 309, 312, 313
Little Agnes, 183, 193, 194
Little Duck, 311, 322, 330, 340
Little Harry, 67
Little Lady, 124
Liverpool (English horse), 63
Liverpool (French horse), 63
Liverpool Autumn Cup, 112
Liverpool Grand National, 91, 93, 188
Livingstone, 138

MAD

Lobanoff, Prince, 43, 102
Loch Ranza (horse), 311
Locke, Captain, 43
Lollipop, 220, 221, 258
'Lombard,' Mr. T., 172, 178
Longchamps (hippodrome), 22, 102–104
Longchamps (horse), 83, 166
Longdown, 148, 151
Lonray, Haras de, 213, 270, &c.
Lord Clifden (horse), 138, 268
Lord Lyon (horse), vi, 156
Lord Seymour (horse), 324
Lorillard, Mr. Pierre, 274
Lorraine, the Chevalier de, 7
Lottery, 26, 63, 64
Louis XI., 329
Louis XII., 329
Louis IV., 3, 5, 7, 96
Louis XV., 8, 96, 356
Louis XVI., 9, 42, 96, 356
Louis XVII., 42
Louis XVIII., 3
Louis d'Or, 255, 314, 336
Louis Napoléon (Bonaparte), Prince, 23
Louis Philippe, 4, 5, 21, 33, 170, 353
Louisa, 101
Louise Victoria, 244
Loustic, 187
Louvre, the, 7
Lowther, Mr., 124
Lowther House, 244, 343
Luc, 315
Lucien Bonaparte, Prince, 254
Luisette, 190, 196, 197
Lunel, M. H., 130, 183
Lupin, M. Auguste, ix, 49, 53, 57, 68, 103, 145, 190, 212, 228, 229, 239, 244, 262, 326, 343, and *passim*
Lycisca, 69
Lydia, 18, 30
Lyra, 138

MACADAM, 220, 265, 272
Macaron, 208
Macaroni, 137, 215
Macaulay, Lord, 42
Macgregor, 175
Machalo, the Chevalier de, 42
Mackenzie-Grieves, Mr., 43, 49, 104, 345, and *passim*
Macmahon, Marshal, 163, 329
Macquinez, 332
Madame II., 278
Madelaine, M. G., 106
Mademoiselle Clairon, 244, 245
Mademoiselle de Champigny, 116, 124

MAD

Mademoiselle de Chantilly, 76, 81, 108, 112, 335
Mademoiselle de Fligny, 164
Mademoiselle de Mailloc, 191, 195
Mademoiselle de Senlis, 278, 279
Mademoiselle de Vendôme, 119
Mademoiselle Duchesnois, 130
Madrid, Château de, 6
Madrid, Haras de, 38, 101
Mahomet, 61
Maid of Mona, 76
Maiden, 163
Maillé, Mademoiselle Henriette de, 329
Maillot, La Porte, 37
Maisons-Laffitte, 41
Malapert, M., 282, 330, 345
Malibran, 280, 290
Malines, 15, 101
Mameluke, 26
Man-at-Arms, 128
Manette II., 180
Manille, 190, 195, 197
Mannington, 197
'Man of the Mountain,' The (M. Vincent), 328
Manolo, 187
Mans, Le, 120
Mantille, 243
Maravedis, 158
March, Lord ('Old Q.'), 9
Marengo, 157
Marianne, 108
Marie Stuart, 209
Marignan, 115, 116, 130
Marin, 187
Marion, MM., 344
Mariquita, 315
Marix, M., 304
Marks, Mr. ('Antidote'), 359
Marmot, 213
Marshall, Mr. R., 208
Marske, 10, 163
Martel-en-Tête, 81, 108
Martin, M. de Francisco, 314
Martin Pêcheur II., 318
Martingale, 317
Martinvast, Haras de, 144, 345
Maskelyne, 271
Massa (formerly Négro), 112
Massinissa, 177, 187
Master Richard, 143
Matchem, 9, 10, 334, 337
Mate (American), 223
Matelot, 195
Mathilde, the Princess, 39
Maubourguet, 124
Maulmont, M. de, 98
Mauvaise-Tête, 362
Mavrocordato, the Princess, 329

MON

Mazeppa, 129
Meëus, Count, 282
Meiklejohn, Mr. (detective), 238
Melbourne (Young), 95
Mello, the 'Haras' de, 325
Merlin, 34, 40
Merry May, 331
Merry Monarch, The (horse), 320
Merry, Mr. (James), 201
Messager, 195
Messine, 63
Metcalfe, Mr., 200
Meudon (haras), 3, 14, 18, 21, 37, 38, 100
Meudon (horse), 64, 345
Meynell, Mr. Hugo, 9
Mic-Mac, 331
Middleton, 40
Mignonette, 155, 208, 209
Milan, 163, 258, 263, 266, 270, 282
Milan II., 258, 263
Mineral (dam of Kisbér), 218
Minette, 206
Minister, 205
Minotaure, 177
Minting, 327, 340
Minuit, 40, 63
Mirabeau, M. de (the Count), 11, 14
Miss Annette, 30
Miss Buckland, 205
Miss Caroline, 74
Miss Cath, 82, 108
Miss Gladiator, 147, 345
Miss Hervine, 192
Miss Jummy, 328
Miss Toto, 205, 207, 210, 215
Mr. (Mister) Wags, 26, 62, 66
Mite, 101
Modena, 208
Moissonneur, 197
Moldavia, 152
Mon Etoile, 110, 111, 129, 144, 321
Monarchist, 73
Monarque, 27, 70, 71, 85, 93, 102, 146, 336
Monarque (Young or Y.), 158
Mondaine, 155, 217, 241
Monitor, 163
Monmouth, the Duke of, 6
Monseigneur, 178, 179, 186, 188, 192
M. (Monsieur) de Fligny, 163, 215
M. (Monsieur) le Prince, 192
M. (Monsieur) Louis (hurdle-racer), 187
M. (Monsieur) Philippe, 249, 251, 335
Montagnard, 163
Montargis, 184, 209, 335
Mont de Marsan, 118

MON

Monte Carlo, 255
Montécot, Viscount Guy de, 364
Montford, 196
Montgeroult, Haras de, 345
Montgomery, M. (Count) A. de, 137, 345, and *passim*
Montgonbert, 157, 161, 187
Montrachet, 187
Montreuil, M. de, 354
Moore, Mr. Jack (bookmaker), 365
Moore, Sir J., 87
Moreau-Chaslon, M., 345
Morisco, 34
Morizet (Russian), 223
Morlaix, 101
Morny, the (Count) Duke de, 43, 53, 74, 94, 103, 113, 130, 132, 142, 345
Morok, 63
Morris, Mr. J. B., 358
Mortemer, 162, 163, 165, 174, 178, 189, 261, 335
Moscowa, the Prince de la, 31, 32, 43, 98
Moscowa, the Princess de la, 32, 34
Mosselmann, M. Hippolyte, 53, 72, 344, 354
Mothe, M. de la, 89
Mouchy, M. de, 354
Mould, Mr., 179
Moulins, 72, 344
Moulsey, 155
Mourle, 243
Moustique, 69
Mundig, 99
Murray, Mr. Edwin (convict), 238
Muscovite, 68
Musgrove, Mr. (jockey), 269
Musket, 174
'Mus' (Mr. Lefèvre's dog 'Muscat'), 254
Myosotis, 221
Myszka, 64
Mythème, 64

NABOB, the, 49, 146, 165
Naiade, 74
Namur, the Viscount de, 123
Nancy, 69
Nanetta, 63
Napoleon (horse), 64
Napoléon I., 14, 15
Napoléon III., 31, 39, 113, 170, 353
Napolitain, 195, 336
Narbonne, the Count de, 98
Nassau, the Prince de, 97
National Guard, the, 33
Nativa (ex Lanterne), 63, 102
Nautilus, 23, 57, 62, 63, 65, 66
Navarette, 187

ODE

Neasham Hall, 214
Negro, 197, 205, 335
Négro (afterwards Massa), 112
Nélusko, 164, 166, 174, 180
Neméa, 156
Nemours, the Duke de, 21, 24, 36, 41, 229
Neptunus, 191
Nethou, 193, 194
Neva (Russian), 223
Newmarket, 8, 9, 13, 39, 62, and *passim*
Newmarket (horse), 290
Newmarket Handicap, the, 80
Newmarket Whip, the, 314, 336
Newminster, 59, 67
Nexon, the Baron de, 109, 344, and *passim*
Ney, Edgar, 31, 43
Ney, Joseph Napoléon, 31
Ney, Marshal, 31
Neys, the, 32, 43
Nichol, Mr. A., 331
Nicolet, 159
Nightingall, Mr., 251
Niobé, 88
Nivernais, Le, 49
Nivière, the Baron L. de, 35, 107, 354, and *passim*
Nivière-Fridolin, the confederacy of, 140, 148
Nivière-Lagrange, the confederacy of, 107, 113, 114
Noailles, the Count Manuel de, 107
Nobleman, 175
Noë, 129
Noélie, 142
Nonant, 188; (another), 310
Norfolk, the Duke of, 7
Normandie, the Duke de, 42
Normandie, M. de, 42-44, 102
Normandy, 66
North, Mr. (jockey), 54
Northumberland (horse), 10, 334
Nougat, 167, 213, 217, 282
Nougats, 85
Novateur, 203, 207
Nubienne, 162, 345
Nuncia, 81, 108, 112
Nuncio, 58, 59
Nunnykirk, 57, 58, 83
Nutbourne, 111

OAK Stick, 62
Oaks, the English, 126 and *passim*
Oaks, the French, 22, 32, 55 and *passim*
Océanie, 258, 261, 266, 272, 282, 336
Odette, 56

INDEX

Odette II, 312
Odine, 127, 136
Old England (horse) 320
'Old Q.,' 9
'Old Tat,' 356
Ontario, 278
Opoponax, 161
Optimist, 128
Orlando, 321
Orléans, Duchess d', 353
Orléans (Egalité), the Duke d', 9, 97
Orléans, house of, 24, 27
Orléans (son of Louis Philippe), the Duke d', 5, 21, 22, 23, 37, 38, 51, 62, 65, 102, 170, 229, 236, 342, 353
Orléans, the Prix d', 80
Ormonde, 152, 327
Orphelin, 136, 138, 183, 184
Orthodoxe, 187, 188
Osborne, Mr. J. (jockey), ix.
Ossian, 214
Otage, 332
Otho (Emperor), viii
Otho (horse), 10, 334
Oulgouriska, 250
Ouragan II., 165

PACHA (steeplechaser), 93
Pacific, 263
Paganini, 178
Pain, Mr., 356
Paladin (two), 77, 193
Palaiseau (haras de Villebon), 343, v. Villebon
Palaiseau (horse), 115, 116
Palamède, 313
Palestro (ex Coquet), 116, 117, 130, 317, 335
Palmer, Mr. (detective), 238
Palmer, Mr. (sportsman), 34, 53, 357
Palmer, The (horse), 161
'Palmer's New Betting Rooms,' 34, 357
Pandour, 167
Pangloss, 10
Panique, 266, 272
Pantal, Mr. (jockey), 108
Papillon, 69
Papillotte, 113
Paradox (the elder), 40
Paradox (the younger), 310, 316
Pardon, 258, 266, 272, 345
Paris, the Count de, 37
Paris, the Grand Prix at, 55 and *passim*
Paris, Grand Prix de, 55 and *passim*
Paris, Prix de la Ville de, 55
Parlement (horse), 341

Parole (American), 266
Partisan, 114
Pateen (or Po-teen), 364
Patrician (horse), 9
Patricien, 83, 113, 158, 160
Pauline, 127
'Pauline Z.' demands a tip, 326
Paul's Cray, 259, 262
Pavis, Arthur, 23, 54
Pavis, Edgar, 23, 54, 342
Payment, 145, 343
Paysanne, 222
Pearson, General, 134
Peau d'Ane, 324
Peck, Mr. R., 251
Pecq, Le, 7, 96, and *passim*
Peel, General, v, 251
Peel, General (horse), vi, 113
Perceval, M. de, 65
Pergola, 136
Périer, MM., 98
Périgord, the Count de, 354
Péripétie, 167
Perla, 198, 207
Pero Gomez, 134
Perplexe, 208, 209, 212
Perplexité, 262, 270
Perregaux, Viscount E., 65
Persigny, the Duke de, 32
Peter (horse), 251, 253
Peter (steeplechaser), 91
Peter Simple (steeplechaser), 91
Petit-Gris, 334
Petit-Sérans, M., 344
Petrarch, 218, 223
Peu d'Espoir, 73, 75
Peut-Être, 86, 210, 211, 212, 282, 335
Phantasmagoria, 101
Phantom, 101
Phantom Cottage, 244, 343
Phénix, 81, 259, 262, 266, 335, 345
Phenomenon, 125
Philip-Shah, 64
Phœbus, 315
Phœnix, 81
Physician, 64
Pierrefonds, 110
Pin, Le, 14, 50, 55, 89, 93
Pi-Ouit II., 309
Pirat (German), 224
Pistole, 191
Place, le Chevalier de la, 41
Placida, 226, 258
Plaine de Sablons, the, 8, 96
Plaisance, 340
Plaisante, 222, 266
Plaisanterie, vii, 117, 239, 315–320, 331, 332, 335
Plaizel, M., 363

PLA

Planète, 203
Planner, Mr., 179
Plessis du Vernet, 6
Plover, 65
Pluton, 222
Pocahontas, 23
Poetess (the elder), 26, 30, 65, 66, 71, 102, 321, 343, 352
Poetess (the younger, dam of Plaisanterie), 321
Poilly, M. de, 354
Polyeucte, 341
Pompadour (Jumenterie de),15,342
Pompée II., 331
Pompier, 163
Pontalba, M. (the Count) Célestin de, 64, 65, 345
Pope Joan, 101
Porte de Boulogne, La, 37
Porte Maillot, La, 37
Porter, Mr. J., 251
Postérité, 191
Poteen (or Pateen), 364
Pot8os, 337
Potocki, 58, 77
Poudrière, 203
Poule d'Essai, 55, 288
Poule des Produits, the, 56
Poulet, 259, 263, 266, 273, 335
Pourquoi ?, 270
Prado, the Count de, 108, 344
Pradt, the Abbé de, 15, 101
Prat, MM., 251, 345 and *passim*
Pratt, Mr. Charles, 54, 152, 175
Pratt, Mr. George, 152
Preakness (American), 223, 224
Précurseur, 108
Prédestinée, 63, 144
Premier, The (steeplechaser), 93
Premier Argonaut, 187, 192
Present Times, 309, 316
Presta, 340
Prétendant, 110, 112
Prétentaine, 328
Prétentaine II., 188
Prime Warden, The, 57, 108, 120
Prince Arthur, 139
Prince Charlie, 203, 209, 211
Prince of Wales (horse), 175
Printanier, 188
Printemps, 321
'Prisonniers de Guerre, &c.,' 40
Prix du Nabob, 288
Prix d'Orléans, 80
Prix des Princes, 96
Prix du Roi, 96
Prix Greffülhe, 288
Prix Royaux, 96
Problème, 332
Prologue, 259, 267, 282

REI

Prométhée, 269, 271
Prophète, 222
Provocateur, 125
Prudence, 316
Prud'homme, 259, 273, 281
Prunet, M. Pierre (jockey), 55
Pryor (or Prior) and Pryoress (or Prioress), 78, 79
Pumpkin, 163
Puritain, 196
Purity, 163
Pyroïs, 10, 334
Pyrrhus the First, 109
Pythagore II., 270
Pythonisse, 188

QUEENSBERRY ('Old Q.'), the Duke of, 9, 20, 27
Queen's Plates, 336
Qui Vive, 332
Quoniam, 23

RABAGAS II., 243, 324
Rabion, M., 98
'Rabot,' the Prince du, 32
Races, French (names altered of), 171
Race-courses, French, 96, 97, 102, 105
Radcliff, Mr. J., 188
Rafale, 178
Rainbow, 18, 33, 100, 357
Ramadan, 73
Ranger, The, 138, 194
Rataplan, 23
Ratopolis, 64
Ravenshoe, 197
Rayner, Mr. C., 251
Rayon d'Or, vi, 234, 250, 259, 261, 264, 267, 282, 334, 335, 336
Réalité, 188
'Reciprocity,' 133; the cry for, 216
Reciprocity (horse), 216
Recorder, The (horse), 175
'Red House at Battersea,' 20
Red Rover (steeplechaser), 93
Regain, 288, 292, 309
Regal, 206
Régalade, 222
Regalia, 152, 153, 197, 261
Régane, 196, 197, 203
Regimentstochter (German), 224
'Régine' (the opera), 32
Régis, M. Th., 345
Register of thoroughbreds (French stud book), 4
Regrettée, 267, 269
Reine, 84, 144, 189, 194, 196, 202, 334
Reine Berthe, La, 86, 131

REI

Reiset, M. Jacques, 53, 345, 354
Reluisant, 313, 316, 318
Rémus, 70, 73
Rennes, 120
Renonce, 65
Restitution, 162
Restoration, the, 3, 14, 15
Retento, 124
Réussi, 273
Reveller, 264
Rêveuse, 292
Révigny, 183, 193, 194
Revolution of July, the, 4, 5, 15, 62
Revolution, the Great, 3, 5, 11, 62, 334
Richard II., 13
Richelieu (horse), 290
Richepance, 332
Ridotto, 264
Rieussec, M., 15, 18, 31, 32, 97, 357
Riseber, 79
Rivière, M. Jules, 63, 344
Robert Macaire (horse), 310
'Robert Milton,' 253, 324, 361
Robert the Devil, 263
Robien, The Count de, 283
Robin, M. Jules, 53, 126, 129, 169
Rob Roy, 225
Rochette, the Baron de la, 49, 344
Rockingham, Lord, 10
Roederer, Count P., 344
Roffignac, the Marquis de, 53
Roger, the Baron, 270
Roi de la Montagne, 243, 324
Roi des Bohémiens (horse), 364
Roi-Fou, 330
Rolfe, Mr. (jockey), 269
Rome, 13
Romulus, 23, 82
Ronce, 152
Ronzi, 73–79
Roquefort, 137, 167, 169, 204, 222
Roscoff, 239
Rosebery (horse), 238
Rosebery (Lord), 219
Rosicrucian, 162
Rosières (aux Salines), Haras de, 15, 101, 342
Rothschild, Baron Alphonse de, 217 and *passim*
Rothschild, Baron Antoine de, 99
Rothschild, Baron Gustave de (with Baron Alphonse), 217 and *passim*
Rothschild, Baron J. de, 100
Rothschild, Baron N. de, 49, 53, 65, 345
Rouge, 10, 334
Rous, Admiral, 7, 132, 153, 224, 228
Rowlston, 3, 11, 18, 100

SAL

Roy, M. Ernest Le, 41, 43, 228
Royal Hampton, 310
Royallieu, Haras de, 179
Royallieu (horse), 121, 124, 128, 150
Royal Oak, 26, 27, 30, 31, 56, 102
Royal-Quand-Même, 69, 90
Royaumont, 273
Royères, M., 15, 97
Royston, Lord (Earl of Hardwicke), 359
Rubens (horse, the elder), 101
Rubens (horse, the younger), 287, 288, 292
'Running Rein,' 56, 268
Russia, 39, 167, 223
Ruy Blas, 162
Rymill, Mr., 327, 356
Ryshworth, 168

SABATIER, M., 344
Sabinus, 174
Sablons, the Plaine de, 8, 96
Sablonville, 29, 102
Sabre, 36, 207, 209
Saccharometer, 127, 137, 138
Saffery, Mr. H., 358
Sagan, the Prince de, 326
Saint-Aignan, 126
Saint-Albin (Lagayère), M. de, 361
Saint-Christophe, 163, 197, 225, 226, 239, 240, 241
Saint-Clou, the Marquis de, 88
Saint-Cloud, 6, 362
Saint-Cyr, 130, 212, 213, 217
Saint-Firmin, 267
Saint-Gatien, 311
Saint-Georges, Haras de (Brittany), 101
Saint-Georges, Haras de (South), 328, 344
Saint-Germain, 43
Saint-Germain (horse), 64
Saint-Germain-en-Laye, 6, 96
Saint-Germain, the Count de, 354
Saint-Honoré, 327
Saint-James (horse), 278, 291
Saint-Petersburg, 60
Saint-Romain, the Count de, 354
Saint-Sauveur, the Marquis de, 346
Saint-Victor, M., 2
Saint-Victor's Barb, 2, 364
Sakountala, 340
Salamander (steeplechaser), 95
'Salon des Courses,' the, 34, 357, 358
'Salons de Paris, Les,' 28
Saltarelle, 155, 207, 208, 213
Saltéador, 155, 260
Saltram, 125

SAL

Salvanos, 188, 195, 335
Salvator, 212–214
San Donato, the Count or Duke of, 39
Sans Marque, 332
Sansonnet, 287
Saraband, 316
Sarrazin, the Count de, 98
Satisfaction, 222
Sator, 196
Satory (horse), 292, 309
Satory (Versailles), 22, 50
Saumur, 58, 89, 93
Saunterer, 79, 81
Sauterelle, 327
Savernake, vi, 156
Savile, Mr. H., 134, 194, 197, 198
Saxifrage, 340
Sayers, Tom (prize-fighter), 154
Scandal of the 'Running Rein' sort, 56
Scapegrace, 162, 256
Schickler, the Baron A., 49, 53, 144, 164, 345 and *passim*
Schickler, M. (the Baron) J. G., 98, 101
'Scission,' the Lagrange-Lefèvre, 244
Scobell, 270
Scott, Mr. W. (of Pennsylvania), 282
Scottish Chief, The (horse), 139
Scroggins, 62
Secretaries of the French Jockey Club, 106
Sedan, the Man of, 177
Seesaw, 162, 216
Seigneur II., 330
Seillière, Baron Frank de, 324, 326
Seillière, Baron Raymond de, 323, 324, 363
'Selwyn' (Jesse's), 9
Selwyn, George, 19, 27
Sémur, racing at, 5
Sénégal, 332
Senlis, 40
Sérénade, 63, 144
Serge II., 291, 309, 336
Serious, 77
Serpolette II., 269, 270
Seul, 183
Seymour (horse), 213
Seymour, Lord H., 19, 20, 27, 30, 31, 37, 38, 51, 53, 56, 62, 98, 102, 321, 353, 356
Shannon, 177, 189
Shark, 337
Sharper (horse), 60
Shipton (near York), 361
Shotover, 134

STI

Siberia, 148
Sidi Mahmoud (Barb), 101
Sidonia, 218
Sigurd, 341
Silex, 308
Silvio, 134, 226, 235, 253, 259, 322, 330, 340
Sina, Baron, 329
Sir Bevys (horse), 252, 256
Sir Tatton Sykes (horse), 73
Sire, 197
Skye, 291
Slane, 30
Slapdash, 160
Sly Fox, 179
Snake, 95, 200
Snake mare, The Old, 200
Société d'Encouragement, the, 2, 19, 34, 43, 60, 102, and *passim*
Société - Générale des Steeple-chases, 351
Société pour l'Amélioration du Cheval Français de Demi-sang, 351
Société Verviétoise, the, 65
Solitaire, 332
Soltykoff, Prince, 245
Somno, 191
Sonchamp, 131, 136
Songstress, 343
Sorcerer, 101
Sornette, 35, 108, 110, 112, 121 174–176, 191, 336
Soubeyran, the Baron de, 344
Souchey, M., 98
Soukaras, 292
Soumise, 136, 155
Soupçon, 208, 324
Sourche, Château de, 100
Sourire, 330
Souvenance, 188
Souvenir, 125, 126, 129, 169
Souveraine, 128
Spa, 90, 92, 94
Speculum, 162
Speed-the-Plough, 72
Sphynx, 10
Spinaway, 332
Sporting papers, French, 361, 362
Spreoty, Mr. (jockey), 54, 67, 68
Squirt, 163
Stamford, Lord, 130, 138
Standard-bearer, 174
Star, 264
Star and Garter, Pall Mall, 45
Stathouder, 155
Staub, M. A., 213, 270, 346
Stebbings, Mr. W., 320
Stentor, 136
Stilton, 67

STI

Sting, 26, 58, 68
Stirling, Capt., 251
Stockholm, 292, 311, 336
Stockwell, 23, 232
Stracchino, 239, 240
Strada, the Marquis de, 23
Stradella, 128, 131, 136
Strelitz, 263, 264
Strongbow, 57
Stud Book, the French, x, 4, 21, 38, 41, 57
Stuhlweissenberg (stud), 118
Sturt, Mr. Gerard, 195
Suavità, 64
Succès, 208
Successes in England (French), 334 et seq.
Sue, Eugène, 2, 99
Suffolk and Berkshire, the Earl of, 7, 154, 241
Sugarloaf, 222, 226
Sultan, 73
Sultan (the younger), 158, 336
Summary, a, 333 et seq.
Surinam, 195
Surplice, 77
Surprise, 110, 116
Sutler, 267, 273, 291, 310
Sutton, Sir R., 134
Suzanne, 196
Suzerain, 164, 165
Suzette, 222
Sweepstakes (horse), 9
Sweetsauce, 112
Sweet William, 337
Swift, 245, 247, 248
Sycomore, 340
Sylla, 192, 196
Sylvain, 108
Syphon, 163

TAFFRAIL, 345
Tafna, 260, 267, 273
Taje, 128
Talhouët, the Marquis de, 120, 294
Talon, Viscount A., 89, 90
Tambour, 179, 204
Tambour-Battant, 363
Tandem (ex Multum in Parvo), 101
Tape-à-l'œil, 331
Tapestry, 137
Tarbes, 50, 120
Tarrare, 63
Taster, 9
Tattersall, MM., 236, 355
'Tattersall's,' 356
'Tattersall's,' the French, 34, 356
Teddington, 67
Teissier, the Baron de, 62

TWO

Teissière, M., 113
Télégraphe, 125
Terves, M. de, 53
Tetotum, 56
Teucer, 10, 334
Thannberg, M., 41
Thatched House (St. James's), 15
Theodoros, 195
Thiers, M., 21
Thormanby, 111
Thorp, Mr., 179
Thurio, 245
Tim, 40
Tim Bobbin, 168
Tim Whiffler, vi
'Times,' the, 228
'Tiny' Wells, 67
Tippler, 107
'Tipton Slasher,' the, 154
Tivoli, 19
Tocqueville, the Count de, 15, 50, 97, 101, 345
Todleben, 151
Tolla, 86, 173
Tolstoi, Count, 354
Tomate, 40, 63
Tom Fool, 137
Tomlin, Mr., 43
Tontine (the elder), 56, 342
Tontine (the younger), 262
'Tontine scandal,' the, 57, 66
Tooley, 100
Toucques, 138
T(h)oulouse Barb, the, 2, 364
Tourbillon, 197, 206
Tourmalet, 151, 155
Tournament, 36, 85
Toxophilite, v
Trafalgar, 146
Trajan, 337
Tramp, 108
Trance, 101
Trembleur (steeplechaser), 93
Trent, 208
Triboulet, 363
Trimmer, Mr. G., 251
Tristan, 270, 292
Trocadéro, 83, 156, 162, 173, 178, 322, 335
Trombone, 197, 205
Tronquette, 64
Trouvère, 332
Trumpeter, 159
Trust, 69, 70, 352
Turcos (horse), 128
Turenne (horse), 188
Turf (horse), 10, 334
Turnus (bred in Germany), 63
Tuscany, the Grand Duke of, 39
'Two Thousand,' the, 83

C C

'Two Thousand,' the French, 56
Two-year-old racing in France, 352
Tyrolienne, 36, 212

UDINE, 341
Umpire (American), 111, 143
Underhand, 159, 161
Union Jack, 108
Upas, 340
Ural mines, the, 39

VALBRUANT, 76
Valenciennes, 92
'Valenciennes, Histoire du Siège de,' 32
Valentin, 309
Valentine (horse), 128
Valentine, Hardaway, and Topping, MM., 359
Valentino, 188
Valéria, 69
Valois, 173
Vandyke Junior, 101
Vanteaux, M. de, 53, 98, 344
Vauban (horse), 161
Vaublanc, the Count de, 43
Vaucresson, Haras de, 343
Vaugiraud, the Marquis de, 101
Vellon, 324
'Vendanges de Bourgogne,' the, 28
Vendôme, MM. de, 7
Vendredi, 30
Venison, 91
Ventre Saint-Gris, 81, 82, 86
Véranda, 190, 193, 194
Verberie, Haras de, 344
Vercingétorix, 270
Verdière, 327, 340
Verdure, 75, 189, 196, 336
Vergogne, 65
Vérité, 75
Vermeille (ex-Merveille), 75
Vermisseau, 331
Vermout(h), 39, 75, 85, 146, 165
Vernet (horse), 292
Vernet, Plassis du, 6
Verneuil, 163, 218, 222, 226, 239, 240, 260, 335
Verny, 362
Verry, M., 126
Versailles, 15, 22, 33
'Versailles of the Condés,' the, 354
Versigny, 200, 262, 263, 267
Vert, 10, 334
Verte-Bonne, 287
Vertu-Facile, 126
Vertugadin, 75, 151, 152, 155, 162
'Vertus militaires, les,' 36

Verulam, 162
Verviers, Société de, 65
Vésinet, Le, 7, 96
Victor Chief, 252
Victorieuse, 156, 157
Victorine, 162
Victot, Haras de, 66, 71, 146, 321, 342
Viennois, 313, 330, 341
Vigilant, 270
Vigogne, 187, 190, 331, 341
Villafranca, 83, 128, 131, 136
Villebon, Haras de, 35, 176, 282, and *passim*
Villeneuve, 316
Vincennes, the royal park at, 9, 50, 62, 96
Vincent, M. (of Tarbes), 328
Vincent (horse), 198, 200, 210
Vineuil, 146
Violette, 113
Virago, 69
Virgil (Roman poet), 22
Virgule, 159
Viroflay, Haras de, 15, 18, 33, 49, 100, 343
Viroflay (horse), 112
Vis-à-vis, 331
Viveur, 269
Vivian, Lord, 224, 228, 235
Vivid, 86, 126, 140, 155
Vizir, 268, 269
Voilette, 262, 267
Volage II., 213
Volante, 18
Voltella colt, The, 218, 226
Volturno, 208
'Voyage dans la Russie Méridionale,' &c., 39
Vulcan, 197
Vyner, Mr., 311

WALES, the Prince of, 150, 364
'Wallace v. the Attorney-General,' 28
Walpole, Horace, 8, 9
Walton, Mr. 'Plunger' (American), 291, 310
Walton (horse), 101
Warren Hastings (horse), 226
Warwick, 92, 108
Wasp, 187
Waterloo (battle), 68, 146
Waterloo (steeplechaser), 93
Water-Nymph (dam of Kincsem), 252
Weatherbound, 111
Weatherby, Messrs., 45
Weathergage, 68

INDEX

Webb, Mr. (jockey), ix ; (another) 54
Wedding, 81, 108, 116
Welland, 128
Wellingtonia (horse), 321
Wells, 'Tiny' (jockey), 67
West Australian, 59, 72, 99, 149
Westminster, the Duke of, 134
Wharton, the Hon. Thomas, 6, 7
Wheel of Fortune, 256, 332
Whip, the Newmarket, 314, 336
Wigginton, Mr. T., 328
Wild Charley, 150
Wild Cherry, 216
Wild Oats, 168
Wild Thyme, 292
Wild Tommy, 222
Wilde, Mr. T. (bookmaker). 365
William III. (The 'Dutchman'), 14
Wilton, Lord, 336
Wingrave, 155
Wings, 343
Winkfield, 69
Winnings (in money) of French horses in 1871, 189–192
Wirthschaft, 37

Wizard, The, 59, 111
Womersley, 58
Wood, Mr. C. (jockey), ix
Wright, Mr. W. (bookmaker), 359

XAINTRAILLES, 310, 311, 313
Xurullo, 128

Y ELECTION mare, 56
Y. Emilius, 74
Y. Melbourne, 95
Y. Monarque, 158
Yes, 187
Ypsilanti, the Princess, 329
Yvrande, 308

'Z' Pauline (demands a 'tip'), 326
Zambesi, 149
Zichy, the Countess, 329
Zoological Gardens, 18
Zoraïde (Russian), 223
Zoroaster, 101
Zouave (son of the Baron), 81, 82, 108, 112
Zut, 234, 251, 267

www.ingramcontent.com/pod-product-compliance
Lightning Source LLC
Chambersburg PA
CBHW031418150426
43191CB00006B/321